D0891762

FOR LIBERTY AND EQUALITY

FOR LIBERTY AND EQUALITY

THE LIFE AND TIMES OF
THE DECLARATION OF INDEPENDENCE

ALEXANDER TSESIS

OXFORD
UNIVERSITY PRESS

OXFORD
UNIVERSITY PRESS

Oxford University Press, Inc., publishes works that further
Oxford University's objective of excellence
in research, scholarship, and education.

Oxford   New York
Auckland   Cape Town   Dar es Salaam   Hong Kong   Karachi
Kuala Lumpur   Madrid   Melbourne   Mexico City   Nairobi
New Delhi   Shanghai   Taipei   Toronto

With offices in
Argentina   Austria   Brazil   Chile   Czech Republic   France   Greece
Guatemala   Hungary   Italy   Japan   Poland   Portugal   Singapore
South Korea   Switzerland   Thailand   Turkey   Ukraine   Vietnam

Published by Oxford University Press, Inc.
198 Madison Avenue, New York, New York 10016
www.oup.com

Oxford is a registered trademark of Oxford University Press

Library of Congress Cataloging-in-Publication Data
Tsesis, Alexander.
For liberty and equality : the life and times of the Declaration
of independence / Alexander Tsesis.
p. cm.
Includes bibliographical references and index.
ISBN 978-0-19-537969-3 (alk. paper)
1. United States. Declaration of Independence.   2. United States—Politics and
government—Philosophy.   3. United States—History. I. Title.

E221.T74 2012

973.3'13—dc23

2011048264

9 8 7 6 5 4 3 2 1
Printed in the United States of America
on acid-free paper

For my Dedushka Abrasha

The Declaration supplies the principles giving character and motion to the machine.... The powers under the Constitution are no more than the hand to the body; the Declaration is the very soul itself.

SENATOR CHARLES SUMNER

What is the American ideal? It is simply and precisely stated thusly in the Declaration of Independence—"We hold these truths to be self-evident, that all men are created equal, that they are endowed by their Creator with certain inalienable rights, that among these are life, liberty and the pursuit of happiness!" This noble language, fortified by the implementing language of the 14th Amendment, makes the picture complete.... Isn't it about time that it be made a reality?

CHIEF JUSTICE EARL WARREN

CONTENTS

1

INTRODUCTION

The Declaration of Independence is often idolized, canonized, and even worshiped, with little understanding about the extent to which it has influenced American culture and law. Many people are riveted by the Declaration's statement of human equality, but the indictment of George III seems to be no more than a relic of an ancient event. A closer look at more than two centuries of speeches and writings reveals that the Declaration of Independence has had a remarkable influence on American policy making. Politicians and social groups—composed of various races, ethnicities, occupations, genders, coalitions, religions, and levels of education—have shaped the significance of the document. Reformers have found it meaningful for advocating greater inclusiveness and equality. At every stage of American history, the Declaration of Independence provided a cultural anchor for evaluating the legitimacy of legal, social, and political practices. Not only civil rights activists have drawn inspiration from its proclamation of inalienable rights, but individuals decrying governmental abuses have also turned for support to the document's enumeration of British "tyranny."

For nearly two and a half centuries, the Declaration has been recited at innumerable Independence Day celebrations. Millions upon millions of Americans have heard, read, and internalized its message. The Declaration's staying power is clear from how its rhetoric resonates with ordinary people. Today the federal government protects the Declaration at the National Archives Building in Washington, D.C., under armed guard in the same exhibition hall as the Constitution and the Bill of Rights. The clarity with which the Declaration was written has preserved the value of inalienable rights for posterity, though it be decades and even centuries removed from the disputes of the American Revolution.

The nation's extraordinary rise to power came from an improbable rebellion. A small group of colonial statesmen agreed on the Declaration's explanation of their decision to throw off the reins of the British Empire. The document ascribed the power of forming a government to the people. It posited that their participation in representative democracy was necessary to identify and safeguard core inalienable rights, including "life, liberty and the pursuit of happiness." Down to the twenty-first century, that announcement of national purpose provides a basis for principled decision making. The manifesto's formal recognition of natural human rights, being those inborn characteristics that are essential to human dignity, remains a moral ballast for fair decision making.

The Declaration of Independence has been essential to the development and enforcement of norms within and outside the legal system. Its statement of sovereign purpose created baseline standards for lawmaking, adjudication, and regulation. In this book, I concentrate on the various ways politicians, associations, groups, and individuals have relied on the Declaration of Independence to justify changing policies, laws, and customs. Dialogue about public values, aspirations, and purposes have set the path to social and political renewal. The Declaration's terms are broad enough to allow for differing opinions, but what is steadfast is the Declaration's statement of human equality, which is irreconcilable with discriminatory regulation, adjudication, and law enforcement. The manifesto has played a significant role in so many milestone events of United States history that it is demonstrably no mere ornament of the past but rather part of an ongoing national dialogue about rights and governmental powers.

Of course, some speakers have manipulated the document for grandiloquence, exploiting this readily recognized rhetorical tool to achieve political or economic ambitions. The existence of occasional empty rhetoric, however, does not diminish the Declaration's genuine contribution to the cause of human rights. Its words have sparked popular imagination, energized mass movements, presented opportunities for coalition building, and created political divisions. These movements built on the Declaration's statements of natural rights and reinterpreted them within the context of their political, civil, and social causes. The document's statement of innate equality has inspired many politicians, and conversely exposed the short-sightedness of others.

My aim is to examine the evolving relevance of the Declaration of Independence. Throughout the country's history, its underlying meaning has remained the justification for American sovereignty—the establishment of a representative polity committed to protecting inalienable rights. The nation's greatest shortcoming has been its failure to fulfill the manifesto's pledge of equal liberty. America's strength lay in its moral commitment to civic and entrepreneurial mobility. The principle that all persons are equally entitled to seek their happiness inspired diverse groups and served as a standard against which government actions could be assessed. Unlike the European society from which the colonists sprang, there was no official hereditary aristocracy to prevent farmers, artisans, craftsmen, laborers, and shopkeepers from entering politics. The Declaration's preamble provides a ready formula for challenging class-based discrimination.

The Declaration of Independence tethers national identity, and contemporary culture informs popular opinion about the nature of inalienable rights and representative government. The framers' decision to incorporate universal statements about humanity gave birth to an instrument that transcends the ancient conflict between the British Empire and one of its colonial satellites. The consistent reappearance of the manifesto's normative values indicates that it was more than merely a legal brief for independence, as some constitutional scholars claim.[1] To the contrary, the document created a recognizable creed for government conduct that went beyond procedural fairness.

Repeated reliance on the Declaration's principles—in debates ranging from abolition of slavery, suffrage, and immigrant rights to recognition of newly independent nations and acquisition of federal territories—indicates that they establish policy-making norms rather than merely assert glittering generalities. More significantly, however, the claim that all persons enjoy equal liberty has animated debates and brought on constitutional changes.

Prior books about the Declaration of Independence have primarily focused on either its philosophical framework or its relevance to the revolutionary generation. There are several excellent intellectual studies of the document, most eminently Carl Becker's *The Declaration of Independence: A Study in the History of Political Ideas.* It has gone through multiple print runs since its first publication in 1922 and remains available today. Morton White's and Michael Zuckert's books delved even more deeply into the natural rights philosophy that informed the Declaration's signers.[2] Jay Fliegelman's book *Declaring Independence: Jefferson, Natural Language and the Culture of Performance* took a different approach, contextualizing the Declaration's oratorical flourishes within contemporaneous rhetorical styles.

In one of the most notable recent books on the subject, *American Scripture: Making the Declaration of Independence,* Pauline Maier expanded Becker's textual analysis of the Declaration of Independence. She also elaborately examined state ratifying conventions. Maier argued that the Declaration was primarily a statement of national sovereignty, placing significantly less weight on clauses about individual rights. Her approach differs from mine. From my perspective, the Continental Congress did not need the Declaration of Independence to separate from Great Britain. In fact, it had voted for independence two days before the signing of the Declaration. In the pages that follow, I emphasize the document's ideological content more than its statement of liberation from colonial rule.

Unlike other authors who have written books on the Declaration of Independence, I focus on how a variety of social movements incorporated its message into their reform efforts. Throughout this work I have mainly followed a chronological scheme. My aim has been to tell the story of the Declaration of Independence without engaging in academic polemics. My research is mainly based on primary sources such as newspapers, diaries, letters, transcripts of speeches, and congressional records. I focus on domestic topics but where applicable also discuss the Declaration's influence on international affairs, a line of research initiated by David Armitage in *The Declaration of Independence: A Global History.*

The story of the Declaration of Independence is both inspiring and disillusioning. Since its signing, Americans have expressed their deep admiration for the document's principles. They have raised the banner of inalienable rights for the world to see. Government by consent has allowed ordinary people to pursue meaningfully free and happy lives. Failures to live up to professed commitments, however, have raised doubts about the validity of the country's self-image as the bastion of basic liberties.

In this book, I try to uncover the extent to which the Declaration's readily recognizable statement about self-evident truths has influenced the course of history in the United States. I investigate whether the document's guarantee of equal liberty is substantive or merely ornamental. The humanitarian ideals on which the nation was founded have not always withstood the pressure of special interest groups. The document's message of universal freedoms nevertheless continues to be the national manifesto of representative democracy and fundamental rights.

The pages that follow trace the many ways in which social groups relied on the Declaration of Independence as a popular constitution. It inspired patriotism, provided a recognizable statement of fundamental rights, and established the people as the source of governmental power. The actual Constitution is a technical document—filled with legal terminology about writs, amendments, jurisdictions, rules, and regulations—while the Declaration is an easy-to-follow narrative about how the country was created and about the protections for life, liberty, and the pursuit of happiness it was meant to secure.

In recent years, references to the Declaration of Independence have primarily been historical. Since the 1970s, most books, speeches, and court decisions that mention it have construed the document as a lustrous artifact of U.S. history rather than a statement of a living creed. Arguments that integrate the Declaration's principles into current affairs are rarely encountered. One hears about its original meaning but rarely hears arguments as to how the American people can understand its paragraphs on self-government and inalienable rights to address contemporary policies. I have written elsewhere about the Declaration's relevance to current affairs.[3] This book demonstrates how, from the time of independence through the late 1960s, ordinary people, politicians, and organizations construed its meaning to advocate for reforms that would make the Declaration's promises of liberty and equality a reality.

2

BECOMING INDEPENDENT

THE AMERICAN COLONIES BEGAN COOPERATING POLITICALLY AGAINST British rule even before they adopted the Declaration of Independence. In 1774, delegates from twelve of thirteen colonies gathered in Philadelphia for the First Continental Congress to decide how to respond to coercive British laws. Passions ran high against acts permitting British officers to requisition private property for billeting soldiers and cutting off seaborne trade to Boston. Initially, most delegates hoped to mend relations with England, while only a small faction favored independence. At that point, British leaders probably could have negotiated mutually favorable terms to resolve colonial grievances; instead, a power struggle ensued that resulted in the American Revolution.

All the colonies except Georgia sent representatives to the First Congress. Members were inching their way toward the treasonous proclamation that Congress derived "all its power, wisdom and justice, not from scrolls of parchment, signed by Kings, but from the People." The most radical leaders came from Massachusetts and Virginia. For almost two years, moderates from New York, South Carolina, and Pennsylvania controlled the pace of negotiations with the Crown, anticipating that King George III would respond favorably to American petitions protesting parliamentary decrees. In the first year of intercolonial governance, few Americans shared the pessimistic concern of Samuel Adams, the popular leader from Massachusetts, that "if the British administration and government do not return to the principles of moderation and equity, the evil which they profess to aim at preventing by their rigorous measures, will the sooner be brought to pass, viz:–*the entire separation and independence of the colonies.*" Yet even Adams continued to express hope for "permanent union with the mother country, but only on the principles of liberty and truth."[1]

John Adams, Samuel's cousin, and other Massachusetts delegates arrived in Philadelphia on August 29, 1774, ready to participate in the first session of Congress. An entourage made up of gentlemen from various colonies emerged from the city limits to greet them. Straightaway, they all headed to a tavern to refresh themselves after the tiresome journey. Other delegates joined them there.

Congress first met in Carpenter's Hall on September 5, with Peyton Randolph as its president. Delegates could peruse books from the excellent library housed in the building, which provided resources to consult for their deliberations. Within a week, Congress appointed a committee to look into the "state of Rights of the Colonies in general." Radical committee members, who wanted to clearly signal a rupture with England, clashed with conservatives, who were still committed to the British Empire. Some on the committee agreed with Virginia's Patrick Henry that a variety of conflicts had thrown the colonies into a "state of nature," no longer obligated to follow British laws. Others sided with the sentiments of New York's James Duane that rights had to be grounded "on the laws and constitution of the country from whence we sprung ... without recurring to the law of nature." At the heart of their disagreement was whether Americans should draft a new social contract or remain bound by their allegiance to the King.

The committee's initial draft tried unsatisfactorily to combine the opposing views, asserting that Americans' rights derived from "the laws of Nature, the principles of the English Constitution, and charters and compacts." In October, Congress adopted a Declaration of Rights, which proclaimed the colonies' powers to legislate, tax, engage in internal politics, and be free from parliamentary control. The document also asserted that Americans were "entitled to life, liberty, and property," of which they could not be dispossessed without their consent.[2]

Thomas Jefferson, the eventual author of the Declaration of Independence, was not present at the first Congress, which dissolved on October 26, 1774. In June 1775, a month after the Second Continental Congress convened, Jefferson took his seat as a delegate from Virginia. In a letter written almost half a century after their first meeting, John Adams remembered that although Jefferson was then only in his early thirties he already had "a reputation for literature, science, and a happy talent for composition."[3]

When Jefferson arrived, he found that many patriots were still too hesitant to seriously consider independence. Although the first skirmish of the Revolution had taken place on April 19, 1775, in Lexington and Concord, Massachusetts, the prevailing consensus was still to await the Throne's magnanimous response to colonial entreaties.

The first session of the Second Continental Congress gathered on May 10, 1775, at the Philadelphia State House, later renamed Independence Hall. Though not all members were present on a daily basis, in all sixty-five men participated, fifty of whom had been members of the First Congress. Benjamin Franklin was the oldest delegate at seventy-one, but several were considerably younger. After independence many of them became leaders of the new nation. John Jay, who was a youthful thirty, went on to become the first Supreme Court chief justice. Forty-year-old Patrick Henry would become governor of Virginia. Roger Sherman, a shoemaker by trade, whose prestigious involvement in politics included the signing of the Articles of Association, the Declaration of Independence, the Articles of Confederation, and the Constitution, was fifty-four at the beginning of the Second Congress. Many others in the pantheon of Revolutionary iconography, including the uniformed George Washington and the aristocratic Richard Henry Lee, were also actively involved in the proceedings of the Second Congress. Although the Second Congress felt the pressure of an impending war with England, it was able to effectively exercise executive, legislative, and judicial authority.[4]

By September 1775, John Adams was regularly imploring delegates to desist from conciliatory petitions and pass a declaration of independence. Despite his best efforts, Adams was still unable to convince most of Congress to budge. Instead, the Congress's primary focus was on supplying and organizing the armed forces. It established the Continental Army, commissioned Washington to be the commander-in-chief of the Army of the United Colonies, and bought the munitions needed to supply it. To finance these appropriations, Congress issued continental currency (backed by bills of credit whose value diminished throughout the war). When this funding proved to be insufficient, Congress turned to foreign creditors. Despite the fairly united consensus to take up arms, most delegates continued to believe that King George III would side with them against Parliament's heavy-handed interference in colonial affairs. Delegates nevertheless began exploring ways to enter diplomatic relations with foreign nations, recruit Native American tribes, and negotiate peace with the British.[5]

With no end to the fighting in sight, a political commentator expressed surprise at members of Congress who were still unwilling to consider ending colonial rule. Meanwhile, the gulf was widening and political hostility between Britain and the colonies was becoming irreparable. Calling for a boycott of British goods in late October 1775, General Nathanael Greene of Rhode Island observed, "People begin heartily to wish a declaration of independence." Likewise, Franklin stated that with the continued use of force colonists would "be obliged to break off all connection with Britain."[6]

Mass publications began openly attacking the Crown and increasing awareness about the political dispute. The press's influence cannot be overstated. The newspapers would also be important in reprinting the Declaration of Independence. White literacy was higher in America than Europe, and the written word was essential to winning popular support for the independence. In Virginia and Pennsylvania, approximately two-thirds of males could read and sign their names, but only about half that number of women were literate there. The literacy rate in 1750 New England was over 70 percent for men and about 45 percent for women, but in the southern colonies it was lower for both genders, at about 50 to 60 percent for men and 40 percent for women.[7]

In his January 1776 pamphlet *Common Sense*, Thomas Paine demonstrated the enormous impact of rhetoric, using passionate, everyday language to arouse a popular revolt against a hereditary, monarchical government. Paine vividly described colonial grievances, unabashedly denouncing what he considered to be tyrannical British rule and calling for independence. Within six months of its publication, three hundred thousand copies of his call to revolt had been sold.

Paine framed a theory of popular government in such affective language that it influenced ordinary Americans to cast off centuries of allegiance to the King. Samuel Adams praised Paine in 1802: "Your *Common Sense* and your *Crisis* unquestionably awakened the public mind, and led the People loudly to call for a Declaration of our national independence." By the mid-1800s, *Common Sense* was regarded as "the book of Genesis ... From this book sprang the Declaration of Independence." In 1876, without providing definitive proof but expressing accepted lore, a journalist likewise asserted that "no single cause was more effective in producing the Declaration Independence than his *Common Sense*." So great was Paine's influence on the changing popular sentiment against the distant, hereditary sovereign that over the centuries to follow there were many who erroneously believed he had authored the Declaration of Independence.[8]

A month after Paine's *Common Sense* first appeared, Richard Price published a pamphlet in London condemning parliamentary infringement on the colonists' political and civil rights. Within a year, sixty thousand copies of Price's pamphlet were in circulation in England, and American printers from South Carolina, New York, and Pennsylvania were reprinting it.[9]

By the first months of 1776, the Continental Congress was deeply immersed in lawmaking. It began to regulate commerce, appoint magistrates, and provide colonial courts with guidance for resolving admiralty cases. Colonies such as Virginia, Maryland, and North Carolina received permission from Congress to export products to foreign countries. Delegates also sent three commissioners—Franklin, Samuel Chase, and Charles Carroll—on an unsuccessful, albeit important, mission to Canada. Even without a formal call for independence, by British standards these acts were treasonable.[10]

On April 12, 1776, North Carolina became the first colony to instruct its representatives "to concur with the delegates of the other colonies in declaring Independency."[11] According to one North Carolina representative, the colony's bold step came in response to Royal Governor Josiah Martin's public encouragement of slaves to escape from bondage and aid England in quelling the American rebellion. Martin subsequently fled for his life.[12]

South Carolina's chief justice, William Henry Drayton, charged a grand jury on April 23, 1776 "that George the Third, king of Great Britain, has abdicated the government ... that is he has no authority over us, and we owe no obedience to him." He impaneled the grand jury "to regulate your verdicts, under a new constitution of government, independent of royal authority." Drayton further explained that governance is "founded upon so generous, equal and natural a principle ... [to be] expressly calculated to make the people rich, powerful, virtuous and happy." This statement contained elements of the philosophy that Jefferson would soon incorporate into the Declaration of Independence, proclaiming men's natural right to enjoy "life, liberty, and the pursuit of happiness." South Carolina did not, however, immediately adopt Drayton's views on independence.[13]

Debate persisted about the value of petitioning the King. That same month an author under the pseudonym "Moderator" wrote excitedly of a congressional proclamation to expand free trade: "The ports are now as open to all the world as they would be by an actual declaration of independence." Merchants found routes around the British naval blockade against foreign commodities. The separation of America from England was now almost inevitable. In May, even a supporter of Great Britain argued that it would be nonsensical to drive the colonies "to that last shift, a declaration of independence"; that measure would result in even greater conflict. Loyalists rejected claims that "the authority of the people" demanded opposition to the Crown.[14]

Colonial cooperation prior to adoption of the Declaration of Independence provided incalculable experience in running a federal nation. On the tenth of May, Congress recommended that colonies lacking governing bodies "adopt such government as shall, in the opinion of the representatives of the people, best conduce to the happiness and safety of their constituents in particular, and America in general." Acting even more treasonably, on May 15 Congress published a preamble explaining that given the Crown's failure to respond to "humble petitions" it was "necessary that the exercise of every kind of authority under the said crown should be totally suppressed, and all the powers of government exerted, under the authority of the people of the colonies, for the preservation of internal peace, virtue, and good order, as well as for the defence of their lives, liberties, and properties." The historian Gordon Wood has argued that the "May 15 resolution was the real declaration of independence" because it established new governments opposed to Great Britain. He is only partly correct because the Continental Congress had not yet issued a statement of national unity, which would become a core component of the Declaration of Independence. By mid-1776, eight colonies evinced varying degrees of willingness to vote for independence.[15]

Charlotte County, Virginia, unanimously expressed its sense that any further remonstrance to England would be futile. The statement, sent to the county's delegates preparing for the upcoming Virginia Convention, asserted the inevitability of adopting a declaration of independence to allow Virginia to cast "off the British yoke" and enter "into commercial alliances" with friendly foreign nations. The Virginia General Assembly, with Edmund Pendleton as its president, did not disappoint. On the fifteenth of May, the Virginia Convention required its delegates at the Continental Congress to initiate a resolution to "declare the United Colonies free and independent states, absolved from all allegiance to or dependence upon the Crown or Parliament of Great Britain." Francis Lightfoot Lee, one of two members of his family to sign the Declaration, blamed England for forcing Virginia into this momentous decision. News of Virginia's declaration traveled far and fast; by July, it had made its way into the pages of a Scottish magazine.[16]

On June 7, 1776, Richard Henry Lee introduced the Virginia resolution, calling for the Continental Congress to declare any allegiance with Britain to be severed and all colonies to be "free and independent States." John Adams seconded the motion. Their agreement on the subject was no surprise since the two had developed a tight political alliance. Among the delegates, the pair held some of the more radical views on independence. Even though their agendas and oratory were closely matched, the two men were strikingly different. Adams was rather corpulent while Lee was tall, lean, and handsome, despite suffering from a debilitating injury to one of his hands. Adams never employed slaves; Lee, along with at least seventeen other signers of the Declaration of Independence, held property rights in slaves. So leery were the delegates of being charged with treason that although the *Journal of the Continental Congress* reproduced the motion, neither man's name was mentioned.[17]

The motion for independence failed to garner the immediate support of several key delegates. Of those, the most prominent were John Dickinson and James Wilson of Pennsylvania and John Jay, Robert Livingston, and James Duane of New York. These five sought to better prepare the public, exhaust their entreaties to the King, and increase the likelihood of obtaining foreign support. Those already in favor of independence, by contrast, argued that a formal declaration was the only means of gaining aid from France and Spain as well as initiating commercial exchanges to make up for the losses of British imports and exports. Congress, they argued, needed to demonstrate its leadership at a time when military storms rendered it impossible to live again as Englishmen.[18]

Dickinson's disapproval was most significant because of his renown as a colonial pamphleteer. His *Letters from a Farmer in Pennsylvania*, published in 1767, had been the most circulated work of its type, helping defuse an earlier conflict with Parliament. Congress would later appoint him to draft the Articles of Confederation, which he then presented to Congress eight days after its approval of the Declaration of Independence. Rather than arguing that colonists had a natural right to revolution, Dickinson opposed British policies because he regarded them as contrary to English laws. He never signed the Declaration. While Adams called for immediate dissolution of allegiance to Great Britain, Dickinson argued that such a measure would lead to increased hostilities and was in any case inopportune given the divergent colonial policies. Opposition to independence briefly carried the day, with delegates from Pennsylvania, New Jersey, South Carolina, Delaware, and New York unable to commit to the rupture, and those from Maryland only tentatively willing to cooperate.[19]

Rather than force matters, the proponents of independence decided to be patient. On June 10, Congress postponed debate on Lee's resolution until July 1. But not wanting to waste any more time since the momentum was toward independence, on June 11 it appointed a committee to draft a declaration. Lee would have been a logical pick, but he returned home the very day the committee was appointed, to care for his severely ill wife. Congress chose Franklin, John Adams, Livingston, Jefferson, and Sherman. Amazingly, one of the five, Robert Livingston, never signed the Declaration of Independence because he was away at the New York Provisional Congress.[20]

While the committee worked on its draft in Philadelphia, the Virginia Convention continued to promulgate reforms. On June 12, Virginia adopted the Declaration of Rights, which newspapers circulated across the colonies. With its strong natural rights undertone, the Declaration of Rights began with this preamble:

I. That all men are by nature equally free and independent, and have certain inherent rights, of which, when they enter into a state of society, they cannot, by any compact, deprive or divest their posterity;

namely, the enjoyment of life and liberty, with the means of acquiring and possessing property, and pursuing and obtaining happiness
and safety.

II. That all power is vested in, and consequently derived from, the
people....

III. That government is, or ought to be, instituted for the common benefit,
protection, and security of the people, nation or community; of all the
various modes and forms of government that is best, which is capable
of producing the greatest degree of happiness and safety....[21]

There is little doubt that this formulation influenced Jefferson, who had
a copy with him while he drafted the Declaration of Independence; he may
have even paraphrased from it.[22]

The Declaration of Rights' high-sounding statements, however, should
be taken with several grains of salt. The Declaration stated that "all men
are by nature equally free and independent," though the statement was not
indicative of most Virginians' real lives. George Mason, who is credited
with composing the original draft of the Virginia declaration, was, like
Jefferson, a wealthy slaveholder who opposed importation of foreign slaves
but never freed his own. Numbering about 165,000 in 1776, Virginia's slave
population was the largest of any colony. Virginia also curtailed the basic
rights of other groups. Women, whether married or unmarried, had been
denied the right to vote since 1699. The same stricture was reenacted in a
1769 Virginia statute that also excluded free blacks, Indians, and racially
mixed blacks from the voting rolls. These groups' political participation
was relegated to indirect influence through private conversations, public
meetings at taverns, and election day festivities. Nor was the right to vote
universal for all white males. In 1776, a white man could vote only if he
"owned one hundred acres of unimproved land or twenty five acres with
a house." To prevent more indigent, migrant workers from coming into
the state, Virginia also passed an antivagrancy act that year. The power
of Native American groups living in the Chesapeake Bay had withered
and their numbers had dipped since the early seventeenth century, when
the colonization of Virginia began. The year he wrote the Declaration of
Independence, Jefferson also spoke of removing the Cherokees to reserva-
tions to punish them for supporting the British.[23]

As the drafting committee continued to work, other colonies came to terms with the impossibility of reconciling with the Crown. The Connecticut General Assembly, without any reference to Lee's motion, instructed its delegates to propose that the Continental Congress

> declare the United American Colonies Free and Independent States, absolved from all allegiance to the King of Great Britain, and to give the assent of this Colony to such declaration when they shall judge it expedient and best, and to whatever measures may be thought proper and necessary by the Congress for forming foreign alliances, or any plan of operation for necessary and mutual defence.[24]

Some colonies were more reticent. On June 15, New Hampshire's General Assembly instructed its delegates "to join with the other colonies in declaring the thirteen united colonies a free and independent State." Even Pennsylvania, which remained uncommitted, expressed a "willingness to concur in a vote of the Congress, unanimously declaring the united colonies free and independent States" as long as the colony retained its sovereignty. Despite some continuing opposition, the die was cast. At one point in a debate, while hearing someone else read of the popular support for independence, a North Carolina member of Congress raised "both his hands to heaven" as if in a trance and shouted, "It is done! And I will abide by it." In an 1813 letter, Adams savored the memory of that odd behavior: "I would give more for a perfect Painting of the terror and horror upon the Faces of the Old Majority at that critical moment than for the best Piece of Raphaelle."[25]

In 1823, Jefferson recalled how the Committee of Five appointed him, its youngest member, to create the initial draft. There is some discrepancy between his account, written in 1823, and John Adams's, a year earlier. Adams remembered the committee choosing both of them to come up with a draft but himself having personally convinced Jefferson to go through the task alone.[26]

Jefferson drafted his masterpiece in a rented apartment, on the second floor of a three-story Philadelphia building. Having finished the initial draft, he presented it for editing to Franklin and Adams. They made few changes. Its author then reported the document to Congress on Friday, June 28.[27]

FIGURE 2.1 *Harper's Weekly*, July 3, 1897, vol. 41, no. 205, cover/p. 1. (Image courtesy of the Library of Congress.)

Vehement debate on Lee's resolution for independence began on the following Monday. Adams, as Jefferson would recall, was the "colossus of that debate." Despite their best efforts, a clear split occurred. New Hampshire, Connecticut, Massachusetts, Rhode Island, New Jersey, Maryland,

Virginia, North Carolina, and Georgia voted for it. South Carolina and Pennsylvania cast votes against it, Delaware's two delegates were divided, and the New York delegates declared they were ready to vote for the resolution but believed their instructions forbade them from doing so.[28]

The next day, July 2, a momentous change took place. An additional delegate for Delaware, Caesar Rodney, who had been riding on horseback all night in the rain, arrived to break the tie, voting for independence. In his diary, John Adams describes Rodney as "the oddest-looking man in the world; he is tall, thin, and slender as a reed, pale; his face not bigger than a large apple, yet there is a sense of fire, spirit, wit, and humor in his countenance." This unusual-looking fellow is reputed to have ridden a remarkable eighty miles, changing horses along the way, and entering Independence Hall in his boots and spurs, still dusty, shortly before the doors of Congress were shut at the opening of the day's session. Members of the South Carolina delegation had come to a consensus to vote for Lee's motion. Pennsylvania had nine members who were seated in 1775, but only seven of them were present in the hall on July 2; two of them were no longer active in Congress. One of those two, Andrew Allen, had left in June and would become a British Loyalist; the other was on his deathbed. The "yea" vote for Pennsylvania was cast by only three of the delegates who were present, with two others voting against it. John Dickinson and Robert Morris were in the hall but abstained from voting, allowing the affirmative vote to stand. That left New York's delegation. But it did not vote either way, adding its support only several days later. Congress had now resolved "that these United Colonies are, and, of right, ought to be, Free and Independent States; that they are absolved from all allegiance to the British crown, and that all political connexion between them, and the state of Great Britain, is, and ought to be, totally dissolved."

This was the actual declaration of independence. The document that has come to be known by that name was instead an explanation of Congress's decision to absolve its allegiance to England on July 2.[29]

Half a year after Paine bedazzled the colonies with his *Common Sense* and fifteen months into the war for independence, Congress voted to create a new nation. Writing his wife, Adams mistakenly predicted when Americans would commemorate independence: "The second day of July, 1776, will be a memorable epoch in the history of America. I am apt to believe that it will be celebrated by succeeding generations as the great

Anniversary Festival." This date has now largely been forgotten, with Independence Day being celebrated annually on the fourth of July, the date Congress adopted the committee's resolution.[30]

Having decided the highly contentious question of independence, Congress turned its attention to Jefferson's draft declaration. The document was an explanation of why the newly formed states decided to separate from England. Rather than begin with a statement of grievances, the document first espouses a higher law of governance, metaphysically existing, independent of any state and designed for the betterment of humanity. Jefferson's preamble to his proposed declaration masterfully synthesized extant natural rights philosophy, espousing the universal right of the people to seek independence and put an end to tyranny.

According to Jefferson's *Autobiography*, most of the second, third, and fourth of July were spent debating his draft. An apocryphal story, which midnineteenth-century historians attributed to Jefferson, tells of the delegates' haste to complete deliberations on the document. As they worked, swarms of flies from a nearby livery stable gained access through an open window and bit the delegates' legs through their silk stockings. Even as they delivered speeches, delegates regularly swiped flies away with handkerchiefs. Debate on the Declaration of Independence might have been prolonged, but delegates ended it early to flee from the biting pests.[31]

Other authors, including Carl Becker and Pauline Maier, have done such a thorough textualist analysis of the document that it would be redundant for me to do so again. Therefore, I offer only a sketch of its wording.

As early as 1822, an anonymous author of a newspaper article meticulously described changes that the Committee of Five and Congress had made to the document.[32] Jefferson was incensed at the "pusillanimous idea" of eliminating passages censuring the English people, believing they had violated their friendship with the colonists. Of even greater moment was Congress's willingness to placate Georgia and South Carolina slave importers by striking Jefferson's clause "reprobating the enslaving of the inhabitants of Africa." Northern delegates, Jefferson claimed, "felt a little tender" by this censure, having been so often the mercantile carriers of kidnapped Africans. The decision to omit the clause condemning the international slave trade allowed it to continue until 1808, when the Congress passed legislation criminalizing the practice. Until that year, the U.S. Constitution had protected the slave trade against federal intervention.[33]

Alterations to his draft so irritated Jefferson that Franklin, whom he sat by, consoled him with an anecdote. "I have made it a rule," began Franklin,

> whenever it is in my power, to avoid becoming the draughtsman of papers to be reviewed by a public body. I took my lesson from an incident which I will relate to you. When I was a journeyman printer, one of my companions, an apprentice hatter, having served out his time, was about to open shop for himself.—His first concern was to have a handsome signboard, with a proper inscription. He composed it in these words: 'John Thompson, *Hatter, makes and sells hats for ready money,*' with the figure of a hat subjoined. But he thought he would submit it to his friends for their amendments. The first he showed it to, thought the word '*hatter*' tautologous, because followed by the words 'makes hats,' which shew he was a hatter. It was struck out. The next observed that the word '*makes*' might as well be omitted, because his customers would not care who made the hats; if good and to their mind, they would buy, by whomsoever made. He struck it out. A third said he thought the words '*for ready money*' were useless, as it was not the custom of the place to sell on credit; everyone who purchased expected to pay. They were parted with, and the inscription now stood, 'John Thompson sells hats.' '*Sells hats?*' says his next friend; 'why nobody will expect you to give them away. What then is the use of that word?' It was stricken out, and '*hats*' followed it, the rather, as there was one painted on the board; so his inscription was reduced ultimately to 'John Thompson,' with the figure of a hat subjoined.

Franklin's tale spoke to both authors' sense of accomplishment and of the scrutiny they receive from external reviewers. Jefferson may have felt his text had been denuded, but Congress actually made relatively few changes to it.[34]

The formally adopted version of the Declaration of Independence contains a moral statement of governance and a series of indictments against George III. The document begins with a general defense of revolution, saying that certain events compel the people to dissolve all allegiance to their former sovereign and form a separate political entity. The next paragraph, commonly known as the preamble, makes the natural rights case for a government with the people retaining their equal and inalienable rights, which include "life, liberty, and the pursuit of happiness."

The phrase about human equality was not an empirical statement about the human condition, but a normative guarantee of national policy making. It drew on a natural law tradition that posited the existence of a common human aspiration to pursue happiness. Representative government was thought to be essential to the fulfillment of a social compact executed by the people. Government's primary purpose was to promote the people's well-being. Inclusion of these sentiments, as Abraham Lincoln later said, "was of no practical use in effecting our separation from Great Britain; and it was placed in the Declaration, not for that, but for future use."[35]

Much academic and political criticism has been leveled at the claim that men are created equal, with most denouncing the inaccuracy of saying that intelligent and imbecilic, rich and poor, young and old are equally endowed with the same talents, abilities, and social stations. But to nineteenth-century statesmen the "self-evident truths" adopted in the document seemed reasonable, indisputable, and fairly commonplace, derived as they were from time-tested philosophers such as Cicero and Locke. To Congress the phrase "all men are created equal" at least meant that aristocratic birth would no longer guarantee any special privilege, and on a broader level that all people share the legitimate political aspiration to be free.

Whether members of the Continental Congress intended for the phrase to include anyone other than property-owning white men is disputable. Many scholars believe it did not apply to blacks, women, aboriginal Americans, or white men without encumbrances. Literature of the period indicates otherwise. As we will see in the next chapter, popular and political authors often invoked the phrase to denounce unequal treatment of black slaves. Less frequently, others, including Abigail Adams and Benjamin Rush, also understood equality to extend to women. As for aboriginal tribes, the newly formed states, like the British before them, treated native peoples as sovereign nations whose inhabitants were their natural equals. Indian removal had not yet become official U.S. policy. In practice, white males benefited disproportionately from the Revolution, but in time the ideology of the Declaration of Independence became a quasi-constitutional statement of universal, popular sovereignty. Although the

Declaration technically lacked the force of law, social groups understood it to provide baseline national commitments that were incorporated into the Constitution.

The preamble of the Declaration of Independence further posited that representative governments should protect people's safety and welfare. The decision to set aside old alliances should not, however, be undertaken lightly. Under the circumstances, the document justified revolution as necessary to end the "long train of abuses and usurpations."

The introductory statements are followed by a series of accusations against George III, meant to demonstrate why perpetration of "repeated injuries and usurpations" forced the colonies to cast off tyrannical rule. The list of charges blames the Crown for intruding on colonists' political, property, privacy, procedural, sovereignty, and commercial rights. After laying out the case against continued British rule, another section lists the colonists' concerted but ineffectual efforts to petition the Crown and settle grievances.

Having set out a vision of national independence and the case against continued colonial rule, the Declaration concludes by "appealing to the Supreme Judge of the world for the rectitude of our intentions ... and by the authority of the good people of these colonies" to dissolve all bonds to Great Britain and to function as "free and independent states."

The people are said to be the source of authority, empowered to determine when government is acting tyrannically and to replace it with another. The statement of liberation from colonial rule is not made in the separate voice of each colony; rather it claims that "one people ... dissolve" the bonds of political alliance between America and Great Britain. The Declaration's central doctrine assumes a state of nature in which all men are created equal, each a rational being who is capable of meaningfully participating in representative governance. Even the phrase "when in the course of human events" is meant to invoke a popular, democratic period of deliberation. But Jefferson identified no mechanism for accurately gauging public sentiments about the propriety of independence. Neither did he furnish any means of resolving conflicts of opinion about how best to affect the national interest. He nevertheless stated unequivocally that "Representatives of the united States of America" declared the colonies to be independent "by Authority of the good People of these Colonies."

Thomas Jefferson was only thirty-three when he drafted the Declaration of Independence. Several other young men also signed the manifesto. Thomas Heyward, Jr., who had received his formal legal education in London during the conflicts of the late 1760s and early 1770s, was but twenty-nine years old. Among the others who placed their signature on the document, Benjamin Rush was thirty, Elbridge Gerry thirty-one, James Wilson was thirty-three, and Arthur Middleton of South Carolina and William Hooper representing North Carolina were both thirty-four. They all must have known the grave risks of signing an act of treason. Adding humor to otherwise grave proceedings, the heavy set Benjamin Harrison turned to Gerry, who was slender, and said, "When the time of hanging comes I shall have the advantage of you. It will be over with me in a minute, but you will be kicking in the air half an hour after I am gone."[36]

Time often alters history in the popular mind. An American folktale spread—fueled by journalists, teachers, Independence Day orators, and Jefferson's mistaken memory—claiming that all fifty-six signatures were affixed to the Declaration on the Fourth of July, but closer analysis rules that out. On July 4 only John Hancock, then president of the Continental Congress, and Charles Thomson, its secretary, signed it. Hancock (who already had a $2,500 bounty on his head) was rumored to have risen from his seat as he boldly put his hand to the parchment: "There, John Bull, can read my name without spectacles—he may double his reward, and I set him at defiance."[37] Most of the men probably signed on August 2, 1776, when an official version of the Declaration of Independence was engrossed on parchment pursuant to an order of Congress.

New York delegates' signatures appear on the Declaration, but until July 9 they were not authorized to even vote for independence. As of July 4, some signatories had not even been appointed to Congress. Five of the Pennsylvania signatories–George Ross, George Clymer, Benjamin Rush, James Smith, and George Taylor–were elected to Congress only on July 20. Another of the Pennsylvanians, Robert Morris, had voted against the Declaration on July 4 but signed the document. Similarly, George Read of Delaware signed despite his contrary vote on the fourth. Maryland delegates Samuel Chase, who later became an associate justice of the Supreme Court, and Charles Carroll of Carrollton were not present in Congress on July 4. Matthew Thornton, a delegate of New Hampshire but born in Ireland, put his name below the Declaration's text when he took his congressional seat on November 4. One signatory, Thomas McKean of Delaware, was present on July 4 and even beckoned for Caesar Rodney to hastily come to Philadelphia to cast that colony's tie-breaking vote but McKean did not sign until 1777 or 1781.[38]

Independence had national and international implications. The Continental Congress strengthened its hand to draft the Articles of Confederation, formulate internal policies, and negotiate treaties. The Declaration's statement of national ideology fired up the army. The commitment to a government beholden to the will of the people became the cornerstone for the revolutionary generation and the newly founded country.

3

THE NATION'S INFANCY

THE DECLARATION OF INDEPENDENCE LISTED REASONS TO SEPARATE from Britain and principles for the new American polity. The decision to become politically autonomous of England was coupled with a framework for a new governmental structure beholden to the will of the people. However, the political, social, legal, and economic culture of the day did not match the Declaration's idealism; the document's contemporaries understood as much. The Declaration of Independence signaled an unwavering willingness to end the privileges of aristocracy, yet blacks, unpropertied white men, and women were barred from participating in representative democracy. The revolutionary generation began tackling its own shortcomings but left fulfillment of its legacy to future generations.

The original printed version of the Declaration, known as the "Dunlap Broadside" of July 4, 1776, listed only John Hancock and Charles Thomson as signatories. They received the honor, along with the intrinsic risk of capture, in their separate capacities as the president and secretary of the Second Continental Congress. Not until January 18, 1777, did Congress order that the Declaration be republished with the names of subsequent signers, which had until then been cloaked in secrecy. In the meantime,

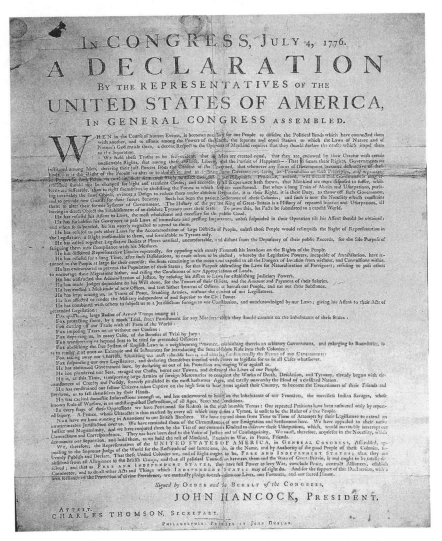

FIGURE 3.1 Dunlap broadside, "Declaration of Independence," July 4, 1776. (Image courtesy of the U.S. National Archives and Records Administration.)

the document's proclamations of sovereignty and natural rights were disseminated throughout the states.[1]

After voting for the final text of the Declaration, Congress informed Americans and potential overseas allies and trading partners of its content. The newborn nation had expressed its sovereignty and principles. The text was read publicly on the eighth of July, 1776, in Philadelphia, where the Continental Congress was meeting. The honor fell on Colonel John Nixon, a sheriff and member of the Council on Safety. He later became president of the Bank of North America. Nixon read the document to loud applause in the State House Yard, later renamed Independence Square. The first copy of the Declaration was also fastened to a pole for public display. The First Battalion, stationed in Easton, Pennsylvania, along with a crowd of ordinary citizens heard a reading of the Declaration on July 8, 1776, followed by the marching of infantry, "with drums beating, fifes playing." Throughout the other states the document was likewise read to both civilians and soldiers. The message was as much a call to arms as it was a statement of national purpose.[2]

Because of its close proximity to Philadelphia, the inhabitants of Dover, Delaware, received word of the achievement by post on July 5 or 6. One of the state's delegates, Caesar Rodney, sent a letter with details of the decision to break from the allegiance to Britain. An election for the battalion officers was stopped so that the letter could be read to a regiment of soldiers and a gathered crowd. Those in attendance let out three loud huzzahs to signal their approval. Then, following a parade of the light infantry, the Committee of Safety of Delaware ordered the burning of King George III's portrait. On July 27, 1776, the Delaware Assembly met and appointed delegates to a state constitutional convention in response to the break from colonial dependence.[3]

The first reading of the Declaration of Independence in New Jersey took place on July 8, in Trenton. On July 9, independence was also proclaimed at the main building of the College of New Jersey (now known as Princeton University), to the firing of "a triple volley of musketry." Writing from a military fortress in the state, Major F. Barber reported in a letter that on July 16 his colonel gave the troops time away from their assignments in order to hear the reading of the Declaration followed by "the fire of three cannons from the fort, three huzzas, and this sentence,—'God bless the United States of America.'" The men also enjoyed a treat of three barrels of grog. The news traveled like wildfire to other parts of the state, indicating that the revolution enjoyed widespread support. Frolickers in Bridgetown, New Jersey burnt the king's coat of arms, as the celebrants had done in Philadelphia. Those in attendance then heard a speech from a renowned physician from West Jersey, who solemnly proclaimed that they were entering a great but terrible period and adjured the audience against using their new freedom as an excuse for "disorder and licentiousness."[4]

While Americans internalized news of independence, the pressing military situation called for decisive action. Colonial troops pitched bulwarks against a predicted British attack. By July 12, Admiral Howe, accompanied by thousands of supporting soldiers, arrived on Staten Island, preparing to attack New Jersey and New York City. Breastworks were also built up around the Long Island coastline, there being no certainty where the British fleet might press its assault.

George Washington, commander-in-chief of the Army of the United Colonies, had already received news of the Declaration's passage on July 9. On that date, he ordered several Brigades to gather, and officers to read the document to troops on the Commons. Soldiers had heard the reading of the Declaration of Independence in the city of New York three days earlier. Decades after the event, a veteran remembered how the general looked onto the hollow square where officers were mustered in parade formations. That evening a large assembly gathered around a statute of George III, posed on horseback, that stood at Bowling Green; they pulled the statue down. Forty-two thousand bullets were later made from its metal. Hearing of the country's independence changed allegiance from Great Britain to a nation as yet undefined by anything other than its declaration of independence.

On the ninth, the Provincial Congress of New York, meeting in White Plains, approved of the Declaration of Independence and changed its name to Convention of the Representatives of the State of New York. Three days later, a private stationed in New York wrote his father a letter: "I most heartily congratulate you on the Declaration of Independence, a Declaration which happily dissolves our Connexions with the Kingdom where the Name of King is synonymous to that of Tyrant, and the name of Subjects to that of Slaves."[5] Remarkable in this report is not only the zeal of a soldier but the extent to which it melds with faith that the Revolution was a means to liberation.

On the eighteenth of July, the Declaration was read to the general population of New York at the City Hall. Many British loyalists continued to disapprove of independence and held out hope for reconciling with the mother country. But their sentiments did not carry the day. The reading of the nation's nascent manifesto of sovereignty, which was making its way through all of the states, was like a battle cry and a call for unity. The existence of a document explaining the reasons behind the fight for

FIGURE 3.2 *Harper's Weekly*, Saturday, July 9, 1870, p 1 (vol. XIV, no. 706), cover page/ page 1. First Reading of Declaration of Independence In New York. (Image courtesy of the Library of Congress.)

independence and the need for a new, centralized government gave soldiers and ordinary citizens alike something more concrete to coalesce around than a mere abstract concept of liberty.[6]

For many, however, liberty remained no more than a byword. On August 9, 1776, the *New York Journal* reported a reading of the Declaration of Independence where a toast was raised to the "Liberty to those who have spirit to assert it." Advertisements in the same issue starkly showed how narrowly some understood those words. John Mitchel offered a reward for capturing a runaway "mulatto slave named David." Benjamin Pitney offered a reward for the capture of "a negro man named Samson," and Jacob Wilkins advertised to pay for the capture of "a negro man named Jack" who was born in Guinea and spoke broken English. The incongruity between the message of universal rights and the fact of slavery seems to have been lost on the newspaper editor.[7]

New England states, with considerable populations who supported abolition of slavery, came out strongly for independence. The document was read to large, joyful crowds in New Hampshire on July 18. For an unknown reason, the document was not read publicly in Connecticut. Instead, the state's General Assembly simply approved the Declaration in October 1776.[8]

The earliest celebration of the Declaration in Massachusetts appears to have taken place in the city of Worcester "on the green near the liberty pole." After a boisterous celebration, the crowd made its way to the King's Arms tavern, and demanded that the sign be removed. Twenty-four toasts were made; among the more humorous ones were "Sore eyes to all Tories, and a chestnut burr for an eye stone," and "Perpetual itching without the benefit of scratching, to the enemies of America." In Boston, the Declaration of Independence was read from the State House balcony on July 18. This same structure was where Samuel Adams, John Adams, James Warren, John Hancock, and other colonial radicals delivered their fiery speeches in the 1760s and early 1770s. Just beyond its walls, the gunshots of the Boston Massacre had set the colonies aflame.

The toasts that followed the readings reflected the Declaration's dual federalism. First, patriots drank in honor of the newly proclaimed national sovereignty, to the "prosperity and perpetuity to the United States of America." Another toast was offered for the underlying aspirations of the revolution, "the universal prevalence of civil and religious liberty." Yet another toast to the Massachusetts legislature indicated the burgeoning dual sovereignty of the newly constituted united states. Celebrations also took place at Watertown for people who were unwilling to travel to Boston for fear of contracting smallpox, which was then raging through the city. At another celebration, a pageant of drums and ringing bells followed the reading of the Declaration of Independence. As elsewhere, the assembly indicated its approbation for the document with "repeated huzzas, firing of musketry and cannon, bonfires, and other demonstrations of joy." With each reading the country was becoming more acquainted with its station among nations and the aims of Revolution.[9]

Meanwhile, the Declaration was read in the Baltimore Court House on July 22. There were gunfire salutes, and the city was illuminated at night. The next month a convention gathered at Annapolis to frame a state constitution. And in November 1776, the Continental Congress moved to Annapolis.[10]

Revolutionary leaders focused their efforts on cities, likely realizing that they would draw larger and more diverse audiences than in rural areas. In Virginia, on July 25, the Declaration was read at three government buildings in Williamsburg, which was then the state's capital and seat of the College of William and Mary, Thomas Jefferson's alma mater. On the fifth of August, the Declaration was read in Richmond, to which four years later the state capital would be moved, regaling in the toasts and congratulations of property owners and militiamen.[11]

The many contemporary reports of parades, gun salutes, huzzahs, and general festivities throughout the colonies indicated that a large portion of the population supported independence and the ideals stated in the Declaration of Independence. John Hancock's request of the states to disseminate the document was echoed in North Carolina by the Council of Safety, which ordered that town and county committees proclaim the Declaration in the "most public manner." Cornelius Harnett, president of the Council of Safety, whom Josiah Quincy once called the Samuel Adams of North Carolina because of his prodigious efforts prior to the Revolution in organizing opposition to British taxation, received the honor of reading the document. He recited the document's content before a jubilant throng in the town of Halifax, which was then the legislative seat of the North Carolina General Assembly. The raucous crowd started cheering as the document was opened, but a hush then fell over the audience, allowing

Harnett to complete the reading. After hearing the final words ring out, with their pledge of the people's lives and fortunes to independence, tremendous shouts of joy, flag waving, cannon firing, and boisterous street parties broke out.[12]

The day after these festivities, on July 26, the Kentish Guards and their commanding officer, Colonel Richard Fry, organized themselves in parade formation at the State House at Greenwich, Rhode Island. After hearing a reading of the Declaration, the crowd entered Arnold's Hall for a light meal. Toasts were made to all thirteen states, to the Colonial Army, and to Rhode Island. Militarily and politically, the state was becoming part of a unified government of sovereign states. A participant also lionized the international implications of liberation: "May Liberty expand her sacred wings, and in glorious effort diffuse her influence o'er and o'er the globe." Thus, at a time when Americans were celebrating unity of the states, they were also speaking in terms of human rights. In Providence, salutes were made for the "Independent States of America forever [to] be an asylum for Liberty." An octogenarian named George Brown was chosen to read the Declaration "on account of the 'compass of his voice.'" A crowd gathered along the street to hear him articulate a vision for nationhood.[13]

In the Deep South, men and women of all ages gathered in Charleston, South Carolina, on August 5 around the Liberty Tree to hear a reading of the Declaration. That same spot had been a revolutionary gathering place since the time of the Stamp Act protests. The beating of drums, playing of music, and waving of flags added to the independence festivities. Following the recitation, the Episcopalian Reverend William Percy delivered a patriotic address in the sweltering heat, during which his slave fanned him. A foreigner, writing home of this strange sight, could not help but notice the hypocrisy of reading of liberty while being cooled by an individual bound to perpetual slavery.[14]

Georgia, last among the original thirteen colonies to receive the Declaration, voiced its support for natural liberty on August 8. During a mock funeral in Savannah, to symbolize the interment of George III's political existence, the eulogist called on fellow citizens to renounce the King for trampling "the constitution of our country and the sacred rights of mankind." This formula expressed contempt for the monarch because he infringed on colonists' positive and innate laws. Participants of the procession accused the King of tyranny and resolved "to fight for our rights and privileges."[15]

Public readings of the Declaration of Independence offered a unifying battle cry that helped bridge the manifold differences among thirteen sovereign entities spread across a largely pristine frontier. Partly because of the difficulty of traversing such distances, there was little communication among the various citizens. Travel by coach and on horseback was common, but the sea offered the most direct path for transport. In the South, journeys by land were often slowed because many waterways lacked bridges, making them formidable natural barriers that frustrated individual riders and businessmen. Covering distances between the waterways was also difficult because of the rutty, sandy, and tree-strewn condition of roads in those days. Rivers, rivulets, and streams were even less reliable because they were subject to flooding and their shoals were not well mapped. Little trade transpired among merchants who shipped their goods along the Potomac, Susquehanna, Santee, and Roanoke Rivers. The Allegheny and Appalachian mountain ranges rendered communications irregular between the eastern seaboard—where the major cities of New York, Baltimore, Boston, Philadelphia, and Savannah had been built—and western villages irregular at best.

In the nascent nation, the Declaration of Independence and the constitutional infrastructure of national governance played important unifying roles among thirteen diverse and loosely linked states. Canals, steam engines, and trains would eventually link the country in a manner that was unforeseeable at the time of the Revolution. In the early republic, communication and travel between states was crude and laborious because of the many fords, mud holes, rickety bridges, washed out roads, and ruts, a common ideology as it was expressed in the Declaration of Independence provided a dispersed people with shared beliefs about representational governance and individual rights. Interpretation of those themes would cause much debate in the halls of Congress, state and local assemblies, and local taverns, but the Continental Congress's decision to include a statement of human rights in the Declaration made it pertinent to conversations that extended far beyond liberation from British colonial rule.

Prior to ratification of the Constitution, the Declaration of Independence defined the character of a national community committed to protecting people's life, liberty, property, and pursuit of happiness. Thereafter, it became associated with a national ethos that influenced the rhetoric of politicians, social organizations, and ordinary citizens.

Advance copy from

OXFORD
UNIVERSITY PRESS

198 Madison Avenue, New York, NY 10016-4314

**Title: For Liberty and Equality: The Life and Times
of the Declaration of Independence - $29.95**

Author: Alexander Tsesis

Publication date: 06/01/12

Cloth ISBN: 9780195379693
Cloth price:

Samuel Adams, who was one of earliest agitators against British colonial policies, recognized that congressional decisiveness was crucial for strengthening interstate confederation. On July 15, 1776, Adams rejoiced that "our Declaration of Independency has given Vigor to the Spirits of the People." Writing to Dr. James Warren, Adams expressed wonder that "beyond our Expectation" all the colonies approved "our declaration of Independence."[16]

The Declaration changed the nature of combat, transforming a civil war into a revolution. It became clear that the states would not desist from hostilities without the complete withdrawal of British troops and administrators. An assemblyman from Sussex County, New Jersey, who eventually joined the British army initially wrote enthusiastically to his cousin, a future New York representative to the Continental Congress, that separation from the King would provide the people with clarity for the "heart and hand" to move together. Also confident that the Declaration would help build resolve in the newborn country, a future Massachusetts senator congratulated one of the document's signers, Elbridge Gerry, for "the late full declaration" that cast the die leaving none doubting "on which side it is his duty to act." Another of the Declaration's signers, Benjamin Rush, wrote of the Pennsylvanian's increased military morale, being certain that "I think the declaration of independence will produce union and new exertions in England." The sense of monumental achievement was broadly accepted, but the statement of independence also created a rift among the colonists.[17]

Independence put British Loyalists in America on their heels. In some parts of the country, tarring and feathering, imprisoning, and threatening English sympathizers became cruel sports, which resulted in an outward migration that had already begun in 1775. The Declaration caused a sharp political shift of support from Tories (who supported imperial policies) and moderate factions to the revolutionaries.[18]

Despite much opposition in England, the newly founded United States was greeted by unexpected support there. In 1776, the former governor of West Florida, George Johnstone, asserted at a session of the British House of Commons that although "he was far from being pleased with the Americans for their declarations in favour of independency," he nevertheless "saw clearly that they were driven to the measure by our vigorous persecution of them." Similar sentiments were voiced in a London opposition newspaper, *The Public Advertiser*. It pointed out that the Declaration of Independence proved the disparaged Americans were "manifestly not those cowards and poltroons which our over-hasty, ill judging, wrong-headed Administration styled them."[19]

The more common response to independence, however, indicted Americans for their hypocrisies. The English lexicographer Samuel Johnson remarked that among Americans the "loudest yelps for liberty" came from the "drivers of Negroes." *The Gentleman's Magazine* in September 1776 mocked the Declaration's proclaimed "self evident" truth that all men are created equal: "In what are they created equal? Is it in size, strength, understanding, figure, moral or civil accomplishments, or situation of life? Every plough-man knows that they are not created equal in any of these." Another London newspaper disparagingly recounted the event at which a South Carolina clergyman read the Declaration of Independence while a slave fanned him and held an umbrella shielding him from the sun.

Thus, even the opposition took up the Declaration as a national statement of purpose against which American conduct could be measured. At the tail end of 1776, a supporter of the Crown drew attention to the Declaration's incomplete account of history: it mentioned the colonists' humble petitions but silently passed over the Boston Tea Party; the destruction of Loyalists' properties; Virginia's and Maryland's capture of British ships, which began even before the signing of the Declaration; and attempted invasions into Canada during 1775.[20]

The many mentions of the Declaration of Independence in American and British documents indicate its influence in the early republic. During that period, the document's statements about sovereignty and equality often appeared in the writings of prominent American politicians.[21]

The extant evidence indicates that the Declaration indeed affected the Early American Republic. Between 1776 and 1812, the full text of the document was republished countless times and read even more often at Fourth of July celebrations. Multiple discussions of the Declaration during that interval concerned both America's emancipation from British rule and the mandate to protect the people's unalienable rights. The instrument was understood as a decisive break from England and as a statement of individual rights.[22]

Contemporaries immediately recognized that the Declaration's justification of revolution validated taking up arms against England. In 1777,
an author stated that the reasoning of the Declaration justified the colonists' decision to break with Great Britain. War echoed the message on
parchment. The unalterable nature of the rupture was also understood
overseas. On November 7, 1777, British Prime Minister Lord Frederick
North explicitly stated before the House of Commons that the Declaration
of Independence had pushed British subjects in America to take extreme
measures against what he considered to be legitimate use of Parliamentary
authority. Two years later, an Edinburgh, Scotland, newspaper reported
that "the declaration of independence staggered her most zealous friends"
because it threw off colonial authority and annihilated commerce with
England.[23]

America's founding generation came to regard the Declaration as more
than an assertion of sovereignty over land and waterways. In the midst
of revolution, a committee of the Pennsylvania General Assembly found
that an oath of allegiance to the king of England was incompatible with
the Declaration's assertion of freedom and independence for the state and
"the present glorious struggle for Liberty and the natural Rights of mankind." The document gave voice to deeply held political philosophy that
renounced aristocracy and social hierarchy. "The same act that announced
the existence of our Republic, proclaimed also the principle on which it is
erected," wrote Henry Steward, referring to the "principle of equality contained in the declaration of Independence . . . [a] principle essential to every
rule of Justice, but never before made the basis of any government." The
Declaration's statement of sovereignty was only part of its popular draw. It
also asserted the people's nonnegotiable demand that government protect
their essential rights irrespective of their social standing. The nation's duty
to abide by ordinary people's will was not optional, as it had been under
monarchy, but a centerpiece of the new republic.

The extent to which the Declaration's rhetoric of equality was a reflection of the popular ethos appears in accounts of Independence Day celebrations, which were filled with musical performances, public readings of the
Declaration, and religious services. Exultation for the document came at
the local, state, and federal levels. Toasts offered at "the old Coffee-House"
in New York City were indicative of the public sense of unity and public
safety in the early days of nationhood. Glasses were raised for "the United

States of America—May they be the abode of peace and of freedom, and may their prosperity evidence to the world, that in the union of liberty and of law consists the respectability of government, and the happiness of the individual" and to "the Rights of Man—May they be clearly understood and fully enjoyed.... The great Family of Mankind—United by one common nature, may they feel and know that they have one common interest, 'The happiness of each other.'"

These and similar toasts celebrated not merely the Declaration's significance to nationhood but also the standard it set for protection of human rights. Merchants meeting for the Fourth of July at the popular Tontine Coffee House showed the same enthusiasm. They cheered, for upholding "equal rights," which were conceived as the political end that gave "each man his due." These merchants also remembered the continuing suffering of slaves and expressed the hope that "the soil of America be consecrated by the genius of universal emancipation." Independence celebrations of mechanics and tradesmen demanded that "the hammer and hand ever be uplifted to beat off the shackles of slavery and weld fast the federal union." Celebrants differentiated American statehood from tyrannies throughout the world. The hopes they expressed for an end to monarchies transcended American borders in the hope that "the citizen of the world enjoy equal liberty."[24]

Authors of books, pamphlets, and articles articulated commitment to the Declaration's creed about government's obligation to protect the people's "equal right to life, liberty, and pursuit of happiness."[25] Antislavery advocates adopted the preamble's statement of national principles. Other contemporary polemicists also perceived that the preamble's statement of principles made the proclamation of national sovereignty only one of the Declaration's purposes, extending its relevance to matters of social policy and morality.

The Declaration of Independence readily became part of the collective American consciousness because its description of rights restated widely accepted political thought. Thomas Jefferson's formulation of the "self-evident" truth that "all men are created equal, that they are endowed by their Creator with certain unalienable Rights, that among these are Life, Liberty and the pursuit of Happiness" echoed the mainstream political thought of his day. In drafting the Declaration,

Jefferson relied on contemporary understanding of universal rights. As his political star rose, the public mind came to associate these principles with its author.

Years after independence, two of the most prominent signers of the Declaration accused Jefferson of copying the document from other sources. Richard Henry Lee and John Adams drew attention to its lack of originality. Jefferson shook off these accusations. In his defense, he wrote that the Declaration of Independence "was intended to be an expression of the American mind," not personal opinion. Lee, a catalytic delegate to the first Continental Congress and a signer of the Declaration, claimed that Jefferson "copied from Locke's treatise on government." For instance, the preamble's language resembled John Locke's assertion that persons "by nature, [are] all free, equal and independent." The erudite Adams, who along with Lee had been one of the most influential figures of the Continental Congress in 1776, wrote to Timothy Pickering with undeniable irritation that there "is not an idea in" the Declaration of Independence "but what had been hackneyed in Congress for two years before."[26] The aspersions were partisan and not entirely objective, but Lee and Adams accurately described the depth to which public consensus influenced the drafting of the nation's founding statement.

Jefferson was one of many authors who tied revolution to a higher cause. Revolutionary indignation against British interference stemmed from the notion that as English citizens Americans had natural rights that their government was bound to respect. With the War of Independence, this sentiment was universalized beyond the English Commonwealth to all mankind. The thought of breaking away became tenable because the people's interest in common happiness came to outweigh their allegiance to the Crown. The Reverend David Griffith, who became chaplain of the Third Virginia Regiment, wrote in 1776 that God did not require obedience to the king, whose acts were destructive to human happiness. Providence and reason did not require citizens to be subject to arbitrary laws that undermined their rights and overall welfare.[27]

Revolutionary adulation of the Declaration focused both on the nation's military achievements and on its political ideals. Mercy Otis Warren, a historian, wrote that the people retained the power to check governmental entities whose function was to protect their happiness and safety. Unlike aristocracies, which aggrandized private interests, a republican form of government's purpose was to preserve the community's property, life, and liberty. An observer of an Independence Day celebration in Philadelphia regarded the country's greatest achievement as outshining victories through the ashes and violence of battle. It was, rather, a celebration "of knowledge over ignorance, of virtue over vice, and of liberty over slavery." Likewise, a newspaper columnist wrote from Salem, Massachusetts, that the Fourth of July ought not "to be celebrated, merely as affecting the separation of one country from the jurisdiction of another: but as being the result of a rational discussion and definition of the rights of man, and the end of civil government; and as opening the fairest prospect of political happiness, that ever smiled upon the world." The article went on to call for immigration to the land where mechanics and farmers alike could rest secure in the fruits of their labors. During these early years of nationhood, in southern cities such as Baltimore, Maryland, there was talk of liberation from arbitrary domination that had thwarted the human ability to enjoy inborn equal rights and freedoms.[28]

A quandary facing the nation was how to safeguard human liberty and equality while allocating adequate powers to a central government. The Declaration of Independence created both a country beholden to the will of the people and principles for organizing a new government capable of protecting their safety and happiness. The authority of government, the framers believed, derives from the people's willingness to grant it a limited set of functions. A government that is answerable to all its citizens can best preserve "the natural equality of mankind." Laws subordinate particular individuals' interests to a civic system capable of administering justice and not favoring any "classes of men."[29]

The principles asserted in the Declaration of Independence were aspirational decrees to end aristocratic rule; at the time of the Revolution, this was a radical ideal. Creation of a national state on the premise that persons had equal rights at birth, as was popularly accepted in the late 1770s, meant that government had an obligation to exercise its power to preserve natural rights.[30] The often-stated refrain about inborn equality and government's duty to protect human happiness is a clear indication of general acceptance of the natural rights philosophy behind the Declaration of Independence's phrase "all men are created equal." Polemicists knew that this language was likely to strike a chord with ordinary people. Creation of government was understood to be a collective decision to join forces for the benefit of the whole.

By elaborating on the reasons for undoing the bonds of monarchy and aristocracy as a whole, the founders distinguished their new government from autocracies around the world. Henceforth, governance was to be based on the people's will and administered for their benefit. Americans' decisive step toward republican government had a profound effect on world history.

4

YOUTHFUL REPUBLIC

REVOLUTIONARIES COMMITTED THE GOVERNMENT TO PROTECTING natural rights. They believed monarchical hierarchies to be incompatible with the statement on equality enshrined in the second paragraph of the Declaration of Independence. The radical claim that human rights are innate rather than privileges granted by rulers set a fire that helped raze privileged social hierarchies in favor of representative governance. "Human nature," as Benjamin Rush said, "is the same in all ages and countries."[1] For him and most other politicians of his generation, this meant there are inborn characteristics that are inalienable, irrespective of a person's level of education, social and political station, or religious affiliation. The belief that everyone is entitled to fair treatment also had direct ramifications for the limits of governmental power. The Declaration of Independence rendered protection of human rights a quintessential aspect of governance, but pragmatic domestic and foreign considerations counterbalanced those ideals with policy making tradeoffs.

The influence of the Declaration on early nation building went well beyond its original purpose. A document that was first meant to announce and justify U.S. independence wound up influencing state and federal policies. The Declaration's statements on rights and self-governance extended its significance beyond announcing nationhood. States found no difficulty reconciling the document's passages on sovereignty with their own

constitutional developments. But participants in proto-antislavery movements condemned states that retained slavery because the institution was
so evidently contrary to the Declaration's assertion of universal liberty.
Early women's rights advocates also took inspiration from the document to
indict existing practices. The statement on rights created a national ethos
that deepened the sense of unity in the new country and established an
aspirational norm of equality.

A period of nation building followed on the heels of the Revolution. The
process of allocating powers between federal and state governments
unfolded gradually. The Declaration variously influenced a number of
states' constitutions. Georgia included a passage in its 1777 constitution
justifying the exercise of power to create a new government on the basis
of "the independence of the United States of America ... declared on the
fourth day of July, one thousand seven hundred and seventy-six." This
clause relied only on the Declaration's statement on sovereignty; little more
could be expected from a state committed to retaining slavery and including only white males in its voter rolls. The next year South Carolina, another
state where the Declaration's statement on rights would have seemed out
of place given strong support for domestic slavery and privileges for free-
holders, similarly explained that drafting a new constitution was necessary
after the momentous change brought about by the declaration "dated the
fourth day of July, one thousand seven hundred and seventy-six."[2]

Vermont, which was not one of the original signatories of the Declaration
of Independence, nevertheless relied on the document for its statement
of existential purpose. The state's 1777 constitution outlawed slavery; its
reliance on the Declaration of Independence was sensitive to the document's statement on inalienable rights in a way that the Georgia and South
Carolina constitutions were not. The Vermont constitution of 1777 was
ideologically closer to the Declaration of Independence than those of the
two Deep South states because it combined the concepts of representational government and universal rights.

On January 15, 1777, a convention of representatives from various counties and towns formed a new state pursuant to the Continental Congress's
decision "on the 4th day of July" to "declare the United Colonies in
America to be free and independent of the crown." A half year later,
Vermont followed its explanation for independence with a clear statement

of rights, closely resembling the Declaration of Independence: "All men are born equally free and independent, and have certain natural, inherent and unalienable rights, amongst which are the enjoying and defending life and liberty; acquiring, possessing and protecting property, and pursuing and obtaining happiness and safety." By diffusing the Declaration's promises into its constitution, Vermont granted state subdivisions the power to enforce ideological portions of the national document.[3]

Like Vermont, New Hampshire's 1784 bill of rights also reflected the Declaration's ideological commitments to protection of individual rights, collective self-governance, and equality: "All men are born equally free and independent; therefore, all government of right originates from the people, is founded in consent, and instituted for the general good. All men have certain natural, essential, and inherent rights—among which are, the enjoying and defending life and liberty; acquiring, possessing, and protecting, property; and, in a word, of seeking and obtaining happiness."[4]

The New York constitution of 1777 integrated the entire Declaration of Independence into its text. But unlike the case of Vermont and New Hampshire, slavery was abolished only gradually in New York, where pragmatism won the day over principle. This was commensurate with the conventional belief throughout most states that despite the country's commitment to universal liberty the possibility of racial insurrection and protection of property rights made it impossible to eliminate the institution immediately, if at all.[5]

Other states did not explicitly include language from the document but unmistakably adopted its political ideology. For instance, in Thomas Paine's opinion Pennsylvania's 1776 constitution was "conformable to the Declaration of Independence" because it granted "every freeman" voting rights. Benjamin Franklin presided over the state's constitutional convention, which afforded poor and propertyless men voting privileges. This republican alteration was meant to reflect the revolutionary contributions of ordinary citizens by excising a 1700 Pennsylvania Assembly requirement that voters own at least fifty acres of land or possess fifty pounds of "lawful money." This form of self-governance was distinct from the accusations of autocracy leveled in the Declaration against King George III. The 1776 constitution not only reiterated some of the same grievances the Declaration of Independence asserted against the King but also used language similar to its principles: "A Declaration of the Rights of the

Inhabitants of ... Pennsylvania: 1. That all men are born equally free and independent, and have certain natural, inherent and inalienable rights, amongst which are, the enjoying and defending life and liberty, acquiring, possessing and protecting property, and pursuing and obtaining happiness and safety." A new state constitution came into effect in 1790, containing similarly reminiscent language to the effect that "men are born equally free and independent, and have certain inherent and indefeasible rights."[6]

The prologue of the 1780 Massachusetts constitution also contained a bill of rights, written by John Adams, dramatically proclaiming: "All people are born free and equal, and have certain natural, essential, and unalienable rights; among which may be reckoned the right of enjoying and defending their lives and liberties; that of acquiring, possessing, and protecting property; in fine, that of seeking and obtaining their safety and happiness." Those sentiments represented the radical formula of universal equality and unalienable rights of the Declaration of Independence, in part reflecting Adams's role in editing Jefferson's first draft of the document while serving with him on the Declaration drafting committee. In an 1841 letter published in an abolitionist paper, John Adams's son and former president John Quincy Adams wrote: "The virtuous principle of the Revolution of American Independence was human liberty—universal human liberty. This was emphatically the principle of the Declaration of Independence. It was the paramount principle of the Declaration of Rights forming the foundation of the Constitution of the Commonwealth of Massachusetts." Demonstrating the effectiveness of these principles when translated from the Declaration of Independence into a formal state law, Chief Justice William Cushing for the Massachusetts Superior Court decreed that slavery contradicted the state constitution's principled commitment to the natural freedom and equality of all men.[7]

As the country grew and spread westward, other states' constitutions adopted similar natural rights language reminiscent of the Declaration of Independence. They associated the American social contract with a government obligation to protect the general welfare.[8]

The newborn states understood they were more likely to survive in a national union than they could on their own. Drafting the U.S. Constitution would define the branches of governance, about which the Declaration of Independence only intimated. Having created a country and by 1783 having gained international recognition from France, the Netherlands, and

Spain, the United States still needed to demonstrate that it could function as a unified federal system. The Constitution was a binding expression of public will that, a contemporary said, "transplanted ... the precious maxims of the Declaration of Independence." In the words of another, "In 1787, the patriotic fathers," at the Philadelphia constitutional convention, "held the same sentiment" as the sages of 1776. The documents were complementary but not identical. The Declaration of Independence was to the Constitution what the Constitution is to statute: a general statement that becomes increasingly detailed.

The Declaration established the overall structure of representative government, while the Constitution specified its operation and allocated its powers. The Declaration created a unified national government. The Constitution went much further, detailing the composition and the functions of its three branches—executive, legislative, and judicial. The Declaration of Independence's approval of government by consent was translated into the Constitution as an adoption of representative rather than majoritarian democracy. For instance, the Declaration established a national polity composed of states, while the original Constitution granted states the authority to run their own day-to-day operations.[9]

There was also a marked contrast between them. Unlike its forerunner, the original Constitution did not explicitly acknowledge the existence of inalienable rights. The Declaration's preamble was a statement of national consensus about the equality of inalienable rights, but until the late nineteenth century the Constitution's statement of protected rights, known as the Bill of Rights, did not even apply to states' actions. The Constitution claimed to be the creation of "we the people of the United States," but much of U.S. history has been an effort to reconcile the Declaration of Independence's statement about the equality of inalienable human rights with the disparities countenanced by the Constitution. During the nation's first hundred years, the greatest humanitarian effort was mounted against slavery. Abolitionists and feminists tended to rely on the Declaration because the original Constitution made no mention of equality. A Constitution "ordained and established" in order to "promote the general Welfare, and secure the Blessings of Liberty" appeared to circle back to unalienable rights, but the ninth section of its first article protected slave importation for twenty years after ratification. The Continental Congress had rejected Thomas Jefferson's effort to include a paragraph in the Declaration of Independence condemning the British king for slave trade into the colonies, but it took the Constitution to affirmatively protect slave importation from federal intervention. The Three-Fifths Clause, which gave slave-holding states extra legislative representation, countenanced hereditary racial exploitation of African slave labor, thereby protecting a racial aristocracy irreconcilable with the Declaration's condemnation of social hierarchy. The Declaration asserted that all men are created equal, while the Constitution allowed states to maintain inequalities based on prejudices and gender stereotypes, even granting slaveholders the power to pursue and recapture fugitives.

Supporters of the proposed constitution, who were known as Federalists, and its opponents, the so-called Antifederalists, referred to the Declaration of Independence in their debates on ratification of the Constitution. Their reliance on the document to make diametrically opposite points shows the Declaration to have been mutually revered but not given to only one interpretation.

Despite the states' continued governance of day-to-day affairs, the Declaration announced creation of a national identity, attributing its authorship to the "good People of these Colonies." The Constitution similarly purported to be the creation of "we the people." Both phrases spoke to the entire body politic rather than a confederacy of separate and independent sovereignties. Nevertheless, even though the original Constitution lacked any protection of rights, the Declaration's underlying justification for revolution and governance clearly related to a popular desire to safeguard civil liberties.

Antifederalists, such as Major General William Lenoir from North Carolina, argued against ratification because the proposed constitution "secures no right; or, if it does, it is in so vague and undeterminate a manner, that we do not understand it." They believed that including constitutional protections of rights was essential to prevent the excesses of government that the Declaration of Independence had condemned. Antifederalists considered states to be better repositories of popular governance than a national behemoth. Pennsylvanian John Smilie wrote "that unless some criterion is established by which it could be easily and constitutionally ascertained how far our governors may proceed, and by which it might appear when they transgress their jurisdiction," the people's right to abolish government and uphold principles of the Declaration of Independence would be "mere sound without substance." Samuel Spencer, a participant in the first North Carolina ratification convention, complained that "our rights are not guarded." He wanted more than mere commemoration of the Declaration of Independence: "There is no declaration of rights" in the Constitution "to secure to every member of the society those unalienable rights which ought not to be given up to any government." In one of a series of letters, "Cato," whom scholars typically identify as New York Governor George Clinton, wrote that "the power of government is entrusted with those, who are esteemed the most capable of promoting the happiness of the public." In exercising authority, Cato counseled, states must be mindful of the Declaration of Independence's proclamation "that all men are created equal; and that they are endowed by their Creator with certain unaliena-ble rights: that among these are life, liberty and the pursuit of happiness." Cato, just like other Antifederalists, thought positive law to be necessary to enforce the natural rights promised in the Declaration of Independence.[10]

On the other side of the constitutional debate, during the Pennsylvania ratification convention James Wilson read aloud the Declaration of Independence's statement of unalienable rights, equality, and happiness. He emphasized the need to acquiesce to the people's will by adopting the Constitution. Jonathan Elliot, who in the 1830s published some of the debates of state conventions on ratification of the Constitution, also took a Federalist perspective on the Declaration's relevance to federal sovereignty:

> The declaration of the independence of all the colonies was the united act of all. . . . It was an act of original, inherent sovereignty by the peo-ple themselves, resulting from their right to change the form of gov-ernment, and to institute a new government, whenever necessary for their safety and happiness. So the Declaration of Independence treats it. No state had presumed of itself to form a new government, or to provide for the exigencies of the times, without consulting Congress on the subject.

Another group of Federalists believed that the unalienable rights described in the Declaration of Independence were adequately protected by states' bills of rights, with no need for additional national safeguards.[11]

Federalists won the debate by passing the original Constitution without protections for fundamental liberties, but shortly following its ratification they agreed to add the Bill of Rights. On June 8, 1789, James Madison proposed that an amendment be added to reflect that "power is originally vested in, and consequently derived from the people. That government is instituted, and ought to be exercised for the benefit of the people."[12] Though the exact wording was not adopted, its purpose became the Ninth Amendment's guarantee that "the enumeration in the Constitution, of certain rights, shall not be construed to deny or disparage others retained by the people." This provision, as Professor Charles L. Black, Jr. pointed out, should be interpreted to mean that the people retained the unalienable freedoms guaranteed by the Declaration of Independence rather than relinquishing them to the government.[13]

Some of the other amendments directly resembled passages from the Declaration. One of the grievances colonists complained of in the Declaration of Independence was the king's attempt to deprive Americans "of the benefit of trial by jury." To prevent this form of abuse, Article Six of the Bill of Rights provided that all criminal defendants "shall enjoy the right to a speedy and public trial, by an impartial jury." Where the Declaration blamed the king for "quartering large bodies of armed troops among us," the Third Amendment prohibited soldiers from quartering in any house during times of peace without the owner's consent, "nor in time of war, but in a manner to be prescribed by law." The Declaration complained that England had passed laws without regard for the public good, while the Constitution asserted that government was to act for the "general welfare." In 1776, the colonists decried the king's repeated unwillingness to seat elected representatives, and the Constitution guaranteed "to every state in this union a republican form of government" made up of elected officials.

Despite their similarities, an important provision was unstated by the Bill of Rights: the equality of all people. That principle of national identity, with its manifold implications for national and state governance, would be linked almost exclusively with the Declaration of Independence, rather than the Constitution, until ratification of the Reconstruction Amendments.

The Declaration of Independence's statement of equality was carefully parsed by religious ministers, philosophers, and ordinary citizens. Even after ratification of the Bill of Rights, those who invoked the creed of equality turned to the Declaration of Independence. In 1794, Samuel Adams, serving as the acting governor of Massachusetts after John Hancock's death, told both branches of the state's legislature that when "the Representatives of the United States of America" agreed "all men are created equal, and are endowed by their Creator with certain unalienable rights," they proclaimed "the doctrine of liberty and equality" to be the "political creed of the United States."[14]

Bishop James Madison, the slave-holding president of William and Mary College and cousin of future U.S. president James Madison, wrote that "the natural equality of men" was "the only basis on which universal justice, order and freedom, can be firmly built, or permanently secured." William L. Brown, a Scottish minister and professor of moral philosophy at the University of Utrecht, developed one of the most elaborate political theories of his day: despite differences in human abilities and talents, "the grand principle of the natural equality of men ... is the only basis on which universal justice, order, and freedom, can be firmly built, and permanently secured." Even though all people seek advancement through personal achievements, to satisfy their social urges they organize communities to further their welfare. Mankind experiences a greater portion of happiness by benefiting from the combined talents of society. Each person is obligated to contribute socially through his unique skills, rendering each citizen no less worthy of respect than any other.[15]

Richard Price, a moral philosopher with close contacts in the Continental Congress who criticized American slavery and slave trade, explained that the maxim "'that all men are naturally equal,'" reminiscent of documents such as the Declaration of Independence, "refers to their state when grown up to maturity and become independent agents, capable to acquire property and direct their own conduct."

Although the nation was established on the principle of equality, the term was rarely thought to refer to women. Governance by the people's representatives shielded individual rights from the uncertain whims of autocracy, but it favored powerful majorities capable of protecting their interests.[16]

Speaking at a Fourth of July celebration in 1801, William Hunter forthrightly said that women and blacks were denied the vote out of "utility and expediency." He then patronizingly asserted that women were prohibited from participating in the elective franchise because they were so "interesting, fascinating, with power to direct us" that once in politics they were likely to "engross a complete monopoly of power." As for blacks he believed slaves should be excluded from governance because they were "extremely dependent, extremely ignorant, extremely indigent, and fiercely barbarous."[17] Hunter had used his opportunity to address a crowd gathered to celebrate the Declaration of Independence to justify inequality.

From the time of independence, it was evident that lawmakers had no intention of sharing the equal bounties of victory with women. Even before Richard Henry Lee moved Congress to vote for independence, Abigail Adams wrote her husband, John Adams, imploring him to include women in the quest for liberal equality. "I long to hear that you have declared an independency," she wrote. "And ... I desire you would remember the ladies and be more generous and favorable to them than your ancestors." A decade and a half later, Mary Wollstonecraft, who published what many have called the first feminist declaration of independence, took revolutionaries to task for establishing society on the premise of equality while chaining "half of mankind" to gender subordination.[18]

A female speaker at a Fourth of July celebration linked the imperative to end women's subordination with abolition of slavery. This was a very early connection of two causes that abolitionists of the nineteenth century would later intertwine through the binding principles of the Declaration of Independence. The speaker, referred to in published reports only as "A Lady," asserted that people gather to celebrate independence "not on account of the atcheivments [sic] of armies," nor independence from England, but "because the American people have calmly, and deliberately declared, that 'all men are created EQUAL.'" If this phrase "embrace only half of mankind," she went on to say, it amounts to "only half systems, and will not more support the burden of humanity." The Declaration taught principles for sons and daughters to realize their equal competence for great attainment. So too, the "rights of sufferages [sic]" were of equal concern to men and women. Remaining true to the American creed, she also lamented the fate of the "Ethiop! Suffering brother" and implored him to "curse us not—some of us have principles of justice and bowels of compassion....Africa! Africa!... Where we have excited murders, robberies, and burnings, that we might punish them in our won land with endless, hopeless slavery, on the victims of our subtilty [sic] and their innocent posterity—Declaration of Independence! Where art thou now?" Although

America understood the Declaration to end British aristocracy, it retained the privileges of gender and race.[19]

Contrary to the hopes of such prominent revolutionaries as Benjamin Rush and John Jay, adoption of the Declaration's statement of universal rights did not lead to the immediate demise of slavery. The protections in the Bill of Rights against deprivation of "life, liberty, or property, without due process of law," existed side by side with other sections of the Constitution, such as the Three-Fifths Clause, that countenanced human bondage. Compromises were made for the sake of national unity, despite their overt incompatibility with the Declaration of Independence's statement of equal unalienable rights.

Contemporary newspaper advertisements offer a glimpse of the glaring divergence between ideals and practices. A 1780 *Pennsylvania Packet* contained both the Pennsylvania test oath and advertisements for runaway slaves. Oath takers were required to confirm that they had been loyal to the state "since the Declaration of Independence." In the column to the right, on the same page where mention of the Declaration appeared, a Virginia advertiser offered a reward for a runaway slave named Dick in his midtwenties, with "three remarkable scars on each side of his face, being his country mark." He also sought Tom, who was missing two of his upper teeth and had "curious flourishes, or artificial cuts, on one of his arms, being his country mark." Another offered $200 for a slave from Frederick Town, Maryland, who played the fiddle and managed to escape in "an old grey coat, red jacket," and leather pants. In those days, the same paper also published advertisements of reward for the capture of Anglo Saxon apprentices.[20]

More than any major policy debate of the late eighteenth and early nineteenth centuries, the controversy about slavery kept the Declaration in the public eye. The manifesto's statement on human equality stoked widespread conviction that all people had the same natural interest in liberty, which ran counter to the hierarchical roles of masters and their underlings.

The antislavery movement was not, however, a creation of the Revolution. The ideology Americans broadly espoused in the 1770s was nevertheless inspirational enough to hearten black petitioners, soldiers, and litigants to protest against the resilience of hereditary bondage. The revolutionaries adopted a language of universal human rights to set out a more convincing case for independence from the British Crown. Their eighteenth-century social sensibilities, nurtured in a world where women were subordinate to men and slavery was the norm, could not have fully realized the implications of the Declaration of Independence's recognition that all human beings are endowed by the Creator with the same unalienable rights. By explaining the Revolution in rights-protecting terms, the founding generation created an expectation that humanitarian policies would end the British Empire's system of class subjugation, which in many contemporary minds included putting an end to slavery. Historian David Brion Davis has written that "the Declaration of Independence was the touchstone, the sacred scripture for later American abolitionists, for blacks like David Walker as well as for whites like Benjamin Lundy and William Lloyd Garrison." The revolutionary philosophy of individual liberty and human equality combined in a utopian vision of government that inspired generations of American blacks to claim their fair share of the common good.[21]

Many revolutionaries recognized the incompatibility of slavery with their philosophical statements in the Declaration about natural equality. For them, establishment of a nation went hand in hand with ethical obligations.

The same year in which the Continental Congress voted for the Declaration of Independence, a variety of magazines, newspapers, books, and correspondence reprinted the document. Sometimes authors referenced the Declaration simply as a statement about the transfer of sovereignty from Britain to America. Quite commonly, it was also discussed as a universal statement of rights. Explanations about the decision to dissolve ties with England appear in writings to be linked with "the … glorious struggle for Liberty and the natural Rights of mankind." The sentiments of the Declaration were thought of in universal terms before 1790. This was due to widespread consensus that humans have certain rights in common with other persons. In some cases, this was taken to a very progressive level of advocacy. For instance, an author writing under the rubric "Crito" in 1787 asserted that the Declaration of Independence was an indictment against the hypocrisy of slavery:

It was repeatedly declared in Congress, as language and sentiment of all these States, and by other public bodies of men, "that we hold these truths to be self-evident, that *all men* are created *equal:* That they are endowed by their Creator with certain *unalienable rights:* That among these are *life, liberty,* and the pursuit of happiness":.... The Africans, and the blacks in servitude among us, were really as much included in these assertions as ourselves; and their right, *unalienable right* to liberty, and to procure and possess property, is as much asserted as ours. ... And if we have not allowed them to enjoy these unalienable rights ... we are guilty of a ridiculous, wicked contradiction and inconsistence.

In 1785, the *Freeman's Journal* published an anonymous author's letter with similar ideas about slavery. He quoted from and made specific reference to the Declaration of Independence in order to show that "this custom of enslaving and tyrannizing over our fellow creatures disgraces us."[22]

An "American in Algiers," who in 1797 referred to the Declaration of Independence as "the fabric of the rights of man," faulted those who had bound Africans to slavery even as they enjoyed "the Rights of Man." He put the point in verse:

What then, and are all men created free,
And Afric's sons continue slave to be,
And shall that hue our native climates gave,
Our birthright forfeit, and ourselves enslave?
Are we not made like you of flesh and blood,
Like you some wise, some fools, some bad, some good?
In short, are we not men? and if we be,
By your own declaration we are free.[23]

Fourteen years earlier, New Jersey Quaker leader David Cooper underscored the contradictions between Revolutionary principles of equality and the institution of slavery in two side-by-side columns. He quoted from the Declaration in the left-hand column: "We hold these truths to be self-evident that *all men* are created *equal,* that they are endowed by their Creator with certain *unalienable rights;* that among these are life, *liberty,* and the *pursuit* of *happiness.*" Adjacent to this quote, in the right-hand column, Cooper ripped slaveholders for their hypocrisy"

If these solemn *truths,* uttered at such an awful crisis, are *self-evident:* unless we can shew that the African race are not *men,* words can hardly express the amazement which naturally arises on reflecting, that the very people who make these pompous declarations are slave-holders, and, by their legislative [conduct] tell us that these blessings were only meant to be the *rights* of *whitemen* not of *all men*."

The inhumanity of slavery and its incongruity with the Declaration's aspirations became an oft-elaborated theme in antislavery writings.[24]

George Buchanan, a physician speaking at the American Philosophical Society, quoted the Declaration of Independence in order to demonstrate that its claim of fixed principles was incompatible with oppression of "the unfortunate Africans." For men in the antislavery camp, there was a blatant disconnect between the American creed and slavery. The 1793 publication of the New Jersey Society for Promotion of the Abolition of Slavery's Constitution opened with the epigraph, "We hold these Truths to be *self-evident*, that all men are created equal, that they are endowed by their Creator with certain unalienable rights, that among these are Life, Liberty and the pursuit of Happiness." Having a "government founded on the principles of justice and reason," the document went on, is inconsistent with the withholding of "those rights from an unfortunate and degraded class of our fellow creatures." The select group of New Jersey citizens against the degradation of "part of the rational creation" held meetings to express their commitment to the Declaration's humanistic ideology. Within two decades of its signing, the Declaration had made a deep impression in American culture.[25]

Other abolitionist societies, in Connecticut, Pennsylvania, and Maryland, also quoted the document and called for redress of wrongs done to Africans. The New York Society for Promoting the Manumission of Slaves was organized in 1785, with John Jay taking on the role of president. Alexander Hamilton was another celebrated member of the organization. It successfully lobbied for a manumission law, which took effect on July 4, 1799, by appealing to New Yorkers' sense of consistency: "Read the declaration of independence. 'We hold these things to be *self evident* ... happiness.' Are negroes men and did God create them? ... If so, by what conceivable acts, or at what possible time, could they become absolute slaves to their equals. *Every negro in America is, this moment of right, a freeman*."[26]

Quoting from the same passage of the Declaration as had the New Jersey Society, a supporter of Thomas Jefferson, writing for the *North Carolina*

Journal, declaimed the extent to which "prejudice is substituted for justice ... while slavery is supported by law, and part of the human race legally degraded to the condition of the unthinking brute." From Providence, Rhode Island, in 1787 Crito insisted that Africans were included in the Declaration's assertion about the "unalienable right to liberty." And he called Americans to task for regarding "the British in an odious and contemptible light, purely because they were attempting, by violence, to deprive us, in some measure, of those our unalienable rights," while "*at the same time*, or since, we have taken or withheld these same rights from the Africans, or any of our fellow-men." It took gall to display zeal for the preservation of "natural and indefeasible rights," wrote an author calling himself the Pedlar, "while we overlook the condition of thousands of our fellow creatures, held in the most pitiable state of abject Slavery."[27]

A citizen of Delaware, Warner Mifflin, spoke of the anguish he experienced daily thinking about the "tyranny and oppression" against African Americans that was "suffered so readily to prevail in the councils of American rulers, to a degree in no instance exceeded by Britain" before the Declaration of Independence. The United States refused to put an end to the slave trade despite "the laborious production of wisdom of this country" which had produced the Declaration of Independence as the manifest "faith of the nation." Alexander McLeod stated in 1802 that anyone who was so self-interested as to "buy, sell, and enslave for life, any individual of the human race" was likely to be a civil tyrant unworthy of political office. McLeod and others were certain that anyone who rationalized the institution of slavery would be unable to impress a universal sense of equality on the people's minds that the Declaration of Independence had imprinted.[28]

Contemporary writers drew attention to foreign contempt for Americans' high-minded claims to the universality of liberty and virtue while slaveholders ran roughshod over unequivocal statements of the Declaration of Independence. An author warned that persons of African ancestry were no "strangers to human nature" as endorsed by the document and would avenge the humiliating wrongs of bondage; if granted their release as a right intrinsic to human nature, they would avenge themselves for being denied free exercise of their God-given equality. Another writer asserted that "after having proclaimed 'that all have an unalienable right to life, liberty, and the pursuit of happiness,'" it was ignoble to keep "these poor people ... fettered in irons."[29]

Black petitioners also complained that barbaric laws, like the fugitive slave statute passed in 1793, were incompatible with the God given "blessings and benefits granted to us in the enjoyment of our natural right to liberty." Multiple pamphlets of the day forcefully asserted that the Declaration of Independence's statement of equality was incompatible with the dehumanizing practices of slavery. Remarking on the slavery of black people, James Forten exhibited the inspiration of the premise of the Declaration of Independence: "We are men; and though many among us cannot write, yet we all have the feelings and passions of men, and are anxious to enjoy the birth-right of the human race." Instead they suffered the unwarranted punishment of manacles and disproportionate criminal punishments.[30]

Thirty-two years after passage of the Declaration of Independence, at the end of Thomas Jefferson's presidential administration, a statute rendered slave importation illegal in the United States. The prohibition against slavery merged national power with the Declaration's humanistic statements. Writing in response to a Society of Friends letter, Jefferson backed the legislation: "I sincerely pray with you that all members of the human family may, in the time prescribed by the Father of us all, find themselves securely established in the enjoyments of life, liberty, and happiness." He like other supporters of the statute argued that the Declaration of Independence's assertions about human rights placed termination of slavery within the province of the federal government.

Opponents of the new law made novel use of the Declaration. They complained that losing their slave cargo, without being able to bring it from the West Indies to sell in the United States, amounted to the same "important grievance complained of in the Declaration of Independence"; that of "'cutting off our trade.'" These petitioners' rationale demonstrated that even protesters wishing to elevate their property rights above others' liberty interests were able to resort to the document, so long as the rhetoric read out the universal humanism and equality that abolitionists considered intrinsic to the national manifesto. It amounted to selective application of the Declaration to whites alone.[31]

The statement about equal and inalienable rights became the standard against which U.S. domestic and foreign policy could be judged. The document set a precedent for the Age of Revolution, when new countries throughout the Caribbean and North and South America emerged from the yoke of colonial rule. Though the Declaration inspired liberation movements throughout the hemisphere, most foreign declarations of independence in the nineteenth century did not include a statement of human rights as did their forerunner. This difference between the U.S. document and its foreign counterparts indicates that its anticolonialist and self-governance messages had more impact abroad than did the statement about natural human rights. In the United States, revolutionary movements were regarded to be part of the worldwide phenomenon that the American Revolution had set in motion.

5

COMPROMISING FOR THE SAKE
OF EXPANSION

THE DEMOCRATIC-REPUBLICAN PARTY DOMINATED POLITICS DURING
the first quarter of the nineteenth century, with Thomas Jefferson as its
leader for much of that period. This era of seeming political tranquility
was punctured by debates about whether slavery should extend west to the
Missouri Territory. The Declaration of Independence figured prominently
in congressional deliberations, forever altering understanding of the document's central message and the country's self-image.

Beginning with the first decade of the nineteenth century, Federalist
political strategy deemphasized the Declaration of Independence in order
to downplay Jefferson's intellectual contribution to the Revolution. This
was as much a swipe at Jefferson as it was a deliberate, but unsuccessful,
attempt to draw support away from his Republican Party. In 1809, an
author wrote that "no extraordinary ability was necessary" to enumer-
ate accusations against King George III "and as to the principle, it is evidently taken from Locke, without the candour of an acknowledgment."
The acrimony was not about the significance of the Declaration's central
principles of self-governance and liberal equality, but about the status of

its author. Richard Henry Lee and John Adams asserted that Jefferson had lifted Locke's ideas without proper attribution. Jefferson dismissed these charges. He claimed to have incorporated ideas into the document that were widely circulating throughout the colonies in contemporary writings, speeches, and sermons.[1]

Despite their political differences, by the 1820s Jefferson and Adams had resumed their friendship. Both were sought after to be speakers at Fourth of July celebrations. The public looked to them as elder statesmen. The years had taken a toll on the founding generation, and those few revolutionaries who still survived were in declining health. Jefferson and Adams—friends in early middle age, political enemies in late middle age, and pen pals in old age—gave up the ghost on the same day. Almost providentially, they both passed away on July 4, 1826, the fiftieth anniversary of the Declaration of Independence. Their fates, which had been closely interlinked—both men were members of the Continental Congress, foreign ministers, vice presidents, and presidents—became united in the national mind by death. Adams had developed such an affinity for his younger friend that his dying words were, "Thomas Jefferson still survives!" He was mistaken: Jefferson had died about five hours before, at the age of eighty-three. A month later, the *Edwardsville Spectator*, an Illinois newspaper, announced the timing of Jefferson's death to be "a wonderful coincidence! Fifty years from the Declaration of Independence—on the very day...this great man...has breathed his last!...Could he have selected the moment of his departure this would have been the very one which he himself would have chosen." About a week and a half before his death, Jefferson wrote a letter to the mayor of Washington expressing his hope that the "Declaration be to the world what I believe it will be...the Signal of arousing men to burst the chains under which...ignorance and superstition had persuaded them to bind themselves, and to assume the blessings & security of self-government."[2]

Eulogies about their lives provided the occasion to commemorate the achievements of the Revolution. Much discussion at public meetings and in newspaper columns was spent glorifying the Declaration of Independence. As the country celebrated its commitment to freedom, it was about to embark on western expansion. National growth might have been achieved hand in hand with legal restraints on slavery, which so clearly violated blacks' inalienable rights, but instead Congress allowed the institution to spread into the new state of Missouri.

By the time of Adams's and Jefferson's deaths, Independence Day orators commonly expressed nostalgia for the days when the nation's forefathers shook off monarchical rule. After the War of 1812, when the Democratic-Republicans became the dominant force in American politics, the Declaration rarely appeared in substantive legal discussions. It continued to rouse patriotic feelings during Independence Day celebrations, but meaningful references to its principles declined markedly. This changed drastically at the end of that decade, when a controversy over whether Missouri would enter the Union as a slave or free state returned the Declaration of Independence's statements about liberal equality to the heart of contemporary issues.

The U.S. Constitution established a bifurcated government. In the early years of nationhood, clashing opinions existed as to whether federal or state authority should dictate the minting of currency, taxation, banking, treaty making, infrastructure development, and armed service. When the Federalist Party held the presidency, James Madison wrote the Virginia Resolution (1798) and Thomas Jefferson the Kentucky Resolution (1799), defending the right of states to refuse to follow federal laws they considered to impinge on their sovereign prerogatives. Once each took his turn as president of the United States, however, they backed increased federal power to annex land and create a national bank. President Madison overcame strong Federalist opposition to the War of 1812, which he claimed was the second war of independence against continued British oppression.[3]

Madison's protégé, James Monroe, handily won the 1816 presidential election. Following his victory over Rufus King, the Federalist Party became too weak to alter national policy through the executive and legislative branches. Only the judiciary remained a Federalist bastion of power, with John Marshall presiding as chief justice and many other party stalwarts holding lifetime tenure in lower court appointments.

In 1817, Congress commissioned Jonathan Trumbull to do a giant painting for display at the U.S. Capitol depicting the signing of the Declaration of Independence. He completed the work in 1818. The patriotic artwork arrived in Washington only in 1819, after having been exhibited in New York City and Philadelphia. It was immediately praised for its "splendid," "celebrated," and "great" depiction of Jefferson handing the instrument to John Hancock, who was seated at the president's table with Secretary of Congress Charles Thomson standing at his right. Flanking Jefferson are other members of the declaration drafting committee: John Adams, Robert Livingston, Benjamin Franklin, and Roger Sherman. Around the room are many of the other signatories, but some important members of the Continental Congress are missing. Caesar Rodney, who furnished the deciding vote for Delaware, was left out. He was not the only one; Trumbull found no space for Virginia delegates Francis Lightfoot Lee and Thomas Nelson, even though they both seem to have been present for the July 4, 1776, vote.[4]

Americans were nostalgic about their past and curious about the document that described the nation's existential purpose. In 1819, Joseph M. Sanderson published his book proposal to print a collection of vignettes about the men who voted for independence, requesting subscribers to fund the project. His brother, John Sanderson, eventually edited the first two of what would be nine volumes of the *Biography of the Signers of the Declaration of Independence*.[5]

It was during Monroe's presidency that an engraver permanently damaged the signed Declaration of Independence. A facsimile was to be created by placing a sheet of India tissue paper, moistened with water and gum arabic, over the entire document. A heavy proof roller was then run

FIGURE 5.1 John Trumbull. *The Declaration of Independence, July 4, 1776*. Oil on canvas, c. 1832. (Courtesy of the Wadsworth Atheneum Museum of Art, Hartford, Connecticut/ Art Resource, New York.)

over its entire length with weights used to keep it in place at both ends. The paper was next rolled over a polished plate of copper covered in white wax. An exact replica was thereby created—but at the expense of about half the original's ink, rendering much of it illegible for future generations.[6]

Independence Day had long been celebrated with "pomp, shows, games, sports, guns, bell, bonfires, and illuminations," just as John Adams had clairvoyantly (or brashly) predicated in 1776. The 1819 celebration in Springfield, Massachusetts, began at sunrise with the firing of twenty-one guns; the salute was repeated at noon. The Rev. Mr. Chase delivered an oration that called for a variety of reforms, including "Abolition of the Slave trade," which persisted despite a congressional ban against it. At New London, Connecticut, bells chimed and a salute followed at sunrise. The next day, in Baltimore, the commemoration hosted a band performing a national ditty; raised toasts included one by the Abolition Society, which expressed the hope that "the result of our republican institutions—free themselves, Columbia's sons will oppose bondage in every shape." At Burlington, Vermont, "the usual ceremonies were performed" and the "declaration was read." At dinner, various toasts were raised, among them: "African Slavery.—May the waters of the Mississippi, baptize the unhappy African a freeman, and eternally redeem him from oppression. Patriots of South America.—May their wisdom teach them zeal, a true stopping place.... Agricultural Societies.—May they become a nurse to honest wealth, to manly sentiment, and manly energies." There was an undeniable concern about the resilience of slavery.[7]

The debates from 1819 to 1821 about the proposed statehood of Missouri demonstrated the fragility of the Era of Good Feelings, a legendary calm in national politics during the Monroe administration. Blistering arguments divided the country along sectional lines. The dispute centered around whether Congress had the authority to prevent slavery in the portion of the Louisiana Territory that in 1812 was renamed the Missouri Territory. In hindsight, it seemed inevitable that the message of the Declaration of Independence would became central to agitation against the spread of slavery. Debates on the Missouri Compromise intensified the steadfastness, adamancy, contentiousness, and implacableness of abolitionists and antislavery groups.

Despite a brief period of calm after abolition of the slave trade, the dispute over slavery could not be fully silenced because of its incompatibility with the principles of the Declaration of Independence. In 1818, widespread condemnation of slavery decried the injustice of denying others "equal rights and equal privileges" solely because of their skin color. The words invoked the language of the founding document, as no form of the word *equality* could be found in the Constitution. The following year, an author described a slave auction at New Orleans where a fifty-year-old husband, a forty-five-year-old wife, and their two children, of about nine and seven years of age, were separated by sale. In words that were even more closely reminiscent of the Declaration of Independence, the observer noticed that this divided family, possessing God-given "unalienable rights," was headed to new homes where the "blows and stripes" of a cruel tyrant might await them.[8]

Abolitionist organizations, in parts of the South and North, attacked the injustices of slavery. The sixteenth Convention for Promoting the Abolition of Slavery and Improving the Condition of the African Race was held in Philadelphia from October 5 to November 10, 1819. Participants issued a joint statement that "all men are created equal ... our declaration of independence" committed the nation to gradual emancipation. Participants jointly proclaimed that the Declaration's statement of equality was incompatible with the southern demand to legally sanction the westward spread of slavery. Those attending the meeting agreed that the extreme injustice committed against persons of African ancestry could only be righted by freeing them from slavery and granting them "reparations." Slaves were owed lands where they could settle, cultivate, and build homes as well as religious and literary instruction; unfortunately, participants presented no detailed plan about how to administer the restitution owed to a class whose labor had been exploited for two centuries.[9]

Abolitionists differentiated themselves from the American Colonization Society, which was formed in December 1816 for the avowed purpose of expatriating the free black population beyond American boundaries. Speaking at a Society meeting, Elias B. Caldwell from the District of Columbia said that although the Declaration of Independence asserted all men are created equal with inalienable rights, racism made it impossible for whites to live with blacks: "It is considered impossible, consistently with the safety of the state, ... that they can ever be placed upon this equality," laid out by the Declaration, to enjoy "these 'inalienable rights,' whilst they remain mixed with us." Colonization Society loyalists sought to achieve intersectional tranquility through racial separation. This concept was inapposite to the abolitionist call for equality, integration, and reparation.[10]

A more bitter ideological battle was brewing about whether slavery would spread west of the Mississippi river. The immense tract of land Jefferson's administration acquired from France was one possible place to repatriate free blacks, although most members of the Colonization Society would have preferred to ship them to northwestern Africa. The Society was solicitous of slaveholders' support and carefully avoided criticizing the institution itself. This was no surprise given that slaveholders such as Henry Clay and Bushrod Washington were among its leaders. In striking contrast, those committed to genuine black equality regarded the Louisiana Territory as a place where slavery would be forbidden, in accordance with the principles of the Declaration of Independence.

The inhumanity of domestic slavery appeared repeatedly in newspapers, such as one from Charleston, South Carolina, where an advertisement announced the sale of "40 *young Negroes*, at the sign of the *Heart*, consisting of men, women, boys and girls." Another offered sixty-nine "prime gang" Negroes, "principally plantation servants and field hands"; demonstrating the callousness of slavery, the same advertisement listed the sale of "horses, mules, [and] cattle." On the very same page with these advertisements, an author commented on this sad state of affairs. He cringed at the thought that this could be happening "in a land of republican freemen," even though the practice was diametrically opposed to the "principles of a government, whose basis is the equality of man... [Against those principles are the] principles [of slavery] that bear a wonderful contrast to those which actuated their fathers, when they signed the declaration of independence." The Declaration-based argument for ending slavery lost in the Deep South, but there was still a chance that the institution could be contained and prevented from spreading westward, just as it was prevented from entering the northwest through the Northwest Ordinance of 1787.[11]

The first realistic opportunity to end expansion of slavery west of the Mississippi River came in 1819. Congressional debates about the Missouri Compromise were filled with references to the Declaration of Independence. Southerners wanted to admit Missouri as a slave state in order to augment their block of congressional representation and to create new markets for the domestic slave trade.

From the time of the Louisiana Purchase in 1803 through establishment of a Missouri territorial government in 1805, slavery was legal. Congress had already accepted the growth of slavery in the South with admission of the states of Kentucky (1792), Tennessee (1796), and Mississippi (1817). So too the state of Louisiana, which lay at the southernmost tip of the Louisiana Territory, entered the Union in 1812 as a slave state. On the other hand, Congress conditioned admission of Ohio (1803), Indiana (1816), and Illinois (1818) on their abiding by the Northwest Ordinance, which prohibited introduction of slavery or involuntary servitude within a large area. Legislators enacted no such condition for admitting Vermont, but the state's own laws precluded the introduction of slavery.

To admit Missouri as a slave state would have expanded southern congressional representation and created new markets for the domestic slave trade. Admission of the state of Alabama on December 14, 1819, with its constitution explicitly protecting slavery, created an even split in the United States Senate, with two senators for each of the eleven northern and eleven southern states.[12]

During debates about Missouri's admission, a one-term congressman from New York, James Tallmadge, Jr., became renowned for introducing a bill to limit slavery's encroachment into the newly formed state. He had already made his views clear when the House debated the Illinois constitution, sarcastically commenting then on how America's image abroad suffered from perpetuation of slavery: "Our enemies had drawn a picture of our country, as holding in one hand the Declaration of Independence, and with the other brandishing a whip over our affrighted slaves."[13] With no national prominence or political faction to support him, Tallmadge was an unlikely standard bearer.

On February 13, 1819, delegate John Scott of Missouri, who after statehood would be elected to be its representative, offered a bill to enable Missourians to form a state government. Two days later, Representative Tallmadge proffered his amendment to it. He did not propose to free those slaves who were already residing in the Territory, who numbered 10,222 in a total population of 66,586 inhabitants. His proposed statutory amendment provided that after admission of Missouri no more slaves could be brought into the state. All children born to slaves were to be freed at the age of twenty-five.[14]

Rep. Timothy Fuller of Massachusetts, who was in his first term in Congress, having earlier served four years in the state senate, was the first to invoke the Declaration of Independence. He quoted the passage about all men being equal and endowed with inalienable rights to point out that it must apply to slaves like all other people. "It follows," he continued, "that they are in a purely republican government born free, and entitled to liberty and the pursuit of happiness." This set off a firestorm, with several congressmen protesting that it was improper for Fuller to question the republican character of slave states. Fuller excused himself, saying he meant no such offense to states that "held slaves when the Constitution was established." That subject he thought to be outside the purview of the national legislature.

> My reason, Mr. Chairman, for recurring to the Declaration of Independence, was to draw from an authority admitted in all parts of the Union a definition of the basis of republican government. If, then, all men have equal rights, it can no more comport with the principles of a free Government to exclude men of a certain color from the enjoyment of 'liberty and the pursuit of happiness,' than to exclude those who have not attained a certain portion of wealth, or a certain stature of body; or to found the exclusion on any other capricious or accidental circumstance.

Excluding the black population from political freedoms violated the principles of representative government to the same extent as an aristocracy or an oligarchy based on affluence. Fuller considered both to be forms of subordination and domination prohibited by the Declaration.[15]

Fuller and Tallmadge were part of the generation that grew up during the Revolution; by coincidence, both men were born in 1778. Tallmadge began his defense of the amendment in the House on February 15, 1819, by denying that he wanted to question the legitimacy of slavery in the original states of the Union. Neither did he plan to oppose admission of the Alabama Territory since it was proximate to other slave states. But whatever argument could be raised to rationalize slavery there, "all these reasons cease when we cross the banks of the Mississippi." Tallmadge refuted the argument that Congress could place no conditions on admission of a new state into the Union. He claimed his amendment was no different from the congressional requirement that Missouri agree to open its navigable waters to the other states. Congress had also placed conditions on admission of Louisiana, for example, requiring that it guarantee the right to trial by jury. Tallmadge mocked slaveholders' argument that they could not cultivate and occupy Missouri without exploiting slave labor. If there were not enough free settlers to form a state at that time, the inhabitants of Missouri could simply wait until their numbers grew to forty thousand and then reapply for admission.

He then turned to the Declaration of Independence, as he had done during the debate on admission of Illinois. The evil of slavery was "brought upon us without our own fault, before the formation of our government, and as one of the sins of that nation from which we have revolted." Jefferson's original draft of the Declaration contained an indictment of the British king for forcing the slave trade on Americans, but to avoid angering delegates from the deep South the Continental Congress had struck it from the final draft. Unlike the Continental Congress and Jefferson, Tallmadge did not back down, his point being that slavery was an imperial wrong that undercut the integrity of the charter of American independence. Congress had the authority to require new states entering the Union to abolish slavery: "You have proclaimed, in the Declaration of Independence, 'That all men are created equal....' The enemies of your Government, and the legitimates of Europe, point to your inconsistencies, and blazon your supposed defects." His main point was that only by prohibiting slavery in Missouri could the United States avoid the charge of being untrue to its stated purpose for national sovereignty.[16]

Tallmadge called on Congress to apply the ideals of the Declaration of Independence in a location under federal control. The day after his speech, the House passed the amended Missouri bill by a vote of 87 to 76. The Senate, however, turned back the momentum, voting against gradual emancipation by 31 to 7 and against the measure to prohibit further introduction of slavery in Missouri by 22 to 16. On March 2, the Senate passed a differently worded bill authorizing creation of the state of Missouri but with no prohibition against slavery. With the House unwilling to back down, heated debates raged throughout the country.[17]

The public and newspaper polemics about the Missouri bill were more acerbic than the rather genteel deliberations in Congress had been. Representatives Fuller and Tallmadge had laid down the gauntlet, seemingly requiring the South to decide whether the principles of the Declaration of Independence would continue to influence the nation's understanding of republican governance. With Jefferson still alive, the Democratic-Republican Party could not overtly renounce the document without suffering enormous political repercussions. Jefferson realized that the Missouri controversy portended a terrifying threat to the country's existence. In a letter, he said the degree of acrimony awoke him like "a fire-bell in the night" from the repose of domestic tranquility. There was a good deal of saber rattling as some Missourians threatened to rebel from the United States and draft their own declaration of independence rather than join the Union. Southerners also feared that talk of freedom would fuel slave insurrections. Some supporters of slavery actually tried to harness the Declaration of Independence to their side of the argument, much as the slave traders had done seeking to prevent liquidation of their human chattel. A grand jury impaneled by a circuit court in St. Louis complained that the supporters of the Tallmadge amendment threatened to restrict their "free exercise of rights in the formation of a constitution." Such a political encroachment would violate Missourians' "unalienable rights and privileges as a people" and was comparable to the British tyranny and oppression "from which [the] original declaration of American independence" had emancipated the people. This conceived of the Declaration as a model for new states to choose their own property regimes, without the interference of a centralized power.[18]

On the other side of the debate were the supporters of some version of Tallmadge's antislavery amendment. In response to the argument that Congress lacked the requisite power to prevent slavery in Missouri, former Chief Justice of the United States Supreme Court John Jay, who was then in his seventy-fifth year, wrote that "slavery...ought not to be introduced in any of the new states, and that it ought to be gradually diminished and finally abolished in all of them." He pointed to the Constitution's grant of power enabling Congress to prevent migration and importation of slaves into any states. The framers of the Constitution had not used the word *slavery* in providing this power because of the institution's "discordency with the principles of the Revolution; and from a consciousness of its being repugnant to the...positions in the Declaration of Independence" on the equality of mankind. An author writing for a Boston newspaper agreed that the Importation Clause of the Constitution empowered Congress to prevent internal and external slave trade and migration. The writer also drew attention to a constitutional clause requiring the United States to guarantee a republican form of government in every state. "Now I will not stop to ask the gentlemen, where they get a definition of 'a republican government' consistent with slavery," he began facetiously:

> I will not press against them, the words of the declaration of Independence, that Political New Testament of our country, 'that these truths *are self evident, that* all men *are created* equal; that they are endowed by their creator, with certain *unalienable* rights; that among these are life, *liberty, and the pursuit of happiness*: that to *secure these rights*, governments are instituted among them.' I will not urge these words, because the usage of our country has since, by an unfortunate necessity, been in contradiction with their spirit; and we have among us many governments, to which we cannot deny the name of Republican, where this fundamental principle of all republicanism, the equality of men, is unknown.

His brilliant use of negatives implied that slave states were not republican because they overtly violated the inalienable rights of the enslaved population.[19]

In Missouri, the *St. Louis Enquirer* mocked Supreme Court Justice Joseph Story for invoking "the Declaration again!" to charge a grand jury of the Circuit Court of Plymouth, New Hampshire, that slavery "is so repugnant to the natural rights of man and the dictates of justice" that its origin must be in barbarism. The newspaper took Story to task for asserting that because the underlying principle of the United States declared that "all men are born free and equal, and have certain unalienable rights," Africans condemned to perpetual slavery could rightfully ask, "Am I not a man and a brother?" The article condemned Story for applying the universal statements of the Declaration of Independence to slaves.[20]

There were also plenty of voices sharing Story's sentiments. At a public meeting in Cincinnati, which was convened in December 1819, resolutions were passed against Missouri slavery. One of two people opposing the decrees asserted that all blacks living in the country should be slaves. Several gentlemen repelled him, with one indignantly asserting that Congress had the duty "to secure to every being who draws the breath of life, whether white or black, those rights which the Declaration of Independence asserts to be natural and unalienable." Citizens of Hartford, Connecticut, who met at the state house the same month, resolved that slavery was "repugnant to the spirit and principles of a republican government" and could be proscribed by Congress at the time of a state's admission to the Union. They further resolved, "That in the opinion of this meeting, the peculiar phraseology of the preamble to the Declaration of Independence, declaring that 'all men are created equal, &c.' shows conclusively that the illustrious authors of that document, never contemplated the farther extension of Slavery in these U. States." The Hartford remonstrances were later communicated to the U.S. Senate. Instead of abolishing slavery, wrote the *Connecticut Journal*, the proposed Missouri constitution protected "the power to hold in bondage, to buy and sell humans...which is a denial of every axiom of our Declaration of Independence." Taking their cue from the first congressional debate on the Tallmadge amendment, both sides dug in for a sustained dispute about the meaning of American freedom.[21]

About the same time, the speaker of the New York State Assembly, John C. Spencer, told his fellow state legislators of a caricature on exhibit in England "representing an American holding a scroll in one hand, containing the words of our declaration of independence, 'all men are born free and equal,' while the other hand is employed in lashing a miserable female slave!—Who does not feel humbled at the gross inconsistency?" Despite this powerful indictment, Spencer believed the United States was founded on principles that counseled her to overcome the inherited, colonial infamy: "I rejoice that we may retort back upon England the cruel jest, and that although we have enough to answer for in continuing the foul stain, yet that our hands did not stamp it upon our character." The historian David Brion Davis has pointed out the disingenuousness of British criticism of Americans' failure to fully act on their proclaimed allegiance to the rights of man. In England of the 1820s, wage laborers who quit their work were subject to imprisonment, and women and young children worked in cramped mines and stifling factories. In time, wage laborers in the United States would find that the egalitarian ideals of the Declaration of Independence could be marshaled for their causes, as they were to confront slavery.[22]

On December 29, 1819, soon after Congress reconvened, the Senate returned to its debate on admission of Missouri. Congress controlled a vast tract of land; the available resources could sustain an immense population.

Those who opposed slavery argued national tranquility required that "every new State received into the Union, should be admitted on the broad principles of liberty and equality of rights, announced to the world in the declaration of independence.... If Missouri is permitted to hold slaves the die is cast.—No future so favorable as the present, will occur for restricting the evil." Americans continued to point the finger at England for the inception of slavery in the New World, but their arguments were not overt defense of the institution: "The evil as it now exists does not owe its origin to us." This excuse for retaining slavery was unconvincing forty-three years after independence. "The period has arrived when we must appeal, either as a nation struggling to extricate itself from a mischief entailed upon it by a former government," wrote a citizen from Illinois, "on the one hand declaring to the world as self evident truths, 'that all men are created equal.'... and yet, on the other, with strange inconsistency, holding in despotic slavery a large portion of their fellow beings; and when they have the power to check, fostering the monstrous hydra, by giving it ample scope for extension. If it must be so, I shall indeed have to blush for my country." Rufus King, a senator from the state of New York, regarded the concession to the original slave-holding states to have been a "necessary sacrifice to the establishment of the constitution" at the nation's founding. He, like Tallmadge, agreed that Congress lacked the constitutional mandate to end slavery in the original thirteen states. Congress's available authority over U.S. territories, however, needed to be practically used to advance the vital theory of American government, with its commitment to preservation of the equality of rights as the best policy for securing public and individual liberties.[23]

Sen. Jonathan Roberts of Pennsylvania introduced an amendment to the Missouri bill forever prohibiting slavery there. He was concerned with the institution's spread to the entire region west of the Mississippi: "And here, what an abyss for reflection opens! Shall we depart from, those truths that lighted our fathers to independence and liberty?" Daniel Raymond, a member of the Colonization Society, believed that "a more momentous question has never been agitated in this country since the declaration of independence." He offered the pragmatic solution of transporting blacks to Africa; otherwise, he feared that extending slavery west of the Mississippi river would increase the threat of insurrection. He also feared creation of an "unlimited mart for the sale of slaves" that would "encourage avaricious planters to endeavour to increase their multiplication, as they do cattle for sordid gain."[24]

Driving this debate was the question of whether national union was possible, or even desirable, without the protection of inalienable rights promised by the Declaration of Independence, especially in areas of congressional control. If the document implicitly mandated creation of republican government in the new territories, logic led to the conclusion that any states retaining the institution of slavery were not representative of their entire population. Lack of representation of blacks went against the concept of self-government by the will of the people. The terms of the Declaration of Independence were neutral, while slavery was emphatically racist. A further aspect of the Missouri debate was the willingness to sacrifice these principles for the sake of national union, another intrinsic purpose of the Declaration. When it came to slavery, these driving strands of the Declaration were irreconcilable.

Congressional debates often returned to whether the national legislature should and could set ideological conditions for statehood. Unsurprisingly, there were two diametrically opposing schools of thought on this matter, with the antislavery proponents quoting the Declaration as if it provided mandatory standards and the defenders of southern property rights downplaying the manifesto's significance to the conflict.

Opponents of slavery argued that all the inhabitants of new states to the Union deserve "the rights, happiness and liberty of millions of the human race." Congress, they believed, could condition statehood on adoption of constitutions with provisions protecting inalienable rights. Accordingly, even though states remained sovereignties they were also members of the United States and therefore were obligated to comply with the "great political principles upon which all our institutions repose." The ideals of the Declaration of Independence applied to the entire national community. All its members, according to this manner of thinking, were obliged to comply with the Declaration's formulation of the social contract between government and the people. Congress was not required to grant any territory statehood unless its laws prohibited forced subjugation of people.[25]

At the opposite end of the spectrum, Delaware Senator Nicholas Van Dyke, Jr., rejected the antislavery view as a novel interpretation of national commitments that threatened to dissolve social bonds. Slavery continued to be legal in Delaware, although it lacked the same degree of support it enjoyed in the Deep South. No one could anticipate during the time of independence, Van Dyke believed, that "the recital of abstract theoretical principles, in a national manifesto in 1776 would be gravely urged at this day, to prove that involuntary servitude does not lawfully exist within the United States." This raised an interesting question about whether the Declaration was solely an ideological text with no legal force or the founding law that bound the national government to humanistic conduct.

Robert R. Reid, a representative from Georgia who had previously been a state judge, picked up on Van Dyke's theme. He discounted the nationalistic claim that the Declaration of Independence allowed Congress to reject a territory petitioning to be a slave state. In support of his position, he contended that the Ninth and Tenth Amendments provided that the people of each state could create a new constitution to their liking and that states would be sovereign over domestic matters, such as property, without federal interference. In his view, these constitutional clauses trumped any abstract argument derived from the Declaration. This states' rights approach even received backing from some northerners. Before the New York Legislature, a speaker professed that although "the preamble to the declaration of independence...has been incorporated into the constitution...we ought...to be cautious how we meddle with the concerns of other people" who reside more than fifteen hundred miles away.[26]

Southerners assiduously claimed a right to own slaves. It was at this time that slavery, which had long been considered a necessary evil, began to be spoken of as a positive good. One of the most distinguished senators, William Pinkney, passionately defended Missourians' political prerogatives. He gained international and domestic renown long before the Missouri conflict; President Jefferson had appointed him to be a co-minister to Great Britain, and President Madison had called on him to serve as the attorney general of the United States. In the debate over Missouri, Pinkney believed that the Declaration of Independence's principles of human rights were inapplicable to slaves; they were to be treated like any other property rather than people. Pinkney's renown allowed him to attack the ideology of the Declaration of Independence without fearing political repercussions: "The self-evident truths announced in the Declaration of Independence are not truths at all, if taken literally; and the practical conclusions contained in the same passage of that declaration prove that they were never designed to be so received." Representative Reid thought that Northerners' references to "the sublime doctrines of [the] Declaration of Independence" were no more than a farce because no one would accept the logic of their own arguments, which would include legitimization of intermarriage.[27]

Sen. Nathaniel Macon of North Carolina mocked the notion that "a clause in the Declaration of Independence" granted Congress the power to free slaves. To him the claim that "the Declaration of Independence gave authority to emancipate" slaves seemed dubious because "the patriots who made it never proposed any plan" to achieve such an end. Similarly, South Carolina Sen. William Smith defended the institution of slavery on religious grounds, thinking it to be a divine curse visited on Africans. Like other defenders of slavery, his perspective dehumanized blacks, relegating them temporary denizens to whom the Declaration's statement of human rights did not refer. He rhetorically asked northerners, many of whom came from states where emancipation was achieved gradually rather than immediately, "If this was a declaration of independence for the blacks as well as the whites, why did you not all emancipate your slaves at once?" When the Declaration was adopted, Smith continued, Africans were imported into the country as "our personal property" and were not members of the body politic.[28]

The Declaration of Independence played a central role throughout the course of the Missouri debates. Participants marked positions about the nature and scope of governance that would take center stage during the pre-Civil War period. If the Declaration were to be understood literally, it could only signify the guarantee of universal freedom of all people. National purpose had been set on parchment, but the rejoinder against extending the principle of liberal equality to blacks was that slavery persisted even after independence. Creation of new states in the territories constituted a means to at least put the brakes on slavery's extension throughout the country, although this should have been extended to general abolition of slavery.

Against the notion that only states could regulate slave property, Walter Lowrie, a Pennsylvania senator, argued that the Declaration's maxim about human equality is a self-evident truth implying that owning hereditary slaves "is not among the natural rights of man." Lowrie's message was that the natural right to freedom proclaimed by the Declaration was incompatible with the notion that whites could exert absolute dominion over blacks. The future Massachusetts Chief Justice Lemuel Shaw similarly wrote that "the incalculable evils which slavery inflicts on society" are "irreconcilable with any notion of natural justice." Rufus King echoed the sentiment of the Declaration of Independence that "all men being by natural law free and equal...one man could not rightfully make another his slave." Neither could a "social state" confer a mandate to new states that would allow them to sanction hereditary servitude within their borders.[29]

With so strong a disagreement, it was necessary to find common ground. Resolution to the tempest in Congress ended on March 6, 1820, with adoption of a law that placed no restrictions on authorization for Missouri to form a state government and draft a constitution. The Tallmadge amendment gained the needed votes in the House, but not the Senate. In return for the concession on Missouri, Maine was to enter as a free state. Slavery would henceforth be prohibited north of the 36°30' latitude in the Louisiana Territory, and permitted to exist south of that geographic coordinate.[30]

Elected Missouri delegates met in the dining room of the Mansion House Hotel in St. Louis to create the first state constitution, signing it on July 19. Unsurprisingly, their final product granted slavery the imprimatur of law. The U.S. Congress accepted the constitution without any restrictions on slavery. Shortly thereafter, President Monroe announced that Missouri had met the conditions for statehood, and it was admitted into the Union on August 10, 1821. The argument that the Declaration mandated Congress to prohibit further extension of slavery had been defeated.

6

JACKSONIAN ERA DEMOCRACY

COMPROMISE ON THE MISSOURI TERRITORY WAS ONLY A TEMPORARY patch for the persistently strained political relations between the North and the South. Geographic, class, economic, and ethnic differences created both tensions and alliances for the control of federal, state, and local resources and public offices. Although lacking any enforcement provision, the Declaration of Independence's statement of natural rights continued to be invoked in a slew of policy debates. Even though the Bill of Rights explicitly protected liberties against federal encroachment, social reformers buttressed their claims by invoking the Declaration of Independence's statement on equality. New strains of the argument became popular in the national dialogue too, with the refrain that people can more effectively exercise the Declaration's guarantees of representative self-governance through state rather than federal lawmaking. Memory of the Revolution became a thing of an increasingly distant past, but the principles at the core of national independence remained the cornerstone of national identity.

During the Jacksonian period of American history, the Declaration of Independence was incorporated into the mission statements of various antielitist causes. The document's statements about popular government offered interest groups a framework for demanding greater voice in politics and reduction of social distinctions. In the short run, however, it was white males rather than society as a whole who benefited most from rising democratization.

Jacksonian America became increasingly industrialized, as urban centers grew and markets expanded, helped along by new forms of transportation and mechanization. With the growth of commerce between states, the Declaration became a centerpiece for divergent movements: on the one hand it was a patriotic standard raised to celebrate the nation's expansion and interstate connection through new canals and railroads, but on the other it inflamed the sentiments of those who were leery of the growing power of federal government.

By voting to allow Missouri into the Union as a slave state, Congress helped to legitimize human bondage. The supporters of state sovereignty triumphed over those congressmen who argued for limiting slavery on the basis of the human rights principles of the Declaration of Independence.

The popular consensus that slavery was a temporary evil had faded by the 1820s. Writing to a newspaper editor in 1820, a discouraged, elderly author reminisced how he "used to hear, and read, as the sentiments of slaveholders, that slavery was a curse which they were anxious to remove, and control, by every practicable means." In the Early Republic, even those who retained slaves complained the practice was "an outrage upon the rights of humanity, which they abhorred and deplored, and were solicitous to remedy as fast as possible—in conformity with the spirit of our Declaration of Independence." With the passage of time, however, the author found their aversion for slavery and their affinity to human rights to be no more than a pretentious sham. Attitudes had changed so drastically that he wondered whether consistency required altering the document "which we are in the habit of reading on the 4th of July."[1] His pessimism was somewhat overstated.

Some slaveholders not only manumitted slaves but even became adamantly antislavery advocates. Edward Coles moved to Illinois from Virginia in order to free his own slaves. He soon became governor of the state after a hard-fought election in his adopted state. From 1823 to 1824 Coles waged a vigorous and successful battle against the proslavery faction to keep the state free. An elderly supporter of Coles's administration admonished young voters that they should turn back efforts to legalize the institution in Illinois: "All willing slave-holders, and those desirous

to be such, together with all bacchanals, gamblers, swindlers, house rob-
bers, kidnappers, &c. would fain be called true Republicans; but that
character doth belong to them; the appellation Tory, belongs to them, see
the Declaration of Independence." In a sign of changing times, Thomas
Jefferson, whose Declaration of Independence had explained the immediate need to be free from British tyranny, wrote a letter to Coles expressing disappointment that the younger generation did not show adequate
zeal for ending slavery. He nevertheless counseled Coles not to free his
slaves in Illinois immediately but wait "until more can be done for them."
Coles did not heed Jefferson's advice, not only setting his seventeen slaves
free but even giving each family a small farm as a start to economic independence. Reflecting on these events, an official publication of the Illinois
State Historical Library concluded that Coles's action attested that he was
"imbued with the principles of the Declaration of Independence, that all
men are created equal."[2]

Exploitation of African labor remained the accepted norm in the Deep
South, despite written protests that tyrannical laws, such as those prohibiting anyone from educating slaves, violated the basic tenet that "'we are
all born equal' [as] says the declaration of independence."[3] In discrete
parts of the South, there was still strong support for gradual emancipation, an end to the slave trade, and education for slaves, but realities on
the ground differed from the aspirations of idealists. The Presbyterian
Synod of Kentucky unsuccessfully proposed a gradual abolition plan for
its state. It drew attention to the incongruity of "the exalted truth in our
Declaration of Independence" with the deprivations of liberty, personal
security, and property ownership associated with the state's system of slavery. Antislavery sentiments were also openly expressed in Tennessee. In
1821, the Manumission Society of Tennessee proposed several laws amel-
iorating slavery. In response, the Committee on Slavery of the Legislature
of Tennessee unanimously resolved that slaveholders should be able to
emancipate their slaves if they be convinced by "the language and spirit
of the Declaration of Independence, that all men are and ought to be free."
With a future state supreme court justice, Jacob Peck, acting as chairman,
the committee cautioned that any such law should include a provision that
would prevent "unfeeling and avaricious" slaveholders from freeing elderly
and infirm slaves in order "to rid themselves of the burden of supporting
the aged slave[s]." It also recommended passage of a law against separating

slave husbands and wives through sales. During this same period, an Englishman wrote, of his travels through America in 1822 and 1823, "In Kentucky and Tenessee [sic], the admission of free blacks is prohibited, while that of slaves is allowed...notwithstanding their famous Declaration of Independence, in which liberty is mentioned as a natural and inalienable right." The Declaration continued to influence petition writers, but they were unable to break its choke hold south of the Missouri Compromise line.[4]

The content of a newspaper published in July 1826, the Fiftieth Jubilee of American independence and the month of the deaths of Adams and Jefferson, indicated just how murky the Declaration's ideals had become to southerners. The *Torch Light and Public Advertiser*, which was published in Hagerstown, Maryland, printed one article containing the toasts raised at an independence celebration and another article about the hour of day at which the Declaration of Independence had been signed. Yet on the very same page, the editor printed an offer of a $50 reward for the capture of "Three Likely Negro Women": Nelly, the advertisement went on, had already purchased her freedom, Harriot left behind a six-week-old infant child, and Juno left wearing homemade cotton clothes. Also appearing on the page was a report that the mayor of Natchez, in southwest Mississippi, had rescued four boys kidnapped from Philadelphia, the city where the Continental Congress signed the Declaration, to be sold off as slaves. Another story involved two black women and a child who were kidnaped on a schooner from Baltimore; its captain offered the three of them for sale. The paper provided no details about the end of their ordeal. These newspaper items displayed the country's two-sidedness: on the one hand it was a nation firmly committed to the principles of the Declaration of Independence, but on the other it was unwilling to outlaw an institution diametrically opposed to the ideals of equality and liberty. In these points of opposition lay the country's potential and its moral failure.

The antislavery movement was only one social cause that identified with the principles of the Declaration of Independence. Increasingly, between 1800 and 1830, various politically disempowered groups relied on the manifesto to agitate for change. Their causes ranged from civil and religious liberties to public education, free press, suffrage, and abolition of debtor prisons.[5] Without any constitutional recourse and sometimes even unable to identify politicians who might take interest in their causes, they turned to the common man for support. The Declaration of Independence was a readily recognizable statement of rights and government responsibilities. The liberation statement of 1776 was more readily understandable and rhetorically powerful for ordinary people than the technical jargon of the original Constitution, and even the Bill of Rights.

The manhood suffrage movement made one of the most compelling cases for securing the rights of the people proclaimed in the Declaration. At the beginning of the century, laborers living on low wages were typically ineligible to vote because they could not meet the property requirements for elections. Roger Sherman, a signer of the Declaration of Independence who was a shoemaker by trade, became a hero of the movement that aimed to expand public office to persons on the basis of character and intellectual attainment rather than wealth. An author complained that suffrage to men with property did not accord with the Declaration's rejection of wealth-based governance:

> What! Are not life and liberty as dear to the honest laborer and the industrious mechanic, as they are to the wealthiest Nabob of the land? Are these inestimable rights, in a land of liberty, in a Republican Government, to be held at the will of a privileged, pampered, and overgrown Aristocracy? Who contributes to the real substantial wealth and prosperity of a country? *Who fights her battles?* Not the haughty Aristocrat, who rolls in wealth, and feeds, and fattens, and riots, upon the wretchedness of the poor and the toils of the industrious. But the laborer, the mechanic, the farmer's son.

Writing about political equality in 1800, James Cheetham interpreted the Declaration of Independence's words that "all men are created equal" to include "the political equality of man." From this followed the principle that "the right of suffrage cannot...belong to a part without belonging to the whole." Without any constitutional clause mentioning equality, agitators for an end to political aristocracy invoked the Declaration of Independence.[6]

Reformers could not, of course, expect to convert everyone to their perspective. In 1820, an author writing for a New York newspaper who went by the name of "Franklin" was unconvinced by the natural rights arguments bandied about on behalf of an expanded voting franchise. He regarded voting to be like any other privileges that government could grant, regulate, take away, or deny altogether. The "Declaration of Independence said 'all men are created equal, &tc,'" he conceded, but this did not delegitimize a host of restraints on natural freedoms: galloping of horses through streets and splitting wood on boardwalks were prohibited in cities; Hudson and Albany, New York, outlawed smoking pipes after sunset; and New York City and Philadelphia barred slaughtering cattle, making soap, and tanning leather outside zoned areas. These disparate examples of how government limits human liberties were meant to support the writer's central point that adoption of the Declaration of Independence in no way implied states' governments lacked authority to retain freehold requirements on voting, which continued to be enforced in Virginia, where several of the illustrious framers of the Declaration of Independence had lived. Virginia would be the last holdout state to drop its property requirements, retaining a modified form of freehold requirement until 1850.[7]

Throughout much of the United States, Franklin's sentiments were becoming antiquated. Georgia had already opened its franchise to all white males in 1798, Delaware dropped property requirements in 1792, and Maryland first ended property qualifications for state offices in 1801 and to all other elections in 1810. A Baltimore citizen reminisced how "in the year 1801, the principles of *Seventy-six* triumphed in Maryland" with the passage of the "universal" suffrage act. Such a change was necessary, he went on, to vindicate the "principles asserted in the Declaration of Independence" by protecting poor men who stood "most in need of the protection of equal law" from the excessive political influence of the rich. The year after Franklin published his article, Massachusetts dropped its property qualifications altogether, after debates that relied in part on the Declaration of Independence. Elsewhere, citizens meeting in the town of Enfield, New York, passed resolutions condemning the aristocratic design of their state's voting restrictions. They asserted that prejudice against the laboring poor in the exercise of elective franchise was against "the principles set forth in the spirit of our declaration of independence." Heeding popular support for reform, in 1821 New York also eliminated property qualifications for white male voters but required that they pay taxes. Blacks living in New York could vote, but only if they held an unencumbered freehold estate worth at least $250. The decision to drop the property requirement for whites, explained former U.S. Sen. Nathan Sanford, was meant to end the aristocratic practices traceable to England. "Property," said another delegate to the New York constitutional convention, "when compared with our other essential rights, is insignificant and trifling. 'Life, liberty, and *the pursuit of happiness'*—not of property—are set forth in the declaration of independence as cardinal objects."[8]

Opposition to plutocratic governance, a central theme of the manhood suffrage movement, also led to popular demand for abolishing the system of imprisonment for debt. In 1830, five in six people imprisoned in New England and the Middle States had allegedly failed to repay creditors; most owed less than twenty dollars. The inability of so many people to repay so small an amount also demonstrates why property voting requirements negatively affected citizens' ability to enjoy the Declaration's promise of self-government. Imprisoning anyone unable to satisfy the demands of creditors, wrote one petitioner, violated the human and equitable standards of the Declaration of Independence. U.S. Sen. Richard M. Johnson, a hero of the War of 1812 and an advocate for workers' rights, adopted this cause. He successfully proposed a law denying federal courts the jurisdiction to sentence debtors to jail because the practice granted political advantage "to one class of citizens over another," contrary to "the great principle of equal rights that the Declaration of Independence and the Constitution of the United States." As in the case of political enfranchisement, the Declaration of Independence was a normative tool for faulting a system of wealth privilege. The document had an impact on populist movements even before Andrew Jackson's presidency.[9]

The woman suffrage movement was another example of how a social group that sought to end subjugation turned to the Declaration of Independence where no constitutional provision was available to it. Suffragettes' incorporation of the Declaration shows the extent to which it was a living document whose original meaning served as a historical baseline to launch evolving understandings of equal citizenship.

Suffrage had expanded in the United States from the days of the Revolution, when only propertied men could cast a ballot. The only state in which women had the right to vote after the Revolution, New Jersey, deprived them of the vote in 1807. This backward turn was highly revealing of the Revolutionary Age's attitude toward women. Although the Declaration of Independence used the generic "all men are created equal" rather than "all males," even progressive leaders did not initially extend this premise to suffrage for every adult American. The founding generation, which initially did not see past the privilege of property voting restrictions, was even less aware of gender inequalities. Laboring men did gain the privilege during the Jacksonian Era, but women remained outsiders to the formal political arena.[10]

The dominant perspective in America during the early nineteenth century downplayed women's status. They were often referred to in paternalistic terms. The stereotypes were not necessarily negative, but they were preconceptions that hindered women from fully exploring their potential and achieving their goals. A toast at an 1825 Independence Day celebration in Huntsville, Alabama, was to the Home, the "best reflector of woman's brightness." This gallant praise disguised how in that state and throughout the country the stereotype of women's frailty was invoked to rationalize restraints against their right to receive an equal education, obtain a divorce, engage in politics, and pursue a professional occupation.[11]

Throughout the United States the Declaration of Independence existed side by side with gender inequality. Women's property rights were controlled by law in several states. During the midnineteenth century, the trend among states was to increase married women's control over family property. Under the federalist model of sovereignty, some states permitted married women to alienate their property, while others granted that right only to the male head of household. In many of these states, the Declaration coexisted with accepted norms of gender discrimination. For example, the Declaration of Independence appeared on page one of Connecticut's 1835 statutory compilation. Within the book's pages, a law required husbands to countersign for wives desiring to alienate real property, but it did not prohibit husbands from selling their property unilaterally. Six years earlier, Delaware likewise printed the Declaration in the same book as the Constitution of the United States and its state laws. Among Delaware's substantive provisions, though, was a prohibition against married women disposing of real and personal property through wills and testaments. In Rhode Island, married women could not devise, give, or dispose of property without the husband's consent. There too the state officially reprinted the Declaration of Independence.[12]

The defenders of the gender status quo periodically took the Declaration of Independence into account, but only to rule out its application to women's rights issues. One author sought to explain women's legal inequality by resorting to a narrow understanding of natural rights that was often repeated in the context of similar restrictions on blacks' liberties. In an 1845 treatise, a retired Cincinnati College professor expressed his belief that the Declaration of Independence correctly asserted that life, liberty, and the pursuit of happiness were the primary rights. Someone holding this perspective might have also regarded voting and property ownership to be equally inalienable for men and women. Instead, the author explained that women should be subservient to their husbands and politically disempowered because the Declaration's words were never meant literally. An article in the *Yale Literary Magazine* was even more explicit in vindicating inequality despite acknowledgment of women's inclusion in the Declaration's statements about the entire American population. To justify the exclusively male composition of government, the author simplified the task of analysis by making a circular argument: women were excluded from politics because they, children, criminals, the insane, and slaves are "such a motley multitude" that their exercise of rulership would be unimaginable. Scores of articles and speeches compared women's status to that of children, who were citizens but not political participants.[13]

Supporters of women's rights were on firmer analytical ground; not needing to explain away the text of the Declaration, they applied its "principle that all men are born free and equal" in gender-neutral terms. From its earliest days, the New England Anti-Slavery Society regarded "the first principles of the Declaration of Independence" to enjoin all men and women to vindicate the natural rights of all humanity. In her two-volume treatise *Society of America*, Harriet Martineau asserted that on the basis of "one of the fundamental principles announced in the Declaration of Independence" the source of legitimate governmental authority was consent of the governed. This concept was incompatible, Martineau went on to say, with one-sided use of official powers to tax women, imprison them, and grant men divorces while withholding from women the power to own property and engage in politics. A contemporaneous review of Martineau's book commented that in light of the Declaration's proclamation of principles there was no plausible reason to deny women political rights while demanding their obedience to the law.[14]

Many comparisons were made to the colonial rebellion that led to the great battle cry "no taxation without representation," and to the suffragist claim that voting rights were women's due because they were taxpayers. Men made laws without any formal input from women, which was analogous to British parliamentary actions imposed without the colonists' involvement. In her autobiography, the physician Harriot K. Hunt of Boston described how she sent a protest to the city treasurer along with her taxes. Her sense of justice and passion for liberty, she wrote, were grounded on the Declaration of Independence. Any legitimate construction of the document, Hunt went on to say, construed it to be a statement about the inalienable rights of all humanity.[15]

The United States was entering an era of expanded commercialism, democratization, and trade. Consequently, the Declaration provided an anchor for unified patriotism even as it helped various protest movements raise questions about the country's failure to live up to stated ideals. Improved means of transport, communication, and distribution were essential for meeting the evolving demands of interstate commerce. Americans debated whether states or the federal government should take on the funding, planning, organizing, and building of infrastructure. John Quincy Adams became the standard bearer for federally funded improvements, while Andrew Jackson carried the torch for those who clung to a state-oriented framework for commercial growth.

One of the greatest inventions of the early nineteenth century was the locomotive. On July 4, 1828, in a ceremony symbolically planned for Independence Day, construction of a railroad began in the city of Baltimore heading west, with the ambitious name of the Baltimore & Ohio Railroad. The guest of honor, who turned over the dirt at the groundbreaking ceremony, was Charles Carroll, the sole surviving signer of the Declaration of Independence. An official Deputation of Blacksmiths presented the tools needed to break the soil, remove it, and then pour the cement. The presenter was not remiss to note the specialness of the occasion: "The day that gave birth to a nation of freemen—the day, venerated sir," he said referring to Carroll's involvement with the Continental Congress and the Declaration, "with which you are so conspicuously identified, the day that shall be the polar star to future ages, advertising them, that men dare declare themselves a free and sovereign people, that republics can exist, that they neither require the royal diadem or military rule to direct the great helm of state in safety." He connected past to present and the Declaration's promises of individual liberty with the nation's expanding market.[16]

Carroll had been friends with, and still reminisced about, Thomas Jefferson, John Hancock, and John Adams. He was fond of telling his captivated audience about Benjamin Franklin's wit and good humor. Although more than ninety years old, Carroll's faculties were unimpaired on the whole, though his sight had grown too dim to read. His gait was nearly as spritely as that of a fifty-year-old. Though his hair was silvery white, his voice continued to possess the vigor of manhood, and he spoke with articulate distinctiveness. Like the document itself, Carroll had aged physically but intellectually he remained fresh. Two years before, at the nation's half centennial, he had thanked God for surviving to see that day, recommending "to the present and future generations the principles of that important document as the best earthly inheritance their ancestors could bequeath to them, and pray that the civil and religious liberties they have secured to my country may be perpetuated to remotest posterity and extended to the whole family of man." In his words, laying the first stone of the B&O Railroad was "among the most important acts of my life, second only to my signing the Declaration of Independence, if even it be second to that!"[17]

The Maryland legislature chartered the Baltimore and Ohio Railway Company in an effort to regain some of the western trade that the Erie Canal was diverting from Baltimore to Philadelphia and New York. There were many signs that Americans believed freedom of travel and interconnection were linked to American independence—the freedom to pursue happiness far from their place of birth. A link between Independence Day and the liberty of new technology offered was also made earlier, on July 4, 1817, when the anniversary of the Declaration of Independence was celebrated jointly with commencement of the Erie Canal project, which officially opened for boat travel on October 25, 1825. Stretching from the Hudson River in New York to Lake Erie, the completed canal stretched 363 miles. On the forty-ninth anniversary of the Declaration of Independence (July 4, 1825), standing just west of Newark, Ohio, Governors DeWitt Clinton of New York and Jeremiah Morrow of Ohio turned the first shovel of dirt, commencing work on the Ohio & Erie Canal. The orator of the day announced to more than seven thousand spectators that this "Jubilee of American Independence" heralded the start of an era of navigation and improvements. The President of the United States, John Quincy Adams, attended the opening festivities of the Chesapeake and Ohio Canal. He spoke of three epochs of American history: the first being acceptance of the Declaration, the second unification of states under the federal government, and the third construction of internal improvements through canals and other arteries of commerce. His belief in the federal government's ability to support growth of the American system was not shared by his successor, Andrew Jackson, who regarded Indian removal and not internal funding for highways to be essential for national expansion, never pausing to reflect on the discontinuity between the anticolonial principles of the Declaration and colonization of aboriginal lands.[18]

Jacksonian populism enabled a growing number of white men to participate in democratic politics. Election reformers understood the Declaration of Independence to be a nationwide statement against aristocratic rule. In the popular mind, President Jackson became linked with Jeffersonian agrarianism and the cause to secure equality for common people. The year of Jackson's death, in 1845, his former secretary of the navy and secretary of the treasury, Justice Levi Woodbury, claimed that "the great author of the Declaration of Independence" believed Jackson to be a man who rose from the ranks of the people to become "his country's glory." Jackson's journey from an orphan, who survived through his extended family's generosity and his own hard work, to president was a symbol of the equal potential for all workingmen to rise from obscurity to greatness.[19]

In the late 1820s and early 1830s, the Democratic Party backed governance by numerical majority rather than by property ownership, drawing support from a large segment of the population. Writing anonymously in 1839 for the *United States Democratic Review*, an author identified the Declaration of Independence to be "the origin of democratic liberty." The nature of democracy is "the supremacy of the people, restrained by a just regard for individual rights." Going further into the doctrine of the Declaration, the article claimed that the foundation of democracy was "perfect equality of rights among men." Praise for popular rule took on quasi-religious terms, with Jefferson being praised as the "apostle of Democracy" who had covered the country with the "mantle of the Declaration of Independence." "The principles of Democracy contained in the Declaration of Independence," asserted George Bancroft, a renowned historian and prominent Jackson supporter, "possess vigor to revive the decaying energies of ancient states; to enfranchise the world; to renew the youth of the nations."[20]

What went almost unstated was that Jacksonian populism did not accept that the Declaration's universal statements could refer to women, blacks, or aboriginal Americans. To the contrary, it was a Herrenvolk (master race) democracy that accepted the romantic notion of leveling but limited its beneficiaries to white males. The notions of anti-elitism and patriotic unity, therefore, were noninclusive of many groups for whom the Declaration's assertion of inalienable rights remained an aspiration but not a reflection of reality. Majority politics, without imbedding the Declaration's statement on human equality, provided only unfulfilled hope for those without access to the institutions of power.

Neo-Federalists of the period, such as Fisher Ames, drew attention to the inconsistency of the Democrats' claim that the people's will should always prevail and their acknowledgment that "the mere will of the majority is inefficient" for proper management of government. The problem with democratic rule, Jackson's detractors believed, was that it leads to anarchy in which the most bombastic, connected, and aggressive factions dominate social and political minorities. Although there was no politician who could sidestep broad electoral support for democratic politics, there was much reason to doubt that Jackson accepted the Declaration's principle of universal human rights.[21]

Indeed, there were many Americans who equated Jackson with King George III rather than Thomas Jefferson. For instance, prominent politicians and investors expressed misgivings about Jackson's closing of the Bank of the United States and depositing the federal funds into state banks favorable to his administration, the so-called pet banks. Those who decried the president's refusal to abide by the federal charter of the bank regarded this executive decree to be autocratic because he failed to follow the will of the people's representatives in Congress. A South Carolina correspondent asked rhetorically whether Jackson's "rotten" supporters "believe that the real sovereignty resided in the King or government? Our Declaration of Independence asserts that Governors derive just authority to rule only from the consent of the governed."[22] For the Whigs and other opponents of the administration, the Declaration's indictment of autocratic rule became a key component for attacking Jackson. In a very different setting than the one that gave life to the document, it continued to lend context for evaluating whether the country's leader was acting according to the will of the people.

Neither was Jackson's withdrawal of deposits from the Bank of the United States the only charge against him for violating the Declaration's standards of representative governance. Accusations of being an autocrat also related to his rejection of congressional funding for internal improvements such as national roads, his use of postmasters to suppress opposition mailings, his approval of malicious and dehumanizing rumors about aboriginal American tribes to advance plans for their removal from native lands, and his rejection of judicial interpretation of constitutional matters. This picture differs from the standard narrative that attributes to Jackson an administration beholden to the will of ordinary people.[23]

The leveling ideals of democracy did inspire political action groups, such as trade union movements, which were intent on ending conditions likened to slavery, including monopolization and proscription of collective bargaining. But ending black chattel slavery was not on white labor leaders' agenda, evincing another example of an organization that narrowly interpreted the precepts of the Declaration of Independence.

Labor organizations that had previously operated for benevolent and charitable purposes began to strike for higher wages, reasonable working hours, and improved working conditions.[24] The diverse entourage of an 1818 Fourth of July procession in Newark, New Jersey, put the widespread celebration of independence into relief. The military marched in front, followed by working tailors mounted on a horse-drawn wagon. Close behind were a variety of other craftsmen such as stonecutters, bricklayers, mason tenders, and carpenters. Also taking part in the procession were bakers, smiths, lace weavers, sawyers, watchmakers, silver platers, hatters, cabinet makers, candle makers, trunk makers, boat builders, and coopers. After the parade, a crowd gathered to hear the speech of the day, a reading of the Declaration of Independence, and oratory from female scholars, a teacher, and others.[25]

For laborers the Declaration of Independence was more than a patriotic statement of a bygone era. *The Working Man's Declaration of Independence* of 1829 began with passages from the original Declaration's first two paragraphs. After setting out a statement on men's equality, it listed specific grievances against oppressive monopolies. Workers' parties, like those in Philadelphia, New York, and Cincinnati, also found the Declaration of

Independence instructive for formulating petitions against the opulent rule of Federalists and the corporate favoritism of Democrats.[26]

For some, such as one founder of the Working Man's Party of New York, the equality spoken of in the Declaration of Independence could be achieved only by first confiscating property from those who extorted labor and then redistributing it to manual laborers. But redistribution was an extreme demand that few agreed with, and President Jackson came out against it. His message to the Senate, delivered upon his vetoing the bank rechartering bill, stressed that "distinctions in society will always exist under every just government. Equality of talents, of education, or of wealth cannot be produced by human institutions." The dominant strand of labor protest spoke not in terms of equalizing wealth but of improving the lives of workers and their families. This, like distribution, was a revisionist interpretation because the Declaration of Independence never addressed class conflict. It did, however, implicitly recognize the equal right to own property without arbitrary interference. Another labor activist claimed that using private riches to pay for universal education was what "the Declaration of Independence meant when it declared all men 'to be born free and equal.'" These interpretations of the document overlay existing social issues on the concepts of the aging parchment. According to the Working Man's Party, the Declaration of Independence was "the political text book for republican Working Men: a practical illustration of its principles" was what they demanded. Seth Luther, who traveled throughout New England to protest dangerous industrial conditions, argued that labor unions were as legitimate as any other association. No one argued that fire fighters are illegal, "but if *poor men* ask Justice, it is [said to be] a most horrible combination. The Declaration of Independence was the work of a combination, and was as hateful to the Traitors and Tories of those days as combinations among working men are now to the *avaricious* Monopolist and *purse proud* Aristocrat."[27] Luther related the labor movement's campaign against monopolies to the anti-aristocratic strains of American independence.

By importing the Declaration of Independence into the realm of labor relations, the workers' rights movement sought to demonstrate the manifesto's relevance to people's everyday lives. They regarded the pursuit of happiness in individual terms of acquiring property. The Declaration of Independence to them was a document promulgated by the people for the security of personal rights.

FIGURE 6.1 *New York Herald*, Sunday, July 6, 1845. (Image courtesy of the Library of Congress.)

Unions viewed the Declaration of Independence as a statement of personal and associational empowerment, but the document also played an interpretational role in defining national sovereignty. The Missouri Compromise could not put to rest debate about whether national ideals enumerated in the Declaration of Independence could or should trump states' laws regulating property. The decision to prevent slavery from spreading above the 36°30' parallel demonstrated congressional recognition that the Declaration's statement of universal rights informed national policy, even though constitutional provisions like the Fugitive Slave, the Three-Fifths, and the Insurrection Clauses protected slaveholders' property rights. The level of generality with which the Declaration of Independence defined government and its obligation to the people led to clashes between state and federal priorities.

The American manifesto appeared at the heart of many controversies involving states' rights in the midnineteenth century. A prominent conflict foreboding future instability stemmed from South Carolina's November 1832 nullification of the import tariffs of 1828 and 1832. The state's legislature passed an ordinance declaring federal duties and imposts on imported goods to be null and void. South Carolina was an agricultural state whose revenue relied heavily on the export of items such as tobacco, cotton, and rice along with importing most of its finished commodities from Europe and the North. The tariffs increased the price of foreign consumer goods available to southern merchants and consumers. They also afforded the North a protected market, allowing industrialists to increase retail prices while decreasing foreign sellers' ability to undercut them.

The proponents of nullification were states' rights champions who argued "that South Carolina, by the Declaration of Independence, became, and has since continued, a Free, Sovereign and Independent State; that, as a Sovereign State, she has the *inherent* power to do all those acts, which, by the law of Nations, any Prince or Potentate may of right do." This theory regarded the relationship between the states to be a "compact between independent sovereigns." The foremost exponent of the compact theory of governance, John Calhoun, authored the South Carolina nullification ordinance while he was vice president in Jackson's first administration. The governor of Virginia, like many others in the South, agreed with the general proposition that "it was not a Declaration of Independence by the Congress, as a body possessing authority, but by the several States themselves, assembled in Congress." The states-centered conception of government diminished the republican nature of Congress and inflated the role of individual states to reject unfavorable federal regulations.[28]

The nullification movement relied on formulations of the Virginia Resolution and the Kentucky Resolution, authored by James Madison and Thomas Jefferson, respectively. The two resolutions and their status among the founders (especially because one of the drafters was also the man who wrote the Declaration of Independence) gave South Carolina authoritative statements of state autonomy. Madison, who was still alive during the Nullification Crisis, disclaimed use of his resolution for dividing the states, but by then it had taken on a life of its own.

Nullificationists emphasized the Declaration's condemnation of tyranny, which they related to Congress's imposition of unwanted imposts on the South. Supporting the South Carolina ordinance in principle, Virginia Rep. John M. Patton said that the general government of the United States was acting tyrannically by insisting that an unwilling state comply with federal statutes. The Declaration of Independence, according to Kentucky Sen. George M. Bibb, created "free and independent States...not as a single nation," allowing each to be self-governing. Bibb believed that the Constitution did not change the nature of the relationship between the states, which remained independent sovereigns rather than subordinate members of a unified country.[29]

John Quincy Adams, having by then become a gadfly in the House of Representatives, argued that the compact theory of states overlooked the existence of a unified American people who through their representatives in Congress could set economic policies for the whole nation. He warned that if South Carolina's intimidating tactics were to prove successful in changing federal policy, "the Declaration of Independence will become a philosophical dream, and uncontroled [sic], despotic sovereignties will trample with impunity, ... at interminable or exterminating war with one another, upon the indefeasible and unalienable rights of man." He regarded the document in national rather than state terms. A meeting, held in Philadelphia, claimed that the Declaration of Independence created a country with the authority to protect manufacturing, agricultural, and commercial interest. Although Adams was Jackson's nemesis, the two men agreed on this issue. The latter proclaimed that through the Declaration of Independence "we declare[d] ourselves a nation by a joint, not by several acts; and when the terms of our confederation were reduced to form, it was in that of a solemn league of several States, by which they agreed that they would, collectively, form one nation for the purpose of conducting some certain domestic concerns, and all foreign relations."[30]

Other southerners who otherwise sympathized with a version of states' rights that called for democratic local autonomy and decreased imposts were not willing to buy into the nullification version of the theory. The North Carolina Legislature warned that secession might lead the North and South into violent confrontation. In that case, "this temple of liberty" could "totter to its fall" and thereby leave the rights of man in the dust and the human "capacity for self-government" no more than wishful thinking. The tenor of the North Carolina statement demonstrates how, decades before the Civil War, there was a general consensus among southern states that although South Carolina had raised a legitimate grievance on behalf of its citizens, it could not simply refuse to follow the "general government's" laws. What's more, the need for national sovereignty was explained in terms that interlinked the benefits of federal laws with enjoyment of inalienable rights. The residents of Harrison County, Virginia, conceded that "the right to resist oppression when it becomes intolerable, is one of those unalienable rights consecrated [by the] Declaration of Independence." However, it could be exercised only when the people's liberties were being systematically violated. According to them, the tariff simply did not rise to the level of oppression that justified a rupture of the Union; to the contrary, unity was critical to public safety against foreign aggression and "domestic strife and discord."[31]

Resort to the Declaration of Independence as an article of America's political creed initiated conflict between those who believed that the American people were parties to the government and those who believed that states were at the core of American government. South Carolina Sen. John Calhoun's theory on nullification left disposition of all policy at the behest of states, while Adams nationalists regarded federal supremacy to be the cornerstone of internal and foreign policy. At the end of the South Carolina conflict not a shot was fired, but the rhetorical war, which ended in 1833 with passage of a new tariff that gradually reduced rates to ease the southern burden, split the country into increasingly sectional understandings of nationhood.

Although no other southern states joined South Carolina's effort to nullify federal law, the sectional divide grew more pronounced over the issue of slavery. The movement to expand the institution further west accepted the statements of principles in the Declaration of Independence to be about self-governance. Its leaders demanded that slaveholders either enjoy their property right to bondmen throughout the United States or grant citizens of the territories and new states the right to self-governance, including the choice of whether slavery should be legal. Such a conception of the Declaration rejected the normative claim that the document's statements on representational democracy had to be balanced with its statements about universal human equality.

With slavery limited to the South, slaveholders and their representatives in Congress sought to expand the institution westward. In 1823, most of the slave-holding emigrants flocked into Texas, with Mexico's reluctant acquiescence. By happenstance, that same year Mexico passed a law prohibiting the sale of slaves within its borders and liberating children born into slavery at the age of fourteen. The Mexican Constitution of March 11, 1827, provided that "no one shall be born a slave in the state, and after six months the introduction of slaves under any pretext shall not be permitted." Significant conflict arose in 1833, at the time of the South Carolina crisis. Mexico, under the leadership of President Antonio López de Santa Anna, increasingly enforced its emancipation laws. This was the same year the British Empire prohibited slavery within its realm. By adding Texas as a slave state to the United States, opportunistic merchants wished to vastly expand the slave market to the southwest. With more land on which to lawfully raise slaves, they foresaw increased demand and selling prices for human chattel. Planters and slave speculators bought huge tracts of land in expectation of an economic boom from cotton harvesting. In May 1836, a month after the defeat of Santa Anna in war, Mexico recognized Texas's independence.[32]

Many of those who supported U.S. annexation of Texas adopted a similar reading of the Declaration of Independence to that of the supporters of South Carolina's nullification. Although the two causes were very different, both relied on the claim that the Declaration required that Texans' sentiments on slavery should be binding on the United States.

The Texas declaration of independence of March 1836 was partly modeled on the U.S. Declaration of Independence: "When a government has ceased to protect the lives, liberty and property of the people, from whom its legitimate powers are derived, and for the advancement of whose happiness it was instituted, and so far from being a guarantee for the enjoyment of those inestimable and inalienable rights, becomes an instrument in the hands of evil rulers for their oppression" the people had the obligation to "take their political affairs into their own hands" by severing themselves from the old government and creating a new one. The Texas constitution of 1845, unlike the Declaration of Independence and the U.S. Constitution, explicitly adopted the popular claim that chattel slavery was an inviolable form of property. Section VIII of the Texas Constitution provided that "the legislature shall have no power to pass laws for the emancipation of slaves, without the consent of their owners; nor without paying their owners, previous to such emancipation, a full equivalent in money for the slaves so emancipated."[33]

The Texas constitution discarded the Declaration's universalistic language of inalienable rights. John Quincy Adams decried the exclusion of African descendants and Native Americans from the rights and privileges of citizenship in Texas. Adams differentiated the Texas declaration from that of the United States. He noted that the former embodied the usual guarantees for liberty but contained the hypocrisy of "all the usual guards for the protection of liberty... [but] the constitution of the Republic of Texas... virtually repudiates the sublime doctrine of the natural rights of man" of the Declaration of Independence. On another occasion, he called for an end to slavery in Texas, denouncing the inhabitants' disdain for equality: "I know well that the doctrine of the Declaration of Independence, that 'all men are born free and equal,' is there held as incendiary doctrine and deserves lynching." This typical Southern attitude, he went on to say, "has done more to blacken the character of this country in Europe than all other causes put together." Benjamin Lundy, an abolitionist newspaper editor, dismissed the notion that the Texas insurgents instigated a popular rebellion. He likened the illegitimacy of their actions in Mexico to a considerable number of German settlers in Pennsylvania, who composed a small part of the whole, taking up arms against the general Congress and requesting Europe to recognize and aid their armed struggle.

> It was an acknowledged axiom with the founders of this Republic, that whenever any form of government fails to secure to its citizens generally the possession of their inalienable privileges, in the "pursuit of happiness," &c.—"it is the right of the people to alter or abolish it, and to institute a new government, laying its foundation on such principles, and organizing its powers in such a form, as to them shall seem most likely to effect their safety and happiness." Yet they never promulgated the doctrine, that a small minority in a community should exercise the right to prevent the *majority* from carrying this principle into effect.

Lundy believed the Texas insurgency to be the work of slave-holding elites rather than a popular revolution for the vindication of Mexicans' rights.[34]

Shortly after Texas officially joined the Union as the twenty-eighth state, the New Hampshire Congress denounced the U.S. Congress's willingness to countenance the "propagation of human oppression" there: "New Hampshire holds to the truth of the declaration of independence, that all men are created equal, and to the truth of the same declaration in her own bill of rights; that her voice shall be heard on the side of the oppressed, and against the system of human slavery." At the heart of this proclamation was belief that no new states should be allowed to join the union unless they adhered to the country's founding principles. Supporters of Texas statehood, on the other hand, believed slavery to be a domestic system existing at its residents' discretion. Though New Hampshire placed greater weight on the Declaration's normative standards, Texas emphasized its self-governance provisions and construed them to include the right to own slaves.[35]

New Hampshire was not alone in a humanistic reading of the Declaration. The Connecticut legislature objected to its Sen. John M. Niles voting on behalf of Congress's joint resolution to annex Texas as a state "to extend and perpetuate the system of human slavery," which was "incompatible with the spirit of the Declaration of Independence," the Constitution, and the will of the people. The legislature of Delaware, where slavery was legal, used similar language. It objected to annexation of Texas without first obtaining Mexico's agreement. Then came what might be read as an acknowledgment of Delaware's own shortcomings: "While we admit, in the provisions of the constitution, a solemn compact, recognizing the legal existence of slavery as a domestic institution...we nevertheless deprecate its studied extension and perpetuation, as manifested in the annexation of Texas, as hostile to the spirit of the declaration of independence." Congress's ultimate decision to admit Texas was a triumph for President James K. Polk's expansionist doctrine of Manifest Destiny, without regard to the nation's founding statement of universal rights.[36]

As slavery expanded, the claim that the United States was devoted to "life, liberty, and the pursuit of happiness" looked more and more like grandiloquent but empty rhetoric. Assertions against slavery lacked the needed backing to triumph in Congress. And a well-organized, militant minority was determined to retain slaves. When Arkansas petitioned Congress to enter the Union in 1836, its constitution included a clause retaining slavery as a form of protected property. Massachusetts Rep. George N. Briggs, who unsuccessfully argued against admission of a new state with such a provision, rested his case on the principles of the Declaration of Independence:

I do not look upon that declaration as the mere publication of a truth, beautiful in theory only, and not capable of a practical application. On the contrary, I believe it may be, and in all free Governments should be, carried out in practice. It is based on the principles of eternal truth and justice, and will abide when all existing Governments and human institutions shall have decayed and passed away. Holding these opinions, sir, how can I give any sanction to that highly exceptionable article in the constitution of Arkansas?[37]

Southern demands to allow slavery to spread westward could be countered only by principled policies of nationality. Opponents to the admission of new slave states focused on the humanistic aspects of the Declaration of Independence, while those at the other end of the debate claimed that the document was meant to create separate, sovereign states for the protection of property.

Claims of state self-determination over matters of slavery did not have solely a domestic effect. The United States presented itself to the world as a bastion of inalienable rights where natural equal birth gave every person the opportunity to enjoy the benefits of representative government. But it was clear that the nation's self-image as the embodiment of the principles in the Declaration of Independence was undermined by various state policies belying its statements of human rights.

Foreign diplomats came to festivities, appearing alongside American cabinet members, demonstrating the Declaration's continued symbolism in the United States and abroad. During Monroe's presidency, members of the diplomatic corps joined Secretaries of State John Quincy Adams and John C. Calhoun to hear the document read. The French Marquis de Lafayette, who had served as a major general during the War of Independence, lauded the American creed throughout his life. Speaking in 1821 at the French Chamber of Deputies, with murmurs to his right and applause to his left, Lafayette asserted that Europe was divided between the banners of despotism and aristocracy and liberty and equality. Even before the 1789 French Revolution, "the principles of their immortal Declaration of Independence," he continued, were "received into the bosom of the constituent assembly...amidst the greatest of our patriotic solemnities..., the usurpations of the imperial despotism." At a late-1830 Paris event in honor of American guests, Lafayette asserted that "on the 4th of July was proclaimed the Declaration of Independence...[when] a new era of liberty for the two worlds...was founded upon the genuine rights of the human race." But the persistent existence of slavery during an era touted for its democratic reforms limited the enjoyment of human rights to a privileged group, differentiating on the basis of race, gender, and religion.[38]

Rep. Joshua Giddings, one of the most prominent antislavery members of Congress, quoted from the Declaration's statements on freedom and equality to show how in 1776 the United States "aided by France ... supported freedom." By the midnineteenth century, Giddings believed things had changed to the point where the supporters of slavery portrayed America as a country no longer committed to "the doctrines of '76." The antislavery movement warned of the consequences to America's image abroad. John Quincy Adams believed that the South had no fidelity to the Declaration's principles of freedom and equality. The proslavery claim that the founding document was filled with faux generalities rather than substantive promises placed the United States in a bad light overseas.

Horace Mann, an educational and antislavery activist with a national reputation, warned that even though the Declaration of Independence had brought great changes to the world, its principles had yet to be realized in the United States. He believed the document had helped inspire Europeans, in such nations as France, Holland, Belgium, Naples, and Sicily, to strengthen their protections of civil liberties. As for his native United States, he complained, "To what bar of judgment will our own posterity bring us, what doom of infamy will history pronounce upon us, if the United States shall hereafter be found the only portion of Christendom where the principles of our own Declaration of Independence are violated in the persons of millions of our people?" Henry B. Stanton, a member of the American Anti-Slavery Society, agreed with Mann: "What a stain is the slavery on our country; the boasted land of freedom, the pioneer of liberty; with our Declaration of Independence proclaiming throughout the world, that 'all men are born free and equal,' inviting the oppressed, from other lands to come hither and inhale the pure elastic atmosphere [of our] Republic." As long as blacks are marketed and sold like cattle in the capital city of the United States, Stanton went on to say, the credibility of its ambassadors stationed in autocratic countries like Russia would be undermined.[39]

The Jacksonian period, with the annexation of Texas, admission of Arkansas into the Union as a state, and continued intrusion onto Native American lands, set the stage for a more tense battle of words between abolitionists and the apologists of slavery. Debates between those who regarded the Declaration of Independence as primarily a document about individual rights and those who thought of it as the affirmation of state self-government were the beginnings of a vicious debate that would lead to civil war.

7

SUBORDINATION

POPULAR INVOLVEMENT IN GOVERNMENT AND POLICY MAKING GREW significantly during Andrew Jackson's presidency, but not all segments of society benefited equally. The Declaration of Independence continued to be a clarion call for a wide variety of social movements such as those advocating an end to business monopolies, opening of public lands to settlers, creation of common schools, and expansion of women's rights.[1]

Disparate groups found themselves at loggerheads about whether the Declaration's statement of liberal equality applied to everyone or only to white men. Human rights debates about African Americans' and women's rights were even more contentious than those involving workers. If laborers needed public education to compete in an industrial economy, their grievances paled in comparison with those of slaves to whom southern laws denied the most basic rights (such as literacy), or married women who could not vote, no matter how well read.

Slavery repressed the human drive to participate in community governance. The South's peculiar institution violated the guarantee in the Declaration of Independence that the people have the right to institute government, "laying its foundation on such principles and organizing its powers in such form, as to them shall seem most likely to affect their Safety and Happiness." To the slave population, the manifesto was of far greater moment than positive laws. Natural law principles held the promise of liberation, while statutes and constitutions codified their inequality.

In the breasts of slaves such as William Wells Brown, who had repeatedly fled from bondage, Fourth of July orations "kindle[d] the feeling in favor of freedom which can never be effaced." It inspired him to seek liberation in a way that the Constitution, with its clauses protecting the institution of slavery, could not. To Brown's mind and in the opinion of many bondspeople, the Declaration of Independence clearly condemned slavery, and even its author came under attack: "Who could have anticipated that the apostle of American democracy should himself have been an aristocrat and a despot!...Jefferson based his political opinions upon general principles of human nature." Jefferson's practices were condemned by the ideals he espoused in the Declaration of Independence. In the course of a Fourth of July oration at Salem, Massachusetts, attorney Joseph E. Sprague denounced the "aristocratic spirit in the slave holder," which still survived in a country that professed "that all men are born free and equal." He then asked his audience, with what must have been heartfelt inner turmoil, "How long will this detestable bondage continue to disgrace our country, and remain a standing contradiction of all our professions and institution?" Given the disconnect between reality and aspiration, Brown and other slaves gravitated to the Declaration's statement of self-evident truths.[2]

Throughout the early nineteenth century, until the 1830s, antislavery societies were more active in the South than the North. The issue was of more consequence below the Mason-Dixon Line, where the overwhelming majority of slaves and free blacks lived. During that time several slave states also entered the Union. As a result of natural growth and the addition of new southern states, the slave population increased from 1.2 million in 1810 to nearly 1.5 million in 1820 and 2.1 million in 1830. During the same census years, the slave population in the North decreased dramatically from 27,000 to 19,000 to 3,500. Southern voices for the eventual dissolution of slavery, including those of Thomas Jefferson, Patrick Henry, and George Washington, were muted. In its operation, the Constitution protected slaveholders' interests through clauses like those for reclamation of fugitive slaves, suppression of slave insurrections, and augmentation of the number of representatives for slave states. In those northern states where emancipation proceeded gradually—particularly in Pennsylvania, New York, and New Jersey—the number of persons bound to perpetual servitude diminished as the century advanced. Even after sectional passions were kindled with the dispute over Missouri's admission as a slave state, the American Convention of Delegates from Abolition Societies continued to provide guidance to representatives from northern and southern antislavery organizations.[3] With time, however, the peculiar institution came to be lauded in the South as an economic and culturally uplifting institution. Meanwhile, northern immediatist abolitionist societies and gradualist antislavery associations became more adamant in their calls to end a domestic tyranny opposed to the most basic tenets of the Declaration of Independence.

The outrage against slavery was radicalized at the height of the Jacksonian Era. William Lloyd Garrison, the most caustic abolitionist of them all, mocked the "Southern slaveholders, and their northern abettors" for "the ringing of bells [and] the kindling of bonfires" on the Fourth of July that purported to celebrate the "'self-evident truths' of the Declaration of Independence." If a British three penny tax on tea was reason enough to fight the Revolution, he wrote, "How much blood may be lawfully spilt, in resisting the principle, that one human being has a right to the body and soul of another?" And if the British impressment of some six thousand American sailors could legitimate the War of 1812, "How many lives may be taken by way of recompense, or, in more popular phraseology, how many throats may be cut" to avenge the enslavement of American laborers? Garrison characterized forced impressment of sailors and kidnapping of slaves to be infringements against the inalienable rights glorified by the Declaration of Independence.[4]

On the ninth of July, 1829, before an audience at the Park Street Church at Bennington, Vermont, wearing spectacles and a white collared black suit, Garrison lit into the country for its hypocrisy:

> Every Fourth of July, our Declaration of Independence is produced, with a sublime indignation, to set forth the tyranny of the mother country, and to challenge the admiration of the world. But what a pitiful detail of grievances does this document present, in comparison with the wrongs which our slaves endure!...I am ashamed of my country. I am sick of our unmeaning declamations in praise of liberty and equality of our hypocritical cant about the inalienable rights of many.

Garrison's language was severe, but he refused to remain silent in the face of such a grave injustice.[5]

The incompatibility between the county's self-image and its practices appeared repeatedly in abolitionist publications. Frederick Douglass's newspaper, *The North Star*, ran a letter likewise mocking continued celebration of Independence Day despite the persistence of slavery. Although the assertion that "all men are created equal...sounds lofty," American practices required rewording. To be true to the facts, the author wrote, the preamble of the Declaration should be rewritten to say, "All men are created equal; but many are made by their Creator, of baser material, and inferior origin, and are doomed now and forever to the sufferance of certain wrongs—amongst which is Slavery!" To blacks, the Fourth of July was "but a mockery and an insult." To the advocates of slavery, he surmised, "liberty and equality" meant no more than firecrackers, raised flags, and other raucous festivities.[6]

Garrison and Douglass were inspired by the hopes of 1776, but one elder statesman's caustic attack on slavery was based on his own experiences and memories of the Revolution. John Quincy Adams denounced the spread of slavery and encouraged younger abolitionists in religious-sounding terms:

> I rejoice that the defense of the cause of human Freedom is falling into younger and more vigorous hands. That in the three-score years from the day of the Declaration of Independence, its self-evident truths should be yet struggling for existence against the degeneracy.... The youthful champions of the rights of human nature have buckled and are buckling on their armor, and the scourging overseer, and the lynching lawyer, and the servile sophist, and the faithless scribe, and the priestly parasite, will vanish before them like Satan.

The youthful group that grew into adulthood in the early 1830s—a group that included Garrison, Wendell Phillips, Lydia Maria and David Lee Child, Henry B. Stanton, Angelina and Sarah Grimké—would accept the torch of freedom. All of them lived until after the Civil War to rejoice at the passage of the Thirteenth Amendment to the Constitution, which finally abolished slavery.[7]

In the 1830s, abolitionists grew ever more vocal in their indictment of slavery. Nearing the end of his life, a former Army fifer of the Revolutionary

War, Noah Worcester, lamented the inexcusable failure to live up to the Declaration's "doctrine that all men are born free and equal, and that liberty is one of the inalienable rights of man." He recalled the popular maxims of the Revolutionary fighting force: "It is better to die freemen than to live as slaves" and "Liberty or Death." The conviction in the truisms of those sayings led many "white people" to free their slaves at the end of the war because they believed all along that they had been fighting to vindicate the "principle that liberty is an inalienable right, that all men are born free and equal." National citizenship was bound with principled politics. The Declaration had linked the battle for independence to "liberty and the rights of man." But rather than being consistent in blotting out slavery from the land, the framers included provisions in the Constitution to secure the holding of slaves, "and this in direct violation of some of the most important principles in the Declaration of Independence." Had the Philadelphia Convention expected southerners to come to an understanding the injustices of slavery, Worcester concluded his article, the framers must have been greatly disappointed.[8]

Abolitionists became prominent in the North while southern antislavery movements went underground or fled to escape violence. Yet even in the slave states, the Declaration of Independence inspired slaves such as William Wells Brown who heard it read in public.

Abolitionists believed the statement of natural rights in the Declaration of Independence imposed a national obligation to emancipate slaves. And they counterposed this with the protections of slavery found in the Constitution. For them, the Declaration was the core legal statement of inalienable human entitlements. Any provisions of the Constitution in violation to it were unconscionable compromises. Their devotion to the 1776 statement appears in almost all the abolitionist depictions of the early nineteenth century.

An ingenious artist created antislavery window blinds in the 1830s. One image represented an American Eagle holding the Declaration of Independence in its talons; to the side was a representation of two slaves kneeling and praying for fulfillment of its truths. The independence document played a central role in many calls for reform. In its 1833 Declaration of Sentiments, the American Anti-Slavery Society proclaimed that the preamble to the Declaration of Independence was the "corner-stone" of the "Temple of Freedom." Other abolitionists were more expositive. For instance, the great Unitarian minister William E. Channing's 1835 book *Slavery* explained how forced bondage interfered with individuals' ability to pursue happiness through education. Abolitionists were not swayed by claims of those who prophesied that mass murder of whites would ensue after abolition. The crusade to end the forced deprivation of liberty, as Channing wrote, was a corollary of the Declaration of Independence's grand message that the "meanest individual in society has the same natural rights with the most exalted." Authors often declaimed the hypocrisy of "one day signing the declaration of independence, and brandishing a slave whip the next." There were substantial differences among antislavery groups, but they agreed that God-endowed rights could not be alienated or possessed by another.[9]

This at least was clear to the firebrand William Lloyd Garrison, that each slaveholder knew "that he is a thief and a tyrant" for selling families at auction, refusing to pay laborers fair wages, and denying half the southern population education and religious instruction. As president of the American Anti-Slavery Society, Garrison regarded the Constitution as tolerating oppression. He turned instead to the Declaration of Independence to justify the crusade for freedom and equality. Slavery was a denial of the republican principles of the Declaration of Independence, wrote Charles Elliot in *Sinfulness of American Slavery*. "Every slaveholder," he went on to write, "is, virtually, an absolute monarch to his slaves," just as King George III had been to his colonial subjects.[10]

A few antislavery theorists sought to rationalize the proslavery-sounding clauses of the Constitution, claiming it could not be understood to violate the Declaration of Independence. According to them, even the Fugitive Clause was not about recovering slaves since forced bondage could not be legal in a country founded on the Declaration's statement of human equality.[11]

The Anti-Slavery Society, on the other hand, contrasted the principles of the Declaration from the compromises of the U.S. Constitution. It considered the latter to be a compact to form a *"union at the expense of the colored population of the country."* Even the signers of the Declaration did not escape their barbs: "They were not actuated by the spirit of universal philanthropy; and though in words they recognized occasionally the brotherhood of the human race, in practice they continually denied it." They tolerated or participated in selling humans like cattle while they boasted of their respect for the rights of man. An Underground Railroad conductor, John Rankin, lauded the Declaration's "fundamental principles of republicanism," while denouncing the Constitution for giving slave states an extra congressional representative for every seventy thousand slaves. The very congressmen who gained seats on the basis of slaves entered political office to "strengthen the yoke and tighten the chains of cruel oppression." This denied slaves any effective representation. The principles of the Declaration of Independence were further "trampled in the dust," said an original member of the Anti-Slavery Society, Robert B. Hall, because the Constitution's Insurrection Clause required the federal government to militarily suppress slave rebellions.[12]

Abolitionists throughout the North believed that the framers' decision to create a new nation was not predicated solely on the desire for sovereign independence or even the privileges secured by the British Magna Carta. Nationhood for abolitionists was primarily grounded on the doctrine of inalienable rights in the Declaration, which are "conferred by the Creator, and which they possessed in common on equal terms with all men." Constitutional clauses requiring the return of fugitive slaves and apportionment to the South of extra representatives for three-fifths of its slaves were aberrations that the founding generation believed to be necessary (albeit short-term) concessions. Most abolitionists refused to explain away the founders' constitutional compromises, which "infringe[d] the inalienable rights of minorities or of individuals." At a Fourth of July celebration in Farmington, Massachusetts, Garrison branded the Constitution "a covenant with death and an agreement with hell" and lit it on fire. Then, with a crowd cheering him on, he proclaimed in antimonarchical language, "So perish all compromises with tyranny! And let all the people say, Amen!"[13]

The Declaration of Independence was regarded as much more than a rhetorical device. Many abolitionist societies relied on its statements as "the principles of national justice." The document set standards for individual rights and governmental obligations. The 1834 Convention of the Free People of Color of the United States stated that its members were duty-bound to inform future generations of the divine revelation incorporated into the Declaration of Independence. Even though they continued to suffer under prejudice throughout the country, they kept firm to the principles derived from "the spirit of American liberty." The members of the Rochester Anti-Slavery Society, like many of their counterparts, made a connection between "the Universal Inalienable rights of man" and the will of God. This moral framework conceived of the inalienable rights to be divinely dispensed rather than governmentally granted. The religious doctrine of essential equal rights "spoke in the name of humanity" rather than race or class. Thus the document provided hope in the face of culturally tolerated injustices.[14]

Secular concepts often merged with religious ones to create a blend of abolition and proselytizing. This conception analogized the Declaration of Independence's statement on liberty with the Bible's golden rule. It regarded the persons of all nations to have been created "of one blood...to dwell on the face of the earth." The right to enjoy liberty was an inalienable gift that God had granted to everyone, and no law could take it away. The Declaration was the moral code for government. A variety of prominent men, among them the newspaper owner Lewis Tappan and Harvard professor Charles Follen, believed the Bible should inform the meaning of the Declaration's pronouncement that "all men are created equal" and endowed with the right to pursue happiness.[15]

The Declaration of Independence set out the moral standard that preceded constitution making, against which abolitionists judged the conduct of politicians, governments, and individuals. Garrison and Isaac Knapp, writing in their *Liberator* newspaper, sought to "prick the consciences of the planters." They indicted slaveholders for treating "rational, immortal beings" as if they were livestock, "contrary to the Declaration of Independence and the law of God." No statute, custom, rank, wealth, or power could justify denying fundamental rights to another person.

Not only did the Declaration create individual moral duty; it also supplied the creed for government conduct. Equality at law was both a natural right and a debt America owed its citizens. The country's duty to honor its African American war heroes was a repeated theme. At the 1840 Convention of New York Colored Citizens, an orator spoke of the revolutionary days when the Continental Congress passed the Declaration of Independence. At the time, "dark browed man stood side by side with his fairer fellow citizen" in the field of battle. The principles of the manifesto were "not of partial or local applicability"; they pertained to the entire human family. The observation is fascinating because it so clearly points out that the statement of human rights in the Declaration of Independence has no federalist limitations. The statements about the sovereignty of the American people and unalienable natural rights are as pertinent to states as to the federal government.

The injustice of racial restrictions on elective franchise, notwithstanding the many black soldiers who fought valiantly and shed their blood "on the soil of every battle field" for the sake of American ideals, could not have been more evident. Frederick Douglass, the prolific black abolitionist, similarly believed that to be true to the "noble sentiment set forth in the Declaration of Independence" blacks' payment of taxes and service on battlefields during the Revolution and War of 1812 should have been rewarded by an equal right to suffrage. Denial of political rights, wrote another black author, treated persons of African descent as if they were subhumans, but for purposes of taxation the government treated them as men. The Declaration of Independence stated the truism that only governments formed by consent of the people are legitimately constituted; therefore, preventing blacks from participating in elections excluded them from playing a role in representative politics.[16]

While most Garrisonian barbs were directed at the South, radical abolitionists also decried northern complicity. In 1832, an author reminded New Englanders that "for thirty-two years after the Declaration of Independence, the ships of New England were actively engaged in stealing victims on the coast of Africa." Along with northern participation in the slave market and commerce in slave-made products, some Yankees who moved to the South became outspoken supporters of the institution. The editor of the Irish publication *Dublin Freeman* wanted to increase foreign awareness of the phenomenon. He had no doubt that readers were aware slavery existed in the United States, "whose people declare to the world, in their magnificent Declaration of Independence, that 'all men are born free and equal.'" But the "contemptible prejudice against color, which prevails in the nominally free States of the Union," was less known. This prejudice excluded blacks "from advancement in social life" and condemned them to the most menial occupations, putting into doubt whether the sentiments about mankind expressed in the Declaration were authentic. Even the liberty of black slaves who managed to escape from the South was not ensured. Fugitive slaves who followed the Northern Star to freedom or who benefited from the help of the Underground Railroad were too often handed over to slave-catchers.[17]

Northern laws could be changed only through state-by-state legislative processes; abolitionists believed it would be more effective to attack the federal government's failure to act against slavery in the nation's capital. A variety of groups flooded Congress with petitions demanding it use constitutionally granted power to abolish slavery in Washington, D.C. A petition signed by eight hundred women entered the record of the Twenty-third Congress in 1835, complaining of slavery in the District of Columbia, calling it "unchristian, unholy, and unjust, not warranted by the laws of God, and contrary to the assertion in our Declaration of Independence that 'all men are created equal.'" The framers of America's manifesto "embraced the whole [human] species." The petitioners chose the broadest possible interpretation of the document, recalling that it "spoke of man not as black, or white, but as embracing the entire species, all colors and all complexions." Unlike the Constitution, it offered slaveholders no clause for defending the institution. The next year, a Quaker petition argued that ending slavery in the Capital was essential for respecting the rights, privileges, and immunities expressed in the Declaration of Independence and adopted by states' bills of rights. Another petition drew attention to the negative impact that slavery, practiced in the seat of government, would have on the image of the United States overseas, where its profession of life, liberty, and the pursuit of happiness was regarded to not reflect actual practices. These and other statements, such as one by Judge William Jay, founder of the New York City Anti-Slavery Society, presumed that the Declaration furnished the federal government with its intrinsic mission, predating the Constitution. The purpose of national government, petitioners believed, was incompatible with allowing enslavement in the District of Columbia.[18]

The Declaration's statement on self-evident truths, as Garrison and others understood it, made immediate abolition and Northern reform imperative. They considered calls for gradual emancipation to be "full of timidity, injustice and absurdity." Just as the founding fathers fought for seven years after declaring the colonies to be independent on July 4, 1776, so too the battle against slavery would take years. The long road ahead was no excuse, however, to not seek justice.[19]

Political abolitionists understood that they could not win elections if they were to adopt Garrison's radical demands. They expressed confidence that the evils of slavery could be resolved in the context of existing constitutional institutions. Immediatists, on the other hand, refused to rely on political horse trading. Judge Jay, for instance, lamented the willingness to appease slave-holding states. He worried that "should *political* Anti-Slavery ever be substituted for *religious* Anti-Slavery the consequences would probably be disastrous to the cause of human rights."[20]

Politicians such as James G. Birney, originally from Kentucky, and Salmon P. Chase of Ohio focused their attention on preventing the spread of slavery into western territories. They condemned the peculiar institution but conceded its legality in existing southern states. This pragmatic faction believed slavery would wither of its own accord because it was economically wasteful and contrary to the nation's core commitments. The more conciliatory antislavery movement became modestly popular and ran candidates in popular elections, first as the Liberty Party (1840), then as the Free Soil Party (1848), and finally ending up the Republican Party (1854), under whose banner Abraham Lincoln captured the presidency.

Political abolitionists were less vitriolic than Garrisonians. They too relied on maxims from the Declaration of Independence but called for a gradual end to slavery. Both groups described the cruelty and oppressiveness of the institution, but they broke ranks on the need to enter into compromises to achieve their mutual purpose. The supporters of gradual antislavery policy making, like the Presbyterian Synod of Kentucky, were no less opposed to slavery, but their strategy was to gain public backing through more modest proposals.[21]

The Liberty Party steadfastly opposed new slave states entering the Union and proposed ending the internal slave trade. Its philosophy was grounded "on the broad basis of the foundation principles of our government, as developed in the declaration of independence and in the constitution." In 1840 the Liberty Party's presidential candidate, Birney, received a mere seven thousand votes nationwide. Though the initial successes of antislavery politicians were modest at best, their candidacy in elections offered an opportunity to disseminate the antislavery message where it might not have otherwise reached. The Liberty Party's platform of 1844 stated "that the fundamental truths of the Declaration of Independence" were so important that voting against slavery was "a moral and religious duty." Although the Party received a tiny minority of the vote, its members persevered, believing that every ballot advanced them one step further to deliverance. A vote for the principles of the Declaration of Independence was a statement against slavery in the District of Columbia, a rejection of the notion that slaves were things rather than people, and a statement that no one "has a better right to his own body, and its labor, and to his wife and children than any other person on earth." Political rallies, such as one convened by New York black voters where speakers repeatedly stated that all men are created equal and guaranteed inalienable rights, were empowering. In a letter to members of the Liberty Party, Alvan Stewart, who along with several other radical constitutionalists claimed the Constitution was an antislavery document, also thought "the Declaration of Independence to be an elementary law, the law of laws, the rock of first principles." Slavery contravened this essential truth and was therefore illegitimate.[22]

The Garrisonian message was internally suppressed in the South; however, antislavery party platforms and speech made their way into southern newspapers because they were considered to be part of mainstream politics. For instance, despite overwhelming support for slavery in South Carolina, a newspaper there published a speech made by the Whig candidate and soon-to-be governor of Ohio, William Bebb. He argued that "our colored brethren" should receive "those rights and immunities that are granted to us" through the "Declaration of Independence." Despite its antagonism to this message, the newspaper also reprinted specific measures he planned to take as governor: black children should be able to attend common schools on a par with white children, and the legislature should repeal laws requiring blacks to pay a surety for their good behavior. That such explicit statements against racism led to Bebb's victory in 1846 by a vote of 118,869 to 116,484 demonstrated that many Ohio voters shared his sentiments. Publication of his views in South Carolina, far removed from Bebb's electoral base, exposed a hostile audience to his views, leaving the possibility of persuading those who remained open-minded.

Political abolitionism also offered blacks the opportunity to take part in policy making. Frederick Douglass was chosen to be a delegate to the Free Soil Party Convention of August 11, 1852. While traveling by steam ship to Pittsburgh, he was forced to sleep on deck and then denied access to a dining cabin for breakfast. The second leg of his trip was by train, and when it stopped at a town for dinner, Douglass was turned out of a hotel dining room. On witnessing this racial injustice, other Free Soil delegates to the convention walked out of the dinner and refused to return.[23]

Those who fought to make the Declaration's ideals a reality found the path meandering and filled with indignities, personal affronts, supremacist confrontations, and inequalities; but they gained solace from the moral rightness of their argument and its link to the principles of American nationhood.

Although the Garrisonian approach of moral suasion differed from the political antislavery movement's efforts, both factions relied on the Declaration of Independence to oppose the American Colonization Society's proposal. The latter's solution to slavery was for blacks to leave the United States. The effort to colonize blacks into Liberia was based on the conviction that peaceful racial cohabitation corrupted black morals, made them seditious and contentious, led to amalgamation of the races, and degraded white labor. Abolitionists decried colonizationism, condemning it as a paternalistic ruse aimed at ridding America of free blacks. Its real object, they believed, was to strengthen the South's peculiar institution by eliminating the imagined threat of a joint free-black and slave revolt.

Henry Clay was one of many prominent politicians in the colonization movement. He first gained national notoriety in 1820 as the Speaker of the House by developing and mustering support for a sectional agreement that became known as the Missouri Compromise (see Chapter 6). It allowed Missouri to join the Union as a slave state, Maine as a free state, and slavery to spread west below the 36°30' longitudinal line. As president of the Colonization Society, Clay expressed his continued belief in equality laid down by the Declaration of Independence, but only in "principle" and not in reality. Nowhere in the United States, he declared, did the "black man, however fair may be his character, and from however long a line of free colored ancestors he may proceed, enjoy an equality with his white neighbors." Rather than resolve the problem here, Clay advocated relocation to Africa. Abolitionists denounced Clay as "the arch Kentucky compromiser, and the haughty despiser of the colored race," for his liberal spirit toward slaveholders and his support of colonization. The American Anti–Slavery Society took him to task. Clay claimed that blacks and whites could not live together because "the liberty of the descendants of Africa in the United States is incompatible with the safety and liberty of the European descendants." This, delegates at a Quaker meeting house asserted, was "no less tyranical [sic] than the doctrine held by the Autocrat of Russia, or the

Algerines [sic]; but stands directly opposed to all right principles, and repugnant to the doctrine held forth in the Declaration of Independence" about human equality.[24]

The positions taken by the supporters of colonization were not homogeneous. Among them were those who argued that free blacks alone should be voluntarily repatriated. Others advocated compensating slaveholders to emancipate and then forcefully shipping their former laborers to Liberia. Some proposals included passages denouncing the institution. An author reminded the public that Jefferson's original draft of the Declaration of Independence condemned those who introduced slavery into the American colonies and expressed concern that "the misfortune, the disgrace remains." The plea then worked out the expense of compensated emancipation and presented sale of western territories as a means for raising the needed federal revenue. Ultimately, colonization failed for lack of resources and inadequate support, especially from free blacks and southern enterprises that depended on their economic output.[25]

Colonization was an attempt to resolve tensions that were endemic to forced racial bondage, legal inequality, and culturally sanctioned discrimination. The overwhelming majority of free blacks reacted adversely to colonization proposals because they disparaged African Americans' right to live, labor, and raise a family in their native country and states. Their ancestors, as many of them explained in print and at meetings, had fought valiantly, shoulder to shoulder with white soldiers, during the Revolutionary War and the War of 1812, and like any other Americans they were attached to the land of their nativity. Several black New York citizens expressed their desire to stay put. And at a time when the prospects for their posterity looked bleak, they were seemingly able to muster confidence: "We do not believe that things will always continue the same. The time must come when the Declaration of Independence will be felt in the heart, as well as uttered from the mouth, and when the rights of all shall be properly acknowledged and appreciated." The Free People of Color of the Borough of Wilmington, Delaware, presented their "decided and unequivocal disapprobation of the American Colonization Society, and its auxiliaries" for seeking to "deprive us of rights that Declaration of Independence declares are the 'unalienable rights' of all men." A speaker at the African Church in Temple-street, New Haven, said that to deny the "sons of Africa" freedom and equality, despite the Declaration's statement of inalienable human rights, was to treat blacks not as men but as "baboons or some other dumb beasts." To suggest that blacks move to Liberia because of their skin color ignored their brave service to the country. The black abolitionist minister Nathaniel Paul, who was born in Exeter, New Hampshire, and later moved to Albany, New York, to lead the Union Street Baptist Church, also let loose his opposition. In 1833, speaking at the Great Anti-Colonization Meeting in Exeter Hall, Paul decried the cruelty of seeking to expel hundreds of thousands of innocent people from their country despite their brave patriotism: "To rob the colored men in that country of every right, civil, political or religious, to which they are entitled by the American Declaration of Independence" was a terrible injustice.[26]

However, the vehemence of the opponents of slavery was not commensurate with their numbers. By the end of the Jacksonian Era, Garrisonian abolitionists and the political antislavery movement held relatively little influence. The revolutionary certainty of slavery's eventual demise had given way to a trend toward defending slavery as a morally good institution that the South had every right to preserve.

The proslavery movement was even further removed from abolitionism than were colonizationists. The Declaration of Independence held the least sway among the apologists for slavery. Politicians who spoke openly in favor of the institution laid their stakes on the Constitution instead. Slavery's apologists drew legal rhetoric from several provisions of the Constitution, including the Fugitive Slave and Insurrection Clauses. On the other hand, abolitionists tended to locate their rationalizations in the statement of universal rights in the Declaration and often condemned the founding generation for the constitutional compromises they had made for the sake of union. Few in the antislavery movement framed the Constitution as antislavery, and those who did struggled to explain away sections such as the Three-Fifths and Importation Clauses.[27]

Some of slavery's defenders acknowledged that it was an evil but believed that emancipating persons who had been subjected to ignorance, violence, and exploitation was dangerous. They warned that freed slaves would exact vengeance for the wrongs they had suffered. Closely allied to them was a group who agreed that slavery was undesirable but who decried federal efforts to stop its expansion, believing that only states could decide on the question of bondage. Another group, characterized by a more cocksure supremacism, said that slavery was part of the natural or divine order in which whites ruled over subservient blacks. The latter group considered slavery to be a positive good for society, beneficial to blacks and whites who gained culturally and materially from the enforced subjugation.

By the early 1830s, it was in vogue for southerners to mock the wording of the Declaration of Independence. Skepticism about the document's statements on natural rights had their origin in the Revolutionary period. The proslavery argument maintained that involuntary servitude was like any other form of labor subordination. Slavery's apologists regarded the self-evident truths to be no more than exaggerated statements in urgent need of qualification. Just as the maxim of the Declaration of Independence did not apply to differences in wealth, education, and skills, the supporters of slavery argued that it was irrelevant to unequal treatment of blacks. There were, after all, burdens on foreigners, women, and people of color. The natural state of human equality was no more than hypothetical; in a complex government "a state of slavery is fundamental." Unsurprisingly, perhaps, the supporters of slavery infantilized blacks. They believed that by "all men" the Declaration of Independence referred only to adult white men. Even if before God they were equal, they rejected out of hand the possibility that blacks could match the achievement and intellect of whites.[28]

The fact that some of the men who signed the Declaration of Independence were slaveholders emboldened those who believed that the document's statement about equality applied only to white males. The framers' failure to explicitly condemn slavery in any portion of the Declaration of Independence or Constitution also provided an argument for those who believed the institution to be solely a matter for private conscience rather than a subject of social concern.

Aside from the claim that blacks were nonparties to the Declaration, there were those who regarded it as a monument of a bygone era. Though recognizing its historic relevance, they asserted that "the Declaration of Independence has no claim whatever to be considered in the controversy of our day."[29]

The South's best-known and most formidable defender of slavery was John Calhoun, whose career stretched across a number of elected offices. In the early stages of his public career, he was a nationalist. As a member of the House of Representatives, he drafted the language for the statute creating the Second Bank of the United States. He supported maintenance of an army while he was the secretary of war in the Monroe cabinet. During the South Carolina nullification crisis, after being elected to the office of vice president in 1828, he changed direction and drafted a resolution supporting every state's right to nullify any federal legislation averse to its economic interests. Until the end of his life, Calhoun was an outspoken supporter of slavery, worried about abolitionism, British emancipation policies, and slave rebellions like the one led by Nat Turner in 1831.

Calhoun led a popular southern faction that not only denounced the Missouri Compromise but also urged extension of slavery westward to the Pacific Ocean. He mocked the Declaration of Independence's claim of equality of the "human races" as being an error inherited from the writings of British philosophers John Locke and Algernon Sidney. Of far greater moment, he believed, was the northern conflict between capital and labor than southern challenges to retention of slavery. The notion of "universal equality," he wrote, was a fallacy "that *deforms* our Declaration of Independence—if one can say so of a document the extravagance [sic], and inaccuracies of which are only to be palliated by the excitement from which they sprang." Neither was the doctrine of natural rights palpable to him since it placed individuals above political communities, which Calhoun believed had primacy over their members. Liberty was not a birthright, he thought, but "a reward reserved for the intelligent, the patriotic, the virtuous and deserving, and not...to be bestowed on people too ignorant, degraded and vicious." This perspective was derisive to persons of African descent as well as uneducated whites. Calhoun disparaged the abolitionists' interpretation that the Declaration was meant to recognize that everyone, irrespective of race, was born free and equal. To the contrary, "instead of all men being created equal, or all men being equally free" he welcomed "the greatest disparity." In response, abolitionists such as Daniel O'Connell, speaking at the 1840 Anti-Slavery Convention in London, argued Calhoun's position was untenable in light of "the first clause of the American charter of Independence, which declares all men equal." At its core the disagreement pitted those believing that race was irrelevant to the existence of rights against a group that considered racial distinctions to be indicative of the subordination of blacks to whites.[30]

Calhoun's advocacy focused on the political relationship between states and the federal government. Another prominent branch of the proslavery movement relied on religion. A Baptist church pastor from Culpeper

County, Virginia, Thornton Stringfellow, regarded slavery to be God's gift to blacks. He reckoned the institution to be divinely ordained for heathen redemption. Stringfellow shed crocodile tears because whites had to be the "masters and guardians of slaves." He went so far as to claim that "in drafting the Declaration of Independence" the framers had "made this outrage one of the prominent causes for dissolving all political connection with the mother country." Nevertheless, rather than calling for abolition of this admitted "outrage," Stringfellow counseled southern whites to Christianize and civilize "these degraded savages" but not to release them from bondage.[31]

Another southern minister, Rev. Frederick A. Ross of Alabama, who was at one point a pastor in East Tennessee and then in Huntsville, Alabama, scoffed at the Declaration's claim of human equality. As proof that inequality was part of God's natural order, Ross pointed to the biblical creation story. "It is not a truth," he wrote, nor is it "self-evident, that all men are created equal." The Bible is clear, according to him, that "God created the [human] race to be in the beginning TWO, a male and a female MAN; one of them not equal to the other in attributes of body and mind, and…not equal in rights as to government." Both were to remain in the station of their creation. The natural differences between blacks and whites were also part of the Creator's carefully wrought scheme of "original inequality." Thus, he summed up, the "five sentences in that second paragraph of the Declaration of Independence are not the truth," since they ran contrary to the biblical account, and anyone who resisted this presumed reality was fighting not against an unjust system of governance but against God's plan for man. He had made men as unequal as "leaves of the trees, the sands of the sea, the stars of heaven." According to Ross the beauty of the Declaration of Independence was its "simple statement of the grievances [of] the colonies," not "these imaginary maxims" about a supposed self-evident truth.[32]

When James Kirke Paulding became involved in the proslavery movement after a visit to the South, his fame as a poet and novelist helped to boost its popularity. He too wrote of the "Supreme Being" in the context of "the inalienable rights of nature." Unlike Ross, however, Paulding conceded the Declaration's assertion that "all men are created equal" but justified the hierarchical structure of slavery by relating it to war captives' forfeiture of their inborn equality. Though he correctly characterized the contemporary law of war, Paulding's explanation was illogical in the context of the thousands of Africans captured during peacetime raids and driven overseas from their birthplaces. Not interested in historical fact but exposition of doctrine, Paulding also sought to square the declaration that all men had an inalienable right to happiness with hereditary bondage. He analogized the gloom and loss of liberty associated with criminal punishment to slavery in order to show that restrictions of liberty were not anomalous to a democracy. But nowhere did he demonstrate that antisocial, criminal behavior was comparable to enslavement on the basis of ancestry and physical characteristics. Evidently unaware that free blacks and slaves seeking their freedom had fought in the Continental Army and various state militias, Paulding wrote that such an "ignorant race [was] incapable of appreciating or enjoying the blessings of national happiness" because they had "taken no part in acquiring them."[33]

Paulding was not the only author who accepted the statement of human equality in the Declaration of Independence but argued that it was compatible with slavery. The northern Episcopalian minister Samuel Seabury described slaves and masters as natural equals possessing differing civil liberties. Seabury admitted there were many strictures on slaves' rights to self-determination, but he claimed that they, like slaveholders, enjoyed an equal liberty of reason, judgment, and religious devotion. This line of reasoning could be satisfactory only to persons born in freedom, but not to those who were born into hereditary bondage. Along the lines of Seabury, the prolific Rev. Thomas Smyth patriotically recounted how the drafters of the Declaration of Independence went to church "with their negro man-servant and maid-servant walking on either side of them."[34]

The proslavery movement either condemned the Declaration's statements on equality or acknowledged but found them inapplicable to blacks. The former was a more aggressive ideology, advocating nullification of national laws that placed restraints on the spread of the institution. The second embraced the Declaration but denied it had anything to say about slavery.

With political abolitionists finding limited success at the polls, proslavery politicians were able to enact several federal measures suppressing dissemination of antislavery literature. In 1835, New York abolitionists developed a mass newspaper mailing campaign meant for the South. President

Andrew Jackson's postmaster general, Amos Kendall, who advocated on behalf of states' prerogatives over slavery, was determined to prevent antislavery voices from attacking local practices. To thwart abolitionists, Kendall unofficially allowed local postmasters to refuse delivery of the writings. Samuel J. May, in his capacity as secretary of the Massachusetts Anti-Slavery Society, protested the suppression of ideas. Speaking at a rally in Boston, May defended the letter campaign: the pamphleteers had done no more than assert "the words of the Declaration of Independence that 'ALL MEN are created equal'" and described God's unalienable gift to all men. A correspondent in the *Boston Daily Advocate* remarked that the Jackson Administration's policy could classify a pamphlet carrying the text of the Declaration of Independence as being incendiary. Even before conflict over the prohibition on mail service broke out, abolitionists had claimed that to southern slaveholders and slave dealers the statements in the Declaration of Independence had a "seditious tendency."[35]

Searching for an alternative, abolitionists redoubled their petitioning efforts to Congress. In response, under Calhoun's leadership in 1836 Congress passed a gag rule requiring antislavery petitions, memorials, or resolutions to be received but immediately tabled without reading or debating them in Congress. The editor of the *Boston Daily Advocate* likened congressional censorship to Tsar Nicholas I's repression of the press in Russia on matters related to serfdom and autocracy. The editorial also compared the gag rule to the French prohibition of criticism instituted at the coronation of Louis Philippe.[36] Such censorship seemed out of place in a country that had fought for independence to protest the British monarch's rejection of colonial petitions. The gag rule was nevertheless reenacted yearly until 1844. Supporters of the rule claimed they sought to restore tranquility and avoid sectional conflict; opponents argued that it violated Americans' basic right to petition their representatives. John Quincy Adams was its foremost opponent.

By 1836, Adams had become a pillar of American politics. He was then a member of the House of Representatives from Massachusetts. He had served in many important public offices in the United States. Among his greatest accomplishments were one term as president, eight years as secretary of state under Monroe, five as a senator from Massachusetts, five as minister to Russia, and two as minister to Britain. In 1811, President Madison nominated and the Senate confirmed Adams to the Supreme

Court of the United States, but for personal reasons he turned down the honor. Though he was never formally a member of the antislavery movement, almost invariably it cheered his pitched congressional battles against the leading proponents of slavery. To many, Adams was "a sentinel on the watch tower of the nation." He seemed to derive genuine pleasure from the thousands of letters he received from abolitionist organizations. Writing to congratulate Adams for his 1838 reelection, the correspondence secretary of the Rhode Island Anti-Slavery Society praised Adams for vigorously standing by the ideals of the Declaration of Independence at a time when slaves suffered under the lash in the South and northern abolitionists worked under the threat of physical attacks. In his response, Adams denounced the "convulsive agonies of slavery, clinging to her human victims." This was not, he continued, "the covenant to which we pledged our faith in the Declaration of Independence."[37]

Adams was more politic than immediatist abolitionists. Unlike them, he spoke in terms of gradual abolition. He thought slavery would end only with the masters' recognition of its inhumanity. William Lloyd Garrison criticized Old Man Eloquent, as Adams came to be known, for not doing enough, even on campaigns like the abolition of slavery in the District of Columbia, where Congress had sole jurisdiction. Adams and antislavery groups did find common ground in the belief that the Declaration's statement on self-evident truth communicated the injustice of human chattel. Adams corresponded with antislavery leaders such as Lewis Tappan, Joshua Leavitt, and Theodore Weld. And Weld admired Adams for raining "blows upon the head of the monster." But Adams kept all of them at arms length, fearing his many enemies would otherwise portray him as a radical.[38]

Adams's jarring speeches in Congress, letters to his constituents, and newspaper articles regularly invoked the principles of the Declaration of Independence. He decried the "ignominious transformation of the people who had commenced their career in the world by the Declaration of Independence, into a nation of slave-traders and slave breeders, for sale." He thought it wrong to prevent members of Congress from condemning the gross inconsistency between "the principles proclaimed in the Declaration of Independence and the practice of holding human beings in perpetual and hereditary bondage." Government was instituted to safeguard the rights of life, liberty, and the pursuit of happiness; that was the doctrine the colonies relied on to justify renouncing their allegiance to Great Britain. Without the Declaration's statement of self-evident truths, Adams believed, the American Revolution would have been but a rebellion against legitimate authority.[39]

Adams was a master parliamentarian who relied on procedural devices to circumvent the congressional rule prohibiting introduction of abolitionist petitions. For instance, he periodically read petitions denouncing slavery aloud in Congress without being overt enough to trigger the gag rule. At one session, he asked the Speaker of the House for permission to read a petition from the Lutheran Church in New York "praying Congress to secure to all the inhabitants of the District of Columbia the benefit of the laws and the rights of the Declaration of Independence." Congress decided this was an abolitionist petition and tabled it, but its content was already in the record. At another date, he requested to enter a petition into the record overtly requesting that the gag rule be rescinded and another sarcastically calling for the Declaration of Independence to be expunged from the minutes of the early Congress. Both were tabled.[40]

At the tail end of 1838 and early 1839, Adams published descriptions of 825 petitions Congress had refused to hear or refer to committees. The National Intelligencer, Washington, D.C.'s foremost newspaper, printed them in five installments. Petitioners from various states had sent them during the Twenty-fifth Congress's third session. The multicolumned airing of censured materials included petitioners' names, their place of origin, and the subject of their prayers. Congress's dominant majority, Adams wrote, had suppressed the people's natural right to political expression. According to him, the First Amendment's guarantee of free speech lay in the Declaration of Independence. He reminded readers that "the last and heaviest charge in the Declaration of Independence against the King of Great Britain was that the repeated petitions of the people of the colonies for redress had been answered only by repeated injuries." Congress, he implied, committed the same injustice for which the framers of the Declaration blamed King George III. Adams was not the only one who recognized the disparity between the nation's founding ideals and its practices. He and the abolitionists understood that government conduct so similar to the actions for which the colonists condemned George III violated the anti-autocratic principles of the Declaration of Independence. They claimed that since the nation's founding the right to petition had been recognized to be an inherent prerogative of Americans; the gag rule was setting it aside in deference to the tyranny of slavery.[41]

On very rare occasions, apologists of the gag rule referred to the original intent of the American manifesto of independence. During one of many congressional debates on the subject, Rep. Mark A. Cooper of Georgia, who was then in his first term in Congress, invoked the Declaration of Independence for a very different purpose than did Adams. He relied on the document to decry the antislavery agitation. Those who petitioned Congress to end slavery, he said, were inciting slave insurrections. The Declaration had likewise accused King George III of advocating "domestic insurrections" by offering freedom to slaves willing to take up arms on the British side. Once they became states, another Congressman asserted, the legality of slavery became solely the prerogative of each state. The emphasis of these assertions was on states' independence rather than the people's independence. As a one-time member of South Carolina's Nullifier Party, Rep. John Campbell, said, so many of its signers were slave owners that "the expressions used in the Declaration of Independence, that 'all men are by nature equal,' &c, were intended to have no reference whatever to our slave population." Campbell wanted to prove that slavery was part of the American tradition, while Adams's efforts were meant to show that the institution was an aberration from the doctrine of the Declaration of Independence. Though Campbell relied on the framers' contradictory practices, Adams found substance in the principles of the Declaration.[42]

Gag rule loyalists grew exasperated with the gadfly, John Quincy Adams. Amid calls to expel him, charge him criminally, or issue a congressional censure, Adams refused to desist. In 1842, southerners attempted to censure Adams in Congress after he presented a petition of forty-six citizens from Haverhill, Massachusetts, calling for immediate dissolution of the Union. Petitioners advocated dissolution to prevent the South from further diverting valuable funds to protect its peculiar institution at the expense of the country's welfare. Adams immediately created a row. From the Senate, Henry Clay (who had been secretary of state in Adams's presidential administration), pressed Kentucky Rep. Thomas F. Marshall to bring a censure motion before the House. On January 24, 1842, Rep. Thomas Walker Gilmer brought the official motion to censure Adams. The trial proceeded, with Adams relishing the fight. Opposition to the

Haverhill petition united the supporters of slavery. They argued that the petition clearly linked "abolitionism and dissolutionism."[43]

Adams began his defense on January 25, 1842. Two astute abolitionist authors, Joshua Leavitt and Theodore D. Weld, provided him with invaluable research assistance. The tension of the debate was audible in Adams's high-pitched voice. With his notorious temper nearly boiling over, he ordered the clerk of the House to read the first paragraph of the Declaration of Independence. Adams knew that many congressmen would find it contrary to existing protocol to invoke the document in the context of slavery. He meant to demonstrate how close the wording of the Declaration was to the offending petition: both, after all, called for separation from national government. Without waiting for a reply from the clerk, Adams repeated his demand to hear the nation's founding principles: "The first paragraph of the Declaration of Independence!" After the clerk had finished, Adams called for the second paragraph, "Proceed, proceed, proceed, down to the 'right and a duty.'" Having laid the foundation of his argument, Adams repeated that if the government becomes despotic the people have the "right and duty to alter or abolish it." The lesson he drew from this was that the people's right to dissolve government at least implied that they have the natural right to petition for dissolution of an oppressive government. The press made Adams's speech broadly available throughout the country.[44]

For two weeks, Adams kept up his assault against Congress's policy to suppress petitions in the interest of slaveholders' sensibilities. By attempting to censure him, the South had accidentally given Adams a forum for laying out the argument for why the House was obligated by the terms of the Declaration of Independence to accept abolitionist petitions. From his perspective, petitioning was a means for the people to voice their concerns about perpetuation of despotism, which was far safer than the remedy of revolution asserted in the Declaration of Independence. One of the proslavery school's most able defenders, Rep. Henry Wise, called Adams "the acutest, the astutest, the archest enemy of southern slavery that ever existed." Adams, no doubt, would have accepted Wise's words as a compliment. In the end, on February 7, 1842, the House decided that voting to censure Adams was tantamount to prohibiting legislators from exercising their obligation to voice the concerns of their constituents. A vote was taken, and Adams was acquitted.[45]

By 1842, supporters of the gag rule held only a four-vote majority, and a three-vote majority in 1843; the following year, after Adams made his motion against reenactment, a twenty-eight-person majority voted against the rule.[46]

The gag rule debate demonstrated yet again how a document that might have been no more than a statement of national sovereignty had retained force in congressional debates. It continued to be a central component in analysis of the critical issue of the day, slavery. Had Jefferson and the Continental Congress not included a statement about human rights and the people's primacy in governance, the document might have gone into obscurity; becoming nothing more than a national relic of the country's achievement in 1776. This was indeed the case with multiple Latin American declarations of independence that contained no statements of natural rights. Instead, the U.S. Declaration of Independence remained deeply pertinent three-quarters of a century after it had been brought to life. Although its provisions lacked any enforcement power, seemingly without any authority to alter legal culture, the Declaration of Independence was the principled framework for debate about laws, society, congressional decorum, and civil liberties.

The antislavery movement was not exclusively focused on black civil rights. Arguments on behalf of women's rights were prominent in abolitionist platforms. Activists often participated in joint events. Women played central roles in organizing antislavery petition drives, which made their way into the hands of congressmen such as Rep. John Quincy Adams and Sen. Charles Sumner. Those efforts earned the respect and gratitude of their fellow supplicants. When women were denied the right to participate officially at the 1840 World Anti-Slavery Convention in London, William Lloyd Garrison sat among the female spectators rather than joining the meeting, in a show of solidarity. That year at a gathering "held by the colored people" in New Bedford, Massachusetts, those in attendance agreed to a resolution condemning the "spirit of prejudice" directed at women, the "well-tried friends of the slave." Such a divisive tendency, the official report went on to say, was "as foreign to freedom and equality, as the slave code of Georgia is to the Declaration of American Independence."[47]

Returning home to the United States, an experienced feminist, Lucretia Mott, and an up-and-coming one, Elizabeth Cady Stanton, joined forces.

Their effort had been anticipated by some of the natural rights and social contracts arguments of Judith Sargent Murray, Frances Wright, Emma Willard, Sarah Grimké, and Margaret Fuller. On July 19 and 20, 1848, they organized the first U.S. women's conference at the Wesleyan Chapel in Seneca Falls, New York.

The Seneca Falls Convention agreed that a broad range of changes were needed to secure for women social, legal, and religious rights. At the end, the meeting participants adopted the Declaration of Sentiments, which relied on core national concepts of liberty and equality. The document drew inspiration from the Declaration of Independence but expanded the earlier manifesto's relevance to clearly include women's interests. Organizers adopted much of the language of the preamble to the Declaration of Independence to better ground their demand for women's suffrage on the nation's founding ideology: "We hold these truths to be self-evident: that all men and women are created equal; that they are endowed by their Creator with certain inalienable rights; that among these are life, liberty, and the pursuit of happiness; that to secure these rights governments are instituted, deriving their just powers from the consent of the governed." But in its radical reinterpretation, the Declaration of Sentiments avowed "that woman is man's equal." Its principled stance on gender equality rejected the accepted norms of the revolutionary and contemporary generations. The document juxtaposed the treatment of women by male patriarchy with the British monarch's treatment of colonists:

The history of mankind is a history of repeated injuries and usurpations on the part of man toward woman, having in direct object the establishment of an absolute tyranny over her. To prove this, let facts be submitted to a candid world.

He has never permitted her to exercise her inalienable right to the elective franchise.

He has compelled her to submit to laws, in the formation of which she had no voice.

The Seneca Falls Convention relied on the Declaration of Independence to evoke women's rightful place in republican governance. Sixty-eight women and thirty-two men signed the Seneca Falls Declaration and eleven resolutions on women's rights, but only one man, Frederick Douglass, voted to adopt Stanton's resolution that women should be granted the right to vote. Judge Cady, Stanton's father, read a newspaper account of his daughter's part in the Declaration of Sentiments. Coming to Seneca Falls, he said, "I wish you had waited until I was under the sod before doing such a foolish thing." Despite this condemnation, the movement was born.[48]

Along with the call for women's rights, the Convention also agreed "that the equality of human rights results necessarily from the fact of the identity of the race in capabilities and responsibilities." Hunt had also condemned the outrage of slavery. The *Liberator*, which was the foremost newspaper of immediatist abolitionists, expressed its aversion for voting restrictions that burdened women unequally because they ran counter to the statement in the Declaration of Independence that "all government derives its just power from the consent of the governed."[49] Wendell Phillips, Garrison's closest associate and the husband of feminist abolitionist Ann Terry Greene, often relied on the document to accentuate and clarify his comments to audiences. In multiple speeches, which the *Liberator* often republished, Phillips decried the absurdity of excluding half of humanity from the Declaration of Independence's formula of natural equality. Not all abolitionists subscribed to Phillips's and Hunt's views; some were more conservative in their family outlook. An article in the *Colored American* began by stating, "Abolitionists hold with the Declaration of Independence" but ended with the premise that the natural order of humanity required women to be subject to their husbands.[50]

Feminists found a national statement of rights in the Declaration of Independence. This was crucial to their cause because many of the core areas they addressed—property ownership, voting, and family autonomy—were traditionally reserved to the states. They were left to changing laws state by state, turning to the Constitution, or relying on the Declaration of Independence. The state-by-state approach was not only tedious but provided no unified theoretical grounding, holding instead a diversity of positive laws. The Constitution contained nothing on gender equality, although a convincing argument could be made that the Bill of Rights applied to persons regardless of gender. Neither of these approaches was as convincing as incorporation of statements in the Declaration of Independence about equality and government by consent into advocacy for women's suffrage.

Irrespective of the Constitution, Ernestine L. Rose told a Boston audience, women's entitlement to an equal opportunity to enjoy liberty, life, and the pursuit of happiness was an essential component of "the higher laws of humanity." Rose's oratorical ability to interweave the philosophy of natural rights into abolitionist and women's rights causes was especially remarkable because English was not her first language; she was a Polish Jewish immigrant. To exclude women from the ideals of the Declaration, she asserted, on the basis of presumed superiority was to "libel and insult humanity."[51]

In the fall of 1850, a convention held in Worcester, Massachusetts, made a "collective protest against the aristocracy of sex," which Rose and other female immigrants had sought to leave behind in Europe. The terms of protest analogized the class conflict of the Revolutionary Era to persistent gendered aristocracy. A statement emerged from the event pointing out the undemocratic principles of those who proclaimed that "'life, liberty, and pursuit of happiness' are 'inalienable rights' of only one moiety of the human species." Those in attendance, numbering about one thousand men and women with prominent abolitionists among them, proclaimed that the framework of the Declaration of Independence opened the door to women being informed voters, executives, legislators, and judges at the local, state, and federal levels. Equal status could be achieved only through access to primary, secondary, and higher education, and fair remuneration for productive industry. According to the October 1851 Woman's Rights Convention, also meeting in Worcester, the injustices women suffered were "contrary... to the Principles of Humanity and the Declaration of Independence." The Business Committee, with Ohioan Emma R. Coe as its chief, asserted that women's inalienable rights could not be secure against "barbarous, demoralizing, and unequal laws, relating to marriage and property," until they were granted the ballot to elect public officials.[52]

The Seneca Falls Declaration of Sentiments became the primary model of midnineteenth-century woman's suffrage statements. Two years afterward, a resolution unanimously adopted at the April 1850 Salem convention proclaimed that the precept "all men are created equal and endowed with certain God-given rights" was a universal dictate of "God himself." From that axiom, without explaining the connection between divine and human decrees, the convention stated that excluding woman from lawmaking prevented her from "pursuing her own substantial happiness by acting up to her conscientious convictions." Those in attendance, who numbered roughly two thousand, went further than politics alone in resolving that "social, literary, pecuniary, religious or political customs and institutions, based on distinction of sex, are contrary to the laws of Nature." What's more, judicial precedents rendering woman subservient to her husband were "unjust and degrading, tending to reduce her to a level with the slave, depriving her of political existence, and forming a positive exception to the great doctrine of Equality, as set forth in the Declaration of Independence."[53]

More than seventy years of national independence had elapsed since the drafting of the national charter of freedom. Despite the towering principles that were a part of the nation's public and private discourses, women had no official say in political matters, blacks remained enslaved in the South, families continued to be auctioned like cattle, the lash augmented the injustices of an unequal system of criminal justice, and slave codes codified white supremacism into law. In the North, too, segregation was common in public conveyances and schools.

To add complexity to the mix, President James K. Polk's war with Mexico raised multiple domestic controversies about the spread of domestic slavery. Mexico ceded nearly 530,000 square miles to the United States through the 1848 Treaty of Guadalupe Hidalgo. Controversy soon arose about whether slavery could be introduced into the new western territories. The relevance of the Declaration of Independence was often a component of the heated dialogue.

The document remained a manifesto of national identity, even though the signed original continued to decompose, from prolonged exposure to sunlight in the U.S. Patent Office, where from 1841 until 1876 it was prominently displayed in a window.

8

THE UNRAVELING BONDS

OF UNION

In the decade and a half leading up to the Civil War, the nation experienced a series of intense internal struggles. The United States incorporated an enormous amount of land to the west after victory in the Mexican American War. Heated debates in Congress, the press, and public then arose about governance of the newly acquired territories. Slavery was the most divisive issue of them all. On one side were those who argued that the Declaration of Independence and its principle of liberal equality prohibited expansion of so inhumane an institution. In the other corner were polemicists who asserted that slaves were not protected by the Declaration's statement of inalienable rights. The latter group argued that the Declaration was meant to protect only whites, their property, and their right to legal self-determination.

A political movement arose to protect laborers from being treated like slaves, and to defend U.S. territories against encroachment by the South's peculiar institution. With the ascent of the Republican Party, a variety of reform causes, ranging from abolitionism to women's rights, were absorbed into the mainstream in the North but were greeted violently in the South. Reformers regarded the Declaration of Independence to be the anchor for social movements struggling to end the vestiges of injustice, which lingered unabated despite the revolutionary message of the American manifesto. Interestingly, proslavery forces also showed an interest in the Declaration as a statement of popular governance, allowing each state and territory to decide whether slavery should be legal. Clashes about the manifesto's relevance to nineteenth-century America came up often in debates on the Compromise of 1850 and the Kansas-Nebraska bills.

Southerners and Northerners held ever more divergent understandings about the functions of U.S. government. Rather than the singular purpose set out in the Declaration of Independence, the two sections gravitated to incompatible ideologies. The rift was mainly about the extent to which Congress had the power to administer U.S. territories. The dominant southern theory insisted that Congress lacked the authority to tamper with the institution of slavery in any existing states and in the territories. To the north, on the other hand, the commonly accepted view conceded that existing slave states be permitted to regulate the peculiar institution within their borders but rejected calls for its westward expansion.

A sharp divide separated those who believed that blacks as much as whites enjoyed the innate rights named in the Declaration of Independence, and those who argued that the signers of the document never meant the phrase "all men are created equal" to apply to anyone of African descent.

Renewed debate over the growth of slavery in the middle of the nineteenth century threatened the sectional calm that had been achieved through the Missouri Compromise. Opponents to President James K. Polk's expansionist policies framed their critiques on ideological grounds. Sen. Charles Sumner regarded belligerence against a foreign state as an expansionist violation of the "baptismal vows" of the Declaration. Rep. Daniel R. Tilden of Ohio was convinced that President Polk's mission to protect Texan slavery against Mexican interference was incompatible with the statement on equal rights. Orations to the same effect resounded at Independence Day celebrations in cities big and small. But this was not the sentiment everywhere. Speakers at Fourth of July ceremonies held in Monticello, Florida, and Raleigh, North Carolina, praised Polk, demonstrating that celebration of the Declaration of Independence could give way to militant patriotism.[1]

By waging war against Mexico, Polk sought to violently resolve a key political debate of the 1844 presidential campaign, which took place shortly after Texas had declared its independence from Mexico. Polk's Democratic Party demanded acquisition of Texas. The Whig candidate for president, Henry Clay, at first opposed annexation but later waffled on the issue in hope of attracting southern voters. Clay's change of heart actually had negative political repercussions, though, costing him potential northern supporters, many of whom were adamant that a new slave state would cut into the democratic rights espoused by the Declaration of Independence. Contrary to the statement that "all men are created free and equal, and are by nature endowed with certain inalienable rights, among which are life, liberty, and the pursuit of happiness," an anonymous author decried,

> a system is to be sustained and perpetuated, which cuts off, at a blow, every one of those rights—which devours and swallows up life with fearful rapidity—which annihilates liberty—which leaves no room for happiness, but in the grave—which divests man of his God-like attributes, drives him to the shambles, and makes him a *brute*—a THING—which tramples under foot all social and domestic relations—which invades the sanctuary of female virtue, and pronounces *woman*, PROPERTY.

In Connecticut, the state legislature issued a resolution condemning one of its U.S. senators after he voted for annexation. His vote was "incompatible with the spirit of the Declaration of Independence, with the compromises of the Federal constitution, and with the great purposes for which it is declared by the people to have been ordained and established." Cause for concern increased after Polk was sworn in and entered the presidential mansion. A group of citizens in Roxbury, Massachusetts, opposed to the annexation, adopted the conclusion that "a vast majority of the people of the free States abhor slavery, as alike inconsistent with the Declaration of Independence, the feelings of their humanity," linking the American ethos with its manifesto of liberty.[2]

Tremendous uncertainty about the expansion of slavery settled on the country when the war came to an end on February 2, 1848, with the signing of the Treaty of Guadalupe Hidalgo. For the price of $15 million, Mexico ceded an enormous tract of land to the United States that was later divided into the modern states of California, Nevada, Utah, most of Arizona, and significant portions of New Mexico, Colorado, and Wyoming. Disagreement about disposition of the land arose even before the Senate ratified the treaty. The Free Soil Party condemned the hypocrisy of those Democratic leaders who professed "devotion to the principles of Human Rights proclaimed in the Declaration of Independence" even as they backed legislative efforts to introduce slavery into the newly acquired areas. Free Soilers meeting in New York stressed the need to halt legalization of slavery on land where it had been abolished nearly twenty years before by the Mexican government.[3] The stakes of the congressional debate grew after news arrived that California wished to be admitted as a free state and that the New Mexico territory and Texas were embroiled in border disputes. Two other points of heated contention were whether slave trading should be abolished in the District of Columbia and whether northern states should be permitted to place legal barriers on the capture of fugitive slaves.

The core disagreement underlying these otherwise disparate topics was whether it was within Congress's power to impose human rights standards on newly acquired territories. Congressmen repeatedly invoked the Declaration of Independence, as they had nearly thirty years earlier during debate on the Missouri Compromise. Some Democrats and Whigs who condemned introducing slavery on land newly acquired from Mexico also invoked Jefferson's memory. They recalled that his original draft of the Declaration of Independence condemned the British monarchy for imposing the slave trade on the United States. Even though the Continental Congress struck the clause from the final draft of the Declaration, Jefferson's accusation was meant to show that allowing slaveholders to introduce the institution into the free territory of Mexico would be no different from the evil Britain had injected into the American colonies.

Opponents of the administration believed it was Congress's, rather than the President's, prerogative to develop policies for governing the territories. In several speeches, they told colleagues that Jefferson had drafted both the Declaration of Independence, with statements on human equality, and the Northwest Ordinance, with its explicit prohibition against slavery in so large a tract of land that it later split into five states and a portion of a sixth. They wished to show that the Declaration's principles were entirely consistent with a ban on slavery in congressionally administered territories.

Against this line of thinking, Rep. Henry C. Murphy of New York pointed out that Jefferson had lived and died owning slaves. But Murphy's statements showed only that Jefferson's practices were not in line with his ideology, leaving unanswered the argument that Congress could govern the territories to accord with the Declaration's statements on natural rights.[4]

Unable to convince each other of the rectitude of their divergent views, various factions began to formulate an acceptable compromise. Moralistic overtones reflected the elevated place America's founding document continued to enjoy. A speaker at an 1847 Fourth of July celebration expected the Declaration of Independence to be as enduring to the history of civilization as the pyramids of Egypt. Those who considered it to be consequential to the human race as a whole understood the great imperative of applying its egalitarian principles throughout the United States. Yet Independence Day for blacks, as a correspondent to Frederick Douglass's newspaper pointed out two years later, was a time for reading the lofty language of the Declaration while suffering "insult and irremediable outrage from despotic oppressors." Year after year, blacks heard "the absurd prating about American liberty and equal rights"; meanwhile they continued to be "a living and suffering witness to American oppression and wrong."[5]

Plans to resolve the congressional impasse were drawn up by several congressmen. Virginia Sen. James M. Mason proposed a fugitive slave bill, and Missouri Sen. Thomas H. Benton proposed demarcation of the Texas boundary. But these plans did not garner nearly enough support for passage. An omnibus bill, negotiated by Senators Henry Clay and Stephen Douglas, sought to resolve all the border disputes at once. President Zachary Taylor, who followed Polk into the executive office, opposed their omnibus bill. In private meetings at the White House he fumed at those southerners, including his son-in-law, Sen. Jefferson Davis, who openly threatened secession. Taylor's sharpest rebukes were directed against Davis's plan to extend the Missouri Compromise boundary to the Pacific, which would have made slavery legal in much of New Mexico and California. One plan proposed moving the slave line from the 36°30' latitude north to 42° in Utah. President Taylor opposed that change as well; he believed "the principles laid down in our Declaration of Independence" sustained Californians' and New Mexicans' right to adopt constitutions prohibiting the introduction of slavery.[6]

Unwilling to settle for the written text of the Constitution as the sole or even primary source of Congress's authority over the territories, Sen. William

Seward's widely disseminated 1850 speech appealed to a "higher law" as a guarantee of the people's inalienable rights. His wording implied that the written Constitution had to be supplemented by a core philosophy that could be supplied only by the type of statements found in the Declaration of Independence. Seward afterward sought to downplay the wording, at the prompting of his political advisor, who feared it might negatively affect Seward's chances for election to national office. (In fact it may have cost him the presidential election of 1860.) Others with lesser ambitions were not so cautious. A newspaper editor from Janesville, Wisconsin, expressed the view that the Declaration established a higher law for government, above any positive enactment, which enjoined the spread of slavery into new territories. A Presbyterian pastor in Brooklyn asserted that the universal principles of the Declaration of Independence protected the people's right to revolt against oppression, which must have sounded to southerners like a call for slave insurrections. In a letter to the editor of the *Wisconsin Free Democrat*, Rep. Charles Durkee attacked those supporting the compromise for "voting down the Declaration of Independence." They regarded the manifesto to be "humbug," he wrote, and set a deathtrap resembling Haman's gallows. Anyone who had read the biblical book of *Esther* might have been concerned about this allusion; Haman's would-be victims preempted his genocidal plan by slaughtering his henchmen. Durkee's biblical allusion seemed to imply that the same fate might befall slaveholders.[7]

After President Taylor died in office from food poisoning, his vice president, Millard Fillmore, became president. He immediately voiced support for Senator Douglas's strategy of compromise on the basis of sectional blocs and various swing votes. Congress then passed the omnibus bundle of five statutes in 1850. It allowed California to immediately enter the Union as a nonslave state, provided that New Mexico and Utah could eventually be admitted into the Union as either free or slave states; it resolved the border dispute between slave-holding Texas and the New Mexico territory; it abolished slave trading, but not slavery, in the District of Columbia; and it passed a stringent fugitive slave act. Theodore Parker, a preeminent Unitarian social reformer, was startled that "in this Republic, with the Declaration of Independence for its political creed, neither of the great political parties" was uncompromisingly "hostile to the existence of slavery" in the United States.[8]

The Fugitive Slave Act caused the greatest outcry after passage of the Compromise of 1850. The statute was designed to help slaveholders recapture the twenty thousand or so fugitives holed up in the North. The law could be executed without any proof of legal title. A claimant merely had to swear out an affidavit claiming ownership. Federal commissioners were authorized to determine cases "in a summary manner" without a jury trial. Before the Act went into effect, an irate senator pointed out that the Declaration of Independence attributed one of the causes of the Revolution to be denial of jury trials to Americans, and now the Fugitive Slave Act sanctioned the same procedural injustice. The law empowered commissioners to return respondents to a life of slavery that was immeasurably more domineering than what framers endured in 1776. Furthermore, not only did the law require federal marshals and deputies to participate in recapture (as well as fining those who refused) but it also required the public to take part in posses formed to recapture fugitives. A Trenton, New Jersey, newspaper wryly remarked: "It is thought they have got a new edition of the Declaration of Independence at the South, especially calculated for the latitute [sic]. The following is said to be the beginning of the precious instrument: 'White men are born with considerable freedom and endowed with inalienable rights, among which are life, liberty, and the *pursuit of niggers!*'"[9]

In 1850, just eleven years prior to the Civil War, neither mainstream Whigs nor Democrats were overtly hostile to slavery even though they differed fundamentally about the status of those slaves living in western territories and arriving clandestinely in the North. Immediatist abolitionists could rely on only a handful of senators—William H. Seward, John P. Hale, and Salmon P. Chase—and representatives—Joseph M. Root, Joshua R. Giddings, David Wilmot, and Horace Mann—to present resolutions against the spread of slavery.[10]

Passage of the Fugitive Slave Act triggered a popular response that relied heavily on statements from the Declaration of Independence. Members of the Social Fraternity of New Ipswich Academy, meeting in a small New Hampshire city, resolved that northern "members of Congress who aided in the passage of the recent Bill for the *proscription of Inalienable Rights*, are unworthy [of] a single vote for re-election." New York Baptists, meeting in Brockport, "passed resolutions *repudiating* the fugitive slave law as contrary to the Declaration of Independence, and opposed to the direct grants of the Constitution to every citizen, and to the law of God." Participants to the convention pledged not to become members of any *posse comitatus* gathered to aid marshals in recapture.[11]

For those who actively opposed the law, rescuing fugitives was justi-fied by the same higher law "that our political fathers appealed to" in the Declaration of Independence. Abolitionists such as Wendell Phillips, Frederick Douglass, and William Lloyd Garrison saw themselves as the defenders and "practical believers in the doctrine of the Declaration of Independence," pitted against great odds to save those who had escaped to freedom and others who were still locked in the shackles of bondage. A British nobleman, the Earl of Carlisle, wondered at the failure of Americans to live up to the paramount duty of the Declaration of Independence. Delivering a lecture at the Mechanics' Institution in Leeds about his earlier travels to the United States, he expressed certainty that the Fugitive Slave Law would not deter anyone whose life's mission was to aid runaways.[12]

William Wells Brown, a fugitive slave himself, published a book about his escape to Europe. He reprimanded Americans for claiming to adhere to the creed of the Declaration of Independence while legislatively support-ing slaveholders' efforts to control one-sixth of the nation's inhabitants in bondage. To demonstrate that the fault was national rather than sectional, Brown pointed out that the Fugitive Slave Law could not have passed with-out the votes of northern congressmen. In Syracuse, New York, a racially mixed man named Jerry who had been confined in jail asked abolitionist visitors, "in the name of the Declaration of Independence" and God, "Why am I bound thus, in a free country? Am I not a man like yourselves? ... Give me the freedom which is mine because I am a man, and an American." The irony of the situation was undeniable: "What was his crime?" asked an agent of the New York Abolitionist Society. "A love of that liberty which we all declared to be every man's inalienable right! And this slave was quoting the Declaration of Independence in chains!" Douglass, who had likewise escaped from slavery, condemned the United States in a Fourth of July ora-tion in 1852 for being "false to the past, false to the present," and by passing a new law that flexed federal muscle for the return of fugitives the nation was "false to the future."[13]

A meeting held in Syracuse in January 1851, with Douglass presiding, poured its contempt and hatred onto the Fugitive Slave Clause. Participants recalled "the immortal writer of the Declaration of Independence." They warned that if slaveholders did not voluntarily opt for emancipation, slav-ery in the United States would spark mass rebellion every bit as violent as the slave revolt in Santo Domingo had been at the turn of the century. For them the law of recapture was a violation of the principles laid down by the Declaration of Independence. Neither statutory nor constitutional law sufficed without the higher law found in the national founding document. Only a return to the natural rights principles espoused at the time of the country's independence could deliver the United States from the injustice of hereditary, forced labor.[14]

Charles Sumner, who was elected to the Senate the year after the law was enacted, waited patiently for the opportunity to use his formidable oratorical skills to present a case for abolishing the law. A chance presented itself during debate about a general appropriations bill for funding presidential execution of federal law. Sumner moved to amend the proposal to prohibit any funds from being used to enforce the 1850 fugitive slave provision and to repeal that law altogether. His amendment never had a chance, but introducing it provided Sumner with an occasion to make an antislavery speech and, as he would do throughout his decades in the Senate, to invoke the Declaration of Independence. He argued slavery was incompatible with the federal government's obligations. National political acts, he believed, were not only constrained by the Constitution; even more ancient "was the Declaration of Independence, embodying, in immortal words, those primal truths to which our country pledged itself with baptismal vows as a Nation. 'We hold these truths to be self-evident,' says the Nation: 'that all men are created equal.'" This statement of national conscience, according to Sumner, informed the meaning of the Constitution.[15]

By the time Sumner made his remarks, there was no legal way to prevent enforcement of the Fugitive Slave Act. It had too much support on both sides of the political divide; both Whigs and Democrats hoped it would achieve long-term sectional stability. The provision was to remain in effect until the Civil War. But abolitionist efforts against it marked the first massive political attacks on slavery since the 1820 Missouri Compromise to rely on rhetoric about universal and inalienable rights.

Women's rights advocates connected the higher law to a related issue. Like opponents of the Fugitive Slave Act and other slave laws, feminists decried systematic political and legal inequalities. Both groups found the Constitution to be insufficient for articulating the purposes of their causes. There was also a great deal of overlap, with many feminists being committed abolitionists and vice versa. Separately and jointly they rallied around the universal statements of equality and national vision in the Declaration of Independence.

On June 9, 1854, Lucy Stone called a meeting of the New England Woman's Rights Convention. In attendance were some of the most notable abolitionists of their day, including William Lloyd Garrison, Emma R. Coe, Pauline W. Davis, Harriot K. Hunt, and Wendell Phillips. They had gathered to mourn the fate of Anthony Burns, who seven days earlier had been convicted as a fugitive slave and sent back to Virginia. Talk at the meeting went far beyond the injustices of fugitive slave returns to other pressing matters. Stone, the president of the meeting, offered resolutions condemning women's exclusion from suffrage and limiting their property rights at marriage, which she said were not in harmony with the self-evident truth of the Declaration of Independence. For them the struggle against slavery went hand in hand with the commitment to gender equality.[16]

No sectional compromise could disguise how alienating the subject of slavery had become. In 1854, the Republican Party entered the political arena with a platform of protecting free labor and halting the spread of slavery. Party rhetoric was filled with references to the Declaration of Independence. Few of its members were abolitionists, but Republican leadership regarded slavery to be an infringement on life, liberty, and the pursuit of happiness, and whose westward movement needed to be blocked. The South, in turn, became ever more suspicious that the North intended to diminish the slave states' national representation.

The Republican Party emerged united against the Kansas-Nebraska Act of 1854. The newest firestorm was set off by a congressional bill, introduced by Stephen A. Douglas of Illinois, who was the chairman of the Senate Committee on Territories. He sought to garner southern support for chartering a railroad with a northern route to link Midwestern commerce to emerging western markets. To that end, his bill proposed dividing the remainder of the land acquired by the Louisiana Purchase into two new territories, with the inhabitants deciding whether to be free or slave. Part of the land lay to the north of the Missouri Compromise coordinates, where slavery was "forever prohibited" by statute. Kentucky Sen. Archibald Dixon added an amendment to Douglas's bill to repeal the Missouri Compromise.

To the Republicans, expansion of slavery was an outrageous violation of the Declaration of Independence. Abraham Lincoln, a former one-term

Whig congressman from Douglas's state, asserted in 1854 that slavery was "a great moral wrong." Lincoln called for a return to the Declaration's "fundamental principles of civil liberty." Sumner, on the Senate floor, explained that he opposed local sovereignty over slavery because the will of the majority could never legitimize gross deprivation of liberty, which was "an infraction of the immutable law of nature, especially in a country which has solemnly declared, in its Declaration of Independence, the inalienable right of all men to life, liberty, and the pursuit of happiness."[17]

Proslavery leaders, on the other hand, claimed that the document's statement of equality applied only to white men. Their arguments stressed clauses of the Declaration pertaining to popular sovereignty. The Detroit *Free Press*, for instance, supported the populist provisions of Douglas's bill. The newspaper's editors regarded federal attempts to prevent territorial inhabitants from managing their own affairs to be as oppressive as the British authoritarianism condemned in the Declaration of Independence. Casting the Declaration as a bulwark of independent state decision making was commonly done during the antebellum period and into the Civil War. Delaware Sen. John M. Clayton traced the principle that inhabitants should govern their own affairs, using the Compromises of 1820 and 1850 as illustrative examples, to infer that the "great principle" of popular rule directed Congress to permit the settlers of Kansas and Nebraska to decide whether to legalize slavery. The Kansas proslavery party actually borrowed rhetoric from the Declaration, asserting that denying the right of the majority to decide whether to legalize slavery would be an outrageous governmental abuse resembling the wrongs enumerated in the Declaration of Independence.[18]

Dehumanizing rhetoric went hand in hand with the effort to elevate popular state rule above congressional, territorial authority. Following a criticism dating to the late-eighteenth and early-nineteenth centuries, an 1855 tract mocked the literal "prate about 'liberty and equality.'" Supremacism not only degraded blacks but also conceived of human equality as applying only to whites, for "negroes are not men, within the meaning of the Declaration." Racism was not confined to political books and pamphlets. In the well of the Senate, John Pettit of Indiana was determined to "contradict or dispute the language of the Declaration of Independence," pseudoscientifically claiming that blacks had half the brain volume of Northern Europeans. Although he conceded that people of the same race have differing intellectual attributes, he claimed that no native African or American free black was on par with whites: "He is not my equal. There is no truth in this declaration," he said, referring to the Declaration of Independence. An author encouraging introduction of slaves into Kansas believed blacks were not whites' equals just as "the helpless idiot, the cripple, the blind, are not the equal to the bright [and] beautiful."[19]

Abolitionists rejected the assertion that the Kansas-Nebraska Bill reflected the will of legitimate government by consent. They denounced the "revolting...ridiculous and contemptible" notion, which a newspaper article attributed to the Pierce Administration, that self-government prevented passage of "slave-prohibiting agreements, compacts and law." Governmental accession to the wishes of one group wanting to exclude another, said a speaker at a public meeting in Providence, Rhode Island, violated the principle that "every man has a right to himself." Another claimed that the Constitution did not use the words *slavery* and *slave* because the Declaration's "self-evident truths 'that all men are created equal'" had been incorporated into the Constitution. In response, California Sen. John B. Weller quipped that the North preached from the Declaration of Independence and its congressmen were ready to remind the country that "all men are created 'free and equal'"; meanwhile, many of their states prohibited blacks from voting, excluded them from jury rolls, prevented their election to state legislatures, and even refused to interact with them as friends much less to consider legalizing intermarriage.[20]

The Kansas-Nebraska Bill passed Congress, and President Franklin Pierce signed it into law. Pierce believed the nation to be composed of "confederate states." "In the language of the Declaration of Independence," as Pierce put it, "each State had 'full power to levy war, conclude peace, contract alliances, establish commerce, and to do all other acts and things which independent States may of right do.'" His approach to the executive branch allowed states to decide their own affairs and conduct toward "subject races, whether Indian or African," except in collective matters such as foreign policy.[21]

In the aftermath of the 1854 debates, the Republican Party grew rapidly. Its members envisioned using federal policy making to slow the expansion of slavery and improve the lives of laborers. It quickly became a formidable political player despite the established bureaucracy of the Democratic Party, which had been a national force ever since Thomas Jefferson's presidency. Republicans emerged as the main opposition party, especially after the demise of the anti-immigrant and anti-Catholic Know Nothing Party, which had experienced surprising successes up to the early 1850s. Rufus Choate, a renowned conservative lawyer and former senator from Massachusetts, warned that if the Republican Party were to gain the reins of national power on the basis of an antislavery platform, the South would reject it. Worse yet, the South would regard it as alien and hostile to its interests. Choate castigated antislavery politics for being predicated on "the glittering and sounding generalities of natural right which make up the Declaration of Independence." He warned that such a state of political affairs would be "the beginning of the end" of the union.[22]

The dispute over slavery could no longer be confined to the political arena. In March 1855, armed bands from Missouri entered Kansas illegally to vote for the first territorial legislature. An eyewitness to the violence described how anyone unwilling to vote for the proslavery ticket was forcefully driven from polling places: "And all this, for what?" he asked. "Why, to kill out if possible the spirit of '76—to blot out the pure sentiments of our fathers as expressed in the Declaration of Independence, and the Constitution of the United States. It is to establish human bondage in one of the fairest portions of the earth's surface." In one voting district with 232 legal voters 1,034 ballots were cast; in another with 25 registered voters 330 total votes were cast; and in yet another district, representative of the same trend, although there were 150 qualified voters the final tally of votes was 964.

Strong-armed tactics and outright electoral deception did not correspond with the popular sovereignty that the Douglas Act had promised. After being elected by fraud, the proslavery legislature convened in Lecompton, Kansas, and, in short order, passed laws against harboring fugitive slaves; requiring officeholders, jurors, and attorneys to swear their support for slavery; and providing a death penalty for specified antislavery activities. Republicans regarded Pierce's recognition of the Lecompton government as an outrageous bowing of federal policy to slave interests. They believed that by passing the law Congress had relinquished its constitutional power over territorial governance to the control of armed bandits. The opposition fervently rejected the politics of force and placed greater emphasis on the government's obligation to safeguard natural rights in the territories and comply with the provisions of the Declaration of Independence. They further believed that, despite the document's consent clauses, Congress could enjoin voters in the territories from passing measures to undermine the rights of others.[23]

As with every issue, there were opposing perspectives. The opponents of slavery regarded its expansion to be a violation of human rights, but the South believed restraints on the growth of slavery, throughout North America, interfered with the property rights of slaveholders.

In the first month of 1857, Kansas's proslavery legislature enacted a bill to convene a constitutional convention. Against the advice of two of the state's territorial governors, John W. Geary and later Robert J. Walker, the legislature first refused to provide for a popular referendum on the Lecompton convention's recommendation. When it finally acceded to the referendum, even the supposed no-slavery constitution that emerged from the convention prohibited only importation of slaves but not retention of those in the territory at the time of statehood. The Lecompton Constitution contained a clause asserting the inviolability of slave property, entirely discounting the Declaration of Independence's value as a statement of human rights. The Board of Commissioners, convened by Kansas's territorial governor and legislature, determined that 2,720 votes out of 6,226 for the slave constitution were illegal and fraudulent. An alternative Free Soil referendum rejected the Lecompton Constitution.[24]

President James Buchanan, when he took office on March 4, 1857, proved himself beholden to the South just as Pierce had been. Electoral victory in fourteen of the fifteen southern states—including staunchly proslavery Alabama, Mississippi, and South Carolina—gave him victory at the polls. Buchanan proved his willingness to comply with the slave region's demands; he was especially intimidated by its growing calls for secession. With the battle lines drawn, Buchanan sent Congress the Lecompton Constitution along with a recommendation for the state's admission.[25]

A supporter of the Lecompton Constitution mocked the notion that the state constitution needed the full elective participation of the voting population. After all, he quipped, even the Declaration of Independence was submitted not to the people but only to the delegates of the Continental Congress.[26]

The argument didn't carry the day. Senator Douglas came out strongly against legitimizing the fraud by forcing "this constitution down the throats of the people of Kansas." Even supporters of slavery, such as

Rep. Laurence M. Keitt, who would soon take up arms against the Union as a ranking officer in the Confederate Army, rejected the Lecompton charade. Keitt agreed with the 1854 premise that pursuant to the Declaration of Independence the people can choose a slave or free government. But he believed the result in Kansas was not representative of the popular will. Representative Giddings, an avid opponent of slavery, denounced the "usurpation and brute force...of extending and supporting slavery." Giddings's tone was moralistic as he warned of impending "civil war, devastation, and bloodshed." He believed that arguing that slaves were a protected form of property in the territories was "precisely the opposite" of what "the distinguished sages who signed our Declaration of Independence meant."[27]

The joint opposition of northern and southern congressmen destined the Lecompton Constitution to failure. Kansas entered the union as a free state on January 29, 1861.

Passage of the Kansas-Nebraska Act demonstrated a newfound political will to allow voters rather than Congress to decide on the legality of slavery within territorial and state borders. The U.S. Supreme Court added to the slave controversy that marred Buchanan's presidency. In an extremely unusual move, Chief Justice Roger B. Taney actually found that the Declaration of Independence's natural right guarantee to own property extended to slave chattel.

Dred Scott v. Sandford, one of the most notorious Supreme Court cases, involved a slave's freedom claim. Dred Scott filed a federal lawsuit claiming that he had gained his freedom when his slaveholder took him to live in the free state of Illinois and later the free Wisconsin Territory. The Missouri Compromise governed Wisconsin. Scott asserted that he had a different state citizenship than did his slaveholder, John Sanford. This legal device was necessary for a federal court to assert subject matter jurisdiction over what otherwise was a state law dispute.

Taney, then in his twenty-second year as chief justice, wrote the lead opinion in the case. In previous cases, he had voted to uphold the constitutionality of the Fugitive Slave Act and to overturn a state personal liberty law, thereby facilitating recapture of fugitives. Yet his record was decidedly mixed. In 1818, he was the defense attorney for a Methodist minister who had been charged in Maryland with the misdemeanor of inciting slaves to insurrection. In his remarks to the jury in that case, Taney invoked the Declaration of Independence:

> And hard necessity, indeed, compels us to endure the evil of slavery for a time. It was imposed upon us by another nation, while yet we were in a state of colonial vassalage. It cannot be easily, or suddenly removed. Yet while it continues, it is a blot on our national character, and every real lover of freedom, confidently hopes that it will be effectually, though it must be gradually, wiped away; and earnestly looks for the means by which this necessary object may be attained. And until it shall be accomplished: until the time shall come when we can point without a blush, to the language held in the declaration of independence, every friend of humanity will seek to lighten the galling chain of slavery, and better, to the utmost of his power, the wretched condition of the slave.

Adding a further layer of complexity to Taney's attitude toward slavery, he once owned slaves but had manumitted them and even granted them pensions.[28]

The change in his thinking was clear from his 1857 *Dred Scott* decision. Taney might have dismissed the case for lack of subject matter jurisdiction, after finding no federal court was authorized to hear Scott's claim to freedom. Instead he wrote tortured dictum in an effort to resolve decades of conflict about the institution of slavery. As part of his opinion, the Chief Justice proclaimed that the signers of the Declaration of Independence never intended blacks to be citizens of the United States or of any individual state. When the Declaration was adopted and the Constitution ratified, he wrote, persons of the "negro African race" were "considered a subordinate and inferior class of beings, who had been subjugated by the dominant race." Blacks were so unfit for association with whites that "they had no rights which the white man was bound to respect." He thereby denied that the natural rights statements of the Declaration of Independence applied to all persons, irrespective of race. The upshot of the decision was that Scott had not gained his freedom by living in free territory. He remained a slave with no inalienable rights. On a grander level, Taney had denied both the possibility that blacks could be citizens of the United States and that the humanistic statement of the Declaration of Independence applied to them.

In his dissent, Justice Curtis categorically rejected Taney's exposition of revolutionary history. At the time of independence, free blacks had been citizens of several states—New Hampshire, Massachusetts, New York, New Jersey, and North Carolina—that granted them the right to vote. Curtis did not think the Declaration of Independence to be central to the question before the Court, but he was nevertheless of the opinion that the framers' statement "that all men are created equal" was an "assertion of universal abstract truths." He believed they could not have intended to say that God "had endowed the white race, exclusively, with the great natural rights which the Declaration of Independence asserts."

For contemporaries, the most disturbing part of Taney's argument declared a revered federal statute to be unconstitutional. Critics asserted that the chief justice should not have reached the substance of Scott's freedom suit because the matter could have been dismissed on jurisdictional grounds alone. The chief justice, determined to resolve decades of sectional conflict, nevertheless held that the Missouri Compromise violated the right of slave owners to live with their human property anywhere in the United States or its territories.

The *Dred Scott* conclusion, with its holding on citizenship and the Missouri Compromise, only exacerbated sectional tensions. The newspaper responses to it were mixed. The New York *Journal of Commerce* regarded it to be "an anachronism, and a historical absurdity to assert that the Declaration of Independence, when it speaks of the 'freedom and equality of mankind,' intended to comprehend the black race." Eighteenth-century slave-holding communities accepted the Declaration, the article went on to say, and could not have meant to assert their slaves were equals. Senator Douglas, though opposed to the Lecompton Constitution in Kansas, came out strongly in favor of Taney's judgement. In his mind, the decision confirmed the right to popular sovereignty. Had the Declaration applied to persons of African descent, Douglas asserted in the summer of 1857, the framers would have been compelled to abolish slavery. His pronouncement ignored that the northern states did just that in the decades after the Revolution and that many of the leading southern leaders of the day—Patrick Henry and Thomas Jefferson, among others—openly condemned their own hypocrisy. Douglas's campaign speech in 1858, made while he was running for Senate reelection in Illinois, mimicked the chief justice. He agreed that the signers of the Declaration, living in a land where slavery was then legal in every colony, could not have been condemning their own constituents by agreeing that blacks had the same rights as whites.[29]

Running against Douglas for an Illinois senate seat was Abraham Lincoln, for whom *Dred Scott* represented a falling away from the nation's core values. Taney's judgment and Douglas's stump speeches, said Lincoln, did "obvious violence to the plain, unmistakable meaning of the Declaration." He asserted that the framers' structural outline was still binding:

> I think the authors of that notable instrument intended to include *all* men, but they did not intend to declare all men equal *in all respects*. They meant to set up a standard maxim for free society, which should be familiar to all, and revered by all; constantly looked to, constantly labored for, and even though never perfectly attained, constantly approximated, and thereby constantly spreading and deepening its influence and augmenting the happiness and value of life to all people of all colors everywhere.

Although Lincoln and Taney were in complete disagreement about the meaning of the instrument, they both regarded it to be a binding agreement between the people and its government. The real difference was in Lincoln's interpretation of the Declaration of Independence as a statement of equal human rights, on the one hand, and Taney's interpretation as an expression of state sovereignty.[30]

The abolitionist and Republican presses vehemently attacked the decision. Garrison's *Liberator* newspaper wrote that with one blow the Supreme Court had eliminated the citizenship of the entire black population. Taney had misunderstood the plain reading of the text, argued the *Boston Daily Advertiser*. The nation's founders failed to end slavery out of expediency but understood it to be inconsistent with the framework of government they established. The *Boston Daily Atlas* believed that Taney's racial interpretation of the Declaration of Independence made a mockery of its plain language. Other articles defended the character of the founders, arguing they "cannot be supposed to have said what they did not believe, and they cannot be supposed to have believed in any other ideas than that the negro race were mere property and not men" when they spoke of the inalienable rights of man. A Milwaukee paper condemned Taney for "degrading of the Declaration of Independence to a mere sham"

and for advancing slave interests rather than simply answering the jurisdictional question.[31]

Northern state legislatures issued resounding condemnation of the
Supreme Court's interpretation. In New York, a joint legislative committee
was established to address *Dred Scott*. It found the opinion to be "a violation
of the sacred principles announced in our Declaration of Independence."
The Ohio General Assembly agreed, tying the Declaration's principles to
due process in the Bill of Rights. Ohio legislators considered it tenable to
say only that the fathers of the country "intended to assert the indestruct-
ible and equal rights of all men, without any exception or reservation whatever, to life, liberty and the pursuit of happiness." To guarantee that right,
the Fifth Amendment prohibited federal infringement of a person's life, liberty, or property without due process of law. The House Assembly of New
Jersey pointed out that Thomas Jefferson had drafted both the Declaration
of Independence and the Northwest Ordinance of 1787, indicating that
he believed Congress had the right to prohibit slavery in the territories.
The Senate and House of Representatives of New Hampshire issued a joint
resolution, regarding the *Dred Scott* decision as an attempt to strengthen
"the slaveholding interests." Contrary to the Court, New Hampshire lawmakers resolved that Congress possessed the power to legislate in U.S.
territories to "advance the cause of universal liberty," which "cannot be
abandoned without proving recreant to the spirit of the Declaration of
Independence."[32]

The *Dred Scott* decision had the opposite effect Chief Justice Taney
envisioned. It aggravated conflict and sped up the cataclysm between the
North and South. Southern slaveholders grew more fervent in their assertion of property rights. The Republican Party, to the contrary, exploited
popular northern opposition to the Court's interpretation of the nation's
core commitments to equality and liberty.

9

SECTIONAL CATACLYSM

Turmoil within the Democratic Party pitted those who backed the Lecompton Constitution against its detractors. The internal conflict split the party into sectional factions. The Republican Party benefited from the rift, gaining control of the government in 1860.

Two divergent views emerged as to the meaning of the Declaration of Independence. In the South, the future Confederate president, Sen. Jefferson Davis, popularized the view that the Declaration created a state-centered polity. Its statement of rights applied only to members of the polity, none of whom were blacks. Northerners, in the meantime, began taking the lead of Republicans, who spoke of the Declaration as a document containing governmentally recognized protections for civil rights.

Republicans' signature issues were prohibition of slavery in U.S. territories and protection of workers' right to be economically independent through free labor. These commitments were tied through the principles of the Declaration of Independence. Lincoln, like many of his fellow Republicans, thought that slavery engendered inequality and degraded free labor. Opposition to the Mexican-American War and the Kansas-Nebraska Acts had fueled his passion for politics. By 1854, when he was a lawyer in Illinois and soon to be a state legislator, Lincoln formulated a political philosophy that relied on the Declaration of Independence as the wellspring for republican institutions. At a public debate in Peoria, Illinois, against Sen. Stephen Douglas, Lincoln spoke of the need for national rejuvenation. "Our republican robe is soiled....Let us repurify it." Lincoln then merged religious with patriotic allusions:

> Let us turn and wash it white, in the spirit, if not the blood, of the Revolution. Let us turn slavery from its claims of 'moral right,' back upon its existing legal rights....Let us return it to the position our fathers gave it....Let us re-adopt the Declaration of Independence, and with it, the practices, and policy, which harmonize with it.

At this stage of his life, Lincoln was willing to settle for slavery's continued existence in southern states, but he came out strongly against its introduction into western territories.[1]

More prominent Whigs and Free Soilers, among them William Seward, Charles Sumner, Joshua Giddings, and Salmon P. Chase, shared Lincoln's sentiments. They would soon unite in the fledgling Republican Party. These influential men found the Declaration of Independence to be a political battle-axe against slavery. Their speeches during the course of debates about the status of Kansas repeatedly invoked the equality of all men and opposed the notion that the Declaration referred only to white men. The political convictions that drove the early Republican Party had conspicuously moralistic overtones.[2]

The Republican Party platform of 1856 vowed to maintain "the principles promulgated in the Declaration of Independence," the federal constitution, states' rights, and federal union. The most controversial aspect of the platform proclaimed Congress's authority to regulate slavery in the territories. The 1860 platform went a step further, quoting the Declaration of the Independence's statement about equality and the inalienability of rights, concluding that those principles were essential to preservation of the Constitution and the Union. The principles of the Declaration were thereby interlinked with the Constitution's grant of power over the territories. It also proclaimed the Party's readiness to secure "liberal wages" for workingmen, adequate remuneration for agriculture, and sufficient monetary reward for skilled mechanics and manufacturers.[3]

To the South, these statements sounded like a belligerent attempt at interference with states' internal affairs. Even before the presidential election of 1860, Democratic congressmen directed barbs at the Republican platform. Congressional speeches evinced increasing distrust of the federal legislature's ability to forge compromises, especially after the Supreme Court and Congress eliminated the Missouri Compromise. By 1859, the conflict was becoming irreconcilable.

Politicians spoke past each other. In one such exchange, Sen. Clement C. Clay of Alabama denounced the Republican Party's antagonism toward slavery. In response, Sen. Lyman Trumbull of Illinois responded that its platform merely adopted the statement in the Declaration of Independence that rights are God's inalienable gifts rather than governmentally granted entitlements. He conceded that property owners could reclaim fugitives in the territories but denied that this meant Africans did not share in the Creator's bounty. Clay interrupted to say Trumbull's stance on universal rights was irreconcilable with the historical fact that the same group who framed the Declaration of Independence also owned slaves. Trumbull could see no way of gainsaying the argument but to assert that the Declaration offered the ideal, established on the foundation of natural rights, even though the necessity of organizing society led to encroachment of those very natural rights. Such an answer could not ameliorate Clay's disdain for northern moralizing. Sen. Andrew Johnson of Tennessee refused to concede even that Trumbull believed his own argument. He thought party politics was driving the Republican Party's claim, and if they would just drop their partisanship they would agree that Jefferson could never have meant to include blacks within the framework of the Declaration of Independence.[4]

Republicans were intent on achieving a solution through political negotiations, but not everyone in the antislavery movement was wedded to peaceful coexistence with the South. A radical approach beckoned John Brown, a longtime abolitionist who in 1855 had settled in Kansas, to help prevent the incursion of slavery into that territory. He committed himself to violent upheaval after proslavery Missourians murdered one of his sons and imprisoned another. A militant, Brown rationalized acting outside the law in order to vindicate the natural rights principles of the Declaration of Independence.

On October 16, 1859, he led twenty-one men on a mission to capture a U.S. armory located in Harpers Ferry, Virginia. They sought rifles and ammunition, but not for themselves alone. Brown's aim was to arm slaves in the vicinity and then head south with confiscated weapons in order to instigate violent slave uprisings. Although they took control of the armory, victory was short-lived. On October 18, a company of U.S. Marines under the leadership of Col. Robert E. Lee stormed their position, leaving ten of Brown's men dead. Brown was criminally charged with treason, murder, and conspiracy.

After his capture, along with a store of weapons, ammunition, and food supplies, a Maryland militia company found Brown's carpetbag containing documents that revealed his intentions and worldview. Among the items were a copy of the Declaration of Independence and a provisional constitution, which had been adopted and signed in May 1858 by white and black delegates at a convention he had organized in Chatham, Canada. Located in southwestern Ontario, the town had several churches that coupled religion and abolition. Its black population grew steadily in the three decades prior to the Civil War from the arrival of runaways fleeing from the United States. Several of those who attended the convention joined Brown the following year at the Harpers Ferry raid and were executed for it. Others involved in both events went on to serve in the Union Army during the Civil War, and one became a black member of the Congress.

Just as the women's movement had relied on the Declaration of Independence and taken the manifesto's logic a step further for its Declaration of Sentiments of 1848, so too the delegates at Chatham unmistakably modeled their Declaration of Liberties on the 1776 document. The Chatham Constitution denounced the "most barbarous, unprovoked and unjustifiable" slavery of "one portion of its citizens...in utter disregard and violation of those eternal and self-evident truths set forth in our Declaration of Independence." It condemned the *Dred Scott* decision and the Buchanan administration for supporting it. Much as the framers had done in 1776, participants at Chatham proclaimed the right to "break that odious yoke of oppression" laid on "their fellow countrymen" in violation of the self-evident truths of nature that made all men equal. Their chief grievance was the "injustice and cruelties inflicted upon the Slave in every conceivable way." The solution lay in the hands of the people who could amend and remodel their government, pursuant to the revolutionary teachings of the Declaration of Independence, "to secure equal rights, privileges, & Justice to all; Irrespective of Sex; or Nation."[5]

Many of Brown's contemporaries regarded him as a martyr for the natural rights cause. While Brown was on trial, Henry David Thoreau, a renowned American author who had finished writing *Walden* just five years before, made a speech at Concord, Massachusetts, expressing support for Brown and his men. He was a surprising person to fill that role because of his pioneering writing on nonviolent resistance to government policy through civil disobedience. Thoreau had taken the rostrum in place of Frederick Douglass, an eloquent orator who decided not to enter the city after he was warned of lurking danger. Thoreau regarded John Brown to be a hero "who recognized no unjust human law." His actions, Thoreau believed, would stand in American history books as an accomplishment along with "the landing of the Pilgrims of the Declaration of Independence." The men at Harpers Ferry, and Brown in particular, were willing to face death because they understood there were certain reasons for which the danger of death had to be overcome: "No man in America has ever stood up so persistently for the dignity of human nature." Other abolitionists agreed. Even William Lloyd Garrison, who repeatedly advocated a pacifist approach to abolition, eulogized Brown after he was found guilty and hanged in Charlestown. As Brown's coffin was lowered into his final resting place, a family friend sang "Blow Ye Trumpet, Blow!" "Who instigated John Brown?" Garrison asked at a memorial meeting. And then he answered:

> It must have been Patrick Henry, who said—and he was a Virginian— "Give me liberty, or give me death!"…It must have been Thomas Jefferson—another Virginian—who said of the bondage of the Virginia slaves, that "one hour of it is fraught with more misery than ages of that which our fathers rose in rebellion to oppose"—and who, as the author of the Declaration of Independence, proclaimed it to be "a self-evident truth, that all men are created equal, and endowed by their Creator with an inalienable right to liberty."

Brown's devotion to principle resonated with the living. The *Ohio State Journal* found his actions to be illegal and deserving of criminal punishment, "but abstract right and every principle of our Declaration of Independence morally justify John Brown." Brown's devotees rested their arguments on a higher law, asserted in the Bible and Declaration of Independence. They were unfazed by contrary state and federal laws.[6]

Visiting the Young Men's Anti-Slavery Society in Leeds, England, during the month of John Brown's execution, Frederick Douglass referred to him as a "dear old departed saint" who acted in accordance with the Declaration of Independence and the U.S. Constitution. Douglass, however, did not even try to reconcile the Declaration's universal principles with the slave-protecting clauses of the Constitution. The meeting's chairman lauded the end of slavery throughout the British Empire and asserted that the terms of the Declaration of Independence demanded that blacks be admitted to the political, personal, and social privileges available to Americans. The *London Times* looked at both sides of the coin. It denounced Brown's resort to violence but bemoaned America's falling away from revolutionary principles, which led him to pursue the scheme:

> There was a time when the best men in America looked on slavery as merely a provisional and temporary institution, and looked forward to the time when the bonds should drop from the hand of the African, and the assertion of the Declaration of Independence that all men are free and equal should no longer be a mockery and a reproach.

Times had changed, "and the language of the southern slaveholder is now rather that freedom is an exceptional institution, destined one day to be swallowed up in the more natural and more humane rule of slavery." Though Brown's attempted uprising was confined to a small town in Virginia, his ideology reverberated throughout the United States and increased tensions between the North and South.[7]

Republicans refused to join the abolitionist chorus, seeking to distance themselves from Brown's "fanaticism." Democrats could nevertheless point to incendiary speeches in 1858 by such leaders as William Seward, who spoke of an "irrepressible conflict" between free labor and slave labor. That same year, Abraham Lincoln asserted before a state Republican convention that "a house divided against itself cannot stand." No country could endure as long as it was "half slave and half free." After the Harpers Ferry raid, Republicans sought to deny any involvement in it while affirming their commitment to its core principles. Sen. Benjamin Wade denied the claims of those who connected Republicans with Brown but also stressed:

> The Republican party, so far as I know, believes in the Declaration of Independence. They do not believe that it is a tissue of glittering generalities. They do not believe that it is a mere jingle of words having no meaning. They do believe that every man bearing the human form has received from the Almighty Maker a right to his life, to his liberty, and the pursuit of happiness. They do not believe that this right is confined to men of any particular name, nation, or color; but they believe that wherever there is humanity there is this great principle.[8]

At Cooper Union, New York, as a presidential candidate, Abraham Lincoln said that Brown showed great courage and unselfishness but that no one could approve of his resort to violence. Likewise, Seward, who was then also a presidential candidate, made clear in New York that Brown was no Republican. In 1860, Brown's admiring biographer, James Redpath, wrote that Brown despised the Republican Party even though they both advocated an end to slavery. Brown did not think a political solution was possible, wrote Redpath, and instead found his inspiration in the "the Golden Rule and the Declaration of Independence, in the spirit of the Hebrew warriors" rather than pacifist abolitionists. "Where the Republicans said, Halt; John Brown shouted, Forward! to the rescue! He was an abolitionist of the Bunker Hill school."[9]

For the proslavery leaders of Congress, any opposition to slavery—whether militant, pacifist, or political—was inimical to their sense of personal and regional freedoms. The South could not outright deny the Declaration of Independence because it was after all linked to their common revolutionary heritage. But to them it was a statement of state sovereignty rather than a document of national, ideological consensus about human rights.

With his orchestration of the Kansas-Nebraska Act, allowing residents of those areas to choose whether to legalize slavery, Stephen Douglas had become the Democratic Party frontrunner for the 1860 presidential election. But his rejection of the fraudulent Lecompton Constitution cost him Southern support. The Democratic Party thereafter split in half, granting Republicans a golden opportunity.

Abraham Lincoln emerged as the Republican candidate. He had little experience in national politics, having served only one term in Congress, to commend himself to the voters. But they could readily find his antislavery statements in print.

The Declaration of Independence was a central theme of Lincoln's political philosophy. In a letter written at the heat of the Lecompton Constitutional controversy and shortly after the Court rendered the *Dred Scott* decision, he avowed that by "men" the document meant blacks as well as whites: "I believe the declaration that 'all men are created equal' is the great fundamental principle upon which our free institutions rest; that negro slavery is violative of that principle." He nevertheless rejected the claim that the federal government had authority to interfere with slavery in those places in the United States where it already existed. Lincoln's speeches underscore how the provisions of the Declaration, although technically unenforceable, profoundly changed the course of history. Prior to the Civil War, Lincoln disclaimed social and political equality for blacks. Two years before he was elected to be president, he took the fairly nondescript but nevertheless controversial position that "there is no reason in the world why the negro is not entitled to all the natural rights enumerated in the Declaration of Independence, the right to life, liberty and the pursuit of happiness." Slaves were "men, not property ... some of the things, at least, stated about men in the Declaration of Independence apply to them as well as to us." His ambiguity left much to be desired by those abolitionists who were advocating a radical change to the American policy, but had Lincoln taken a firmer position against slavery he would have stood no chance at winning national office. The rights described by the Declaration of Independence, he believed, were objective, imbedded in human nature. From this universal-law perspective, it was not the document that rendered slavery a selfish form of injustice but the institution's violation of primal human equality that made it wrong.[10]

Lincoln's positions were the subject of some ridicule. His principal political opponent, Senator Douglas, elicited an audience's hearty laughter when he said: "I do not question Mr. Lincoln's conscientious belief that the negro was made his equal, and hence is his brother." The audience voiced its disapproval of the Republican when Douglas asserted that Lincoln held blacks to be "endowed with equality by the Almighty, and hence that no human power alone can deprive him of these rights which the Almighty has guaranteed to him." For Lincoln the Declaration of Independence was a central thesis of American politics; for Douglas its principles were an object of ridicule.[11]

The presidential election of 1860 was monumental. As the advocates for a more formal role of the Declaration of Independence in politics gained popularity, the proslavery movement became more intransigent in its demands. The *Dred Scott* opinion, which determined the Declaration was inapplicable to blacks, added force to the constitutional interpretation of slavery's supporters. For the judgment's detractors, the Supreme Court's finding foreboded the unchecked spread of slavery as far north as the state of Maine.

Internal dissensions stood in the way of the Democratic Party's victory. The southern wing of the party, which called itself the National Democrats, supported John C. Breckinridge of Kentucky. Its platform proclaimed the federal government's obligation to protect slaveholders' property rights throughout the public domain. Northern Democrats supported Stephen Douglas and espoused popular sovereignty on the matter of slavery. This second group rejected the natural right to own slaves, believing the institution to be based on legal enactments alone. Both Democratic factions vowed to abide by the Court's decision in *Dred Scott*. A third party, the Constitutional Union, which nominated John Bell of Tennessee, stayed away from the most controversial issue, confining itself to a statement supporting equality of the states through national unity. The Republican Party explicitly espoused the Declaration of Independence as the touchstone of natural rights and equality. Its members, like those meeting at the South Brooklyn Republican Club on August 23, 1860, believed the document's statement that "all men are created equal" meant that nonslave states were under no obligation to recognize the master-slave relationship and that the federal government could keep slavery out of the territories. Journalist Horace Greeley's compendium, *A Political Text-book for 1860*, with its extensive coverage of the slavery issue, made the candidates' views readily available to potential voters.[12]

Republicans were generally unambiguous about why they believed the spread of slavery violated the underlying assumptions and mandates of the Declaration of Independence. Voters were left with little doubt about where the party stood on that issue. Rep. Charles Francis Adams, grandson of John Adams, assailed the Three-Fifths Clause of the Constitution. How, he questioned, could slaveholders be said to represent blacks whom they condemn to perpetual servitude? This form of "despotism" ran against "the idea of a Government professing to be founded on human freedom." The philosophy of the Republican Party, Adams went on to say, was based on "the grand doctrine which the Declaration of Independence enunciated." Its assertion of inalienable rights and equality was a statement about "human nature itself." The South had perpetuated the cruelty of the King of England, whom his grandfather's close friend Thomas Jefferson had denounced for tearing Africans from their homes and forcing them to live as slaves in the colonies.[13]

To a large measure, the election of 1860 was about the future direction of the country and the meaning of its founding charter. Like the Free Soil Party's platform before it, the Republican Party's platform directly quoted from the Declaration of Independence. Free Soilers had never been able to garner nearly as much support nor recruit as many prominent politicians as the Republicans. The platform explicitly denounced the Supreme Court's and the Buchanan Administration's permissive positions on importation of slaves into all the territories. If that stance wasn't enough to rouse the ire of even southern unionists, some Republicans such as Senators Charles Sumner and William H. Seward and Rep. De Witt Clinton Leach went much further, advocating the end of slavery everywhere under federal control. If the Republican Party were to win the election, Leach announced in the House,

> it will be governed solely by the principles promulgated in the Declaration of Independence and embodied by the Federal Constitution. I hesitate not to say, that these principles, faithfully observed in the administration of governmental affairs, will lead to the abolition of slavery in the District of Columbia; to the repeal or essential modification of the fugitive slave law; and to the limitation of slavery to the States in which it now exists.[14]

This hard line was unacceptable to the supporters of both slavery and popular sovereignty. Republican Sen. Daniel Clark of New Hampshire offered an amendment to a bill the same year, allowing the children of any taxpayer, irrespective of race, to attend public schools in the District of Columbia. Speaking in favor of the amendment, Republican Sen. Henry Wilson considered the "blessings of moral and mental culture to the children of the free colored race" to be intrinsic to attainment of "natural equality of all men," but he denied that the Declaration of Independence meant to include political and social equality for anyone who was not white.[15] It nevertheless became clear that if the Republicans ascended to power they would rely on their understanding of the Declaration of Independence to make fundamental changes to federal laws.

That these sorts of proposals could even be heard in Congress, where only sixteen years before the gag rule prevented any advocacy of antislavery, infuriated the proslavery camp. The institution's apologists downplayed the Declaration's statements on inalienable rights and human equality. According to them, the Constitution was the root of American government. In it, they located a variety of protections for slavery, such as the Fugitive Slave Clause. This school of thought deemphasized the Declaration, seeing it as no more than a statement of sovereignty and independence. South Carolina Sen. James Chesnut, Jr., for instance, regarded it as a forerunner to the Constitution in the sense that it announced the existence of a new country and sought international recognition for it. The "anti-slavery party," as he called the Republicans during the 1860 campaign, believed "the Declaration of Independence is the basis of the Constitution, and argue as if the Federal Government derived its powers from that famous instrument, and was organized for the express purpose of carrying them into effect." To Chesnut, this sounded "strange" because he conceived of the federal government as having "no other purposes, powers, or principles, than those derived from the Constitution itself; which are all delegated, defined, and limited." The following year, the Senate expelled Chesnut for participating in the Confederacy, in which he eventually rose to the rank of brigadier general. One of Chesnut's colleagues in the Senate, Albert G. Gallatin of Mississippi, would also join the Confederate Army and eventually be elected to the Confederate Senate. Gallatin likewise believed that the Constitution created a limited federal government with the authority to exercise only enumerated responsibilities. The Declaration, on the other hand, according to Gallatin, was "addressed to the king and the Parliament and the people of Great Britain." That document, he said, simply asserted the states had the requisite authority to call a joint convention for drafting the Constitution. And even if it were true that the Declaration of Independence continued to obligate the federal government to protect inalienable rights, the rights were not absolute but could be limited for the good of society.

It was admitted on all sides, for example, that criminal convictions were appropriate even though they cut short men's pursuit of happiness. Just as the welfare of society required some men to be placed into prison cells and others to be hanged from gibbets, Gallatin concluded, "the good of society requires us to enslave the black man and we enslave him."[16]

At the heart of the states' rights perspective on the Declaration was the conviction that local laws, rather than national principles, should govern the status of slaves. An editorial that ran in the *Semi-Weekly Mississippian* rebuked "the frenzied fanaticism that has possessed the minds of many Northern people, the constant assertion that the Declaration of Independence was designed to cover the black man as well as the white." To the contrary, the letter went on to say, slavery had been legal throughout the colonies at the time of the Revolution, demonstrating the colonists had taken racial hierarchy for granted.[17]

During the 1860 campaign, to speak of equality would have been a losing strategy in the North and the South. The Republican Party was cautious not to alienate voters during the 1860 campaign. Rep. Joshua Giddings explained that "Lincoln was selected" to be the presidential candidate because "his anti-slavery sentiment had been less prominent" than that of his chief rivals. The *New York Times*, which first backed Seward and later Lincoln for president, denied that the party espoused political equality for blacks and women. Democrats such as Rep. William W. Boyce of South Carolina, who would soon retire from Congress to join the Confederacy, found this claim to be disingenuous. The Columbus, South Carolina, *Guardian* could not but agree with its fellow Carolinian. Seeking to expose the Republicans' secret agenda "to affirm that negroes were equal to white men," the newspaper pointed to the prominence of the preamble to the Declaration of Independence in the party's platform. To further prove its point, the *Guardian* quoted one of Giddings's speeches that proclaimed the manifesto espoused equal participation of blacks in politics. Giddings was in fact far more cautious of the Republican platform; he had earlier asserted that it was based on "the devotion of the American people to liberty" to the "fundamental truths which constitute the basis of our political faith, as they constituted the basis of the Declaration of Independence." But "we do not say the black man is, or shall be, the equal of the white man; or that he shall vote or hold office, however just such position may be." Realizing that to adopt the truly just position would result in political defeat, Giddings tempered Republicans' views on equality to mean that "he who murders a black man shall be hanged; that he who robs the black man of his liberty or his property shall be punished like the criminal." Giddings's statement was not reassuring for Southerners who rejected these qualified explanations. For them, any reference to the Declaration in the context of rights amounted to an assault on their peculiar institution.[18]

Discounting Giddings's moderate speeches as a ploy, Democrats homed in on his claim that the Republican platform's inclusion of the Declaration was meant to demonstrate the party's recognition of black equality. Three years earlier, for instance, Giddings had told a Republican state convention, "The negro is a heavenly institution, and it is God-like in men to elevate him to an equality with the white." Fifteen years earlier, another leading Republican, Salmon P. Chase, remonstrated to a black audience in Cincinnati against "that clause in the constitution which denies to a portion of the colored people the right to suffrage." Even more direct was Kentucky abolitionist Cassius M. Clay, an avid supporter of Republicans:

> They (the Democrats) tell you we are for liberating the blacks—for setting the negros free. SO WE ARE! We believe, as do you, that in 1776 "all men were created free and equal endowed with certain inalienable rights".... They meant just what they said, and they repeatedly spoke of the negroes as men and as persons. THEY MEANT THE NEGROES WERE EQUAL WITH THE WHITE MEN!

Pennsylvania Rep. Thaddeus Stevens, another straight shooter, told a New York crowd that Democrats ignored freedom; trampled, ridiculed, and denied the Declaration of Independence; and denied human sympathy to a quarter of the global population. Such talk raised grave concerns among southerners about what might happen if the Republicans acquired presidential power.[19]

As was the case with their 1858 Senate race in Illinois, Stephen Douglas and Abraham Lincoln were fierce debaters. From their long acquaintance, Douglas knew that the Declaration of Independence lay at the core of Lincoln's worldview.

For years, Douglas had claimed Republicans were in league with abolitionists. As he pointed out, both claimed that despite the Supreme Court's definitive ruling on the matter, the Declaration of Independence applied to "the negroes and all other inferior races, and place[d] them on a footing of entire and absolute equality with white men." If adopted into law, he inferred, this position would logically require that every slave instantly be set free. States would then be obligated to grant blacks an equal vote, and to alter their separate constitutions to provide for racial equality in legislatures, courts, and ultimately national offices. Then, he said, seeking to agitate his Springfield, Illinois, audience into a frenzy, blacks would need to be given every privilege of white men, including the right to marry white women. Any claims to the contrary, Douglas told the raucous crowd, were patently false "so long as they quote the Declaration of Independence to prove that a negro was created equal to a white man." He was not averse to the Declaration, but his understanding of it was different: it was not a statement of human equality but of popular self-determination over domestic issues such as slavery.[20]

His perspective of the Declaration's significance, like that of the Supreme Court's, extended no further than his own race: "The signers of the Declaration of Independence, referred to white man, and to him alone, when they declared that all men were created equal." In the late nineteenth century the term *race* signified nationality as well as skin color, prompting a Chicago newspaper to remark: "It appears thus, that in Mr. Douglas' opinion not only the African race, but the German, Italian, French, Scandinavian, and, indeed, every nation except the English, Irish, Scotch and American, are excluded from all part or lot in the Declaration of Independence." But that characterization was misinformed about Douglas's actual view. By *white men* he meant "men of European blood and European descent." By repeatedly returning to this subject, Douglas hoped to gain Democratic votes and diminish Republican prospects in the general election.

Douglas's virulent belief in white exclusivity led German-born Carl Schurz to observe that it reeked of an aristocratic sense of privilege. If the Declaration were to apply to the white race alone, Schurz said to a crowd in Springfield, Massachusetts,

There is your Declaration of Independence no longer the sacred code of the rights of man, written by sages and fought for by heroes, but a hypocritical piece of special pleading, drawn up by a batch of artful pettifoggers, who, when speaking of the rights of man, meant but this privileges or a set of aristocratic slaveholders but styled it "the rights of man" in order to throw dust into the eyes of the world, and to inveigle good-natured fools into lending them aid and assistance.

Schurz, who was then only thirty years of age, would attract the notice of the Republican leadership, serving in the years to come as Lincoln's minister to Spain, U.S. senator, and then secretary of the interior under President Rutherford B. Hayes.[21]

At least four books were published in 1860 extensively quoting from Lincoln's speeches and expostulating on the meaning of the Declaration of Independence. These works contained multiple quotes from the 1858 senate debates with Douglas. Newspapers of the day likewise published the speeches. The selected passages made clear that Lincoln believed the natural rights passages of the Declaration applied to all men, irrespective of their race. Lincoln's campaign was electrified by the public airing of these ideological tracts.[22]

Even before Lincoln was elected, there was talk of secession should he become president. The defense of slavery went hand in hand with a perspective of American federalism that considered states to be exclusively responsible for slave laws. South Carolina Rep. Laurence M. Keitt warned that Lincoln's presidency would result in immediate secession. Keitt was seething with anger: "What does he mean by saying, 'I hold that there is no reason in the world why the negro is not entitled to all the natural rights enumerated in the Declaration of Independence,'" he inquired incredulously of Lincoln's speech at Cooper Institute in Manhattan. Keitt knew that one of those enumerated rights was to liberty; "Does he not declare that the negro has a 'natural right to liberty, and that it has been wrongfully taken away from him?'" This, Keitt understood, threatened the Southern way of life:

> Does he not also declare that the "republican party has been organized to treat slavery as a wrong, and to destroy it?"...It means that the South must be abolitionized, peaceably or forcibly. It means that the "natural right of liberty has been wrongfully torn from the negro," and must be restored to him, though it be over burning homes and butchered masters.

Few, then, could be certain whether Keitt's angry bravado was authentic or hype. He would die four years later as a brigadier general of the Confederate

Army, from wounds suffered at the Battle of Cold Harbor, near Richmond, Virginia.[23]

In late summer 1860, the *Charleston Mercury* projected that Lincoln's victory was inevitable unless the country could be convinced that it would lead to disunion. B. H. Hill, the owner of fifty-seven slaves, cautioned against acting too rashly in a speech he gave before the state legislature in Milledgeville, Georgia's antebellum capital. He thought it better to petition Lincoln, invoking the Declaration as an example, before acting to vindicate property rights in slaves: "The Declaration of Independence, which you invoke for an example, says a decent respect to the opinions of mankind requires us to declare the causes which impel us to separation." After the Supreme Court had determined that Congress lacked the power to prevent slavery in the federal territories, the South regarded Republican demands for free soil to be unconstitutional and despotic.[24]

Agitation turned to action in November 1860, when Lincoln won the presidential election. A South Carolina convention was called for the seventeenth of the month to pass a declaration of independence, asserting, "We hold these truths to be self-evident; that, although all men are created wholly unequal, mentally, morally, and physically, yet they are all equally entitled, under every civilized government, to the full protection of their lives, persons and property." The proposed document borrowed extensively from both Thomas Jefferson's format and wording in the original Declaration of Independence. The South Carolina document listed a purported "long train of abuses and usurpations." They included complaints about the "Northern States of this Union" having for many years demonstrated "relentless fanaticism, which declares that institution to be a moral sin," unwillingness to deliver fugitives to their masters, and zeal to prevent slaveholders from emigrating "with their property into the Territories." The Ordinance of Secession, which the South Carolina state convention adopted on December 20, 1860, interpreted the nation's founding Declaration of Independence as a compact between "free and independent states" with a right to secede.[25]

Throughout the South, blame for the secession was laid on the Republicans' shoulders for choosing a candidate whom the region feared would try to apply the equality ideals of the Declaration to blacks. It was a matter of honor. The South would "never compromise that right" of "property in man" taken away from them by what they regarded to be "the doctrine of the abolitionists…under the Declaration of Independence, that all men are born free and equal." Just as the North had feared that the *Dred Scott* opinion would lead to nationalization of slavery, the South feared a Republican administration would pave the way for emancipation. According to Texas Sen. Louis T. Wigfall's stilted view, the nation's founding principles were grounded in states' rights, not human equality: "We assert that the right of self-government is the only right that was established by the Revolution; that it is the only right that is set forth in the Declaration of Independence; that it is a right inalienable to freemen, and terrible to tyrants only." In contrast with what he perceived to be Northern interference, Wigfall pointed out, no Southerner was wont to "preach agrarianism" or demand Northern factories pay fair wages to the workforce. By February 1, 1861, six more states had seceded from the Union: Mississippi, Florida, Alabama, Georgia, Louisiana, and Texas. But for Wigfall the North was at fault. The very claim that the Declaration's statement that "all men are free and equal" applied to blacks was a cause for war. "The Declaration of Independence declares that when one people dissolve their connection with another people," Wigfall blasted his opponents, "it is but proper that they should give the reasons for their separation."[26]

In salons, newspapers, and books, talk turned to whether the South was justified in seceding on the same grounds for separating from Britain as the colonists announced in the Declaration of Independence. The Republicans' Chicago platform, so went an incendiary editorial, attacked the "social institutions of fifteen States of the Union." Such interference was enough cause for hostilities.

Confederate supporters believed that states had a right to secede and their inhabitants to revolt against the policies of a political party that conceived "the clause of the Declaration of Independence which asserts that all men are created equal" to "embrace all human beings of whatever color or race." Residents of those states "have…the right of revolution," wrote an incendiary author, "the last reserved right of every oppressed people. It is upon this great right the Declaration of Independence is based." A government under the leadership of a president who was opposed to slavery in the territories, so this argument went, was not representative of citizens living in the South.[27]

In the midst of the initial wave of secession, some Republicans sought to defuse the ideological conflict by downplaying their party's reliance on the Declaration of Independence. Sen. James F. Simmons of Rhode Island scoffed at the notion—a product of a "diseased imagination"—that quoting the document in the party platform was meant to be a statement about black social equality. Others were not as politic. Edward Everett, who was President Fillmore's secretary of state, noted an attempt had been made "especially by foreign writers to assimilate the existing rebellion at the South, with the American revolution." He saw no similarity between the revolution against a British king who refused to grant colonists parliamentary representation and the rebellion against a government that gained office through general election. The nation's framers, Everett asserted, had not justified unlimited revolution but believed that government was instituted "to secure the inalienable rights of man, among which are life, liberty, and the pursuit of happiness."[28]

There were in fact those in England who considered the Union's decision to stand up militarily against the Confederacy to be hypocritical. A Boston newspaper republished a lead article from the *London Times*, mockingly questioning, "What becomes of the famous Declaration of Independence and of the theory that Government derives its powers from the consent of the governed? The north now talks of conquest, confiscation and military colonies with all readiness of an Austrian Commandant." The same logic was heard on the floor of Parliament. A radical member of the House of Commons, Peter Locke King, conceded that the North was genuine in its desire to abolish slavery. But by denying the South the right to determine its political fate, "they had destroyed political freedom." He expressed surprise that after waging a war of independence the United States would complain about some of its states asserting their independence:

In their memorable Declaration of Independence what did they say? Why, they admitted that the time might come when in the course of human events it might be necessary for the nation to dissolve those political bonds which united them together. Well, then, the time had come, and the South in their turn, not liking the commercial oppression exercised by the North, felt that they were justified in dissolving those political bonds which united them.

In response, an abolitionist-minded orator argued that "any attempt to make their case analogous to that of our revolutionary fathers, or to find their justification in the doctrines laid down in the Declaration of Independence" when the real aim of rebellion was "boundless extension and absolute perpetuity of their accursed slave system," was "not only futile, but an insult to the memories of the signers of that great charter of human rights." Writing in the same spirit in a U.S. newspaper, an anonymous author contrasted the South Carolina Declaration of Causes with the Declaration of Independence. The latter remained American gospel, said the editorial, because it "appealed to the principle of the liberty and equal rights to all mankind," not because of its listed grievances against King George III. The Declaration of Causes, on the other hand, was an aggressive and unprovoked defense of slavery.[29]

On February 11, 1861, President elect Abraham Lincoln and his entourage departed from Springfield, Illinois, on his inaugural journey headed to Washington, the nation's capital. He could have few illusions that massive challenges lay ahead. South Carolina had already issued its Declaration of Causes a month and a half before, and other southern states had followed suit. In its own Declaration of Causes, issued earlier in February, Texas rejected the "higher law" while listing perceived affronts to its sovereignty. The state could not avoid answering the Republicans' assertions that the Declaration of Independence extended to blacks. To the contrary, went the state's statement, "That in this free government *all white men are and of right ought to be entitled to equal civil and political rights*; that the servitude of the African race, as existing in these States, is mutually beneficial to both bond and free." Mississippi's Declaration of Immediate Causes likewise took a swipe at the Republicans' platform: "It advocates negro equality, socially and politically, and promotes insurrection and incendiarism in our midst." And in its statement of dissolution Georgia complained that Lincoln's party supported "the prohibition of slavery in the Territories, hostility to it everywhere, the equality of the black and white races, disregard of all constitutional guarantees in its favor." Official statements from Georgia, South Carolina, and Texas denounced the North for violating constitutional protections of slavery.[30]

For his part, Lincoln sought to pacify the rebellion, going so far as to promise that the nation would not interfere with slavery in the states where it already existed. But he was unwilling to drop ideals that would later lead to abolition. Stopping in Philadelphia on his eastward journey to the inauguration, Lincoln delivered a speech in Independence Hall, where John Hancock had affixed his massive signature to the Declaration of Independence. In an impromptu speech, he confirmed what the South feared: "I have never had a feeling politically that did not spring from the sentiments embodied in the Declaration of Independence." It was the Declaration that "gave promise that in due time the weight would be lifted from the shoulders of all men." His next words foresaw an awful end. Either this principle would save the nation or "I would rather be assassinated on this spot than surrender it." Lincoln stuck to this perspective after his inauguration, telling Congress, on one occasion the same year, that the Declaration's leading objective—"to lift artificial weights from all shoulders"—applied just as much to the North as to the South.[31]

Those Southerners who found the Declaration to be relevant despite their decision to secede continued emphasizing a different section of the document than the one that attracted Lincoln. North Carolina Gov. John W. Ellis's written request for the state general assembly to convene to establish a confederate government and withdraw from the federal union was primarily concerned with the right to revolution rather than individual rights. His message quoted a portion of the Declaration of Independence, asserting "that whenever any form of government becomes destruction of these ends, (the security of their rights), it is the right of the people to alter or to abolish it." The state legislature heeded his call for dissolution and confirmed the absolute right to slave property. Ellis expressed a popular secessionist refrain that unionists, like the Tories of 1776, sought to govern without the people's consent. The president of the Confederacy, Jefferson Davis, saw matters similarly, arguing that the North violated the sovereignty principles of the Declaration of Independence by imposing itself on states acting according to the will of their residents. Davis's vice president mocked the notion that the preamble of the Declaration of Independence was ever meant to apply universally. "African inequality and the equality of white men," he declared, "were the chief corner-stone of the Southern republic!" Unequivocally he said in Atlanta, "The foundations of our new government are laid, its corner-stone rests upon the great truth that the negro is not equal to the white man; that slavery, subordination to the superior race, is his natural and moral condition."[32]

The Confederate states set themselves apart from the Union by rejecting the universal notion of human equality. This is not to say that the

North was an egalitarian paradise; far from it, but its principal politicians retained the ideals that had guided progressive movements ever since the Revolution. Those values would inform debates on the Reconstruction Amendments. Southern rebellion forced the debate about whether the Declaration of Independence was incompatible with slaveholding into the national conscience.

The Civil War was the greatest challenge to federal unity the country had ever faced. Antagonists held diametrically opposite understandings of American sovereignty. They disagreed about whether the framers meant for the Declaration of Independence to set the basis for a confederation of sovereign states or a national community with centralized legal mechanisms for achieving common weal. Through years of debate on the issue, attitudes hardened in both sections until intractable polarization led to violent conflict. The split was explicitly ideological, with the northern faction embracing equal inalienable rights and national control and the southern section favoring the rights of the white segment of the population and state sovereignty.

Lincoln first tried to follow the appeasement paradigm of Henry Clay. He sought to curry southern favor by backing Rep. Thomas Corwin's proposed constitutional amendment to prevent Congress from abolishing or interfering with state slavery laws. After Congress passed the proposed amendment on March 2, 1861, James Buchanan, in one of his last acts as president, unnecessarily signed it. It was already too late for pacific reconciliation. Those who interpreted the Declaration of Independence as a statement of states' independence had already decided to reject every gesture to reach consensus. On resigning his seat in the Senate, John Slidell of Louisiana declared that the North "ignored the principles of our immortal Declaration of Independence." In his eyes, Lincoln's party sought to reduce the South "to subjection.... This will be war," he said ominously, "and we shall meet it." The proposed amendment was the sort of acknowledgment of local sovereignty that George III had failed to make when the colonists petitioned him for redress. Before the Corwin amendment could garner enough state votes to become an official portion of the Constitution, Confederate guns firing on Fort Sumter on April 12, 1861, heralded the beginning of the Civil War.[33]

The Confederacy was by then committed to the view that states were allowed to halt federal incursions. The historical antecedents of the doctrine were Thomas Jefferson's justification of nullification in the Kentucky Resolutions and John Calhoun's ideology of concurrent majorities. Jefferson Davis was not one to mince words, having threatened secession as far back as 1850 over the issue of slaves in land acquired through the Mexican American War. Ten years later, on the floor of the Senate, he argued that sovereign states could reject national policy. The Declaration of Independence, he and many like-minded congressmen believed, was the work of separate colonies not a collective statement of the Continental Congress. Similarly Davis asserted that the Constitution was an act of separate states, not the people en masse. Davis's ultimate conclusion from these postulates was that states retained the sovereign right to sever ties with the Union. On this view, preventing states from leaving the union was the real violation of the Declaration of Independence's statement on liberty. Davis believed the North was violating the sacred right of self-government in order to exploit the South for its raw materials.[34]

Secessionists emphasized the role of the Declaration in undoing the bonds with England, while the Lincoln administration and Congress pointed to the manifesto's humanistic statements. As the *Richmond Dispatch*, published in the capital of the Confederacy, put it at the height of the war, "The only doctrine of the whole Declaration of Independence which the North can consistently rejoice in is that which asserts the equality of man, and which is the solitary blunder in that great document." Another newspaper published in this city, the *Richmond Enquirer*, put the matter in a way that linked the workingmen's struggle with that of free and enslaved blacks:

> Men are not born to equal rights. It would be far nearer the truth to say that some (the laborers) were born with saddles on the backs and bits in their mouths, and others (the capitalists) born booted and spurred to ride them; and the riding does them good. They (the laborers) need the rein, the bit, and the spur. Life and Liberty are not inalienable. *The Declaration of Independence is exuberantly false.*

The author recognized no similar wrongheadedness about portions of the Declaration he perceived to grant a right to disunion. His sardonic comments about the Declaration of Independence were echoed by others who believed that Thomas Jefferson had been caught up in his generation's romantic enthusiasm for natural law philosophy. Popular authors and church preachers, in places such as Macon, Georgia, proclaimed their allegiance to the Declaration but asserted that Jefferson did not mean to include blacks or even believe that equality among white men entitled those "in the lowest condition of life" to participate in governance.[35]

In a book published after the war, former Confederate Vice President Alexander Stephens surmised that the Declaration of Independence was a statement of states' sovereign authority.[36] Stephens ignored the consistent natural rights principles that had been connected to the document ever since the Revolution. His perspective differed from the natural rights understanding of the Declaration that was commonly shared by the founding and early-nineteenth-century generations.

Stephens made clear that slavery and supremacy were at the heart of the Confederate struggle; a Methodist pastor from Racine, Wisconsin, Wesson G. Miller, demonstrated the very different mind-set of those who hoped the battle would be a form of national redemption. He believed the firing on Fort Sumter was an attack on "the great lesson of universal equality and universal freedom" that was "beautifully set forth in our Declaration of Independence," which formed the "corner-stone of our institution." The belligerence had to be answered, he asserted, to repulse the "opposing doctrine of caste and privileged classes, which finds illustration in American slavery." The battle, as he understood it, was for the sake of human liberty. Not everyone would have agreed. Even among opponents of slavery who would have joined voices with Miller to proclaim that the Declaration's self-evident truths applied to all of humanity, there were those who further believed the document contained the "fundamental political maxim" that forcing states to remain in the union was "coercion and political slavery." Few in the North were able to hold onto these views for long, given the Southern challenge to battle.[37]

For the first time since the early years of the Republic, antislavery leaders were able to capture center stage in the political debate. Wendell Phillips, a devout Boston abolitionist raised in some of the nation's greatest schools to be a lawyer, directly addressed the southern claim that the Declaration allowed the region to secede from the Union:

> I acknowledge the great principles of the Declaration of Independence, that a State exists for the liberty and happiness of the people, that

these are the ends of government, and that when government ceases to promote those ends, the people have a right to remodel their institutions. I acknowledge the right of revolution in South Carolina; but at the same time, I acknowledge that right of revolution only when Government has ceased to promote those ends.

To the contrary, he went on to say to a Cooper Union crowd, the North had made repeated concessions—in Florida, Texas, and elsewhere. Disunion harmed mutual economic and security advantages that the states had promised to each other, and it threatened to sabotage the framers' expectation that even in far-off South Carolina slavery would one day wither from its own corrupt practices.[38]

The *Wisconsin State Journal*, which was published in Madison, the state capital and a stronghold of antislavery politics, claimed it could not understand the point of the argument "that the rebel cause is of the same just and holy character as that for which our forefathers fought, and the Declaration is a justification of the slaveholder's rebellion." Whereas the voices of abolitionists were muffled before the outbreak of belligerence, the very terms the South used to justify its secession made Northern audiences far more open to their arguments than they had been before the war. From the antislavery ranks came politicians in numbers never before seen in elected offices. George W. Julian, for one, a little-known Indiana congressman before 1861, gained national recognition. Since the 1840s, when he was a Free Soiler, Julian had engaged in antislavery and antinativist politics with little success outside his state district. He was an advocate of complete abolition, to begin with the liberation of western territories. Few had dared to side with his radical views, but after Sumter he was regarded as a visionary whom the Speaker of the House of Representatives, Galusha Grow, appointed to the Joint Committee on the Conduct of the War. In that capacity he influenced removal of Gen. George McClellan partly for not making emancipation a leading purpose of the Union Army. In the House, Julian told fellow congressmen that slavery was the "evil genius of government" devaluing Southern lands, decreasing national productivity, and standing in the way of free schools: "It has denounced the Declaration of Independence as a political abomination, and dealt with our fathers as hypocrites, who affirmed its self-evident truths with a mental reservation." The Civil War provided antislavery sentiments with unexpectedly fertile ground for growth.[39]

As the war ground on, Confederates returned time and again to the view that government without consent of the governed was tyranny. In its most sophisticated form, the argument for state self-determination was framed in clauses of the Declaration of Independence. One author compared Republicans to the Tories of the Revolution for forcing union onto them just as the British had tried to do to the colonies. It further compared Abraham Lincoln to George III for both suspending habeas corpus and trying to raise slave insurrections. The main idea was that the South held just as much right to assert its independence as the colonies had in 1776.[40]

This claim, wrote a reporter for the *New York Times*, was a disingenuous interpretation because if correct it would have created a remarkably unstable system of government with carte blanche for any state to leave the Union without even seeking reconciliation. At the core, the disagreement was whether the Declaration of Independence was the product of "the people" of the United States or of thirteen separate states. If it was a collective product of all the people, then it created a national identity; if, on the other hand, each colony agreed to its terms as a sovereign expediency then it created a confederate identity. The Declaration of Independence gave no certain answer to these differing arguments about the structure of government. The Confederate side could point out that the document was the product of the "unanimous Declaration of the thirteen united States of America." On the Union side of the argument, were those who pointed out that in the wording of the Declaration it was "one people" who had "dissolve[d] the political bands" with England. The document was the product of the "Representatives of the united States of America" rather than any particular state. According to the latter perspective, the representatives of the thirteen states confirmed that the newly formed nation had a unified vision for governance. Thus, the Declaration of Independence was a willful act to diminish state sovereignty, which was then further reduced by ratification of the Constitution. In its extreme, a position taken by radicals such as Charles Sumner, this meant that even criminal laws, which states traditionally administered and enforced, had to be consistent with the equality principles of the Declaration of Independence. On this reading, rules of evidence or of jury selection that discriminated against blacks were invalid because they intruded into the federally protected right to equality. A more moderate view was that although the Declaration of Independence prohibited secession it left local matters such as criminal, contract, and property laws intact, even if they were overtly discriminatory.[41]

Propelled by war, the necessity to requisition additional soldiers for the front, and abstract ethical considerations about slavery, Republicans changed their approach from voluntary emancipation to forced abolition. Union Democrats opposed them in Congress, wanting to engage in a limited war that did nothing to alter the relationship between federal and state governments. Those Democrats who remained in Congress sought to appease southern states and welcome them back into the national fold, without effecting any change to domestic control of slavery. For a time, Lincoln too tried to convince the South to reconcile, but as this strategy failed even formerly moderate Republicans began taking on a radical attitude toward slavery.

Congress initially was quicker to attack slavery than the president was. The First Confiscation Act became law on August 6, 1861, authorizing the military to take any property, including slaves, that had been used to support the insurrection. Lincoln backed the measure and instructed his generals to carry it out. Although the act freed only a relatively small number of slaves whom the Confederacy directly enrolled in military tasks, it signaled a clear shift in war strategy. The president remained cautious to the point of rescinding Generals John C. Frémont's and David Hunter's proclamations emancipating any slaves in the areas under their command.[42]

On July 17, 1862, Congress passed the Second Confiscation Act, which freed slaves who escaped or whom the Union captured from any slaveholder, militarily or otherwise involved in supporting the rebellion. For some, enactment of this law was an unambiguous sign of progress. "On the brightest page of the nation's history this act will be written next to the Declaration of Independence," wrote the *Chicago Tribune*, understanding the document to be intrinsically antislavery. Congress claimed the power to confiscate property in self-defense pursuant to a half-century-old Supreme Court decision expounding the congressional authority to declare war. The Declaration was a further interpretive tool. Those slaves who were freed under the new law stood to benefit from the Republicans' doctrine that the principle of inalienable rights in the Declaration of Independence pertained to people of all races. Confiscation of property, as Rep. William P. Cutler of Ohio pointed out, was not the end all, since it still fell short of complete repudiation of the institution. From his perspective, Southern opposition to such a momentous change was irrelevant because the Confederate states had committed representational suicide by showing repeated hostility for the "fundamental dogma of the Declaration of Independence."[43]

To the South and its supporters, the taking of property without compensation was a further affront against state governance and an intrusion on individual rights. A member of the British Parliament likewise questioned, "What becomes of the famous Declaration of Independence and of the theory that Government derives its power from the Consent of the governed?" After all, the owners surely hadn't given consent to confiscation of their property. If the North could do that, so went the opposition's thinking, it would make the South into a military colony much as the British had tried to do to the American colonies.[44]

The Second Confiscation Act came into law on the same day as the Militia Act. The latter was meant to offset the Union's military attrition (running at about one hundred thousand desertions in 1862) and to prevent further war losses, which were particularly bad that year. Lincoln initially rejected incorporation of black troops into the ranks when, earlier that year, Gen. David Hunter recruited and then drafted them in the Southern region under his command. But here too, Lincoln altered his views after receiving congressional authorization and realizing that securing the South could be done only through the course of battle and not at the negotiating table. The Militia Act was still a limited victory. Although black soldiers were recruited, it took several months before they were sent to battlefields. Even more importantly, their military service did not entitle them to citizenship.[45]

Congress had no way of knowing whether its strategy would win popular support. Radical congressmen such as Sen. James Harlan of Iowa, sought to downplay the equality that black soldiers would enjoy. The "friends of emancipation," said Harlan during a debate on the militia bill, were not seeking political or social equality but the "equality…implied in the Declaration of Independence," which referred to no more than men's ability to choose an occupation, benefit from their toil, be compensated for work, and seek legal redress.[46]

The mallet had already been swung, and it would eventually shatter the cornerstone of the Confederacy. President Lincoln would soon take the lead. In July 1862 he informed cabinet members that he was considering compensated emancipation but wanted to put it off until the North made additional gains on the battlefield. Before moving forward, he held a meeting with border-state congressmen, unsuccessfully trying to convince them to accept gradual, compensated emancipation. He also made no progress with a deputation of blacks whom he tried to persuade to abandon the United States and colonize in Central America or some other country. Black participants at a mass meeting in Newtown, Long Island, New York, considered the president's request to serve only the enemy's cause, "who wish to insult and mob us." "We have the right to have applied to ourselves those rights named in the Declaration of Independence" was their unequivocal reply. They proposed a different plan: for the president to declare the rebel states to be free, take the land confiscated under the act of Congress, and give it to free and emancipated black citizens.[47]

Reliance on congressional war powers to pass the confiscation acts and the military recruitment law set the stage for a similar exercise of executive power; after all, the Constitution grants the president the authority of commander in chief of the armed forces. From the first year of the Civil War, abolitionists were calling on "the President [to] declare that the principles of the immortal Declaration of Independence shall be carried out in practice throughout the United States—that the blessings of liberty shall be recognized as the birthright of every human being within our limits." This he could do by "a slash of his pen," which would release "four millions of helpless beings."[48]

Newspapers were ablaze when Lincoln issued the Emancipation Proclamation on January 1, 1863. After much rumination, the president determined that his constitutional authority to free slaves extended only to states that were in rebellion. The proclamation emancipated all slaves except those kept in the loyal border states and several regions that were not in rebellion. By setting about 3.3 million persons free with one pen stroke, wrote the San Francisco *Daily Evening Bulletin*, the nation "enables us to adopt the Declaration of Independence of ours without any mental reservation." At the opposite end of the country, in Middlebury, Vermont, the General Congregational Convention approved the Proclamation of Emancipation, setting millions of the enslaved free. Convention participants further expressed the hope that the dreadful war would lead the entire nation to recognize "the truth so prominently set forth in the Declaration of Independence, that all men are equal." Not only did it signal "the Year of Jubilee" but its promulgation also "dignifies labor, ennobles humanity, honors God." Reverend N. A. Staples of the Second Unitarian Church of Brooklyn gave a discourse, in hopes that "the second great Declaration of Independence" would simplify the struggle by providing "the transcendent brightness of the vision" that gave the revolutionary army its frame of action. Among Lincoln's supporters were those who saw a long road, paved with bullets and military privations, before the Union could make good on the "Proclamation of Freedom[,] the new Declaration of Independence." Slaves who learned of the Proclamation did not wait for an end to the fighting, with many of them escaping for Union lines to gain their liberty by joining the ranks of soldiers, moving with Union troops in makeshift camps, or traveling north. On July 4, 1863, Col. Robert G. Shaw, who only fourteen days later would die in the assault against Fort Wagner, wrote a letter home. He extolled the Independence Day celebration on a South Carolina plantation where a "colored preacher, from Baltimore, named Lynch" gave a "very eloquent" speech. At the celebration, "a little black boy" also "read the Declaration of Independence."[49]

As might be expected, there were many who were virulently opposed to the Proclamation. One author considered the Republicans to be "prescriptive and fanatical" and quoted language from the Declaration of Independence that had originally targeted King George III, for maintaining a "military independent of, and superior to, the civil power." The Lincoln administration, the article contended, had done the same by issuing the Proclamation to make a "mockery of the admonitions of the founders of the Union." Another editorial letter asserted that the Emancipation Proclamation and the administration were doing more to harm the union than "the unmolested institution of slavery" did in nearly a century since the Declaration of Independence was signed.[50]

By late March 1863, the administration had developed a policy for black battlefield participation. Prior to that time, black soldiers were primarily relegated to support functions such as digging trenches, building roads, and guarding encampments. In 1863, varying numbers of black soldiers took part in battles, skirmishes, and expeditions in Arkansas, Georgia, Louisiana, Mississippi, and elsewhere. Black soldiers began receiving loud applause for their valor, but under the Militia Act privates and noncommissioned officers received lower pay than whites of the same ranks. The inequality they faced defending the Union flag and subjecting themselves to every danger led to an outcry and calls to repeal the law:

> As a people, as a government, we give the lie to the Declaration of Independence—our charter of Liberty. We say by our acts that all men are not equal. In bravery, in courage, in devotion to the flag, the colored troops have been our equals at Wagner, Port Hudson, Olustee, Paducah and Fort Pillow. I cannot believe this nation has lost its sense of justice—that it is dead to magnanimity.

U.S. Attorney General Bates was able to equalize black and white chaplains' pay according to existing law. Condemnation of unequal pay among lower-ranked soldiers grew until, on June 15, 1864, Congress equalized pay scales and even made the law retroactive.[51]

On the Fourth of July of that year, the Forty-ninth Massachusetts Volunteers came to an area where black troops were garrisoned. "We are interpreting the Declaration of Independence," wrote a member of the Forty-ninth, "so that mankind, fearing or hoping, believe that 'God hath created *all* men free and equal'....Despairing patriots dash away their tears, and exultingly exclaim, 'Liberty *is* man's birthright!'" Age old prejudices, however, were difficult to shake. Even after black soldiers' pay was made equal, Col. Reuben D. Mussey, who actively raised colored regiments in Tennessee and Georgia and provided their ranks with educational opportunities, fired off a letter acknowledging an invitation to celebrate Independence Day at Fort Gillem, Georgia. He was then colonel of the 100th Regiment, made up of black soldiers:

> I cannot, sir, accept any invitation to a military display where other Colonels march their troops while mine are excluded. The Declaration of Independence, whose formal adoption makes the Fourth of July sacred, affirms us an axiom that All Men are created equal. And until you, sir, and your committee learn this fundamental truth, till you can invite all the defenders of their country to participate in your celebration, be they black or they white, your "celebrations of our National Anniversary" are mocking farces.

Legal change would not be enough. To achieve the goals of the Declaration of Independence, victory at arms would need to be joined by an end to cultural inequality.[52]

More than any other wartime document, the Emancipation Proclamation ignited hope. In the words of Union Gen. Carl Schurz, it was the "true sister of the Declaration of Independence; it is the supplementary act; it is the Declaration of Independence translated from universal principle into universal fact." Most important, it moved the nation to recognition that the war was not merely about land, or even federalism, but about the evisceration of slavery.[53]

Military defeat led to more than a cessation of hostilities. Gen. Robert E. Lee's surrender on April 9, 1865, at Appomattox Court House in Virginia was only part of the story. The North's decisive victory would soon translate into constitutional reconstruction to nationalize America's founding principles into enforceable provisions. Both sections of the country were clear about their positions on slavery. The political scientist Michael Foley has pointed out that death and devastation forced the country to confront its record on human and civil rights.

Lincoln had much to do with this rebirth of freedom because he had so often promised that victory would lead to a renaissance of these national values. His 1863 Gettysburg Address reached to the heart of his administration's war aims. In 1776, he said, "our fathers brought forth on this continent a new nation conceived in liberty and dedicated to the proposition that all men are created equal. Now we are engaged in a great civil war, testing whether that nation or any nation so conceived and so dedicated can long endure." Raising the conflict to an idealistic pinnacle, the sectional crisis became a battle to impose a vision of human equality and national citizenship on the nation as a whole.[54]

The Confederate view of state determination would not yield. Union victory was ensured, especially with enactment of three post-Civil War amendments. However, the view that the revolutionary clauses of the Declaration of Independence authorized states to undermine federal antidiscrimination efforts was now irrevocably part of the document's narrative.

10

RECONSTRUCTION

Hope bloomed at the end of the Civil War that victory would prove the Declaration of Independence's statements about equality, liberty, and happiness to be far more than empty generalities. As at no time since the Revolution, the nation recognized that its tolerance of racial inequality was incompatible with the founding principles. The Constitution would need to be amended to eliminate the force of its slave-holding provisions. The Declaration would influence the dialogue of reform; it was an ancient but living manifesto with universal values, whose principle of equal inalienable rights was informed by the past as well as the wisdom of later generations.

In a eulogy for Abraham Lincoln, after John Wilkes Booth's bullet felled the president, Sen. Charles Sumner was adamant that postbellum America should prevent racial injustice. Sumner rallied the country to live up to the ideals of the American Revolution. Victory over the Confederate States, he said, "will have failed unless it performs all the original promises of that Declaration which our fathers took upon their lips when they became a nation." Sumner called on the nation to fulfill Lincoln's vision, drawing on the Republic's continuing obligation to finish the work of Emancipation "and the promises of the Declaration of Independence unfulfilled." Freedom would be chimerical for blacks without the enjoyment of rights and privileges of free people, including the right to vote. Sumner became one of the most adamant advocates for national reconstruction with Congress taking practical steps to animate the Declaration of Independence's two central tenets: human equality and government by consent of the people.[1]

In April 1865, Lincoln's funeral cortège wound its way from Washington, D.C., to Springfield, Illinois. For a time, his casket was brought into Independence Hall, where the Continental Congress first proclaimed the Declaration of Independence. Reconstruction would proceed without him. The nation would try to achieve the goals of its youth without his effective leadership. The uncompromising abolitionist Wendell Phillips asserted that war "broke up the national hypocrisy, and taught us that only by making the Declaration the corner-stone of the government does God grant us a chance of nationality." The nature of that nationality would need much fleshing out. The Declaration of Independence had become a symbol of a glorious past full of national mythologizing and of a theoretical foundation for the future. In 1864, the *Cincinnati Enquirer* ran a story about the death of an Ohio pioneer who was ten years old at the adoption of the Declaration. The physical document was yellowed with age, the signatures were barely legible, but its inspirational message still enlivened social activism and national policy. Without living, human links to the past, stories of the nation's glories and its accumulated wisdom would be the building blocks for change.[2]

After the Civil War, the nation was never the same. The Reconstruction Amendments altered the federalist structure of government. They increased congressional power to define civil rights, diminished state powers to discriminate against black citizens, elevated equality to its proper place alongside individual liberty, and further incorporated the Declaration's human rights ideals into the Constitution. Yet there was a counternarrative as well, which contended that the Declaration's statements against overbearing government prohibited federal intrusion into state civil and political matters. Both of these modes of thought proved lasting, and they remain part of twenty-first century American political discourse.

African American men who served in the Union Army experienced a rebirth when they came home. Many of them remembered being beaten as slaves, sometimes for such minor infractions as reading a book. For them, even the ability to travel without slave passes was a new experience. Many years after the war, William Henry Singleton, who had served honorably in Georgia and Florida as a sergeant attached to the 35th U.S. Colored Troops, wrote a book of his years in slavery and then the military. He wrote proudly of the Union soldiers' gallant sufferings. They had protected "the country of the Declaration of Independence" and "wiped away with their blood the stain of slavery and, purged the Republic of its sin." A northern newspaper correspondent, who wrote in April 3, 1865, from Petersburg, Virginia, noticed a difference between blacks in uniform and the former slaves they helped to free after the Confederate withdrawal from the city. The demeanor of an African American wearing "the national uniform" or one "employed in non-combatant capacities in the service of the United States...fully realizes that all men are free and equal. His carriage is a constant declaration of independence." As for those who were used to living in that Confederate town, they continued to be extremely deferential, unsure what to expect from the liberators. Being an optimist about the outcome of the war, the correspondent believed the "lesson of freedom...is quickly learned, and in a few days they will have acquired much of the dignity of manhood, and carry themselves as citizens, and not as cattle." At the conclusion of the War, overjoyed by the silencing of the artillery pieces and rifle fire, there was an excited sense that the "the radical ideas of the declaration of independence" would "at last be fully realized."[3]

Leaders wishing to enforce the Declaration's promises of equal rights directed the highest offices of government. Throughout Radical Reconstruction, Sumner was the chairman of the coveted Committee on Foreign Relations. Sen. Benjamin Wade was the chairman of both the Joint Committee on the Conduct of the War and the Committee on Territories. William Fessenden was the chairman of the Senate Committee of Finance at the beginning of the Civil War, and he returned to that post after having served as President Lincoln's secretary of the treasury. Sen. Henry Wilson, a lifelong abolitionist, was the chairman of the Military Affairs Committee from 1863 to 1872. Until 1865, the chairman of the Senate Public Lands Committee was James Harlan, who advocated for Congress to protect a wide variety of civil rights formerly at the sole discretion of the states. They and others in the radical camp repeatedly spoke of how changes to the Constitution must be based on the ideals of the Declaration

FIGURE 10.1 *Frank Leslie's Illustrated Newspaper*, March 19, 1870, p. 9. "The Promise of the Declaration of Independence Fulfilled." (Image courtesy of the Library of Congress.)

of Independence. Sumner, for instance, insisted "that the Declaration is of equal and co-ordinate authority with the Constitution itself."[4]

Advocacy for a constitutional amendment began before the conclusion of the War. Lincoln's Emancipation Proclamation encouraged popular support for additional legal actions to break the back of slavery. The organizers of the 1863 National Convention of German Radicals, meeting in Cleveland, announced that among their chief objects was the "abolition of slavery... [and] revision of the Constitution in the spirit of the Declaration of Independence." They considered the "proclamation of equal human rights by the Declaration of Independence" to be "the only true fundamental law of republican life." "Unfortunately," those in attendance found the principles therein were "disregarded already in the Constitution, and still more in party politics."[5]

The two House and one Senate debates on the Thirteenth Amendment, which abolished slavery, repeatedly referred to the Declaration's Revolutionary ideals. The will to put the ideology of '76 into practical effect energized radical Republicans. In the popular press, the *New York Tribune* called on the country to prove that the North "sought not territorial aggrandizement nor sectional power, but the establishment of the principles of the Declaration of Independence." As a senator from New Hampshire, John P. Hale said abolition of slavery was an essential step for the United States to take in order to disengage from patent inconsistencies that tainted its history. He called on fellow citizens to "wake up to the meaning of the sublime truths" that the nation's "fathers uttered years ago and which have slumbered dead letters upon the pages of our Constitution, of our Declaration of Independence, and of our history." Decades of sectional conflicts over the spread of slavery focused Congress's attention on the "great wrong, in a moral and social point of view" that "was admitted into the organic law" at the nation's founding "under a supposed necessity for union." "Our ancestors," asserted Sen. John B. Henderson of Missouri, had paved the way to civil war by hypocritically preserving their own "inalienable right of liberty unto all men," and "came to refuse it to others" under the guise of expedience.[6]

Supporters of the Thirteenth Amendment repeatedly stated that its doctrinal foundation was laid by the universal language of the Declaration of Independence. As Rep. James S. Rollins of Missouri understood events of the bygone era, American Revolutionaries from every region of the country anchored "the great principle...in the rights of man, founded in reason...without distinction of race or of color." A Democrat from Maryland, Reverdy Johnson, whose support for the Thirteenth Amendment was crucial to its passage, considered the Declaration to be "the Magna Carta of human rights." On the basis of that wellspring of American rights, Johnson believed slavery to be "inconsistent with the principles upon which the Government is founded."[7]

The emphasis on egalitarian policy making was a further indication of the fundamental change in the structure and function of federal government. The head of the House Judiciary Committee, James F. Wilson of Iowa, drew his inspiration from the revolutionary proclamation of "human equality" found in the "sublime creed" of the Declaration of Independence, which demands that all be treated as "equals before the law." The nation would be rebuilt with the union forever changed where *"equality before the law* is to be the great corner-stone" that the states and the judiciary would be unable to undermine. Following ratification of the Thirteenth Amendment, its opponents argued that it was never meant to make blacks equal before the law but only to set them free from the fetters of slavery. This was an attempt to deny that the Declaration's principles had been incorporated into the Thirteenth Amendment.[8]

Part of the uncertainty about the Amendment's wide-ranging grant of congressional authority arose from its narrow wording, allowing for a stilted literal interpretation. In hindsight, the Senate erred when it rejected Sumner's proposed modification to the Amendment. He had sought to add a clause explicitly recognizing that "all persons are equal before the law," which would have made the Amendment's relation to the Declaration of Independence less ambiguous. Other senators thought Sumner's proposed addendum to be extraneous because equality was already implicit in constitutional abolition. Congressional failure to include some mention of equality in the final version enabled congressmen such as Sen. Thomas A. Hendricks of Indiana to argue—even after ratification of the Thirteenth Amendment—that blacks were natural and civil inferiors, without the same legal rights as whites: "It may be preached; it may be legislated for...but there is that difference between the two races that renders it impossible."[9]

The Amendment's supporters, who made up the supermajority of both chambers of Congress, repeatedly expressed a very different view. Their speeches often stressed the equality of every person to enjoy inalienable rights. With the passage of the Thirteenth Amendment, argued one congressman, "The old starry banner of our country...will be grander," because "universal liberty" and "the rights of mankind" will then be protected "without regard to color or race." A year after its ratification, Sen. Lot M. Morrill argued that by passing the Thirteenth Amendment the nation had "wrought" a "change" that "was in harmony with the fundamental principles of the Government."[10]

News spread quickly that the prohibition against slavery had become part of the nation's organic law. The Senate adopted the measure in April 1864, the House at the end of January 1865. Writing of the "vast, thundering, and uncontrollable" tumult of joy that ensued after the speaker of the House announced the vote, a Waukesha, Wisconsin, newspaper characterized the legislative event as "the most august and important...since the Declaration of Independence." The grizzled abolitionist William Lloyd Garrison believed the House vote meant "the Declaration of Independence, [is] no longer an abstract manifesto, containing certain 'glittering generalities,' simply to vindicate our Revolutionary fathers for seceding from the mother country; but it is that Declaration constitutionalized—made the supreme law of the land for the protection of the rights and liberties of all who dwell on the American soil." On December 18 of that year, Secretary of State William H. Seward announced that enough states had ratified the Thirteenth Amendment to make it a fixture of the Constitution. But this was not the end of the story, even though it was a fulfillment of the abolitionist vision. As Samuel May, Jr., Garrison's close friend, admonished, the Constitution and Declaration of Independence would be trampled underfoot unless "American law, justice, conscience, sense of consistency and duty" were brought to bear to make the freedmen full and equal citizens.[11]

After centuries of slavery it was unrealistic to think that the Thirteenth Amendment would eliminate racial prejudices at the drop of a hat. Pressing issues remained unresolved, particularly how stringent the North should be toward the conquered South. An economist advised that if the legislature were to "giv[e] effect to the Declaration of Independence" then laborers would have a better chance to prosper at factories, furnaces, farms, and iron foundries. With black and white workmen, the South's abundant resources could be tapped more efficiently than they had been under the stewardship of an idle, slave-holding class.[12]

To avoid complying with the social transformation the constitutional change was meant to engender, Southern states enacted a series of oppressive laws, known as the black codes. They were meant to establish a system of serfdom, subordination, and peonage. Southern governments remained in the hands of Confederate sympathizers because President Andrew Johnson refused the radicals' demands that anyone who participated in the rebellion should be excluded from government. He issued official pardons to thousands of men who had served either in the Confederate government or in its army. Many of the laws those men enacted sought to maintain the plantation system. The black codes established labor and property restrictions. Mississippi, for instance, prohibited African Americans from buying or leasing lands outside cities. A Louisiana law forbade selling or leasing land to freedpeople but required them to find homes within a certain number of days, thereby forcing them back to the plantations they had fled. Any black "servant" in Georgia who worked more than one month for a "master" was required to sign a contract, forfeiting all his past wages and being subject to a $500 fine if he quit before the agreed period of labor ended. In South Carolina, blacks on plantations could not receive visitors or visit others without receiving permission to do so.

Enactment of laws to circumvent the Thirteenth Amendment alerted Congress to the need to attack the problem at the local level. Such a drastic break from the federal structure of government was precisely what the second section of the Thirteenth Amendment anticipated. "To secure the supremacy of republican ideas, and a uniform principle of local government and ideas is now the only object of Congress," reported a Colorado newspaper. The rapidity with which the southern legislatures passed the black codes gave further proof that "state governments at the South never were republican or democratic in principle, and were constantly drifting from the great doctrines of the Declaration of Independence." Col. David Ullman suggested to Civil War Veterans in New York a way to end the black codes and other forms of disguised slavery by constitutional reform in "symmetrical accord with the Declaration of Independence." Senator Sumner, seeing a long-sought opportunity to change the course of history, implored members of an 1865 Massachusetts Republican Party convention to prevent black codes from harming a whole race. With the Declaration of Independence shining "like the sun in the heavens," the freedmen's political fortunes could be secured against "disloyal white man" who had initiated the rebellion and then created onerous restrictions.[13]

There was much room for debate about whether to immediately allow all southerners to participate in postwar policy making or exclude all those who had engaged in the rebellion. Southerners rarely referred to the Declaration in these years, and those who did usually sought to justify the rebellion as an act of self-determination no different from the war of independence. They argued abolitionists and their friends focused on one sentence of the document to the exclusion of all others, especially those providing government by consent of the governed. On the heels of victory, reformers felt more secure in adopting their views because the opposition's power was so severely reduced. Rep. James Ashley of Ohio demanded that future southern constitutions not be repugnant to the Declaration and

Constitution of the United States. He, like his fellow radical republicans, including Sumner, wanted provisional governors to impose martial law until enough southerners could be found to take an oath of loyalty, in part to "sustain the equal rights, civil and political, of all men, according to the principles of the Declaration of Independence."[14]

Writing from England, the philosopher John Stuart Mill advised against being too gentle with the conquered. He admonished Americans to break the back of the slave-holding aristocracy. An additional constitutional amendment was necessary, he believed, to enable the Supreme Court to set aside state legislation that attempted to reinstate slavery by oppressive laws. Change to the fundamental law of the land would ensure that "the cause of freedom is safe, and the opening words of the Declaration of Independence will cease to be a reproach to the nation." Mill was also a renowned advocate for women's rights, which would become a central issue during the Reconstruction period as well. Wendell Phillips Garrison, son of William Lloyd Garrison, related to a Brooklyn audience how he envisioned a new-found nation "raised upon the basics of the Declaration of Independence" with "no sexual or genetic difference." Advances in racial and gender equality would come after many struggles, not all of them successful, and much compromise.[15]

The Thirteenth Amendment not only abolished slavery; its second section provided Congress with the power to develop a statutory agenda to protect fundamental rights, especially those connected to life, liberty, and the pursuit of happiness. Accordingly, shortly after the states ratified the Thirteenth Amendment, Congress proceeded with a bill "to protect all persons in the United States in their civil rights and furnish the means of their vindication." Enactment of the Civil Rights Act of 1866, less than four months after the states ratified the Amendment, offers one of the most telling indicators of the extent to which reconstruction of the Constitution expanded congressional prerogatives to secure essential freedoms. The Act secured the right "to make and enforce contracts, to sue, be parties, and give evidence, to inherit, purchase, lease, sell, hold, and convey real and personal property...without respect to race or color, or previous condition of slavery." The Freedmen's Bureau Act guaranteed an identical list of rights. These two acts nationalized core civil rights throughout the United States.[16]

Many of the speeches supporting the Civil Rights Act of 1866 connected it with the country's fundamental tenets. Minnesota Rep. William

Windom, who later served as secretary of the treasury under Presidents James Garfield and Benjamin Harrison, believed the bill to be "one of the first efforts made since the formation of the Government to give practical effect to the principles of the Declaration of Independence." As the bill's Senate floor leader Lyman Trumbull put it, 1776's "immortal declaration" of equal and inalienable rights has "very little importance" as merely a statement of "abstract truths and principles unless they can be carried into effect" through concrete federal statutes.[17]

The Civil Rights Act of 1866 applied to "the whole people" throughout the United States without exception, including the "high and low, rich and poor, white and black." From its inception, the nation had "professed" to be governed by "the absolute equality of rights," but it had "denied to a large portion of the people equality of rights." The newly ratified Amendment finally provided Congress with authority to make antidiscrimination regulations enforceable throughout the country irrespective of any state's policies to the contrary.[18]

A supermajority overrode President Andrew Johnson's veto of the 1866 bill. Even before the Civil War, Johnson had sided with those who believed the Declaration of Independence concerned only white men's rights.[19] Many of the speeches supporting its passage argued that prohibiting discrimination was essential for guaranteeing real freedom. Normative arguments during congressional debates relied on the country's founding principles to support congressional civil rights authority; discrimination was asymmetrical with the stable norms of postbellum republican governance. Section 2 of the Thirteenth Amendment granted Congress the dynamic authority to discern and legislate against any abiding or new infringements on the fundamental freedoms of the Declaration. Reconstruction broke from "the dogma that this is the country of the white man, and that no other man has rights here which the white man is bound to respect."[20]

Senator Trumbull clarified that the scope of national authority was not meant to destroy federalism but to secure equal rights for every American. Among these essential interests, he asserted, are "the right to life, to liberty, and to avail one's self of all the laws passed for the benefit of the citizen to enable him to enforce his rights." The newly reconstructed form of federalism emphasized Congress's role in setting legal standards against discrimination. It left intact state powers insofar as they dealt with ordinary legal matters, from labor and transactional agreements to tort and criminal law.[21]

The increased federal power over civil rights came at the expense of state authority. In the throes of victory, the North had no incentive for sectional compromise. A Charleston, South Carolina, newspaper drew up a list of principles it considered the Civil Rights Act and martial law to have violated. One grievance was that although the Republicans were "asserting negro equality" as mandated by the Declaration of Independence, they were "unjustly deny[ing] the like equality to the white race in the South."[22] Members of a privileged group often display indignation when the rights of a disadvantaged group are expanded; they consider equal treatment of a despised group to be an affront to their entitled place in society.

The deposed Confederate President, Jefferson Davis, stood fast by his defense of secession. In interviews, he continued to insist that the rebellion was a justified means of vindicating states' independence as created by the Declaration of Independence. Even as the country made enormous legal strides toward equality, there were still those who claimed that those signers of the Declaration of Independence who were slaveholders would have opposed national emancipation. A decade after the end of belligerence, the North and South began to reconcile for the sake of national unity. Davis's fate was revealing. After leading the South into a war where hundreds of thousands of Americans lost their lives, he was released from jail in 1867 and never prosecuted for treason.[23]

While Davis traveled freely and began life in private industry, black codes restrained African Americans from enjoying their freedoms. In the South the views of state supremacy remained intact. Confederate sympathizers complained they were not being granted the right to self-determination guaranteed by the Declaration. An Atlanta newspaper defended secession. It rejected the Radical Republicans' emphasis on the early passages of the Declaration of Independence, which, the author claimed, "they can distort into an assertion of negro equality, and make this an excuse for the assumption of despotic power." The article instead regarded the founding document to be relevant only insofar as it legitimized breaking the chords of tyranny by revolution. An 1866 article in the *New-Orleans Times* continued to tout language in the Declaration of Independence on the right of the states to decide when to throw off oppressive, centralized government. Racist statements were not confined to newspapers or southerners. During a debate in the House of Representatives, James A. Johnson of California proclaimed that "white men for white men's State governments made the

Declaration of Independence." If this perspective had won the day, white state governments could have rendered abolition meaningless.[24]

Northern Democrats joined the cry against military rule of their southern brethren. Attendees of the Democratic National Convention in New Tammany Hall in New York claimed that it was they who stood for the "great principles handed down in the Declaration of Independence." Horatio Seymour, whom they picked in 1868 to be the presidential candidate, blamed the Republicans for modifying language from the Declaration of Independence: they have "sent hither swarms of Officers to harass our people, and eat out their substance." Seymour's wording was taken verbatim from the Declaration of Independence, which had accused the British of the same wrong. This rhetorical device became popular in that election year. Sen. Willard Saulsbury, Sr., of Delaware listed twenty-seven grievances against the North, many of them alluding to the complaints of 1776: "They were guilty of the following offenses charged in the Declaration of Independence: I. They dissolved Legislatures for opposing with manly firmness their invasions on the rights of the people. II. They obstructed the administration of justice by imprisoning judges and officers of the law. III. They attempted to make judges dependent on their will alone for the tenure of their offices and the payment of their salaries," etc.[25]

These counternarratives to radical reconstruction emphasized state sovereignty to deny the claim that the Declaration's central message is found in its second paragraph, in the statement of equal inalienable rights.

Powerful opposition to radical reforms prompted the Reconstruction Congress to advance another constitutional amendment in lieu of solely attacking state and private discrimination through piecemeal statutes. No matter how adamantly activists and politicians argued that blacks had a right to personal liberty under the Declaration of Independence, their ideology could have little impact on freedpeople's lives without the constitutional power to enforce it. Problems presented themselves in the North as well as the South. Indiana and Oregon along with Delaware and Kentucky continued to place restraints on black liberties by denying them entry into their borders. This undercut the ability of blacks to travel freely throughout the states, which was a privilege enjoyed by other Americans.[26]

Missing from the Thirteenth Amendment was any acknowledgment of human equality. Although it seemed clear to many in Congress that freedom from slavery implicitly included the right to enjoy all the privileges and immunities of citizenship, several factors indicated that the ideal would not be realized. For one, even though Congress had overridden a presidential veto to pass the Civil Rights Act of 1866, there were voices throughout the country, including a minority of the Republican Party, who thought the law to be unconstitutional. That was not the mainstream sentiment, but future congresses could repeal civil rights statutes.[27]

Members of the Joint Committee of Fifteen on Reconstruction, notably Senators Jacob M. Howard, John A. Bingham, and William P. Fessenden, wanted to pass another amendment to the Constitution in order to extend national power over civil rights beyond the protections enumerated by the 1866 statute. The committee determined to clarify the grant of congressional enforcement authority in the Thirteenth Amendment by adding what would become Equal Protection, Due Process, and Privileges or Immunities Clauses to the Constitution. Contrary to nineteenth-century and twenty-first-century Supreme Court decisions, such as the *Civil Rights Cases* and *United States v. Morrison*, the original purpose of these clauses was clearly to reduce state powers by augmenting congressional jurisdiction to prevent individual and state acts of discrimination.[28]

In 1866, when the Fourteenth Amendment passed by an overwhelming majority of Congress, opponents campaigned against ratification by invoking the pre-Civil War framework of state exclusivity in civil administration. Radical Rep. John F. Farnsworth of Illinois was among those who hoped "that Congress and the people of the several States may yet rise above a mean prejudice and do equal and exact justice to all men, by putting in practice that 'self-evident truth' of the Declaration of Independence." The term *self-evident truth* had proven inadequate to prevent the spread of slavery and abridgement of free blacks' rights during the antebellum years. The Fourteenth Amendment was meant to embed the principle into an enforceable provision of the nation's organic law. The last section of the Amendment granted federal legislators authority to create uniform civil rights standards for the nation, a function that earlier was exclusively the states' province.[29]

Supporters of the Fourteenth Amendment had no doubt "as to the power of Congress to enforce principles lying at the very foundation of all republican government if they be denied or violated by the States." Sen. Luke P. Poland of Vermont believed that the Declaration of Independence informed the writers of the Fourteenth Amendment. An Illinois congressman who also linked the new constitutional safeguard to the Declaration of Independence asked rhetorically how anyone could "have and enjoy equal rights of 'life, liberty, and the pursuit of happiness' without 'equal protection of laws?'" The Equal Protection Clause of the Fourteenth Amendment gave Congress the power to enforce one of the Declaration's central principles.[30]

The original Constitution contained no antecedents for the Equal Protection Clause. This clause evolved from years of abolitionist elaboration on the precepts of the Declaration of Independence. Representative Bingham of Ohio, who was the congressional leader in debates on the proposed Fourteenth Amendment, indicated in 1857 that he thought equality to be imbedded in existing legal structure: "It must be apparent that the absolute equality of all, and the equal protection of each, are principles of our Constitution." Despite his claim, Bingham realized, at least after the Civil War, that nothing but an explicit provision of the Constitution could vindicate the equality principle of the Declaration of Independence. Standing alone, the Declaration did not grant Congress the power to pass laws to bring about racially neutral republican governance. The abolitionist rallying cry that "all men are created equal" naturally led to an enforceable guarantee of "equal protection of the laws." Even if applying the clause to all men required, to some measure, disregarding that the author of the Declaration was a slaveholder, it became an anchor for abolitionists and a stumbling block for secessionists. Thaddeus Stevens urged Congress to capture the moment: though "our Fathers had been compelled to postpone the principles of their great Declaration, and wait for their full establishment until a more propitious time. That time ought to be present now." Pennsylvania Rep. George F. Miller thought the first section of the proposed Amendment to be "so just that no State shall deprive any person of life, liberty, or property without due process of law, nor deny equal protection of the laws, and so clearly within the spirit of the Declaration of Independence" that it could not be gainsaid.[31]

Ratification of the Fourteenth Amendment took about two years. Republicans made it one of the central issues of the 1866 congressional elections. The political results were reassuring, with Republicans gaining a two-thirds majority in both houses of Congress, providing them with the votes needed to override Andrew Johnson's presidential veto. And in July 1868 the Fourteenth Amendment came into force.[32]

The Fourteenth Amendment was not comprehensive. Radical Republicans like Sumner faulted Congress for failing to include a franchise clause in it. In 1867, three years before ratification of the Fifteenth Amendment, which would guarantee color-blind justice at polling stations, legislators passed a law prohibiting racial restraints on voting in the District of Columbia. In the absence of a constitutional provision guaranteeing the right to vote irrespective of race, only state-by-state acceptance of suffrage could lead to complete reform—an impossible scenario, particularly in the conquered South. Those who resisted granting blacks the right to vote realized that obtaining the franchise would open opportunities for blacks to serve on juries and work as government agents. Racists also merged the civic with the social, claiming that with the vote blacks would demand to repeal laws against intermarriage. In response to this line of thinking, a Connecticut author defended blacks' right to vote as an entitlement secured by the guarantee of government by consent of citizens in the Declaration of Independence. Speaking to an audience at the Milton, Massachusetts, Town Hall in 1868, Edward L. Pierce, a Treasury Department special agent during the war, told his audience that extending franchise was due to repay blacks for their bravery both on the battlefield and in civilian areas. Unless they were admitted to the franchise, Pierce continued, the world would condemn Americans for failing to live up to the powerful statement in the Declaration of Independence on universal rights.[33]

As was so often the case, the Declaration of Independence established a foundation for constitutional change. Thaddeus Stevens, the chairman of the House Committee on Appropriations, made his mission "the establishment of equal rights throughout the whole country by the recognition of the requirement of the Declaration of Independence." With victory in the Civil War, Stevens and other Republicans pushed the national vision of the Declaration rather than the states' rights perspective of Confederate leaders. Stevens regarded voting to be "one of the inalienable rights intended to be embraced in that instrument." Opponents of imposing voting requirements on states answered that the natural rights statement of the Declaration of Independence was never meant to carry over into the Constitution; furthermore, they argued, suffrage was not even an enumerated natural right. Stevens's claim was controversial even among opponents of slavery who typically distinguished natural rights, like liberty, and political rights, like voting. Others rejected such a broad interpretation of the Declaration of Independence as against the original intent of the nation's founders, who chose not to overtly condemn slavery. Stevens readily acknowledged that the nation had never been "the republic intended by the Declaration of Independence." In his view, although the founders failed to live up to their manifesto to the world, the republican "superstructure" established the foundation of black participation in electing statesmen.[34]

The South was not alone in its need for reconstruction and nationalization of civil rights principles. The Washington correspondent of the *Charleston Courier* mocked Stevens, who "has just discovered that the Declaration of Independence warrants universal suffrage, as the foundation of free institutions." Meanwhile, the legislature of Stevens's home state, Pennsylvania, refused to strike the word *white* from its voting statute. Blacks would not be granted the right to vote in that state until ratification of the Fifteenth Amendment. From a somewhat different angle, Sen. Jacob Merritt Howard of Michigan questioned Sumner's claim that the "Declaration of Independence . . . declare[s] that all men are created equal, require[s] that every created human being shall have the right of suffrage." If the right to vote was intrinsic to the Declaration—on a par with the rights to life, liberty, and the pursuit of happiness—why did Massachusetts grant only literate persons the right to vote? In Howard's state, an 1867 referendum to strike *white* from Michigan's constitutional provision on voting was defeated by 1,315 votes. The same year, a referendum to grant voting rights was also on the Ohio ballot. A supporter of it wrote, "You who have squared your faith by the Declaration of Independence, who have proclaimed to the world the equal rights of men, will not, I am sure, stultify yourselves by refusing to the colored men of Ohio that impartial suffrage to which, by the example of your action in the South, they are so fully entitled." The author counseled voters that they would bring scorn onto the state if they condemned the South for rejecting the "'immortal principle of equal rights'" while themselves denying blacks the right to vote: "In this country the only means by which a man can protect himself against the enactment of unequal or oppressive laws is to have a voice in the selection of the officers by whom they are to be [executed]." The author apparently did not convince enough voters: Ohioans defeated black suffrage by more than fifty thousand votes and passed a law the following year explicitly denying blacks suffrage.[35]

Between 1865 and 1869 enfranchisement referenda were defeated in six of eight northern states, passing only in Minnesota and Iowa. Under these circumstances, nationalization of the Declaration's principles of self-determination required an enforceable law that would protect all U.S. citizens, not merely whites.

Widespread opposition in the North and South to the Fifteenth Amendment placed Republicans at risk of losing congressional seats. The party's willingness to support a relatively unpopular cause belies the historian William Gillette's claim that the Fifteenth Amendment was "primarily" an opportunistic ploy to maintain Republican control of Congress. The number of black votes Republicans stood to gain was smaller than the number of white votes they risked to lose. The Fifteenth Amendment was ratified in 1870, and in 1874 Democrats regained a majority in the House.[36]

References to the Declaration of Independence in Congress were curiously focused on the document's consent clauses, the very ones Confederate officials had relied on to justify the states' right to rebellion. Advocates of the Fifteenth Amendment regarded the Declaration's clauses about democratic consent to be endorsements of the will of the people rather than the policies of states. There was no need for them to resolve whether voting was a natural right that could not be denied by positive law or simply a conventional right within the regulatory power of states. What mattered, in the words of Sen. Joseph Abbott, was that according to the Declaration of Independence "all political power was vested in the people." Various congressmen, among them Senator Sumner and Rep. William Loughridge, related their plea for a constitutional guarantee of voting rights to the colonists' outcry against taxation without representation. One of the Declaration's indictments against King George III was that he had imposed taxes without Americans' consent. At the end of the Civil War, Rep. Charles M. Hamilton, a lawyer and veteran, explicitly connected the right to vote to the wording of the Declaration: "Without the elective franchise; without a voice in the making of laws by which he is controlled and to which he is amenable; without an option as to who shall administer them or how they shall be administered, what insurance has a man of his life, what security for his liberties, what protection in his pursuit of happiness?" Self-government was a vacuous concept to anyone who had been denied the right to cast a ballot. The Declaration of Independence set representational government as a *sine qua non* of national purpose. Denying a large segment of the population the right to self-determination violated Americanism in the way the Declaration of Independence had defined it.[37]

With the Thirteenth Amendment having abolished slavery and the Fourteenth having granted citizenship to all people born in the United States, the country had yet to provide enforceable insurance of free citizens' right to participate in the electoral process. California Rep. William Higby believed that if this approach to government had been followed from the outset and "the principles of the Declaration of Independence been carried out both in letter and spirit at the outset, the civil strife might have been avoided." Debate on the Fifteenth Amendment made clear that bans on black voting were predicated on nothing other than the same prejudice that had entrenched slavery. Only by ratifying the Declaration of Independence into positive law, as Rep. Carman Adams Newcomb of Missouri put it, could barriers restricting black citizens' rights be dismantled. In the context of voting, a moralist explained, the Declaration's statement of equality implied that privileged classes of society could not prevent those less well off from receiving their political voices.[38]

Ratification of the Fifteenth Amendment was a tremendous constitutional achievement for the advocates of political equality. President Ulysses S. Grant extolled the Amendment in a message he wrote to Congress. Its adoption into the Constitution, Grant said, was an unequivocal repudiation of the claim that "'at the time of the Declaration of Independence the opinion was fixed and universal in the civilized portion of the white race, regarded as an axiom in morals as well as in politics, that black men had no rights which the white man was bound to respect.'" The First Ward Republican Club of Washington, D.C., celebrated the achievement on April 1, 1870, by alighting to the Executive Mansion to serenade President Grant and Vice President Schuyler Colfax. A colonel made a speech at the ensuing celebration, expressing his joy that the Amendment "looked like the realization of the Declaration of Independence." The party then made its way to Sumner's residence. Standing before the cheering crowd, the senator related how for years his "hope and object has been to see the great promise of the Declaration of Independence changed into a performance, to see that the declaration became a reality." Sumner sounded a cautionary note to the crowd, calling on them to persist as long as blacks continued to suffer from discrimination in segregated railcars, steamboats, and other modes of conveyance. The senator was thus more perceptive than others. In the elation of the moment, even the American Anti-Slavery Society disbanded.[39]

In response to the Fifteenth Amendment, states opened polling stations to many whom they had formerly excluded. An article ran in the *St. Louis Globe Democrat* in December 1876, America's centennial year, about Nicholas Paroway, a black man who died earlier that month. He was ten years old when the Declaration of Independence was signed. Known familiarly as "Old Uncle Nick," he was born a slave in Baltimore. In deference to his advanced age, when Missouri granted blacks the right to vote pursuant to the Fifteenth Amendment he was the first African American in his district granted the privilege to register. Thereafter, he voted in every election.[40]

As tremendous an achievement as the Fifteenth Amendment was, like the Fourteenth Amendment it had significant internal shortcomings. It prohibited use of only three commonly employed exclusionary categories: race, color, and prior condition of servitude. For all that, it was a valiantly flawed effort; it lacked any prohibition against use of property and literacy voting qualifications.

Several congressmen, notably Senators Willard Warner of Alabama, Oliver P. Morton of Indiana, and Henry Wilson of Massachusetts, warned that including only three criteria in the Amendment would make it possible for the South to hide behind laws seeming on the face of it to be neutral but applied so as to keep blacks from voting and holding elective office.[41] Their fears were not idle. By the early 1890s, states would begin undercutting the Fifteenth Amendment by enacting literacy, gender, and property qualifications on voting, thereby drastically diminishing the Amendment's potential to lead to the equality promised by the Declaration. Its shortcomings wound up severely weakening the Fifteenth Amendment's effectiveness.

Ratification of the Reconstruction Amendments significantly enhanced congressional authority to protect inalienable rights proclaimed a hundred years earlier in the Declaration of Independence. Though augmenting federal power, the three amendments decreased states' powers to arbitrarily discriminate against particular groups. Congress passed several statutes—including the Civil Rights Act of 1866, the Peonage Act of 1867, and the Judiciary Act of 1867—despite the opposition of the Johnson

FIGURE 10.2 *Harper's Weekly* Aug. 12, 1876, p. 657. "Declaration of Equality." (Image courtesy of the Library of Congress.)

administration. Soon, the embers of radical republicanism began dying out as the nation became more concerned with reconciliation between southern and northern states rather than uplifting underprivileged groups. The Ku Klux Klan and the White League relied on violence to sustain a "white man's government."

Senator Sumner spearheaded one of the most important federal efforts of the 1870s to add to the civil rights legacy of Reconstruction. Seeking to thwart the citizenship and equal protection clauses of the Fourteenth Amendment, some businesses segregated patrons by race. Newspaper and congressional records were replete with narratives of blacks being denied equal access to musical halls, train cars, soda water, hotels, theaters, and schools.

Sumner weathered violent opposition before the Civil War and afterward found himself in the seat of power. Few had his sustained energy for achieving equal rights. After the Civil War, he was among a group of white abolitionists who continued the struggle to end unequal treatment of blacks.[42] His efforts to pass a desegregation bill paid off only after his untimely death. Sumner's bill aimed to "secure equal rights in railroads, steamboats, public conveyances, hotels, licensed theaters, houses of public entertainment, common schools and institutions of learning authorized by law, church institutions, and cemetery associations." Initial failure led him to redouble his efforts, and he again offered the bill in much the same form.

In an 1872 letter to the Colored National Convention, Sumner wrote of Congress's obligation to persistently fight injustices; he came to realize that the "establishment of equal suffrage" was a good start but not enough. He advised convention participants to focus their efforts on obtaining equal treatment from any institutions created by law, including licensed businesses. Their best chance at success would be to demand that government abide by the principles and promises of the Declaration of Independence.[43]

Sumner also relied on the foundational document in his Senate speeches to influence the legislative agenda. To the end of his life, he insisted "that the Declaration is of equal and coordinate authority with the Constitution itself." He believed any references to human rights in the Constitution "invoke at once the great truths of the Declaration as the absolute guide in determining their meaning." Sumner explained this by likening the Constitution to a machine: "The Declaration supplies the principles giving character and motion to the machine.... The powers under the Constitution are no more than the hand to the body; the Declaration is the very soul itself." Sumner's core mission was to convince Congress to rely on the Reconstruction Amendments' enforcement powers to pass a desegregation statute. If Sumner was correct, public officials—judges, administrators, legislators—would be obligated to explain their human rights policies on the basis of core commitments to liberty and justice that appeared in the Declaration of Independence.[44]

In response to Sumner's claims about the interpretive value of the Declaration of Independence, Senator Morrill, a Republican from Maine, reminded him that Congress's oath was to the Constitution, not the Declaration. A senator from Wisconsin believed that where there is any conflict between the two, policy makers were obligated to follow the Constitution.[45] The significance of this rather theoretical debate concerned evolving understanding about the scope of the newly created congressional powers to pass civil rights legislation. On its face, the Equal Protection Clause of the Constitution could be understood to tolerate separate but equal public accommodations. On the other hand, if the Declaration of Independence was intrinsic to constitutional interpretation, then the manifesto's unitary statement about the human species seemed to allow Congress to prohibit segregation of the races in places operating under a publicly issued license.

On his deathbed, shortly before he expired, Sumner asked a close friend, Massachusetts Rep. Ebenezer R. Hoar, to "take care of the Civil Rights Bill."[46] The election of 1874 demonstrated that, for the time being, the Republicans had gone as far as they could. Contrary to William Gillette's suggestion that they were acting out of self-interest by standing up for the principle of black suffrage,[47] Republicans lost popular support by pursuing civil rights reform. Far more voters turned against them, many of them motivated by prejudice against black voters, than were gained by pressing for black suffrage. That year Republicans lost an astonishing 96 House seats, with Democrats winning 182 seats to the Republicans' 103. Republicans realized they needed to pass the law before the Democrats took control of Congress. The lame-duck Congress, composed of many of the members who lost the election, enacted the Civil Rights Act in 1875, creating a federal cause of action against segregation.

The first legal action under the statute appears to have arisen in Trenton, New Jersey, against a proprietor who refused to allow two black men into his pool hall. The owner's hotel was also in the same building. The judge dismissed the complaint, finding the proprietor could discriminate against anyone he didn't want to accept as a patron. This negative outcome foretold much greater problems to come. Despite the Reconstruction Amendments' clear mandate to augment federal powers over civil rights, the Supreme Court was determined to prevent the drastic change to federalism that the Constitution envisioned. In 1883, the Court decided the Civil Rights Act of 1875 was unconstitutional. Commenting on the opinion, known as the *Civil Rights Cases*, the aging civil rights leader Frederick Douglass asserted that "the decision is contrary to the Declaration of Independence." His comment indicated a belief in the relevance of the older document's doctrine even after enactment of the Reconstruction Amendments. The Court, however, did not so much as mention the Declaration in its opinion, making clear that the justices rejected Douglass's and Sumner's heuristics.

Because of the Court's narrow interpretation, desegregation was put on hold until 1954. The Court's stilted interpretation left activists almost unable to turn to the Constitution to support a liberal understanding of liberty and equal citizenship. The Declaration of Independence remained the bedrock of American politics, however, and it provided social movements with a principled anchor throughout the Gilded Age.[48]

11

RACIAL TENSIONS

Between May and October 1876, the Declaration of Independence was displayed at the Centennial National Exposition. The document continued to have an iconic mystique, although much of the actual parchment had become so faded as to be illegible. In August of the same year, Congress charged a commission, consisting of the secretary of the interior, the secretary of the Smithsonian Institution, and the librarian of Congress, to restore the manuscript. The committee seems to have done little, other than moving it the following year from the Patent Office to the State Department. There the ink became further eroded because the document was displayed in a room where patrons were permitted to smoke and warm themselves by the glow of a fireplace. As of 1881, there was talk of restoration but almost paralyzing uncertainty about how that could be carried out.[1]

Nostalgia surrounded the charter. Almost all the signatures on it were illegible, but there were other ways of acquiring them. In 1877, autograph hawkers sold Benjamin Franklin's signature for $14, Caesar Rodney's for $9.50, John Hancock's for $10. The signature of John Adams sold for $8 at an 1879 auction. There were also buyers in England, with Queen Victoria reported to have one of the finest collections of the Declaration signers' autographs.[2]

FIGURE 11.1 *Harper's Weekly*, July 15, 1876, p. 573. "Reading the Declaration of Independence by John Nixon, from the steps of Independence Hall, Philadelphia, July 8, 1776." Drawn by E. A. Abbey. (Image courtesy of the Library of Congress.)

The desk on which Jefferson wrote the Declaration of Independence was on display at the Music Hall of Boston on the Fourth of July, 1876. It too came to symbolize the national values of the document that a century before had been born upon it. Jefferson designed the desk himself, and it was built by a Philadelphia cabinetmaker with whom he lodged in 1776 on his arrival in the city for the Continental Congress. In 1825, Jefferson gave the desk as a wedding gift to Joseph Coolidge of Boston, who married Jefferson's granddaughter. Years later, Coolidge bequeathed it to his children. They then presented it to President Rutherford B. Hayes as a gift to the United States.[3]

It was easy enough to laud the Declaration's signers. Of greater moment was the need to live up to its dictates. Speaking at a Civil War veterans' reunion in 1875, Sen. Oliver Morton of Indiana happily proclaimed, "We are now a united country, and the great doctrines of the declaration of independence . . . are now in operation." Despite this rosy picture, the document's symbolic value did not change the fact, as William Lloyd Garrison put it, that although constitutional amendments had nominally bestowed on blacks equal privileges as citizens, the "Declaration of Independence still" had yet "to be carried out" in reality. Garrison also denounced the states for granting women less political power than the British had given the colonists.

When President Hayes withdrew federal troops from the South as part of the Compromise of 1877, violence flared against freed blacks. In the election of 1878, because of racial violence and outright fraud throughout the South—especially in South Carolina, Alabama, and Louisiana—Republicans won only 62 of the 294 Southern counties with black majorities. An editorial in a New Hampshire newspaper bemoaned Hayes's presidency, asserting that he had led the Republican Party away from its "standard," which was planted "on the doctrine of the Declaration of Independence," with its claims of human progress through the "Brotherhood and Equality of Man." For the sake of electoral victory, wrote an author in a Maine newspaper, Hayes violated the party's avowed commitment for "the spirit and letter of the Declaration of Independence ... [to] pervade in the South." Instead, withdrawal of the troops crushed black voters, renewing the terrorist attacks of "county murderers and night raiders and regulators." Representatives of the Colored People's Convention at Atlanta demanded that state courts follow "the truths enunciated by Jefferson in his immortal declaration of independence," which "while founded on theory, have been made literally true" by the Reconstruction Amendments to the Constitution. The promises of the Declaration of Independence could scarcely be thought fulfilled so long as judges doled out "unmerciful punishment" by leasing out black prisoners to labor on plantations while failing to punish white marauders.[4]

The North's zeal for the promises of the Declaration of Independence, which was so common at the time of the Civil War and for several years thereafter, seemed to fade from memory. At soldiers' reunions politicians proclaimed, "the South w[as] just as honest as we were in making the fight." Mention of the Declaration of Independence at these sentimentalized events was typically made to show the need for sectional unity rather than to shame those who remained persistently arbitrary in their treatment of blacks.[5]

President Grant's reassurances to the contrary, the Fifteenth Amendment did not eliminate the view "that the Declaration of Independence reads 'All "white" men were created equal.'" Even before the Supreme Court struck the Civil Rights Act of 1875, segregation flourished. A writer from San Jose, California, decried an 1878 state law requiring black and Indian children to be segregated from white students belying the claim that with Reconstruction "the declaration of independence [had been] vindicated; and the colored children" would be treated like "anybody's children." The leading black educator, Booker T. Washington, started the most famous segregated vocational school, the Tuskegee Institute, on Independence Day 1881. Washington counseled patience rather than an active return to the values of the Declaration of Independence. Similarly, a black member of the Massachusetts state legislature, Ron Julius C. Chappelle, who rested his faith on the rights "forcibly demanded in the Declaration of Independence more than a century ago," counseled patience rather than immediate confrontation. At the time, Chappelle could not have known that in the 1880s Jim Crow was becoming more strident and would persist into the midtwentieth century.[6]

Outrages were committed by businesses as well as individuals. A black patron indignantly questioned executives of a steamship running between New York and Richmond, Virginia, "How in the name of heaven can you and your people—in the face of those immortal words of the Declaration...treat the colored people so badly" as to prevent them from playing a piano and forcing them to eat after white patrons. Frederick Douglass rejected the claim that blacks had caused hardships for themselves. The question was not whether blacks as a whole should change but "whether the American people...have virtue enough in them to adjust the action of the Nation to the fundamental principles of the Declaration of Independence and the Constitution of the United States."[7]

Even though the Fifteenth Amendment technically protected the right of blacks to vote in elections, ratification proved to be insufficient. In 1869, Joseph H. Rainey of South Carolina became the first African American to serve in the U.S. House of Representatives. Between 1869 and 1875, sixteen blacks represented seven southern states in Congress. After Reconstruction, however, only six blacks held congressional offices. The situation was similar in state legislatures. To give just one example, between 1867 and 1869 115 blacks were state legislators in Mississippi, by 1876 16 blacks served in that capacity, and between 1896 and 1965 there were no black Mississippi congressmen. White supremacists found indirect ways to get around the Fifteenth Amendment's express provisions and would continue to do so until the federal government stepped in to enforce it in the late twentieth century.

After President Hayes withdrew federal troops from the South, violence and fraud prevented so many blacks from voting that he admitted the "experiment" of entrusting reform to the former Confederate states "was a failure."[8] Arguments for keeping to the ideals of the Declaration of Independence, which influenced the drafting of the Fifteenth Amendment, were muted as southern states passed legislation meant to deter blacks and illiterate whites from voting. For good reason, newspapers warned that "equal Rights, as promulgated by the Declaration of Independence, and Manhood Suffrage, as attempted to be established by the 15th amendment, are in danger of being permanently destroyed in the South." When the U.S. Supreme Court was called upon to uphold the criminal convictions of several people for murdering blacks who had peacefully assembled at a political rally, it refused to do so. In *United States v. Cruikshank*, the Supreme Court recognized:

> The rights of life and personal liberty are natural rights of man. "To secure these rights," says the Declaration of Independence, "governments are instituted among men, deriving their just powers from the consent of the governed." The very highest duty of the States, when they entered into the Union under the Constitution, was to protect all persons within their boundaries in the enjoyment of these "unalienable rights with which they were endowed by their Creator."

Rather than identifying voting as one of the unalienable rights of citizens, however, the Court dismissed the convictions on technical grounds, refusing to rule on the substance of the case.[9]

Even in the age of reconciliation between the South and North, some columnists remained steadfast in the aspirations of Reconstruction. The *Inter Ocean*, a Chicago paper with obvious Republican sentiments, claimed that southern tyranny against black voters demonstrated its continued failure to embrace "the doctrine of the Declaration of Independence." In a column titled "Cry for Change," an author pointed out that by preventing the colored majority from voting, the white minority was undermining popular rule. And in fact, in Mississippi, South Carolina, and Louisiana, where disfranchisement was rampant, blacks were the majority of the population in 1880. These "Southern methods," the lamentation went on to say, were wrong according to "our Constitution and the Declaration of Independence." That year one of the participants of an Albany (New York) gathering of colored citizens read the Declaration of Independence and solicited the Democratic and Republican parties to henceforth treat black voters as free citizens capable, like any others, of selecting candidates. The black vote was important enough for Republican candidates to remind those potential voters that the party had "emancipated four millions of slaves, and gave them the right to 'life, liberty, and the pursuit of happiness' which the Declaration of Independence pronounced to be the inalienable right of all mankind." Others counseled the Republicans to take the manifesto of equality seriously by giving more blacks an opportunity to run for political office, rather than exploiting them for their votes without advancing their political interests.[10]

As sectional reconciliation became firmly entrenched in the national mind-set, the Declaration of Independence began to go out of vogue in matters of racial politics. In the 1890s, Northern Democrats supported their southern counterparts' overt decision to shut out white illiterates and all black voters. There still were voices that refused to drop the effort to govern with the consent of all the people, no matter whether they were of African, Polish, Chinese, or English descent.[11]

The *New Mississippian* exemplified how some authors nostalgically mentioned the Declaration of Independence without demonstrating any affinity for its principles. A columnist praised Sen. James Z. George's effort to pass a state law "in order that white supremacy may be maintained." George, a former Confederate brigadier general, declared disfranchisement to be second in importance only to the initial push to draft the Declaration of Independence. Unsurprisingly, he made no effort to parse the document's clauses. Mississippi's constitution of 1890 codified several disfranchisement devices, including a residency requirement that worked against migrant farmers and sharecroppers, most of whom were blacks. In addition to the literacy requirement, the constitution enabled registrars to "practice blatant discrimination against Negroes who seek to register by asking spurious and improper questions and requiring higher standards of Negroes than whites." The *Jackson Clarion-Ledger* remarked that a black man could vote in Mississippi "provided he has sense enough to 'read or understand

FIGURE 11.2 *Frank Leslie's Illustrated Newspaper*, July 22, 1876 (no. 1,086, vol. 42), cover/p. 1. "July 4th 1876—The Centennial Celebration in Philadelphia, Richard Henry Lee of Virginia, Reading the Declaration of Independence." (Image courtesy of the Library of Congress.)

the Constitution,' translate Hebrew, parse a little Greek or Latin, square a circle and solve a few other mathematical problems." The 1890 state constitution disproportionately harmed black taxpayers' ability to participate in politics: there were about 190,000 black voters in Mississippi the year the constitution passed, but only 9,000 blacks were on its voting rolls for the 1892 election. References to the Declaration in this process seem to have been made to drum up patriotism while trampling its core principles.[12]

In *Williams v. Mississippi*, the Supreme Court legitimized the new restraints on voting privileges. The Court's opinion energized the disfranchisement movement, which realized that neutral statutory provisions could be used to get around Fifteenth Amendment requirements. In 1890 South Carolina Governor-elect Benjamin "Pitchfork Ben" R. Tillman began pushing for disfranchisement of black voters in South Carolina. Tillman promised his Farmers' Alliance and Democratic voter base the "triumph of Democracy and white supremacy over mongrelism and anarchy, of civilization over barbarism." Five years later he led the state's constitutional convention to "disfranchise as many [Negroes] as we could," as he later merrily reported to the U.S. Senate. Arkansas and Georgia followed suit in adopting white primaries to bolster the Democratic party and prevent blacks from winning political office. To the supporters of disfranchisement, the nation's values applied to whites alone: "While the fathers of our nation, in the Declaration of Independence, kept always before them the noble political ideal of the eighteenth century as the ultimate goal of their hopes," wrote a Northern supporter, "they yet tempered it with sturdy Anglo-Saxon common sense." A rising star in Alabama, Congressman Oscar W. Underwood, called for repeal of the Fifteenth Amendment. He proclaimed his certainty that the author of the Declaration of Independence would have never approved of that Amendment since Thomas Jefferson was a proud slaveholder.[13]

The repeal movement failed, and by the early 1900s all the ex-confederate states were relying on registrars to accept eligible white voters' answers to literacy tests but to reject those of eligible blacks. Former Georgia Congressman William H. Fleming told a 1905 gathering of University of Georgia alumni that the entire system of disfranchisement was built on "fraudulent administration of the law." It was impossible to change the Declaration's phrasing "all men are created Equal," so he explained that "white supremacy" resorted to maladministration to keep citizens and taxpayers from casting ballots.[14]

The voting booth was only one of the places where blacks found overt discrimination. After 1883, when the Supreme Court struck down the Civil Rights Act of 1875 with its provisions punishing business owners who segregated customers by race, states began formalizing what had been private discrimination. From the late 1880s into the late 1890s, Florida, Mississippi, Texas, Louisiana, Alabama, Arkansas, Georgia, Tennessee, Kentucky, the Carolinas, and Virginia legalized segregation. Segregation piggybacked on disfranchisement. With the aid of the Supreme Court, in cases such as *Plessy v. Ferguson,* which found that segregation did not violate the Fourteenth Amendment's Equal Protection Clause, the South swept back the waves of the sea. With blacks unable to enjoy public places on a par with whites, many of the safeguards of Reconstruction seemed like distant memories. After the Court narrowed the scope of the Fourteenth Amendment's protections, it could still be argued that "the Negroes of this country, by the Declaration of Independence, which is greater and broader than the Constitution, are equal to the whites," but little would come of it. Even under these circumstances—with setback piling upon setback, with blacks being shot and arrested for publicly announcing that they "had rights...which white men were bound to respect"—all was not hopeless. The Declaration inspired the conviction that the tide of "steady and triumphant progress" would wash "away barrier after barrier until there shall not be left one stone upon another between men of whatever race or color and their inalienable rights." But reality did not match this hope, as patrons of railcars, taverns, opera houses, theaters, housing, and a score of other facilities were divided by race.[15]

The Declaration of Independence was still a statement of protest, but few policy makers in this era took its assertions of human rights to heart. A columnist from Kansas wrote of the daily discussions in newspapers, poems, and speeches regarding discrimination against blacks, "The real question, the all-commanding question is whether American justice, American liberty, American civilization, American law and American Christianity can be made to include and protect alike all American citizens." The cure to the existing evil, as he saw it, was to live up to the dignity of the "sublime...truth and liberty" announced in the Declaration of Independence by seeking "the advancement of the Negro race." Bishop Alexander Walter of Boston's African Methodist Episcopal Church asserted that the guarantees of the Declaration remained unfulfilled as long as lynch mobs could murder, states could withhold ballots and political offices, and licensed businesses could shut their doors because of race. In the half-century following ratification of the Reconstruction Amendments, which had seemed to incorporate the Declaration of Independence into the Constitution, the states successfully undermined progress.[16]

Unable to achieve the promises of the Declaration of Independence through legal reform, many blacks turned to social groups seeking their uplift and equality. The Niagara Movement—directed by such visionaries as W.E.B. Du Bois, Clement G. Morgan, and Lafayette M. Hershaw—was formed in 1905 to oppose Booker T. Washington's nonconfrontational approach to racial uplift. The Niagara group set the stage for civil rights activism during the twentieth century. Its Declaration of Principles, styled by the authors as a Negro Declaration of Independence, demanded equal education and civil rights, repeal of Jim Crow laws, freedom of speech, equal treatment in courts, and an end to racial discrimination.[17]

Du Bois left the organization in 1909 to help found the multiracial National Association for the Advancement of Colored People. In the year of the organization's founding, the eighth edition of Du Bois's influential book *The Souls of Black Folk* was published; in it he wrote, "there are to-day no truer exponent of the pure human spirit of the Declaration than the American Negroes." He meant that blacks were intrinsic to culture in the United States; they were not outsiders but active interpreters of the Declaration's statement of inalienable rights.

Du Bois's assertive doctrine of self-help distinguished him from Booker T. Washington, who did not openly attack the color line but worked instead for separate racial uplift. For those whites who were willing to accept blacks' vocational progress but not their equality as citizens, it was Washington who was the "exponent of a negro declaration of independence." For others, including the NAACP's founding members, notably the philosopher Henry Moskowitz and settlement worker Mary White Ovington, only direct political and social action would translate the promises of the Declaration of Independence into equal civic status for blacks. The Rev. Harry P. Dewey of the Church of Pilgrims in Brooklyn warned that in the South and the North "there was a menace in continuing to withhold from the negro political and industrial equality" while professing the statements in the Declaration of Independence "that all men are created free and equal." He warned "that the black man was waking up from the lethargy imposed upon him by years of servitude, and was preparing to assert himself."[18]

Direct action was much needed, as passivity had encouraged segregation. Progressivism showed few positive effects on the status of ordinary blacks. Though they were able to organize in labor, women's, and suffrage organizations, their efforts remained outside the white mainstream. Kelly Miller, a professor of sociology at Howard University, condemned states that forced blacks, even those who were decorated war veterans, to ride in Jim Crow railcars. He, like the NAACP, demanded "decisive action" to bring "the American body politic" to "her ancient moorings, the Declaration of Independence, the Gettysburg Address of Lincoln, and the Farewell of Old John Brown on the scaffold." Earlier in this book, I discussed the extent to which Lincoln and John Brown relied on the Declaration as the anchor for the American ethos. To the members of the NAACP, merely allowing blacks to learn skills was inadequate in making up for the white man's burden of righting past wrongs. Kidnapping blacks from Africa and bringing them on slave ships to work under forced conditions, without so much as the comfort of a family, created a national obligation to vindicate past injustices. As a San Jose columnist reminded readers on the fifty-fifth anniversary of the Emancipation Proclamation, "The declaration of independence left us the task of establishing a genuine democracy" by "freeing the negro socially and economically, as well as politically." This required providing fair educational opportunity and protecting universal suffrage against subtle forms of disfranchisement.[19]

The drive to separate blacks from white society was interwoven with political and civil exclusion. John J. McMahan, one of the more outspoken supporters of black disfranchisement in South Carolina, called for repeal of the Fourteenth and Fifteenth Amendments. In 1914, he condemned the state constitution adopted during Reconstruction, asserting that it "contained in strongest terms the substance of all the war amendments, with still additional dogmas of equality, copied from the declaration of independence." In his view, the amendments and the Declaration usurped states' authority to discriminate between groups of citizens. Members of Congress who supported repeal of the Fifteenth Amendment sought the ultimate elimination of African Americans from government service.[20]

Southern supporters of popular governance did not as a rule espouse social equality. To the contrary, after the Supreme Court rendered its opinion in *Williams v. Mississippi*, which upheld the constitutionality of voting restrictions primarily meant to stop blacks from casting ballots, similar racially motivated bars to suffrage appeared throughout the South. By 1892, the number of eligible black voters in Mississippi had been reduced to 8,615 from 190,000 eligible in 1890. In one representative county, with a population of 11,700 blacks in 1900, only 25 or 30 votes were cast in 1908, with the rest disqualified on the basis of educational level; another county had only 175 black registered voters out of a population of 30,000 African Americans. Although disfranchisement was primarily racial, it also had classist components, with the elites seeking to exclude anyone they thought to be inadequately literate. In a Mississippi county with 8,000 whites and 12,000 blacks, the only qualified voters were 400 whites and 30 blacks. State disfranchisement made its way into Louisiana in 1898, Alabama in 1901, North Carolina and Virginia in 1902, Georgia in 1908, and Oklahoma in 1910.[21]

A black physician, Charles V. Roman, writing shortly after Teddy Roosevelt's Progressive Party defeat in the 1912 election, expected "a reasonable interpretation of the Declaration of Independence" to include their consent to governance. He understood this to be intrinsically important to blacks' "right to live, labor, and laugh," which "is the heritage of all men." Rather than achieving that vision, blacks encountered a redeemed South where freedoms achieved during Reconstruction were displaced by Jim Crow laws. Magazine editor Samuel Danziger found the Declaration of Independence to "furnish an infallible test for every important public measure." The doctrine of human equality, he wrote in 1915, "cannot be safely undergone by any of the laws or policies conferring privileges [and] limiting suffrage." This argument was a logical construction of the Declaration, but it made no headway against politicians bent on preventing black citizens from voting and enjoying the privileges of citizenship on an equal footing.[22]

Jim Crow laws and racist customs constantly reminded blacks of the painful period of slavery and their degraded citizenship. The importance of organizations such as the NAACP lay in their determination that "the Negro will make himself felt" until the nation would "realize and recognize the full meaning of the Declaration of Independence and give the Negro as equal an opportunity as the man that has a white skin." The increasing activism came as a response to the perception that "the growth of lawlessness" of lynching "is stimulated through the spirit of jimcrowism whose common source was American Slavery." Using parasitic lawlessness to exclude the race from politics, wrote a correspondent to the black daily newspaper *The Chicago Defender*, threatened blacks' ability to enjoy the statements of human rights in the Declaration of Independence. The same newspaper published a letter by M. Marion Davis to the editor disparaging "this so-called land of liberty." Though the Declaration of Independence proclaimed that "all men are created equal," lynch mobs continued to brutalize black citizens, drive them from their homes, and destroy their property.[23]

12

ADVANCING WOMEN'S CAUSES

CHANGES TO THE RACIAL STATUS QUO OCCURRED ALONGSIDE AN evolving understanding of women's rights. As they had from the inception of the women's rights movement, during the early decades of the nineteenth century activists of the Gilded Age and Progressive Era often looked to the Declaration of Independence to buttress their political message. Although the Reconstruction Amendments provided the national government with added power to make the Declaration's promise of self-government a reality, after the Civil War women's political rights trailed far behind men's.

The Fifteenth Amendment failed to address the central issue of the women's rights movement. Writing during the tumult of the Civil War, Harriot K. Hunt openly described the hypocrisy of battling for a representative government while excluding taxpayers from the voting roles. Had the principle of the Declaration of Independence been "recognized in its essence," she wrote in a letter to the Boston tax assessor, "sex alone could not have monopolized the right of suffrage." Hunt denounced the "shams, cheats, [and] falsities" that embedded the word *male* into the statute books. The "latent principles of the Declaration of Independence," she continued, the "moral and intellectual growth" of the American people required the hugely important subject of suffrage to be understood without the trappings of sex.[1]

Just as the American colonists had been told to trust Parliament to care for their political interests, so too women were asked to trust the beneficence of an all-male Congress. Section two of the Fourteenth Amendment, which dealt with voting privileges, was the first instance of the word *male* being used in the Constitution. The moralist writer Lucinda B. Chandler found that "the second article of the fourteenth amendment violates the letter and spirit of the Declaration of Independence." Chandler pointed out that even a mother who urged her sons to fight for the Union was forbidden from participating in national politics. Elizabeth Cady Stanton warned her cousin (a conductor of the underground railroad), Gerrit Smith, that the second section could "take us a century at least to get it out." A petition drive gathered about ten thousand signatures to keep "male" out of the constitution, but to no avail. Susan B. Anthony demanded that the decision be reconsidered because enfranchising black men alone meant that women were "left outside with lunatics, idiots and criminals."[2]

Unable to turn to the Constitution even in its amended form, feminists, like other progressive activists throughout U.S. history, relied on the Declaration of Independence to develop the parameters of their rhetoric. In the document, they found an organic principle of natural rights to fair treatment. The syllogism was simple, as Lucy Stone put it: men and women are humans, with a common origin and destiny; according to the Declaration's statement of equality "every right which inheres in one human being must inhere in all"; "the human right to life, liberty and the pursuit of happiness implies the right to protect life, liberty and the pursuit of happiness"; and protection of that right could be secured only through equal suffrage. Parker Pillsbury, like Thaddeus Stevens before him, proclaimed that the right to vote "for rulers is a natural, inalienable, irrepealable, inextinguishable right." The promises of the Declaration of Independence would be no more than "glittering generalities," he went on to say, unless women could participate in developing policies for the support and enrichment of life. Another author, the Unitarian minister Thomas Wentworth Higginson, who like Pillsbury had advocated on behalf of women's rights for two decades, believed the "simple principles of the Declaration of Independence" to be as self-evident as axioms of geometry: "If the axioms mean anything for men, they mean something for women." Laws throughout the whole country were to be based on those simple principles, "they stating the theory of our government, while the Constitution itself only puts into organic shape the application."[3]

Suffrage was both a means and an end because it was intrinsic to citizenship while also instrumental to enjoying life, liberty, and the pursuit of happiness. It was essential for enjoying the right to cultivate and use lands, erect homes, labor, purchase products, engage in business, obtain an education, participate in public works, and secure equal pay for equal work. Not everyone agreed to the expediency of addressing these issues at once, fearing that tackling them simultaneously would cause the failure of them all.[4]

At the thirty-second anniversary of the American Anti-Slavery Society, Wendell Phillips told an assembly that one question would need to be tackled at a time: "This hour belongs to the Negro." Phillips hoped "in time to be as bold as Stuart Mill and add to that last clause 'sex.'" Stanton curtly replied to Phillips by letter, "May I ask…just one question based on the apparent opposition in which you place the negro and woman. My question is this: Do you believe the African race is composed entirely of males?" Anthony, in her piquant style, writing in her short-lived but influential newspaper *The Revolution*, demanded that the hour of change benefit everyone. Women needed the vote for the same reason the colonists asserted the right to national independence: to prevent government from acting against the interests of unrepresented segments of the population.[5]

The year after Congress passed the Fourteenth Amendment on to the states for ratification, such influential men as Benjamin Wade, Wendell Phillips, Henry Ward Beecher, Gerrit Smith, William Sprague, and Theodore Tilton petitioned Congress to "apply the principles of the Declaration [of Independence] to women" by allowing them to vote. Suffrage was the only recognized form of consent in a republican government. They pointed out that a woman's acquiescence to laws did not by itself indicate her consent to them because she was prohibited from molding policies. This group, along with other supporters such as William I. Bowditch, interpreted the Declaration of Independence to guarantee full participation of citizens, irrespective of gender. From this view, men and women were parties to the social contract. Bowditch considered it tyrannical to govern taxpaying women, many of whom were qualified to hold office, without the consent that the Declaration of Independence guaranteed to them. An author in Colorado put the argument in humanistic terms. Just as the franchise helped men "maintain their 'unalienable right to life, liberty, and the pursuit of happiness,' it will aid women, unless it can be proved that life and liberty are modified by sex, and that the only happiness to be pursued by women is the happiness of making men happy."[6]

The movement split sharply over whether women's rights should follow efforts to obtain civil rights for blacks. The National Woman Suffrage Association (NWSA) was organized to pursue women's suffrage without any crossover activities on behalf of other disempowered groups. The organizers, Anthony and Stanton, were so single-minded that they turned to a known racist, George Train, to finance their publishing efforts. For abolitionists it was unequivocally wrong for the NWSA to receive funding from a man who mocked the nation's Declaration of Independence for its rejection of the presumed natural and moral gradations among human races. Anthony refused to end her association with Train even after William Lloyd Garrison and other allies asked her to desist.[7] Garrison became an editor of an alternative newspaper, *The Woman's Journal*, on behalf of the second major faction, the American Woman Suffrage Association (AWSA). It was led by Lucy Stone, who continued working to achieve black equality along with woman's rights.

Both groups primarily focused their efforts on suffrage. The late 1860s were also a time when state organizations began efforts that would stretch into the early twentieth century, when a constitutional amendment would be added securing a woman's right to vote. The collective message of suffragists, as it was voiced in 1869 by the Missouri Woman's Suffrage Association, was that "the man...who believes in that declaration cannot justly deny to women the right to suffrage" because they were taxpaying citizens who were entitled to the joint control of government. Bowditch of Massachusetts, a former conductor of the Underground Railroad, similarly quoted from the Declaration of Independence to show that governance without consent of women taxpayers was "absolute tyranny." In New Jersey, where women had been disfranchised since 1807, Stone encouraged the state's legislature at a hearing to stay fast to "the Immortal Declaration." Though the document had inspired people the "wide world round," injustice against women persisted at the state ballot box.[8]

Despite these ideals, it would take decades—and in some places, especially the South, women could not vote until ratification of the Nineteenth Amendment. Majorities in western territories were the first to extend suffrage to women. The Women's Convention in Dayton, Ohio, took special notice that the Wyoming Territory had granted women the right to vote in 1869. Legislators there, said Tracy Cutler in her presidential address to assembled delegates, had fulfilled the doctrine of the Declaration of Independence. She hoped "the little twig which Wyoming has shot up on the Rocky Mountains will cover the whole land!" In February of the following year, Stone called on participants at a women's convention in Columbus to petition the Ohio legislature for suffrage. Women's human right "to life, liberty and the pursuit of happiness implies the right" to be politically active in order to protect those interests, she said. Ohio suffragettes were still too disorganized in 1870, the year of the Fifteenth Amendment's ratification, with no fewer than thirty-one local women's suffrage organizations throughout the state. That year the Utah territory enfranchised women, but the U.S. Congress disfranchised them seventeen years later through the Edmunds-Tucker Law, which prohibited women from voting in all territorial elections.[9]

Unlike those who considered the humanistic principles of the Declaration to be empty generalities, the women's suffrage movement from the time of the 1848 Seneca Convention through the Gilded Age developed the view that the self-evidence of human equality implied the symmetry of civil responsibilities and entitlements. They argued that "even-handed justice, a fair application of the principles of the Declaration of Independence," dictated giving women the vote in such states as Vermont and Massachusetts, where they had to pay taxes and were subject to criminal penalties for malfeasance.[10]

In the 1870s, several women openly challenged voting laws. Virginia Minor filed a law suit when an election official in St. Louis refused to register her. She lost at the Supreme Court level in *Minor v. Happerset*, which decided that voting is not a privilege of citizenship. Rather than initiating a cause of action, Susan Anthony convinced an election official to allow her to cast a ballot and was subsequently arrested. She denied the legitimacy of the New York law, wishing that "the doctrines of the Declaration of Independence" and human equality would extend to "women, our mothers, our wives, our sisters, and our daughters." In Cincinnati, Phoebe Phillips presented herself at the tenth ward polling station. When an election judge told her the Constitution did not provide her with any legal ground against local law, Phillips told him it was the Declaration of

Independence that was enough to provide her with a legally recognizable claim to the franchise.[11]

The 1876 centennial of the Declaration of Independence was an opportune moment for a second declaration of independence, condemning the bondage of inequality and demanding that women be placed on par with men both politically and socially. Carrie Chapman Catt, a historian of women's suffrage and one of its foremost organizers in the early twentieth century, remembered the centennial in a speech she delivered almost six decades after the event. Speaking in Chicago at the International Congress of Women, she recalled how with the celebrations of one hundred independent years "the pride of men mounted higher and higher, but the humiliation of women sunk lower and lower." Though Philadelphia prided itself as the crib of freedom, the laws of Pennsylvania prohibited a married woman from entering into a contract without her husband's confirmation of the agreement.

Determined to have their voices heard, Susan B. Anthony and four other women pressed their way to the vice president of the United States, who was attending a July 4 exposition in Independence Square. Arriving at the platform, with the meeting hushed, Anthony handed the (reportedly "deathly pale") vice president a copy of the Declaration of Rights of the Women Citizens of the United States. The delegation then made its way to the First Unitarian Church of Philadelphia. Eighty-four-year-old Lucretia Mott presided over the five-hour meeting. City officials' refusal to grant them permission to participate in the official Independence Day celebration made this convention necessary. Elizabeth Cady Stanton, one of the dozen or so speakers, read the woman's declaration to the engaged gathering. The extensive statement leaned strongly on the ideology of the Declaration of Independence. The 1876 document expressed the NWSA's faith in "the natural rights of each individual," and "the exact equality of these rights."[12]

In an age when paternalism was the norm throughout society, women's leagues often sought to prove the value of adding the female's unique moral consciousness to politics. This line of argument claimed that only women could reliably champion laws for vocational training, education of disabled children, libraries, school sanitation and lunches, clean milk, and temperance. Being "not nearly as much contaminated by vicious habits and corrupting influences as men," so the argument went, women would not tolerate vice. According to this reasoning, if practical effect were given to the statement in the Declaration of Independence that government derives its power from the consent of all the people, then women would lobby to end such vices as alcoholism and prostitution.[13]

Nothing so clearly connected women's suffragists to the cause of the Declaration's framers as the campaign against taxation without representation. Without the right to vote, a husband could tyrannize his wife as King George III had tyrannized the colonists. From one perspective, the Constitution was a hurdle and the Declaration's statement of universal suffrage provided the alternative source of authority. The Fourteenth Amendment expressly referred to voters as "male" and the Fifteenth Amendment did not list "sex" among the protected voting categories. In their effort to interpret the Fourteenth Amendment's right to citizenship or the Fifteenth Amendment's guarantee of voting rights, women's suffrage advocates turned to the statement in the Declaration that all people, irrespective of gender, have an inalienable right to participate in creating government and its policies. Such a reading ran against the historical record of those amendments, which only two decades before had specifically been passed to end discrimination against blacks. Turning instead to the Declaration of Independence demonstrated how that document could be incorporated into progressive constitutional interpretation. In some cases, as in the writings of two politically influential sisters, the "right of a voice in the conduct of the government" was said to be inherent according to the "true theory" set down by the Declaration. The Constitution could neither grant nor withdraw that inherent ability for self-protection against oppression.[14]

The most profound statements were those that explained how the Declaration's doctrine of government by consent was linked to suffrage. The Fourteenth Amendment's right to life and liberty, as Lucinda R. Chandler explained in 1880 to the Margaret Fuller Society in Chicago, was empty "without a right to a voice in the government institutions." As convincing as her statements were on their face, putting them in the context of "the first and great principle of the Declaration of Independence" added gravity to the society's social and political demand for advancing American civilization. It was a refrain as old as the nation itself, but given new life in the milieu of those who advocated for recognition of women voters.[15]

As with any other natural rights argument, the one in favor of women's suffrage was subject to criticism for being driven by a political agenda rather than authentic interpretation of the foundation for national independence. Just as the opponents of abolition discounted the relevance of the Declaration of Independence by pointing out that slavery existed contemporaneously with adoption of the document, so too the opponents of women's suffrage asserted that the framers "did not perceive any incongruity between declaring that 'all men are born free and equal,' that there should be 'no taxation without representation,' that 'governments derive their just powers from the consent of the governed,' and at the same time relieving women from the responsibility and burdens of government." Those who objected to women's suffrage rejected the claim that voting was an inalienable right within the framework of the Declaration of Independence. They believed, instead, that it was a discretionary privilege granted by local, state, and federal governments.[16]

Advancements in women's suffrage in the American West demonstrate both the effectiveness and the ineffectiveness of arguments relying on the Declaration of Independence. In Colorado women gained the vote in 1893, and in Utah and Idaho they became eligible in 1896. The National American Woman Suffrage Association, which was a merger of the two main women suffrage organizations, enjoined its speakers to rely heavily on the Declaration of Independence while canvassing those three states. There was also much talk about the Declaration of Independence prior to Wyoming's entry into the Union as the first state recognizing women's suffrage in 1890. In 1897, Anthony proclaimed that the U.S. flag should include only four stars, representing "the four states where the real principles of the declaration of independence, that taxation and representation are inseparable, [are implemented]." On the other hand, in the late nineteenth century Nevada and Washington suffragettes also relied on the Declaration to argue for women's suffrage, but women did not gain voting privileges in Washington until 1910 and in Nevada not until 1914.[17]

The argument in the Declaration of Independence did not crop up only in respect to the dignity and self-preservation of voting rights. There were other pressing matters during the Gilded Age. Women were entering the workforce as never before. New educational opportunities, at places like Bryn Mawr, Mount Holyoke, and Radcliffe colleges, allowed female students to enrich their lives by becoming physicians, nurses, secretaries, stenographers, and lawyers. "There never has been a time when women were pressing to the front in so great a number of occupations as now," as one contemporary author put it. "It is in some sense a declaration of independence."[18]

Jobs away from home allowed many women to achieve financial and personal aspirations. Gail Laughlin's statement in 1902 to the Senate Joint Committee on Woman Suffrage made a clear connection between the statement in the Declaration of Independence about "life, liberty and the pursuit of happiness" and the government's obligation "to secure just and equitable industrial conditions." Without the right of suffrage, she explained, women "who stand side by side with the men in…shops and factories" were "easily bullied" into accepting wages below those of their male colleagues. This in turn diminished men's ability to bargain for a living wage. A newspaper editorial writer took it to be a given that woman's "first and inalienable right [is] to fulfill the purpose of her Maker," and likewise, "her right to receive equal compensation with man when the same labor is as well performed."

An independent salary also increased women's marital options. For women who chose to pursue happiness through marriage, familial bliss did not necessarily mean sharing a husband's political views. In rethinking the nature of the marital relationship, radical feminists regarded husbands who denied wives an independent voice to be as tyrannical as George III had been to colonists. Susan B. Anthony advised any young woman interested in marriage to first obtain assurance that she would continue enjoying "life, liberty and the pursuit of happiness, with full permission of using your own faculties and earnings to suit your own tastes and capabilities." Another writer counseled every woman to make her own "declaration of independence" at the altar by refusing to repeat the traditional vow to "obey" the husband. In 1894, a woman filed a petition for divorce in the sixth judicial district of Texas that began with:

> When in the course of human events it becomes necessary for a woman to dissolve the matrimonial bonds which have connected her with her husband, and to assume among the individuals of earth the separate and equal station to which the laws of nature and nature's God entitle her, a decent respect for the opinion of husband and this honorable court requires that she should declare the causes which impel her to the separation.

The petition then recited the inalienable rights of women and men, described her husband's cruelties, expressed her attempt to petition "him for redress," and ended with her intention to free herself of the matrimonial bond and be independent. Hers was yet another example of how ordinary people internalized the ethical message of an eighteenth-century document originally composed as an expression of national sovereignty.[19]

Women's impact on public debate was greater than ever during the Populist and Progressive eras. Yet, despite their increased involvement in political and social issues, they remained civically marginalized. At the turn of the twentieth century, women had full suffrage rights in only four states. The arguments for women's suffrage—at the municipal, state, and federal levels—continued, as they had for more than half a century, "to be found in the declaration of independence." Activists found the document to be an easily recognizable source for recruitment, picketing, and lobbying. The key to success was constitutional change, but this could not be achieved without a formidable philosophical foundation for demanding women's access to full enjoyment of citizenship. Important to the campaign of finally turning the public mind to the legitimacy of women's suffrage was the demand in the Declaration of Independence for legal symmetry between citizens: every argument that could be made for male suffrage applied to women's suffrage. So long as women continued to be treated as dependent inferiors, as the Political Equality Club of New York put it, the Declaration of Independence would remain "a national lie."[20]

By this point in history, the National American Woman Suffrage Association had taken its message onto the world stage. In 1902, the organization hosted an international women's suffrage conference in Washington, D.C. Participants included Carrie Chapman Catt, Susan B. Anthony, and Anna H. Shall from the United States; Vida Goldstein from Australia, and Gudrun Drewsen from Norway. Delegates adopted a statement of principles, "that the ballot is the only legal and permanent means of defending the rights...pronounced inalienable by the American Declaration of Independence, and accepted as inalienable by all civilized nations." The second and third international conferences adopted identical language.[21]

In the Declaration of Independence, suffragists located the "great fundamental truth" recognizing "the equal rights of individuals." As women became more educated, they joined political protests, participated in unions, worked against urban blight, and otherwise freed themselves from the daily drudgery of social inequality. This army of men and women became involved in the struggle for "personal dignity, self protection and self government."[22]

Progress had been slow in coming but there was an undeniable momentum throughout the country, and especially in the West, to codify the view that only a government formed through the consent of the governed met the Declaration's principles. Women's suffragists had reiterated this standard of governmental legitimacy since the midnineteenth century. A 1914 declaration of independence condemned America's failures: "The history of our government is a history of injustice to women (as wives, mothers and wage earners) and of repeated usurpations by men, many of them with the avowed object of protecting women." Rational faculty, not gender, determined one's eligibility for voting. Gender bias in voting statutes deprived equally rational adults of the "supreme rights to change those unjust laws which have debarred women who are marching shoulder to shoulder with man."[23]

Women's suffrage was part of a bigger process in the United States of expanding understanding of equal citizenship to include the right to vote. Even the notion of universal male suffrage did not take hold immediately, and in the early republic property qualifications were the rule in all states. In 1915, California Rep. Julius Kahn told a San Francisco audience of the Congressional Union of Woman Suffrage that "fifty years after the declaration of independence there was an absolute lack of man suffrage in every state." The battle for the ballot had been hard fought. At the time of the Declaration of Independence, the vote was still withheld from Roman Catholics in Delaware and Jews in Maryland. In addition, other states had restricted voting on the basis of race or monotheism. Voting qualifications, like gender, were grounded on moralistic prejudices and therefore against the values of the Declaration of Independence. Whether or not the framers understood the leveling of class and gender implied by the natural rights principle in the American manifesto, the equality ideal it established for a just government was incompatible with restraints on adult access to the voting booth.[24]

The most intense effort among women's groups was in obtaining voting privileges, but there was also an appeal for broader social change. In 1900, the Social Democratic Party of America asserted that economic freedoms were also essential to both sexes' pursuit of happiness. What would have been remarkably radical two decades before now had sufficient appeal to be included in the Republican Party platform of 1896, which supported "the rights and interests of women" to "be accorded equal opportunities, equal pay for equal work, and protection to the home." In the years that followed, a similar sentiment also appeared in the popular media of newspapers and magazines. Particularly indicative of the authenticity of these party sentiments is that they were made when women's vote was very small, confined to the west, and of little practical consequence. As with many advances in civil rights, the effort to provide for "equality of opportunities" for the "human race" relied on classic language from the Declaration of Independence. The efforts of suffragists would crescendo until the ratification of the Nineteenth Amendment finally ended formal gender discrimination at the ballot box.[25]

13

THE CHANGING FACE OF LABOR

A DISCONCERTING ASPECT OF THE NATIONAL WOMAN SUFFRAGE Association's recruitment effort was the leaders' willingness to tolerate prejudice in their ranks. In April 1869, shortly before she became the first president of the organization, Elizabeth Cady Stanton wrote in *The Revolution* that the Chinese and some other foreigners were "lower orders" of men who had no business passing laws affecting the lives of cultured women.[1]

Anti-Chinese sentiments often appeared in dailies and congressional debates. An 1870 article in a popular magazine asserted that the only question more pressing to the nation than women's suffrage was how to deal with the immigration of "heathen" Chinese immigrants to the West Coast. The author claimed that naturalizing them "would work incalculable mischief" on the country's morals.[2]

Racialist opposition to Chinese becoming naturalized citizens was tied to their growing presence in the workforce. In 1850, about forty-one thousand Chinese immigrated to the United States, and more than sixty-four thousand arrived the following decade. In the mid-1860s thousands of Chinese laborers came in response to the Central Pacific Railroad Company's call for workers to build the western portion of the first transcontinental railroad. Chinese workers received a dollar a day, about half the wages paid to white men. Proponents for unrestricted Chinese immigration relied on the Declaration of Independence, arguing that naturalization was needed to prevent Chinese coolie laborers from becoming virtual slaves. Sen. Charles Sumner ignited debate in the Senate and the nation as a whole in 1870 when he proposed eliminating the word *white* from the naturalization law, where it had been since 1790. Sumner's stated purpose was to bring the Declaration of Independence into practical effect.[3]

Arguments against nativist policies were grounded in the notion that the Constitution had to be interpreted through the color-blind language of the Declaration. George Godlove Orth of Indiana reminded his colleagues in the House of Representatives that the Declaration of Independence declared that "all persons have an 'inalienable right to the pursuit of happiness.'" To him this meant American naturalization laws should apply equally to everyone, not merely those of European ancestry. Sumner made a similar point to say that discriminatory naturalization laws violated the spirit of the Declaration, which purposefully avoided any mention of racial color.[4]

Democrats seeking electoral support claimed "the Republican doctrine 'of universal equality for all races, in all things' would lead to an 'Asiatic' influx and control of the state by an alliance of 'the Mongolian and Indian and African.'" An author under the pseudonym "Irish Citizen" published an article in a weekly Georgia newspaper mocking the Republicans' interpretation of inalienable rights: "either the Declaration of Independence requires this nation to open its doors to three hundred millions of obscene yellow rascals, or else does *not* require it to admit the three or four millions of malodorous fetich-worshiped black fellows." Sen. George H. Williams was more circumspect but no less racist when he spoke passionately against any proposed statute that would grant foreign-born Chinese access to U.S. citizenship. His Fourth of July speech denied that "the Declaration of Independence or the Constitution of the United States requires us to admit to naturalization Chinese, or cannibals, or Indians, or anybody." As a newspaper reporting his speech understood it, Williams was grouping Chinese, Indians, heathens, and cannibals into a category of undesirables. In Congress, the refrain used to deny blacks rights, the claim that the Declaration of Independence dealt only with white men's rights, was rehashed in the context of Chinese. More benign assertions claimed the entire matter of immigration to be simply about political policy, not natural rights tied to the Declaration of Independence.[5]

Sumner's proposed amendment to the naturalization law went down in defeat. Debate continued, but members of Congress who argued that the Declaration of Independence proclaimed that the country welcomed immigrants from all over the world never gained a majority.[6]

The spike in immigration during the 1880s swelled the ranks of America's workers. The nation became one of the word's greatest industrial powers, in no small part due to the accomplishments of foreigners laboring in coal mines and quarries and on railroads. Many of them, especially Jews and Roman Catholics, suffered from religious discrimination. Protectionist opponents of immigration condemned the moralizing of anyone who "may try to smother us with the Declaration of Independence and the Constitution."[7]

On the West Coast, the Chinese were the most common objects of bigotry. Attitudes toward them continued to deteriorate after the Senate rejected Sumner's proposal to expand naturalization to nonwhites. Denied citizenship, and consequently the right to vote, it was impossible for Chinese immigrants to establish an effective political lobby. Seeking votes, the Democratic and Republican parties courted some of the champions of Chinese expulsion, among them the leader of the California Workingmen's Party, Denis Kearney.

The xenophobia did not go unchallenged. Although the immigration issue was quite different from those traditionally related to the Declaration of Independence, there were prominent voices who connected the topic to the nation's foundational principles. One author was appalled that the parties' "vie with each other in repudiating...the declaration of independence" by supporting anti-Chinese measures. Debate about whether to limit immigration took the nation by storm. The Executive Committee of American Congregationalists wrote President Hayes to protest the "anti-Chinese bill as a surrender to caste prejudices, an injury to the country...in violation of treaty, [and] the principles of the Declaration of Independence." Octogenarian Thurlow Weed, one of New York's most influential power brokers, wrote that the inauspicious effort in Congress to prohibit Chinese immigration was against the "principles which found expression in the Declaration of Independence." It had "been our pride and boast for a full century that America offered an asylum to the oppressed of all nations," but prejudice had taken root. The supposedly heathen Chinese in fact immigrated from a civilization millennia older than America's. Henry Ward Beecher, a prominent woman's suffrage activist and clergyman, also spoke in favor of Chinese immigration. He advocated use of neutral immigration standards without resort to racial or ethnic categories. Such a policy, Beecher explained, would demonstrate the human rights statements of the Declaration of Independence to be sincere. Weed's and Beecher's protests did not stem the anti-Chinese tide. Modification of the 1880 Burlingame Treaty allowed the U.S. government to deport Chinese laborers.[8]

Even more restrictive was the Chinese Exclusion Act of 1882, which suspended immigration of Chinese laborers for ten years. Degrading statements about the ability of the Chinese to assimilate and be productive were commonplace. Only a minority in Congress, including Senator George F. Hoar of Massachusetts, persistently asserted that the Declaration's statement about human equality included the Chinese, who like persons of any other ancestry should be welcomed into American society. Even widespread outrage against anti-Chinese violence, perpetrated in 1885 and 1886 in cities like Rock Springs, Wyoming, and Tacoma, Washington, which one observer called a "virtual violation of the spirit of the Declaration of Independence," did not stem popular nativism.[9]

Anti-Chinese sentiments gained additional statutory legitimacy in 1888 with the passage of the Scott Act, which banned reentry of Chinese laborers who had traveled abroad prior to its enactment. To its antagonists, the Act was a capitulation to the old view that the statement of equality in the Declaration of Independence applied only to whites, something expressly repudiated through the Reconstruction Amendments. Supporters of Chinese labor expressed hope in the judiciary. The Declaration of American Independence, they said, protected all workers' rights to the "natural migratory pursuit of honestly earned subsistence," not just those who were U.S. citizens. Judges interpreting the Constitution "in the light of the declaration of independence," they hoped, would reject Congress's overt discrimination against Chinese contract laborers. Just the opposite turned out to be the case: the Supreme Court had already signaled unwillingness to protect human rights in 1883, when it overturned a federal desegregation statute in the infamous *Civil Rights Cases*, and it had always underestimated the value of the Declaration of Independence to constitutional interpretation. The Court countenanced racially motivated legislative restrictions on Chinese immigrants in *Chae Chan Ping v. United States* (1889), which upheld the Scott Act, prohibiting the reentry of Chinese laborers. Thereafter, Congress passed further restrictions on Chinese immigration in 1892, 1893, and 1902.[10]

Legislators adopted these nativist protections at a time when American workers were turning to unions so as to bargain and strike for higher wages and better workplace conditions. Several labor platforms explicitly invoked the Declaration of Independence in their demands for an eight- or ten-hour work day, regulation of child labor, modification or abolition of the convict lease system, and minimum wages. A supporter of the People's Party, a powerful labor and agricultural organization, explained how the "political independence which the fathers of the country secured" through "the declaration from the arrogance of British politicians" was pertinent to the "frightful power of concentrated wealth." The Declaration's anti-aristocratic provisions were translated into attacks on the excesses of capitalism. Denouncing "foreign capitalists," the author called on the country to "secure industrial independence" so that the pursuit of happiness would not be a sham for the common worker. Statutes tended to favor prosperity through railroad and financial speculation, and lawmakers did little to protect workers against corporate exploitation.

At the tail end of the nineteenth century, manufacturing overtook agriculture as the leading source of national wealth. The period gave rise to the most innovative economic uses of the Declaration of Independence in half a century. A rising number of Americans worked in sprawling urban slums. Labor activists maintained that by failing to pass housing laws to end the squalid living and working conditions of laborers, states failed "to fully acknowledge the equal and unalienable rights with which, as asserted as a self-evident truth by the Declaration of Independence, all men have been endowed by God."[11]

With a growing number of workers employed by corporations rather than private business owners, laborers complained vociferously of dangerous, tedious, and impersonal conditions. Many workers toiled for twelve, and sometimes even sixteen, hours a day, making it almost impossible for them to pursue personal happiness.

The graduated income tax emerged as a popular cause for redistribution of wealth. So popular an argument for economic equality had not gained broad support since the 1830s, and then it did not enjoy nearly the same backing as it in the 1880s. An official of the Boston, Concord, and Montreal Railroad wrote that the "moral imperative on behalf of the economically weak" is a "corollary of that right to life, which is asserted by our Declaration of Independence, [and] is now making its just demand for the right to work, as one of the inalienable rights of man."[12]

Business leaders opposed collective bargaining. They clung to a libertarian understanding of the Declaration of Independence, regarding it as a safeguard for economic individualism. "Man's right to work," became for them an inalienable right intrinsic to "life, liberty, and the pursuit of happiness." In support of capital, Sen. Leland Stanford of California in 1886 argued before Congress that strikers who prevented willing fellow workers from crossing picket lines intruded on the "equal rights and liberties" of those men who wanted to continue to work through the unrest.

Stanford's views were unsurprising given the immense wealth he had acquired as the executive and cofounder of the Central Pacific Railroad. A newspaper columnist pointed out that Stanford's opposition to strikes was meant to diminish workers' ability to leverage concessions from employers. His understanding of the manifesto of independence was misleading, the article went on to say, because it adopted a one-sided view of the term *pursuit of happiness*. The senator's interpretation favored tycoons whose control of enormous wealth allowed them to drive down salaries and increase hours of labor, but it only hurt "those who perform the labor which creates the property." Workingmen in Newark, Ohio, drew a comparison between labor strikers and the framers of the Declaration of Independence: they maintained that collective action was important to both. Union organizations had to "hang together," like revolutionaries, in order to pressure plutocratic owners.[13]

In a speech on the labor question made in Decatur, Illinois, Fred J. Smith expressed frustration at the dominance of laissez faire philosophy in the context of nineteenth-century industrialization. He believed that the men who drafted the Declaration of Independence meant to protect their own landowning class and showed no interest in wage earners. What was needed, he proposed, was a new way of thinking. Several mass rallies took it in hand to issue new declarations of independence; many of them seeking to improve on the one from 1776 by addressing specific grievances of their own day. These were meant to supplement the original Declaration

of Independence, which was drafted when the economy was far more reli-
ant on agriculture. A meeting of the National Labor Union in 1867, which
led to creation of a political labor movement, was nominally committed to
the original Declaration. But the chief aim of that convention was to attack
monopolies, seek greater access to public lands, and denounce banks' control of currency. Participants did not, however, place any emphasis on the
statement of equality in the Declaration of Independence. In 1873, some
Illinois farmers issued a declaration of independence of their own against
railroad monopolies, unneeded tariffs, low wages, child factory labor
before the age of twelve, and excessive work hours. The document began
with the familiar refrain, "When in the course of human events...." It then
continued, "it becomes necessary for a class of the people, suffering from
long continued systems of oppression and abuse, to rouse themselves from
apathetic indifference to their own interests" without resorting to violent
means. The declaration then recited self-evident truths about the abuses of
monopolistic power. In 1874 the Grange Movement, which was the forerunner of the Farmers' Alliance, explained its aspirations: "What we want
in agriculture is a new Declaration of Independence. We must do something to dispel old prejudices, and break down these old notions. That the
farmer is a mere animal, to labor from morn till eve." An 1883 antimonop-
olist meeting in Chicago, which brought together 250 delegates representing fourteen states and the District of Columbia, gathered "to inaugurate
a new declaration of independence, one which would relieve them from
the power of the monopolies and which was a higher creed than could be
found in either the Republican or Democratic party platforms." In similar
terms, the Unemployed Workmen's League in Chicago demanded a new
declaration of independence to provide them with enforceable rights to
work and habitation.[14]

The labor movement of this period was diffuse. Factory hands, skilled
workers, small manufacturers, and merchants invoked "the fundamental
principles of the Declaration of Independence and the constitution" to
express their opposition to the disproportionate power of moneyed trusts.
References to the nation's manifesto of liberty were an easy way to find
common ground among union members. Everyone could agree about the
rectitude of purging politics "of its corruption and carrying into full effect
the great principles of individual liberty proclaimed in the Declaration
of Independence." However, the substance of the programs—which

according to some labor conventions included government ownership and control of railroads, insurance, telegraph wires, and other public utilities—never gained widespread congressional support.[15]

Anarchists presented an extreme version of the workers' platform, relying on the revolutionary portions of the Declaration of Independence to justify violent domestic insurrection to combat excessive use of police force against strikers. In the words of a speaker at an 1892 anarchist meeting in Chicago, tycoons acted "contrary to the spirit of the American Declaration," and it was the duty of the working class to wage "a war between the producers and the rich idlers." Anarchists blamed the government and company hirelings for the violence. The International Anarchist Congress of 1893 asserted that the unequal legal treatment afforded to the privileged class—through public franchises, debt collection, and selective enforcement of contractual obligations—perpetuated poverty and wretchedness. The government-sanctioned aristocracy of property owners, the International's manifesto stated, was against the government's purpose of securing "to all the people the enjoyment of the natural rights proclaimed in the Declaration of Independence." The leader of the Knights of Labor, Terence V. Powderly, also invoked the nation's founding document, though he deeply opposed use of terrorism, such as the Haymarket bombing, to further workers' causes. He spoke of his organization's belief that "the Declaration of Independence means something more than mere words and beautiful sentences," including opposition to an alien king's oppression of the people. However, Powderly did not clearly connect that statement to the Knights' belief in the rights of the poor to be treated fairly in such a wealthy nation.[16]

A more formal political alliance of labor organizations had been in the works since 1886, when a committee began appointing regional representatives for the Union Labor Party (ULP). Its membership included the Knights of Labor, trade unions, farmers' alliances, soldiers' organizations, Grangers, the Anti-Monopoly League, and any other labor cooperatives that "indorse and subscribe to the declaration of independence." The ULP of Pennsylvania called on "all who desire a pure government, based upon the principles enunciated in the Declaration of Independence and reaffirmed in the Constitution of these United States," to cooperate in the politics of the industrial movement. Such a conglomerate could hope that mention of the Declaration would drum up support, but they needed a far more detailed plan with a unique agenda. Henry George, a popular social philosopher and unsuccessful New York mayoral candidate for the ULP in 1886, was more expositive. His message to make "land common property," which enjoyed an enormous following, stemmed from the conviction that the "spirit and...truth of the principles of the Declaration of Independence" support the "abolition of poverty" and the "destruction of industrial slavery." George proposed that labor should benefit from imposition of communal taxes on land in order to enjoy equal rights to the means needed for a fulfilling life. The "monstrous" chasm between the "very rich and the very poor" prevented ordinary people from partaking in the "equal right to life, liberty, and the pursuit of happiness." George's idea "that all men have equal and unalienable right to the use of the earth" appealed to both agriculture and shop laborers.[17]

The call for an eight-hour work day was the central theme of the 1889 ULP's Independence Day picnic in Milwaukee, Wisconsin. "The American eagle and Gambrinus were about equally honored" at the event where patriotism was coupled with a beer-flowing bacchanalia. The keynote speaker declared that "the principles of Declaration of Independence...had been and were being grossly transgressed upon," especially by mining companies. No sooner had it broken "the shackles of the law from the black race" than "the bonds of slavery to monopoly and trusts had been welded upon the limbs of the toiling millions of whites in this country and placed them in a worse condition of slavery than that from which the black race had been freed."[18]

At its most fundamental level, the labor movement's argument was predicated on the conviction that the statement in the Declaration of Independence that "all men are born free and equal" was instructive about the right to access natural resources. According to this view, monopolies prevented citizens from exercising their fundamental right to engage in meaningful work. Moreover, because the right to meaningful work was essential to the stability of free government and the pursuit of human happiness, centralized wealth ultimately undermined democratic government and society.[19]

The ULP was short-lived, but it gave the labor movement valuable experience for building political coalitions, and inspired other conglomerations with similar messages. As an indication of the widespread appeal local and national unions made to the Declaration of Independence, the American

Federation of Labor (AFL, whose rolls included members of the Beer Brewers' National Union, Bakers' National Union, American Flint Glass Workers' Union, National Federation of Miners and Mine Laborers, Iron Moulders' National Union, Cigarmakers' International Union, and many others) often referred to the document at official rallies. Samuel Gompers, president of the AFL, contended that the Declaration's clause on the rights of "life, liberty and the pursuit of happiness" meant "the right to life and happiness should be a guarantee that employment, remunerative, safe and healthful, is accorded to all." This new understanding of the Declaration, Gompers and his followers believed, was necessary to address industrial workers' grievances.[20]

Without such reinterpretation, industrialists focused on the individual right to property, proclaiming that the Declaration of Independence had nothing to do with strikes or other forms of labor protests against private businesses. Gompers's statement was full of platitudes, wrote a columnist in Houston, and lacked useful detail about whose duty it was to provide "remunerative employment for all." Unlike workers' organizations, industrialists conceived the "life, liberty, and the pursuit of happiness" statement to cover individuals' rights to exercise their capacities. The manifesto was regarded by capitalists such as Stanford to be a statement against government intervention into owners' decisions about the use, exploitation, or rental of property. Other than this general interest, which viewed each actor as an equal individual irrespective of bargaining position, the laissez faire perspective rejected government's role in regulating mines, railroads, factories, mills, or farm prices. Under this scheme, everyone was born with an equal right to exercise his or her capacity, but it was wrong to believe that government policies limiting acquisition of wealth would advance civilization or even uplift those who were in the depths of poverty. Many industrialists saw inequality as a normal byproduct of entrepreneurialism and sound financial foresight.[21]

Social Darwinists rejected altogether the Declaration's statements about the equality of human nature. The Chicago investor and prominent attorney D. K. Tenney expressed this sentiment in an 1894 lecture delivered at a Unitarian church located in Madison, Wisconsin. The premise of his remarks was that, "All Men Are Not Created Equal." This had the same implications for him as for proslavery thinkers in the middle of the century: in Tenney's words, "No generalization was ever more mischievous or misleading than the opening chorus of our declaration of independence that all men are created equal." Populists spread falsehoods, he contended, although "the truth is precisely the other way." Government should leave capital alone and allow the wealthy to acquire more property, which Tenney considered to be "the very marrow in the backbone of every community." In its response, the liberal *Inter Ocean* newspaper criticized Tenney for rehashing old attacks on the premises of the Declaration of Independence. Indeed, one can find similar attacks as far back as the eighteenth century that sought to refute the document's statements by pointing to the variety of human aptitudes, temperaments, and strengths. The *Inter Ocean*, however, asserted that the meaning of the statement "that all men are created equal" is not about capabilities but intrinsic human rights. The editorial staff admitted that trades' unions could also illegally abuse their power, but it stressed the government's obligation to pass legislation limiting the growth of business at the expense of laborers. However, without legislation, the *Inter Ocean* argued, there was no way to protect labor from exploitation or to ensure that workers could realize the American dream by pursuing happiness in accordance with the Declaration's "incontrovertible truth" about human equality.[22]

For those who sought to apply the principles of the Declaration of Independence to changed industrial conditions, the nineteenth century was a period of intense adjustment. Until then, the document had typically been discussed in individualist terms—an interpretation more readily captured by the supporters of capitalistic self-determinism. However, at the end of the nineteenth century, worker's organizations began to read the text with an emphasis on social responsibility.

Building on the unionism of the early nineteenth century, the populist movement began associating the case for equality of opportunity with the joint efforts of workers' rights organizations. The almost unquestioned belief, in the Jacksonian era, that entrepreneurial effort would inevitably lead to prosperity become far less convincing. Trade unions modeled themselves as the new bastion against despotism, which was no longer monarchical, as at the writing of the Declaration, but plutocratic. An Alabama labor newspaper, emphatically proclaimed, "the equal right to life, liberty and the pursuit of happiness can hardly be said to exist in a land of slums and palaces, of child labor and unemployed and unexampled luxury."[23] What had been a fairly radical effort to achieve entrepreneurial equality was undermined by hoarding and workforce exploitation. Workers' organizations began to give greater attention to a social responsibility reading of the Declaration of Independence, one that regarded the document as a positive injunction for government regulation of industrial standards.

Railroad, bank, oil, steel, and harvester trusts had such an enormous influence over policy makers at the turn of the twentieth century that they significantly impaired ordinary people's ability to effectively participate in governance. This created a class-based political oligarchy that progressive groups believed ran counter to statements in the Declaration of Independence about government by popular consent.

Antitrust leagues of the early twentieth century formed to stop companies from aggregating wealth through exclusive land grants. Federal and municipal charters for public services such as transportation, utility, and telephone services were meant to benefit the public. In reality, however, a disproportionate amount of the profits went into company coffers. With the growth of corporate leverage came unregulated low wages, longer hours, and unpaid overtime. As the socialist leader Eugene V. Debs pointed out, the ability of a few wealthy individuals to have an inordinate influence on the national economic, legal, and political systems raised questions about whether the equality principles of the Declaration of Independence provided an adequate ideological basis against exploitative corporate practices. Yet Debs never abandoned the document as a binding statement of national liberty.[24]

Grassroots organizations sought to expand the meaning of the Declaration, asserting that instead of merely prohibiting governmental abuse it imposed duties on the state and federal governments to prevent private trusts from exploiting workers. Participants at the eight-hour-day convention hosted by the Charlotte Typographical Union, No. 228, in 1905 asserted that the end of "human toil" was "the enjoyment of life," which was "one of the self-evident truths" secured by "our declaration of independence." Among the many organizations that took the same stance, the Central Trades and Labor Council of Roanoke, Virginia, argued that eight-hour workdays would give "working men and women of the United States ... opportunities of self-improvement and privileges guaranteed by the Declaration of Independence." Unlimited hours of labor made it impossible for workers to find the time needed to enjoy culture and citizenship.

Efforts to shorten the workday were part of a broader movement to provide ordinary people with enough leisure time to pursue activities that tended to increase their happiness. It was individualism redefined more broadly than simply acquisition and enjoyment of property. A leading proponent of this reconceptualization of American values, Florence Kelley, believed that laws should be enacted against abusive employment contracts. One of government's functions, she claimed, was to protect an individual's right to pursue happiness without being bound to abusive employment contracts for long hours at low pay. Mary "Mother" Jones, the chief organizer for the United Mine Workers, who was once arrested for reading the Declaration of Independence to strikers, also demanded the eight-hour day in order to provide miners with time for leisurely thought and education.[25]

The Supreme Court in 1898 upheld the constitutionality of an eight-hour workday for male miners but thereafter rejected public health legislation meant to protect other male workers, such as bakers, whom the justices did not believe to be pursuing hazardous and dangerous occupations. As for women, the Progressive Era Court upheld and later overturned laws designed to limit them to an eight-hour workday.[26]

Child labor was widespread, even in the most dangerous occupations like shaft mining and coal chipping. Critics charged that children who spent long hours at work lacked the time to play and get an education, necessary to enjoy the "equality of opportunity" to which "the Declaration of Independence committed the American people." Juveniles consigned to work by family or personal necessity lacked the ability to attend school, which was necessary to their development as citizens. Without government funding for public schools, wrote an anonymous author from Wisconsin, "we would repudiate the whole spirit of the Declaration of Independence." Talk of this type incorporated the Declaration's language of rights into efforts to protect children against exploitation. The National Society of the Daughters of the American Revolution wrote that adequate protection for children to pursue happiness required both a federal law to abolish child labor and local requirements for compulsory education. A judge from the Juvenile Court for the District of Columbia, speaking at a conference called by President Theodore Roosevelt in 1909 to discuss the care of dependent children, denounced governmental actors who failed to perform duties essential for securing the inalienable rights proclaimed by the Declaration of Independence. The judge thought it absurd to speak of a child laborer's right to freely contract to work at a factory where her clothes might get tangled in a machine and her body mangled in the process. The contract theory of employment, he said, disregarded the leverage a millionaire owner possessed over a factory girl needing to earn her daily bread. A few girls as young as nine and ten turned or were forced by their families into prostitution to increase wages. Legislation was needed, the judge concluded, to provide for the life and liberty of children to enjoy the Declaration's promise of liberty.[27]

The labor and children's rights movements were fueled by the outrage of ordinary Americans. People who worked in factories, worked at schools, and suffered from overcrowding in tenements found that membership in organizations gave them the institutional voice to press for solutions. The Declaration of Independence provided a unified ideology that was recognizable to Americans of all socioeconomic backgrounds.

In pursuit of these populist measures, supporters turned to the Declaration of Independence for an authoritative statement about the need of the people to retain control of political representation to best secure their rights. These parties' proposals for reform differed, but progressives in the Bull Moose, Democratic, and Socialist Parties regarded the Declaration of Independence as a mandate to participate in popular governance, "but the old autocratic ideas of distrust in the wisdom and ability of the people has served to restrict their full and complete exercise of the power which is vested in them." By 1915, seventeen states had adopted referenda and initiative measures, and eight promulgated recalls of politicians. Although the founding generation of Americans did not grapple with the ills of the industrial revolution, the people's voice became essential for formulating an agenda of workers' rights.[28]

Labor organizations translated the Declaration's eighteenth-century sentiments toward British aristocratic rule into a new formula against the abuse of wealth to the detriment of ordinary people. The document's meaning evolved through Jacksonian populism, through Reconstruction politics, and into the industrial age. The nation had expanded, both domestically and internationally, and with its territorial growth ordinary people found new meaning in the ancient manifesto of independence.

14

INTERNATIONAL IMPACT AND DOMESTIC ADVANCE

AMERICAN CONCERNS FOR INDEPENDENCE ABROAD TOOK ON A NEW urgency with the instigation of the Spanish American War. The Declaration of Independence set the framework for national sovereignty in a changed world that witnessed the United States spreading its influence further abroad than might have been imagined by Thomas Jefferson and his revolutionary generation.

A group of forty-six hundred people yelled themselves hoarse at the Central Music Hall in Chicago in a show of support for the 1895 Cuban declaration of independence, which was issued at the commencement of fighting against Spain. Those in attendance endorsed a resolution that began, "We hold these truths to be self evident, that all men are created equal..." and went on to recite other passages from the U.S. Declaration of Independence. The Chicago statement ended with condemnation of Spain for refusing to recognize Cubans' determination to govern themselves. When William McKinley became president in 1897, Congress and the public clamored to send U.S. troops to support the Cubans' fight for independence. The sinking of an American ship, the USS *Maine*, raised war cries to a fever pitch.[1]

McKinley sent soldiers into the conflict with the express aim of aiding islanders in the fight to govern their own affairs. The Treaty of Paris of 1898 ended the fighting, with Spain agreeing to recognize Cuban independence and ceding Guam, Puerto Rico, and the Philippines to the United States. In exchange, the United States paid Spain $20 million. Filipinos wanted complete independence and objected to the transfer of sovereignty, relying on the proclamation in the U. S. Declaration of Independence to the effect that "governments derive their just powers from the consent of the governed." The list of grievances in the 1898 Philippine Declaration of Independence was patterned after those found in the U. S. document.[2]

The same year, heated debate ensued in the United States about the status of the Philippines, pitting individuals who supported expansion of democracy into new lands against those who regarded colonization to be imperialistic. Opponents of annexation pointed out that there was no constitutional authority for annexing the Philippines. They also opposed forced exportation of American ideology, which they believed contrary to the representative principles of governance found in the Declaration of Independence. The most poignant objections came from Sen. George F. Hoar, who decried America's effort to set up a legislature and executive whom the U.S. Congress and president could overrule by decree. He likened such executive oversight to King George III's repression of colonial legislatures. He believed control of the overall policy and daily affairs of Filipinos to be as great an injustice as what had been condemned by the Declaration of Independence.[3]

The American manifesto's proclamation of human equality appeared to many in Congress to imply that all people, including Filipinos, had an inalienable right to develop sovereign entities without foreign interference. American imposition of constitutional rule appeared to anti-imperialists to be a violation of the fundamental American creed of self-governance. "If there is any one principle greater than another that inspired the authors of the Declaration of Independence," said a North Carolina Congressman, "it was that of local sovereignty of States." Having gone to war with Spain to vindicate the American ethos of independence, it was utterly inconsistent to exert colonial rule in the Philippines over more than five million people living on twelve principal and 1,583 dependent islands. Protest over annexation was not always enlightened by the commitment to equality. Rep. Charles S. Hartman, for instance, was concerned that incorporation would presumptively apply the Declaration's equality principles to new citizens, even though people "like the Chinese, Japanese, Portuguese, and other undesirable races of the Hawaiian Islands are utterly incapable of appreciating the benefits of a free government." Hartman could connect these culturally unrelated peoples only through his paranoia about multiracial pluralism.[4]

The Philippine debate brought attention to the U.S. conquest of North America and its implications for the Declaration of Independence, a topic that had almost never been broached before. An editorial in the *Morning Oregonian* mocked those who trotted out the Declaration's "maxims of liberty and self-government" only when doing so was advantageous. British ancestors, just like the Spanish and French, had conquered the Americas without the consent of the native inhabitants. Adding racialized Social Darwinism to its message, the editorial counseled that "orators of the United States senate, who spout apothegms from the Declaration of Independence" about tyranny in the Philippines, should learn from the colonial period that "the world is not for its inferior creatures, but for those who can use it for the highest purposes and best ends." One of the justifications for instating American law was the presumed need to impose order and civilization on "mongrel" peoples, so that they could enjoy the rights promised in the Declaration of Independence. Senator-elect Albert J. Beveridge argued that the statement in the Declaration of Independence about the inalienable right to found a government by consent was inapplicable to barbarians and savages like Indians and Filipinos. Sen. William Lindsay also resorted to historical diatribe to defend incorporation of the Philippines. He pointed out that the "United States did not ask the consent of the inhabitants of Louisiana, or Florida, or New Mexico, or Upper California" before it annexed their lands. By relying on the U.S. history of forced conquest, speakers inadvertently raised questions about how much land the United States had acquired illegitimately in the eighteenth and early nineteenth centuries.[5]

Advocates of colonial rule referred to other historical facts to demonstrate the rightness of their cause. To bolster claims for annexing the Philippines, Tennessee Congressman Richard Gibson found the conduct of the Declaration's author to be relevant. Gibson noted that Jefferson was president at the time of the annexation of Louisiana. As we saw in Chapter 4, he agreed to that acquisition without obtaining consent from the territorial population.[6]

Until the Philippine-American War, the Declaration of Independence had been considered a banner of self-rule throughout the world. But annexation of the Philippines made it seem to be a statement of selective equality. The notion that the Declaration's maxims would apply to Filipinos and Puerto Ricans only after they were compelled to join the union was antithetical to the very purpose of American independence. People who had just thrown off the Spanish yoke, warned Rep. Thomas Spight, would mock the grand ideals of the Declaration of Independence if they were permanently held as vassals of an American empire. Senator Hoar remonstrated, "When you raise the flag over the Philippine Islands as an emblem of dominion and acquisition you take it down from Independence Hall." Rather than allowing the former Spanish provinces to institute new governments that seemed "most likely to affect their safety and happiness," the American Congress, with little knowledge of the inhabitants' culture and immediate needs, was determined to devise a government for them. Keeping the islands as conquered provinces, as the Populist Sen. William V. Allen of Nebraska pointed out, was antagonistic "to the letter and spirit of the Declaration of Independence," which was "the first great charter of American liberty."[7]

The hypocrisy of the American policy in Manila was not lost on the British media. Filipinos had fought against Spain, wrote an English newspaper, "for the very principles which the Americans...stated in the Declaration of Independence," and in return the Americans battled and killed natives to prevent them from asserting sovereignty. Irish politician and revolutionist Michael Davitt condemned the offspring of the signers of the Declaration of Independence. They were raised on the message of "no taxation without representation" only to become indistinguishable from absolutists suppressing vassal states.[8]

As if to drive home Manila's lack of sovereignty, in 1899 American servicemen and regimental bands led Filipinos in a Fourth of July celebration, complete with a reading of the U.S. Declaration of Independence. The same year, a radical U.S. newspaper with a national distribution in the Irish community marked the disconnect between the document and the decision to wage war in the Pacific: "The shame of it is that the soldiers whom the Filipinos are fighting have been brought up to believe in the Declaration of Independence...[and] are risking their lives...to secure the triumph of a policy which if successful, will make the Declaration of Independence a dead letter." The paper also accused President McKinley of flying "in the face of the Declaration of Independence" and coercing "densely peopled islands, whom we are reducing to Political Servitude by force of arms."[9]

William Jennings Bryan challenged McKinley's policies during the 1900 presidential election. A man with a remarkable gift for inspirational speeches, Bryan repeatedly told crowds on the campaign trail that if elected "no citizen here or foreigner abroad will have any doubt that the Declaration of Independence is the law of this land" by ending American imperialism in the Philippines, Puerto Rico, and the Pacific Islands. One of Bryan's articles, which was reprinted in a campaign book published in 1900, expostulated on why imperialism diluted the justice provisions of the Declaration of Independence.[10]

McKinley's reelection, by about 6 percent of the popular vote and a much large Electoral College margin, left anti-imperialists in disarray. However, their voices were not silenced. And the claim for the vindication of the Filipino's inalienable rights continued to echo for the next several decades. American troops withdrew from Cuba in May 1902 and the Philippines gained their independence on July 4, 1946. In 1962, Filipinos changed the date of their celebration of independence to June 12, to commemorate the country's original declaration of independence of 1898. Puerto Rico and Guam remain self-governing commonwealths of the United States.[11]

Despite its own racial problems at home, the United States justified entering the First World War to spread equality abroad. By the outbreak of hostilities, the United States was well entrenched in its territorial islands. In 1915, detachments of soldiers or sailors were stationed in the Philippines, Oahu, Panama, Guantanamo, and Puerto Rico.[12]

While the country was aflame with talk of exporting democracy abroad, President Woodrow Wilson was segregating government offices at home. The president also enjoyed a movie screening at the White House of *Birth of a Nation*. Released in 1915, the film lauded the Ku Klux Klan as a savior of the white race and the New South and played in theaters to capacity crowds. It portrayed blacks as despoilers of white property, menaces to white women, bestial, and uncontrollable. Newspaperman William Monroe Trotter, who a year before had decried federal segregation during a meeting with Wilson at the White House, led two thousand demonstrators opposed to the movie running in Boston. In Philadelphia, the movie played in the Forest Avenue Theater, which garnered a response from five thousand blacks of various ages to protest the screening. Police were called, and a violent riot ensued. The front of the theater was demolished. A contemporary essayist bemoaned that such a screening should have occurred in Philadelphia, which "gave to us that famous compact, the Declaration of Independence, and the Constitution."[13]

Initially when the European War broke out, the United States remained neutral. Wilson nevertheless began to quickly formulate the national response. In a 1914 Independence Day address delivered in Philadelphia, he proclaimed, "The Declaration of Independence was a document preliminary to war." The Declaration would become meaningless, the president believed, unless it applied to contemporary realities. "Liberty does not consist in mere general declarations as to the rights of man," he continued, but in carrying out the mission of the Declaration of Independence to the rest of the world. Pressure to enter the war on behalf of the Entente mounted after a German submarine sank the *Lusitania*, killing more than 1,198 on board, of whom between 114 and 128 were Americans. Former President Theodore Roosevelt, one of whose sons would later die in air battle after America's entry into the war, spoke against Wilson's complacency, which he contrasted with the determination of the men who signed the Declaration of Independence.[14]

Social tensions did not dampen patriotic fervor, even before the formal U.S. entry into the war. During the war, patriotic statements differentiated European privilege from America's egalitarian protections of life, liberty, and the pursuit of happiness. (American exceptionalism tended to ignore the asymmetries of wealth, race, education, and gender in the United States.) The long-established American Peace Society advocated translating the Declaration's statements about human rights into international norms for conflict resolution. The American Institute of International Law believed the peoples of every nation had the right to survival, independence, and the pursuit of happiness. In its words, "the municipal law of civilized nations recognizes and protects the right to life, the right to liberty, the right to the pursuit of happiness as added by the Declaration of Independence of the United States...the right to legal equality, the right to property."[15]

In response, advocates for military involvement asserted that without the force of the "greatest and noblest nation on the earth" built on the "charter of human rights," no mechanism for ending aggression could feasibly be enforced or even created. They too thought that other nations needed to adopt the principles of the Declaration of Independence in order to achieve "abiding world-peace, prosperity, and happiness." But only negotiations following an Allied victory, this camp claimed, could achieve the conditions needed for spreading the Declaration's democratic principles. Americans differed about whether the country should become militarily involved in Europe. However, with the continued German U-boat attacks on ships carrying American civilians, advocates of a martial solution convinced Wilson to deploy soldiers overseas.[16]

American soldiers did not, however, enter battle as equals. A correspondent of a historically black newspaper pointed out how unconscionable it was to conscript blacks into military service without protecting them against lynchings at home, which the *Birth of a Nation* seemed to justify as a restraint against conjectured black criminality. Although Jim Crow was the rule in the South and some parts of the North, black servicemen were required to put themselves in harm's way to spread democracy abroad. In newspapers and books, authors recounted black soldiers' achievements, from the Revolution to the World War. An American journalist wrote that, given the many examples of black patriotism, Wilson's Democratic Party had no excuse for remaining silent about lynching, the neglect of black education, and the deprivation of black suffrage. The only reason, he asserted, for the lack of moral clarity was the Democratic Party's need to maintain electoral dominance in the South. Yet for the most part blacks who remained stateside (among them W.E.B. Du Bois) nevertheless supported the war effort. Bond drives in black communities included reminiscence of the black forefathers' manifold sacrifices, dating back to the days when the Continental Congress signed the Declaration of Independence.[17]

James Davenport Whelpley, a prolific current events author, regarded America's April 6, 1917, declaration of war as the beginning of a third American epoch against imperialism. He believed it compared favorably with the first two epochs, inaugurated by the Declaration of Independence and followed by the Civil War. At its inception, the United States fought for national independence from autocracy, and the battle oversees was regarded as a declaration of independence against world autocracy. A congressman warned that the drum beats of war should be focused on ending imperialism, explaining that the message in the

Declaration of Independence on human equality was to inform foreign policy. Despite this warning, anti-German sentiment extended against individual Germans and German culture; grammar schools prevented teaching German, and German-run newspapers in the United States were hounded to prove their patriotism. War fever led to odd results under the Espionage Act of 1917 and the Sedition Act of 1918. In the battle of sentiments, a judge sentenced the socialist Henry Aurin for distributing extracts of the Declaration and the Constitution as part of an effort to discredit the administration's conduct. New York District Judge Peter J. Hendrick later released Aurin on a writ of habeas corpus, castigating the government for considering distribution of the nation's manifesto to be incriminating: "Why, that's in the Declaration of Independence. We all believe that, and it is what the united press of the country is urging upon Germany." Just before her conviction for denouncing conscription, the anarchist Emma Goldman reminded the trial jury that "according to that dangerous document, the Declaration of Independence, the people have the right to overthrow [the government]." Supreme Court Justice Louis D. Brandeis would later issue a writ of errors, releasing Goldman along with other anarchists. The period featured groups who relied on the document for diametrically opposed reasons, even though both sides treated it as the defining statement of human liberty.[18]

Vocal proponents of the war believed that the fighting was not meant to impose tyranny, nor to protect the interests of the wealthy. An idealistic patriotism appeared in the writings of those seeking a crushing victory. It seemed to many of the young men headed off to Europe that they would wage a "battle in favor of Democracy" against tyranny. The battle was presented by the mainstream press as a defense against Hohenzollern Germany's effort to expand "militant autocracy." Patriotism was redefined to include feelings for the broad world. Rather than simply avenging the death of American civilians on the high seas, the sirens of war called the country to persist in battle until "an ideal for all the people of the earth will have been attained and 'life, liberty and the pursuit of happiness' will be the heritage, not only of Americans, but of all of the people of all of the earth for all time to come." The principles of the Declaration of Independence were a rallying cry as politicians and newspapers spoke of the German government as a corrupt autocracy that the United States needed to help defeat for the sake of humanity.[19]

FIGURE 14.1 *Lexington Herald* (Lexington, Kentucky) July 4, 1918, p. 2. "New Declaration of Independence Comes From Mouths of Guns 'Over There.'" (Image courtesy of the University of Kentucky Library.)

President Wilson's statements, however, showed an even greater breadth of purpose. His Fourth of July 1917 oration foresaw adoption of an international "declaration of independence and of grievance for mankind" that would "be drawn in the spirit of the American Declaration of Independence." The world declaration of liberty, he explained, would result in "the reign of law based upon the consent of the governed and sustained by the organized opinion of mankind." At a fellowship meeting in London the next year, Winston Churchill, then the minister of munitions, proclaimed that "great harmony exists between the spirit and language of the Declaration of Independence and all we are fighting for now." American victory in the Revolution, he said, created the means to spread the Declaration's principles to the world community.[20]

Some of the most unexpected consequences of the world war against autocracy were the decisions of several European and Asian countries to liberate themselves from colonial rule. Mikhail Terestchenko, the foreign minister of the Provisional Government that briefly ruled Russia from March 1917, told Elihu Root, the head of the American Commission to Russia, that the revolution against the Czar was based on the principles of 1776; "Russia holds with the United States that all men are created free and equal." By November 1917, however, the Bolsheviks had deposed the Provisional Government and begun the rapid totalitarian process of outlawing any political opposition. Finland then issued a declaration of independence by the end of the year, freeing itself of Russian rule and its economic instability, instead aligning itself commercially with the West. The following year Lithuania, Estonia, Czechoslovakia, Latvia, Georgia, and Yugoslavia also issued declarations of independence. In East Asia, Korea declared independence, unshackling itself from Japan's harsh colonial yoke. Jews around the world rejoiced at the British Balfour Declaration that provided for their independent statehood in areas formally colonized by the Turkish Ottoman Empire, even though the state of Israel emerged only after the Second World War.[21]

After the armistice muzzled the dogs of war, the Allied Powers gathered for the Versailles Peace Conference of 1919. They mainly sought territorial reparations from Germany, Austria, and Turkey. Of the victorious negotiators, only Wilson claimed no indemnities or damages for his country. In part it was because the United States had entered at the tail end of the fighting. More to the point, though, was his almost single-minded drive to establish an international body for dispute resolution. He believed the League of Nations could be instrumental in facilitating negotiations and preventing wars. Wilson's supporters at home hailed his fourteen point proposition as "America's Declaration of Independence to the peoples of the world." The president's proposal was part of a developmental process. In 1916, the 105 members of the American Institute of International Law had passed "The Declaration of the Rights of Nations." The institute was composed of five representatives from each of the twenty-one American republics. Members included Secretary of State Robert Lansing, former U.S. Senator and Nobel Peace Prize winner Elihu Root, and Cuban Senator Antonio Sanchez de Bustamante. The document posited that the statements in the Declaration of Independence about the rights of life, liberty, and the pursuit of happiness could be translated internationally. The institute denounced territorial gains through attacks against foreign nations and their indigenous populations. This document and Wilson's practical proposal were meant to establish international mechanisms requiring countries to factor human needs, not merely territorial sovereignty, into their policies.[22]

In an address he delivered at the University of California at Berkeley, Wilson linked the covenant to an opening phrase of the Declaration of Independence: "that out of respect to the opinion of mankind the causes which have led the people of the American Colonies to declare their independence are here set forth." To the president, this phrase was relevant because "America was the first country in the world which laid before all mankind the reason why it went to war" by passing the Declaration of Independence. The Treaty of Versailles, he said was "the exaltation and permanent establishment of the American principle of warfare and of right." In a step away from ancient oppression, the signatories were to apply "the principle that the well-being and development of" colonized "peoples form a sacred trust of civilization." League members were to endeavor "to secure and maintain fair and humane conditions of labour for men, women, and children both in their own countries and in all countries to which their commercial and industrial relations extend." These were conceptual leaps forward from the free-for-all warfare of the past. But no right to self-determination would be granted to the people whom the Allies governed, even though government by consent was a central tenet of the Declaration of Independence on which the Covenant was modeled. The victors denied independence to millions of people. Britain remained a colonial power throughout the world in places as far flung as India, Kenya, Rhodesia, and the Falkland Islands. The French also ruled over distant peoples from Algeria to Lebanon to French Polynesia. And the United States continued to take a role in administering the Philippines, although by 1916 the Jones Act had declared the purpose held there by the United States was to grant the Philippines independence.[23]

The National American Woman Suffrage Association drummed up support on the home front while maintaining its effort to achieve equal suffrage. The National Woman's Party went so far as to picket the White House during the course of World War 1 to demand equality.[24] They were building on the successful state-by-state bid begun on the West Coast of enfranchising women.

Soon after the beginning of the European War in 1914, Montana and Nevada adopted constitutional amendments granting women the right to suffrage, even though success of the state-by-state approach seemed at best uncertain. (In 1915, New Jersey, Massachusetts, Pennsylvania, and New York rejected women's suffrage proposals.) In this more hospitable political context, suffragists continued to rely on the Declaration. An editorialist from New Jersey pointed out that the rights to life, liberty, and the pursuit of happiness, to which women and men had an equal interest, could be protected only by the ballot. The main tenets of this argument stated that opposition to suffrage ran contrary to the doctrine of the Declaration of Independence because it unjustly kept women from casting ballots to affect public policy. Like other American citizens, Florence Allen told the Political Club of Cleveland, women could secure legal equality only by laying "their claim to enfranchisement on the substance of the Declaration of Independence." She and a number of other orators sought progress, not mere historical platitudes. At a rally in Chicago attended by the vice president of the Woman's Suffrage Party of Cleveland, a speaker asserted that it was just as irrelevant to the controversy that women did not participate in drafting the original Declaration as it was that men living in 1914 had no hand in writing it. What mattered was that half of U.S. citizens were excluded from entering the political arena as equals. In Illinois, which in 1913 passed legislation granting women the right to vote in special (but not general) elections, first wave feminist Belle Squire made her own "declaration of independence" by refusing to pay property tax on her piano until she could vote for the Chicago Board of Assessors, which had levied it. The Nevada Equal Suffrage Society asserted that by voting women would demonstrate as much patriotism "as was shown by the men who signed the declaration of independence."[25]

America's slogan, on entering the war in 1917, was "Make the World Safe for Democracy." The National Woman's Party, organized by Alice Paul, sought to hold the country accountable, picketing at the White House with placards reading "Democracy Should Begin at Home," "Mr. President, How Long Must Women Wait for Liberty?" and "A Democracy in Name Only." The suffragists were harassed daily by passersby and arrested for obstructing the sidewalk. Press coverage of middle-aged and elderly women being hauled off to jail helped gain sympathy for the plight of the picketers. On Independence Day in 1917, thirteen picketers were arrested for holding up a banner with abbreviated words from the Declaration of Independence: "Governments derive their just power from the consent of the governed." One of the arrested women, Helena Hill Weed, rejected the idea of being submissive to gender injustice as part of the government's effort to present a unified front in wartime. She pointed out that after the Civil War passivity had left suffragettes empty-handed, and she cautioned women against repeated failure after the World War.[26]

Activism was the order of the day. In response to female antisuffragists who did not want women's maternal instinct to be ensnared in politics, Sen. John F. Shafroth of Colorado asserted that inalienable rights should not be denied because some people did not want to exercise them. Women had won the right to vote in Colorado in 1893. During a 1918 congressional debate on a national constitutional amendment protecting woman's right to vote, Shafroth further denounced America's failure to live up to the democratic principles of the Declaration of Independence. The founding document guaranteed government by consent, whereas much of the female population had no way to pick government representatives to express their political will. Congressman William H. Thomas of Kansas, another state that already guaranteed women the right to vote, drew his colleagues' attention to "the services of women during this supreme crisis of the world's history." While the military conscripted men, he said, women "forge cannon, make guns, and even...use them on the field of battle, and to do man's work wherever necessary for the good of the Nation." Under the circumstances, they deserved suffrage "in recognition of woman's sacrifice in defense of our citizenship and the natural and inalienable rights of life, liberty, and the pursuit of happiness." A businesswoman from West Virginia wrote the chairman of the House Woman Suffrage Committee assuring him that by voting for the women's suffrage federal amendment, the men of the sixty-fifth congress would be remembered "with a measure of the same veneration as we hold for those who could not fail humanity when the Declaration of Independence was at stake."[27]

In the early morning of August 26, 1920, U.S. Secretary of State Bainbridge Colby signed a proclamation at his home announcing ratification of the Nineteenth Amendment. The Declaration of Independence was relevant to this fundamental legal change, but social movements in the Progressive Era coped with problems unforeseen in 1776. Necessarily, they translated these ancient ideals and refashioned them to fit debates about worldwide conflicts, colonization overseas, and a federal approach to suffrage.

The philosophy of the Declaration of Independence had been far more carefully protected than the original parchment, whose pen strokes dimmed over years of display behind glass at the State Department. In 1894, the document had been hidden away at the archives department in Washington, D.C., but its ideas continued to be openly debated in the context of contemporary issues. It helped anti-imperialists expose the hypocrisy of distant colonization while proclaiming loyalty to the document's statement of human equality.[28]

The document was then placed between two plates of glass to keep out air, and it was kept in a steel safe away from lights. In 1920, a committee reported that this was insufficient because the safe was neither fireproof nor uncrackable. The following year, President Warren G. Harding agreed to a suggestion from Secretary of State Charles Evans Hughes to transfer the parchment to the Library of Congress for expert keeping. There it was placed in a shrine with gold-plated bronze doors and protected by twenty-four-hour guard.[29]

The document was much more than an icon, however. For many people, it remained a statement of national purpose, a political ideal, and an authentic commitment to the protection of human rights. On the nation's sesquicentennial in 1926, a black New York newspaper asserted that blacks nationally still had "faith in the Declaration of Independence as an instrument of government." It was a sad statement, the article went on to say, that throughout the country blacks suffered a long "train [of] abuses and usurpations of all kinds" such as disenfranchisement and government-sanctioned segregation. Another newspaper with a similar readership in Chicago appealed to President Calvin Coolidge to use his office to achieve real equality ending "color proscription"; otherwise observance of the sesquicentennial would be a "mockery."[30]

Black soldiers who after World War I heroically returned from the European theater might have anticipated a grateful American public putting extra effort into preventing discrimination at home. Instead, they encountered a country unwilling to confront employment discrimination, segregation, housing disparities, disfranchisement, social inequality, or even lynching. A 1919 editorial appearing in a weekly black newspaper from Atlanta observed that "our leaders and statesmen" need to "look facts squarely in the face," for although they "cry peace, peace . . . there will be no peace until all classes and conditions of men shall have equal opportunities in the race for life, liberty and the pursuit of happiness." The *Houston Informer* was more vehement: "The black man fought to make the world safe for democracy, [and] he now demands that America be made and maintained safe for black Americans." The failure to realize equality for black Americans made

MORE FLORIDA JUSTICE

Florida citizens, peace loving Christians, have again demonstrated their great love of justice and peace by celebrating their Fourth of July by placing a dynamite bomb under the Washington school, which was nearing completion in Miami. These citizens have always demonstrated that they are "friends of the Race" and believers in the American Declaration of Independence, which says that "All men are created free and equal." That's why Floridians have led this country in lynchings, peonage, concubinage and other forms of southern justice. And that is why she has such a high percentage of illiteracy—she just naturally encourages illiteracy.

—P. & A. Photo.

FIGURE 14.2 *Chicago Defender*, July 10, 1926, p. 4. "More Florida Justice." (Image courtesy of the Library of Congress.)

Rufus Choate's cliché that the Declaration of Independence was made up of "glittering and sounding generalities of natural right," an unfortunate reality for many. Ideologically, however, as a black college professor pointed out, "So far as the Negro is concerned...we hold that the Declaration of Independence is a very live document." Therein lay the hope that the country might finally be true to its idealistic anchor.[31]

In 1922 the National Association for the Advancement of Colored People supported immediate passage of the Dyer Anti-Lynching Bill. The group thought it necessary for Congress to pass legislation for safeguarding the "guarantee of life, liberty and the pursuit of happiness." When the House of Representatives passed the bill on January 26, the Galveston, Texas, *City Times* praised the achievement as driven by "the highest principles of American justice...to protect the lives, property, and the pursuit of happiness of its citizens." The Senate, however, never voted on the measure, after the Democrats threatened to filibuster it.[32]

There were some who found it an affront to even speak of the Declaration's statement on equality in the context of black citizens. In 1923, a group from Charlotte, North Carolina, expressed its indignation about Boston Mayor James M. Curley's decision to allow a black honor student, Charles C. Dogan, to read from the Declaration of Independence on Independence Day at the Old State House, where the Declaration had been read aloud from the same location in 1776. In response, Curley reminded the protestors of the patriotism blacks had demonstrated: the first American who was shot at the Boston Massacre was a black man, Crispus Attucks, setting off events that culminated in the American Revolution; black union soldiers were essential to Civil War victory; and black World War I veterans had fought "to make the world safe for democracy." Having served the American flag, Independence Day and the message of the Declaration were just as pertinent to blacks as to any other Americans.[33]

Returning black veterans who demanded respect from whites by refusing to abide by southern segregation norms were sometimes physically attacked, several while boarding public transportation in uniform. Mobs lynched seventy black World War I veterans in 1920 alone. Vigilantes organized most of the mayhem; at times they worked alone or with the aid of local officials. The Ku Klux Klan was reborn in 1915 following the anti-Semitic lynching of Leo Frank, who had been convicted on questionable evidence of raping a white factory girl. The Klan's influence spread rapidly. In 1920, it had only five thousand members. But by 1925, at its peak of popularity, the number skyrocketed to an estimated four to five million, though membership dropped precipitously thereafter because of organizational corruption and state and local government campaigns against its lawlessness. On the whole, Klan chapters targeted blacks, Jews, and Roman Catholics but also attacked whites whom they perceived to be averse to the organization's interests.[34]

Government officials around the country were concerned at the near breakdown of civic institutions. In order to delegitimize the Klan, public figures often quoted from or simply referenced the principles of the Declaration of Independence. When California's Quaker Governor Friend William Richardson signed an antimasking law to expose Klan participants, a state newspaper expressed its support. The editors praised Richardson for putting an end to the "un-American" menace that threatened the personal freedoms set down in the Declaration of Independence and the Constitution. The attitude was the same in Brookshire, Texas, where newspaper editors condemned the Klan's lawless lynching, beating, and forced evictions because they were against the Declaration's statements about equality and freedom. An author from Ogden, Utah, explained that his aversion to the Ku Klux Klan stemmed from its efforts "to usurp the powers of the courts and inflict punishments in striking at the government of this great country of ours, that guarantees the pursuit of happiness to the humble citizen, white or black, Jew or gentile." In its assault on the terror organization, a newspaper from Madison, Wisconsin, compared the Klan with the Know Nothing Party of the midnineteenth century and adopted Abraham Lincoln's opposition to nativist supremacism: "How can anyone who abhors the oppression of the negro be in favor of degrading classes of white people?" Lincoln rhetorically wrote to a friend. "Our progress in degeneracy appears to me to be pretty rapid. As a nation we began by declaring that all men are created equal. We now practically read it, 'All men are created equal except negroes.' When the Know Nothings get control it will read: 'All men are created equal except negroes, foreigners and Roman Catholics.'" Lincoln's warning was relevant to the situation in the early 1920s because of its regressive xenophobia and racism.[35]

Klan defenders also quoted the Declaration of Independence but applied its principles only to Anglo Saxons. As so often in history, racists sought the cover of the Declaration for purely nostalgic reasons without taking to heart its universal statement of rights. For instance, in Janesville, Wisconsin, from the podium of the Cargill Methodist Church, a minister denounced state legislators' attempts to "put out of business the Ku Klux Klan." He rationalized the organization's vigilantism as a legitimate way "to protect its people in the pursuit of happiness." The Klan invoked the Declaration of Independence in official documents as well, though conceiving it to grant only whites equality. As the Klan's leader, Hiram W. Evans, who had become the organization's Imperial Wizard in 1922, put it, Roman Catholics were un-American because they were beholden to the Pope and Jews were un-American because their customs prevented them from enjoying the patriotism of the Anglo Saxon.[36] Like Confederate sympathizers before them, the Klan ignored the Declaration's statement of human equality.

Methodist minister J. G. Robinson, who was the editor of the *A. M. E. Review* magazine, called on President Coolidge to "put into practice for all Americans the principles of the Declaration of Independence before attempting to celebrate its sesquicentennial" in 1926. Living with the possibility of lynching, he said, meant the hopeful words of the document were "a hollow mockery." "Lynch law," stated a Columbus Ohio editorial, was mob violence. Such illegality was a violation of "our great declaration of independence" because it substituted the will of the unruly crowd for legitimate authority. As sesquicentennial celebrations were taking place around the country, on July 4, 1926, a planted bomb ripped through the Washington school in Miami. Yet the federal government refused to provide a remedy against states' intransigence in the face of terror, lynching, peonage, and other injustices.[37]

To the contrary, the Coolidge Administration retained Wilson's policy of segregating federal offices. On July 9, the National Equal Rights League and the United Colored American Committee received an audience with Coolidge at the White House. The event was part of the sesquicentennial. The delegates presented the president with twenty-five thousand signed petitions calling for an end to federal segregation. Three years later, the league and the Race Congress made the same "annual Declaration of Independence appeal" to President Herbert C. Hoover, demanding that he be true to the manifesto's principles by putting an end to segregation. The organizations also called for passage of federal legislation to punish lynching, peonage, and disfranchisement. Their open letter asserted that those were "violations in denial or abridgement of the declaration's principles because of race and color."[38]

Despite the continued failure to achieve the universal equality seemingly demanded by the text of the Declaration of Independence, there were some significant signs of progress for black workers during the 1920s. In industries such as steel, auto manufacturing, and mining their wages began to approach (but were still not exactly on par with) those of white workers. Employers found it useful to play employees off each other, exploiting blacks as strikebreakers in cases of white labor unrest. This interracial conflict was aggravated by the discriminatory policy of the American Federation of Labor, which the NAACP and National Urban League castigated for segregating black union members. The United Mine Workers of America was a more progressive labor organization, welcoming blacks into the high echelons of its elected councils but putting little effort into changing the disparate assignments and wages given to black workers.[39]

Labor organizations like the AFL, the International Union of Journeymen Horseshoers of the United States and Canada, and the United Brotherhood of Maintenance of Way Employes (sic) and Railway Shop Laborers continued to invoke the Declaration in their efforts to increase wages, strike without being under the threat of injunctions to diminish the power of corporate monopolies, and improve work environments. In Mingo County, located in the West Virginia coal country, a battalion of infantry arrived to maintain peace following a gun battle between mountaineer miners and company detectives over the eviction of families. Miners, industrial workers, and farmers argued their rights to life, liberty, and pursuit of happiness were meaningless without government regulation of corporate behavior. As they had from the time of the Jackson Administration, workers regarded their struggle against the abuse of moneyed power to be a direct extension of the colonists' drive to secure their inalienable rights through the Declaration of Independence.[40]

As at every point in U.S. history, the judiciary scarcely invoked the Declaration of Independence. It remained primarily a popular statement of national purpose that disempowered groups turned to when they lacked the legislative tools to support progressive causes. Between 1920 and 1931, during which more than ten thousand federal court opinions were issued, only thirteen written decisions even mentioned the Declaration

FIGURE 14.3 "Judicial Suppression of Labor," 28 *American Federationist*, July 1921. (Image courtesy of the Library of Congress.)

of Independence. Even among that fractional number of cases, the founding document was typically cited only in passing or to support conservative interpretations meant to protect employers' contractual liberties. For example, an appellate court found a statute unconstitutional that granted District of Columbia commissioners the authority to set minimum wage hours for women and minors. The court found the law to be an invasion of the employers' inalienable property interests, guaranteed under the Declaration of Independence, for allowing the government to establish standards where it found that wages were "inadequate to maintain decent standards of living." But for most judges, unlike social activists, the document remained a historical artifact.[41]

Although, the United States experienced a small depression from 1920 to 1922, prosperity followed, built largely on corporate profits and dividends, stock speculation in a bull market, and consumer purchases of new luxury items such as automobiles, motorcycles, and motion pictures. Yet the gap between corporate owners and the working class widened. In 1929, 32.4 percent of the wealth was in the hands of the richest 0.5 percent of the population, and 0.07 percent of nonfinancial corporations possessed 22 percent of the country's corporate wealth. Moreover, from a 1920 high in enrollment, unions experienced a 1.5 million drop in membership by 1923. During this time of prosperity, the business vision of deregulation, which President Coolidge advocated, favored an individualistic exercise of inalienable property rights. Consequently there was little mention of the Declaration of Independence as a statement of social change.[42]

In a novel turn, employers' organizations like the National Association of Manufacturers and the League for Industrial Rights regarded government regulation as a socialistic intrusion on the inalienable right to own and use property. During the New Deal Era, this latter argument gained a tremendous amount of traction even as the government began meeting workers' demands for the pursuit of their own happiness.[43]

At a time of massive unemployment, the notion that government's only role was to protect industrial prosperity did not resound with average Americans. Franklin Delano Roosevelt's election victory in 1932 was part of the public realization that government can play an active role in protecting lives, liberties, and the pursuit of happiness. Although the Declaration of Independence was still a visionary statement of an individual's right to pursue of happiness, translating it into a statement about government intervention became a complex process of reinterpreting American values. The efforts of unions provided the framework for the collective action needed to protect the inalienable rights to the basic necessities of life, such as food and clothing.

Given the extreme economic woes of the Great Depression, concrete programs were needed. Merely connecting the vision of the "authors of the Declaration of Independence" to grandiloquent aspirations of ending "disease, poverty and sin, wrong and injustice and oppression" was too unspecific to be of any practical use to the unemployed. The inability of many to rise above the hardships of the Depression through personal thrift required an expanded understanding of national citizenship (which until then had been primarily thought of in libertarian terms) and its privileges. The problems of poverty—which degraded individuals' lives, liberties, and abilities to pursue happiness—required establishment of governmental duties that surpassed what the revolutionaries could have envisioned in their agrarian world. Advocates of federal economic regulations conceived of government not only as a protector of property rights but also as one "intended to be a conscientious effort to build a Nation for the people, in which all should have the right to share, to create, to acquire wealth and to follow the pursuit of happiness." The Declaration of Independence was important in this synthesis of governmental powers and popular expectations. As a professor at the Wharton School of Economics asserted in a survey on labor problems and industrial unrest, the Declaration was a revolutionary statement of popular will, while the Constitution was a product of a more conservative time committed to protection of property. Yet depression could be ended only through revolutionary actions, not conservative economic policy.[44]

The need for a new declaration of independence, for which labor had advocated since the early nineteenth century, became painfully obvious. With wages dropping and consumer confidence at an all-time low, a supporter of labor wrote: "The Declaration of Independence may still recite that all men are created free and equal, the law may still read that the worker and the employer are free to enter or refuse to enter into contractual relations. But the bread and butter fact...is that the worker who refuses to work on the employer's terms may well starve."

Farmers protested the high prices they paid to the operators of grain elevators and rail transport. The Grange Movement and the Farmers

Alliances of the Gilded Age had developed networks for collective action among this segment of the population. The banker-farmer movement, designed to bring these two segments of the economy into closer cooperation, took the perspective that without adequate business aid "the American farmer, the farmer's wife, and the farm children" were unable to enjoy the full share of "life, liberty, and the pursuit of happiness." Once bank failure made it impossible for farmers to rely on that association to deal with the yearly shortfall in farm prices, obtaining public assistance became critical. One farmer asserted that governmental assistance was essential to those barely able to make ends meet through the produce of the land. He believed the Declaration of Independence guaranteed "every human being" the "right to food, clothing and shelter." Such a claim was novel because it conflated the right to "pursue happiness" with the right "to enjoy happiness," but the call for federal subsidies to provide for the bare necessities of farmers, the poor, and the disabled was much in line with the nation's principal topic of debate.[45]

THE DECLARATION IN A NEW
DEAL STATE

THE GREAT DEPRESSION OF THE 1930S SHATTERED THE ERA OF general prosperity that the United States had enjoyed after the First World War. Labor groups discovered that at a time of great economic distress the principles of the Declaration of Independence informed their efforts for equality. From then through the Second World War, the proposition that government was created by consent of the people to protect inalienable rights continued to energize disparate social movements. Having moved beyond the nineteenth century debates over abolition and women's suffrage, which had so often invoked clauses of the Declaration of Independence, reformers turned to new matters. The supporters of economic and social equality began to petition the federal government to be more active in securing the Declaration's guarantees of the people's right to "safety and happiness."

As the great debates on government relief programs were taking place in the United States, the Second World War thrust the nation in a more international direction. The country rallied to the Declaration as a banner of democracy that was easily juxtaposed with Nazi ideology. Defense of the values of life, liberty, and the pursuit of happiness in the European theater was, however, irreconcilable with Japanese internment and the persistent degradation of racial segregation at home.

In the waning months of his presidency, Herbert Hoover laid the foundation stone for the National Archives Building. Located in Washington, D.C., the massive edifice would eventually house the Declaration of Independence, no longer exposed to the elements but protected in a bronze and marble shrine, with armed guards preventing against theft. Although the document was originally meant only to explain the Continental Congress's July 2, 1776, vote for independence, both its principles and its parchment had long been the object of veneration.[1]

During the Great Depression, the document's whereabouts were of little consequence to people around the country desperately trying to rely on their meager savings to feed, house, and clothe their families. In the months between Roosevelt's popular victory and his oath of office, expectations ran high. Woodrow Wilson's former secretary of the treasury and then U.S. congressman from California, William G. McAdoo, reassured Democratic Party loyalists that Roosevelt would be true to the "shining promises of the Declaration of Independence," courageously blazing "new trails that will lead the country out of its pit and back to high ground."[2]

Hoover publicly projected a positive outlook on the economy; Roosevelt, on the other hand, openly acknowledged its practical collapse in 1929 and the continuing grip of depression in 1933, the year of his inauguration. The president and members of the executive branch, among them Secretary of the Interior Harold Ickes, understood the Declaration of Independence to provide Americans with a guarantee to equal opportunity. New Dealers thought they needed to act on the Declaration's principles. They would be empty platitudes without government programs to provide indigents with the modicum of public support needed to enjoy "liberty and a chance at happiness." Some federal relief was needed to escape the destitution of slums, especially at a time of nationwide depression. Postmaster General James A. Farley told an audience assembled for the dedication of a new Durham, North Carolina, post office building that the incoming administration would seek to make the principles of the Declaration of Independence and the Preamble to the Constitution realities through "reorganization of our economic, social and political life." Farley delivered a similar message in the Chicago Stadium to Cook County Democrats. The New Deal, he said, was "a twentieth-century model of Jefferson's principles of government" as expressed by the Declaration of Independence. The government, Farley said, would promote an agenda of economic recovery. In Roosevelt's 1934 Green Bay, Wisconsin, speech, he explained the New Deal's historical roots:

> It is new as the Declaration of Independence was new, and the Constitution of the United States; its motives are the same. It voices the deathless cry of good men and good women for the opportunity to live and work in freedom, the right to be secure in their homes and in the fruits of their labor, the power to protect themselves against the ruthless and the cunning.

Contemporary writings echoed Roosevelt's sentiment.[3]

The first order of business was to reorganize the banking system, which had been highly decentralized in the 1920s, leading to large-scale bank speculation with depositors' funds. The stock market crash of 1929 left banks without adequate reserves to satisfy the demands of panicked depositors. Roosevelt proclaimed a four-day bank holiday, which put a temporary halt to bank runs, and Congress passed the Emergency Banking Act of 1933 and later the Banking Act of 1933. Critics complained that both laws were beyond the scope of federal authority. For most Americans, however, the increased powers of the Federal Reserve and the newly created Federal Deposit Insurance Corporation elevated confidence in the banking system. The measures enjoyed popular support from depositors as well as legislators because they restrained the negligent behavior of "leading bankers, who control three-fourths of the nations' industries and therefore through the power of money, the lives, liberty and pursuit of happiness of millions of men, women and children." Through members of his cabinet, Roosevelt disseminated the claim that the New Deal was not novel but predicated on the ideals of the Declaration of Independence. In 1934, the economics department of Swarthmore College gathered a conference and compiled a book of essays on economic recovery. Participants included two members of the president's think tank, Adolf A. Berle, Jr. and Rexford G. Tugwell. One of the essayists explained the perceived connection between past and present: "In this country... following the Declaration of Independence," there emerged

> a nation guaranteeing human rights under the law, so, under this New Deal there is the hope that there will emerge a consciousness of

human rights as they are affected by business management; and that business management will see to it, in its own ultimate interest, that selfish considerations will not, shall not, prevail; but that there shall be a recognition of the interdependence of us all.

Members of Roosevelt's cabinet incorporated the ideals the Declaration of Independence into their economic policy making.[4] *Telephony*, the magazine of the telephone industry, labeled the National Industrial Recovery Act of 1933 or NIRA, a recovery statute passed within Roosevelt's first hundred days in office, a tremendous experiment in government, "perhaps the most radical since the Declaration of Independence." The law created the remarkably successful Public Works Administration to supervise public projects, and the National Recovery Administration to develop industrywide codes with the input of private businesses; the law also granted trade unions the right to bargain on behalf of organized workers without running afoul of antitrust laws. The United Mine Workers union claimed it played a central role in developing the NIRA's labor provisions. At an annual meeting, the UMW proclaimed the statute to be based on the natural rights principles that predated the Declaration of Independence. John L. Lewis, the union's powerful president, called for a Declaration of Economic Freedom that would supplement but not supplant "Jefferson's immortal declaration for political democracy" into worldwide, "sound measures of industrial democracy." Lewis went on to conjecture that whereas Jefferson's statement in the Declaration of Independence confronted agricultural aristocracy, under the current circumstances laws were needed to destroy "the financial and industrial autocracy." The International Molders' Union was similarly effusive in its praise of the new industrial codes for being in accord with the Declaration's intention to protect men and women against monopolies. The industrial interpretation of the document went far beyond its revolutionary origins.[5]

An Ohio newspaper published a letter to the editor extolling public works projects for deploying the unemployed to construct irrigation canals, parks, and ships. The writer speculated that the right to labor was an absolute human entitlement linked to the human "right to enjoy life and to strive in the pursuit of happiness." From this perspective, putting an end to poverty and unemployment was a national obligation to the people, not merely governmental discretion. Without infusion of public

July 4, 1935, Marks Advance Toward New Freedom

George Washington

Signing of Declaration of Independence

New Deal congress in session

Franklin D. Roosevelt

July 4, 1935, celebrated as the anniversary of the signing of the Declaration of Independence, although the signers attached their signatures on other dates, is doubly significant this year. A new bill of rights is apparently in the making, guaranteeing the citizens of United States advantages and privileges never possessed by the majority of people before. George Washington was leader of his country when United States was establishing its political independence. Franklin D. Roosevelt is president in this present era when the aims of the government are to establish a new social and economic order of greater security and freedom for the majority.

FIGURE 15.1 *Atlanta Daily World*, July 2, 1935, p. 1. "July 4, 1935 Marks Advance Toward New Freedom." (Image courtesy of the Library of Congress.)

funds, the pursuit of happiness was only a distant dream for the twelve million American wage earners who were unemployed at the beginning of Roosevelt's first term in office. Illinois Congressman Kent E. Keller also praised the public works program because without gainful employment the "man willing to labor is denied that opportunity" to attain the "first principles enunciated in the Declaration of Independence." Government programs were necessary, Keller believed, for giving the idle and under-employed the means of freely pursuing occupations that can bring them happiness. These claims assumed that the Declaration of Independence provided a justification for the federal government to take affirmative steps to alleviate woes plaguing ordinary Americans. This was highly controversial in a country where, until then, laws were typically considered to be negative injunctions against government intrusion, not mandates for legislative and executive action. What's more, popular enthusiasm for the National Recovery Administration faded quickly. Wages did not keep up with rising retail prices. Small businesses had little influence on the code-making process, which allowed large companies to fix prices through official NRA codes. In 1935, the Supreme Court found the NRA to be unconstitutional because it delegated legislative authority to the executive.[6]

The Agricultural Adjustment Act was another program that interlinked local and federal control. The AAA paid farmers to limit their crop outputs and authorized purchase of farm animals for slaughter. By thereby diminishing surplus, the program was meant to raise the prices on farm products. The administration's approach favored landowners at the expense of sharecroppers and farm laborers. The AAA granted local councils the authority to distribute federal funds. Property owners dominated these administrative bodies, which tried to retain their privileged status in the community. The Southern Tenant Farmers' Union, located primarily in the Arkansas delta, was a multiracial organization that sought to expand AAA protections to the non-landowning farmer. STFU leaders, such as Sherwood Eddy and H. L. Mitchell, protested that by subsidizing racist and oligarchic planters the federal government was perpetuating the type of tyranny condemned by the Declaration of Independence.[7]

Roosevelt defended the program in a speech before a small farming community in the village of Concord, Nebraska: "I like to think that agricultural adjustment is an expression, in concrete form, of the human rights of those farmer patriots who stood on the bridge at Concord, when they proclaimed the Declaration of Independence and when they perpetuated an ideal by the adoption of the Constitution." Though the government was trying new tools to end the depression, Roosevelt claimed that his efforts were driven by the desire to protect an age-old commitment to the people's inalienable rights. His attempt to relate New Deal policies to a venerable statement of American principles did not give nearly enough recognition to how experimental it was to pay farmers to reduce their output of crops and livestock. The New Deal shifted interpretations of the Declaration away from the framers' original understanding, applying the document's principles of equality and justice to a world where mechanization vastly increased the risk of overproduction.[8]

In 1936, the Court held the AAA to be unconstitutional. Afterward an article in the *Railroad Trainman* magazine critically remarked that "notwithstanding the Declaration of Independence and the Revolutionary War, sovereignty now rests in the Supreme Court, rather than the people, as expressed through their elected representatives." Much as the criticism of the Supreme Court was warranted, it would have been too rosy to paint a picture of U.S. history that drew any period as a manifestation of equality among all Americans.[9]

Columnists in the black community compared the frenetic pace of the Seventy-third Congress to the period following passage of the Declaration of Independence. A socialist activist called on blacks to support politicians who championed pension plan and employment insurance reform. Both, he asserted, were essential to combat the "economic monopoly and industrial monarchism" that undermined the "guarantee of the 'right to life, liberty and the pursuit of happiness.'" Black workers were hit hardest by the Depression. In the South, they composed a disproportionate number of tenant farmers and sharecroppers, who were not entitled under the AAA to receive payments. In the North, blacks overwhelmingly worked in semiskilled, unskilled, and service occupations, where layoffs were higher than in other segments of the workforce. In 1932, with black unemployment at nearly 50 percent, a celebrant of the Independence Day bemoaned that "the great corporations have crushed the life blood from the Equality, Liberty and Pursuit of Happiness on which this mighty nation was founded."[10]

Southern Democrats supported President Roosevelt during the First New Deal, which lasted from 1933 to 1935. Local control of the AAA and the Tennessee Valley Authority along with business leadership in the NRA provided inadequate oversight against discriminatory disbursement of federal funds. Roosevelt also refused to openly support federal antilynching law even though Harold Ickes, who in the 1920s had served as president of the Chicago NAACP, acknowledged that "mass murders, mob rule, and terrorism are subversive of our most cherished ideals as embodied in the Declaration of Independence and the Constitution." Roosevelt decided not to alienate Southern Democrats, whose support was critical for appropriating funding for his relief programs. Southern disenfranchisement measures, such as literacy tests and poll taxes, drastically diminished politicians' incentives to offer funding to black communities and aid to jobs with high concentrations of black workers. Hundreds of NRA codes contained differential wage scales for whites and blacks, the conditions of TVA workers significantly varied by race, and southern CCC camps were segregated. Yet blacks experienced significant enough improvements during the New Deal to shift their allegiance to the Democratic Party from the Republican Party, which until then had been thought of as the emancipating party of Lincoln. Unemployment was higher among blacks than whites; therefore, a larger portion of blacks benefited from the PWA and the Work Project Administration. Articles published in the NAACP's *The Crisis* lauded the conditions of the CCC, despite racial separation. And black bank depositors, like their white counterparts, received tremendous protections for their assets through the FDIC.

Articles in black newspapers demanding equal employment commonly invoked the Declaration of Independence. At the same time, many journalists disavowed "social equality." Writing in the *Pittsburgh Courier*, the popular editorialist John Wesley Neely stated that blacks sought the rights of U.S. citizens, which he said were ensured by the Declaration's statement on innate equality. But Neely repudiated white southerners' worry that "the Negro wants to mix with the white man."[11]

As with the labor movements during the Jacksonian Period and the Gilded Age, black activists called for "a new declaration of independence." Something new was needed because the nebulous claims of the original Declaration of Independence were unspecific. The document had supplied a general philosophy of the state but not directly addressed the pressing hardships of peonage, lynching, hate crime, insult, ignominy, and discrimination. Moreover, as Robert S. Abbott, the founder of the *Chicago Defender* and a graduate of Kent College of Law, said, America had failed in theory and practice to carry out the self-evident truth that all men are created equal. The new statement of human independence, asserted an author in *The Crisis*, should end with the words of the original manifesto: "And for the support of this Declaration, with a firm reliance on the protection of Divine Providence, we mutually pledge to each other our Lives, our Fortunes and our Sacred Honor." But by itself this would not be nearly enough. With a rebirth of freedom, the nation would have to secure the rights to life, liberty, and the pursuit of happiness for everyone. And it would be another three decades before the federal government got vigorously involved in passing adequate civil rights laws.[12]

Business leaders supported the First New Deal, which granted them a significant role in administering programs. However, Roosevelt lost much of his corporate support in 1935, when his administration exerted greater.control over administration of relief programs. The Second New Deal marked a major shift in the interpretation of the Declaration of Independence. Conservatives seized on the document's statements about tyrannical governance and natural rights to protest federal regulations that burdened property. This individualistic trend was a sharp turn to the right from the historically progressive understandings of the Declaration. Since the nation's founding, radicals had invoked the document to justify demands for equal treatment against powerful private and governmental actors. During and after the Second New Deal, however, Republicans took the Declaration in a different direction.

Former President Herbert Hoover gave repeated speeches denouncing his successor's recovery efforts. According to him, national regulation of the economy was akin to socialism and communism, and therefore undermined the Declaration's protections of property ownership. To his ideological cohorts, "pursuit of happiness" was a euphemism for property rather than liberal conceptions of safeguarding various innate human interests in economic and physical security, family stability, old age pensions, or fair competition in the marketplace. A group of conservatives calling themselves the American Liberty League paraphrased the words of the Declaration of Independence, calling on "all liberty loving citizens" to stop New Dealers from infringing on future generations' ability to pursue happiness through hard work and personal savings.[13]

Critics complained of Roosevelt's concentration of power in the executive branch. As Andrew Jackson's opponents had done a century before, Roosevelt's detractors compared him to the English monarch. Groups and politicians who were outraged at the myriad federal agencies Roosevelt charged with relief efforts liked to quote an anti-autocratic passage of the Declaration of Independence attacking George III: "He…has erected a multitude of new offices and sent hither swarms of officers to harass our people and eat out their substance." The personal-property and business-oriented American Liberty League, with roughly 125,000 members, charged that the "very thing that caused the American Revolution is what is taking place today." It linked Roosevelt's administrative style with the authoritarianism the king of England had exercised prior to independence toward the colonies. The League ascribed "New Deal laws and usurpations of authority" to "autocratic power" in "the course of economic affairs." The group further denounced federal regulations by invoking the "twenty-seven grievances enumerated in the Declaration of Independence." In his unsuccessful bid for reelection to the Senate from West Virginia, Henry D. Hatfield told audiences that the "underlings which the NRA has released upon the land" were as "bullying and meddling" as the British officials whom the framers had condemned in the Declaration of Independence. In the Midwest, Illinois Supreme Court Justice Frederic R. De Young warned that the United States was becoming autocratic. Roosevelt's corporate regulations, De Young continued, caused Americans at least as much grief as the tax collectors whom George III had unleashed.[14]

The rising tide of totalitarianism abroad—with Italian fascism, German Nazism, and Soviet communism firmly in place—provided New Deal opponents with recurrent themes. In the half decade preceding World War II, supporters of state legislation claimed Roosevelt's advisors were "radical Socialists, if not absolute Communists," who had "altered, if not entirely discarded," the purposes of the Declaration of Independence. This use of the document was taken up not only by congressmen and conservative groups but by anonymous editorialists as well. An author brought attention to failure of the WPA, AAA, and Civil Works Administration to stem unemployment, calling them part of "the Raw Ordeal," and concluded that "the New Deal has taken from millions of unemployed 'the Pursuit of Happiness' because it has retarded recovery and employment." Contrary to this claim, in 1935 unemployment among nonfarmers actually decreased to 14.2 percent from 20.6 percent in 1933, but it was extremely high compared to the 3.2 percent unemployment prior to the market crash. Writing in the *New York Times*, Samuel Laufbaun believed that those who often repeated that the New Deal was in harmony with the Declaration of Independence did not believe their own mantra. The Declaration, Laufbaun believed, "wants every American to pursue his own happiness, and guarantees him liberty for that purpose," but "the New Dealers want the government to pursue the happiness of its citizens" by giving them a dole.[15]

Republican National Committee Chairman Henry P. Fletcher, among the most vociferous in the *laissez faire* political camp, tried to find commonality in the interests of businesses and ordinary people. Fletcher could not argue that Roosevelt's programs violated companies' inalienable rights, since they were inanimate objects without lives or happiness, so he claimed the New Deal violated and repudiated the guarantee in the Declaration of

Independence of governance by the people, replacing their will with the regulatory choices of bureaucrats. From this perspective, the New Deal was the type of governmental tyranny described by the Declaration of Independence because administrative agents were unelected. For a century and a half social groups, such as abolitionists, feminists, and unionists, had understood the Declaration to be the source of rights against powerful and subordinating uses of law, politics, and money. The negative response to regulatory programs took a novel tact; industrialists viewed the Declaration of Independence as a statement of economic liberties, which was meant to secure the interests of merchants, manufacturers, and mill owners.[16]

By 1935, Roosevelt faced strong opposition from both sides of the political divide. Business leaders had grown increasingly disenchanted with the administration's policies as their role in governance was reduced. The Supreme Court's adverse rulings on the NIRA and AAA further emboldened the opposition. Progressive senators, notably Gerald P. Nye and Key Pittman, faulted the administration for not doing enough to meet the needs of the "forgotten man." Louisiana Senator Huey Long, whom a bullet felled in 1935, favored a redistribution program for the rich to share wealth with the poor. Like the Working Man's Party theorist Thomas Skidmore in the 1820s, Long regarded redistribution of wealth as the only plausible means of securing the promises in the Declaration of Independence for ordinary people.[17]

Although Roosevelt was determined to bestow additional government largesse to maintain popular support, he rejected socialism. The Social Security Act of 1935 was modeled on private insurance plans, which provided economic and medical aid for retirees. The nationwide pension scheme addressed demographic changes resulting from increased industrialization and urbanization.

The idea of furnishing assistance for the elderly and permanently disabled was not new. In 1931, William Green, the president of the AFL, had endorsed the idea. He believed it to be the government's duty to create a safety net for retirees, stemming from the Declaration of Independence's mandate to "foster, promote and sustain human life." Abraham Epstein introduced and popularized the term "social security." Epstein, a Russian Jewish immigrant, was one of the most important figures of social reform in the early twentieth century. He first met Roosevelt just before FDR became governor of New York. After Roosevelt's election victory in 1933, Epstein changed his organization's name to the American Association for Social Security. Epstein had long expressed the opinion that economic insecurity "weighs down our lives, subverts our liberty and frustrates our pursuit of happiness." At a 1930 House of Representatives' hearing on old-age pensions, Epstein drew on the language of the Declaration in support of poor relief: "What is the whole purpose of our Government? Is it not in order to guarantee equal rights and making possible 'the pursuit of happiness'?" By 1934, twenty-eight states and two territories had enacted laws to furnish various types of public assistance to the elderly.[18]

Unlike Epstein, the Supreme Court did not rely on the Declaration to resolve legal challenges to the Social Security Act. Instead, it found the program to be a legitimate use of Article I, Section 8 of the Constitution, connecting Congress with the general welfare and taxing authority.[19] But for Epstein and the pension movement, the Declaration was a vital affirmation of rights. Without the compunction of judicial mandates, the social security movement, like so many social reform movements before and after it, framed its argument on the clause in the Declaration protecting inalienable rights.

The Declaration's mention of those rights, as syndicated columnist Kelly Miller observed, did not express acceptance of sloth at the public's expense but was instead a mandate for "government to afford every citizen the opportunity to maintain a minimum decent standard of living." Labor organizations had relied on the Declaration of Independence since the early nineteenth century to justify striking against substandard wages. For them, the document presented an evolving social, economic, and political ethos. At a 1936 United Mine Workers meeting, a local chapter paraphrased the Declaration to assert its members' "duty, out of a decent respect to opinion of mankind," to press Congress to pass a statute requiring "financial monarchs" to pay "decent wages" to laborers. A nationalized minimum wage, explained a laundress from Harlem, New York, was critical to enjoying the inalienable rights promised in the Declaration of Independence because such a law would constitute a legally cognizable claim against gender discrimination, untimely disbursement of salaries, and insufficient compensation for exhausting work. An author writing in a magazine dealing with topics relevant to railway conductors stated affinity for the Declaration's statement that "all men are created equal." He found that "the tremendous difference" in the "standard of living destroys the very meaning these words were intended to convey." These efforts led to adoption of the Fair Labor Standards Act of 1938, which set a graduated minimum wage standard throughout the country.[20]

The depression was still in full swing in 1939. Administrators of Roosevelt's programs, such as Interior Secretary Ickes, continued associating the values of the Declaration of Independence with protections against child labor and worker exploitation, minimum wages, "economic security against sickness, unemployment and old age."[21] More than 17 percent of the American workforce remained unemployed, and menacing clouds loomed on the international horizon with the totalitarian expansions of the Soviet Union, Nazi Germany, and fascist Italy.

Accusations that Roosevelt's actions were tyrannical, which often drew comparison of his initiatives with the faults that the Declaration of Independence attributed to George III, rang hollow compared to the conduct of Joseph Stalin, Adolf Hitler, and Benito Mussolini. In the United States, news about the persecution of Jews in Germany drew condemnation on the basis of the Declaration's statement on universal human rights. Already in 1933, as reports of violence and terror against German Jews began circulating in the mainstream press, West Virginia Sen. Matthew M. Neely sought congressional backing for passage of a resolution stating that because the American people "hold sacred the assertion of the Declaration of Independence that all men are endowed with the unalienable rights of life" they viewed with "alarm and regret the persecution of the Jews of Germany by the Nazi administration." In March 1933, a speaker at a rally held in Madison Square Garden, New York, with twenty thousand supporters indoors and another thirty-five thousand outdoors, quoted the Declaration. He asserted that a "'decent respect for the opinions of mankind'" must guide international efforts against German atrocities. The trampling of Jewish rights demonstrated disregard for the document's true statements about universal human rights. At a B'nai B'rith gathering, Supreme Court Justice Frank Murphy warned against allowing anti-Semitism to infect the religious tolerance that the framers wrote into the Declaration of Independence.[22]

Ideological rhetoric ran high in the United States, as Nazi aggression expanded into Czechoslovakia and Poland. Americans' ability to pursue their happiness was counterposed with fascist terror against innocents. After Pearl Harbor and the congressional declaration of war, the effort to defeat the Axis powers became "a gigantic idealistic undertaking." In the words of one author, "If there is any question in any one's mind as to what we are fighting for today, let him get down the Declaration of Independence and re-read the two leading paragraphs." Raymond Clapper, a proponent of U.S. protection of Europe against fascism who would die while reporting on the war in the South Pacific, wrote that the Declaration's principles of the people's rights "live deep in the bones of America."[23]

References to the Declaration of Independence contrasted those governments that were formed by the consent of the people to those run by tyrants. In 1941, shortly after the Axis alliance was strengthened by the addition of Romania, Hungary, Bulgaria, Japan, and the rump states of Slovakia and Croatia, Roosevelt rallied Americans by repeating "the words of the signers of the Declaration of Independence—that little band of patriots, fighting long ago against overwhelming odds, but certain, as we are, of ultimate victory: 'With a firm reliance on the protection of divine providence, we mutually pledged to each other our lives, our fortunes, and our sacred honor.'" On another occasion, with Independence Day 1941 approaching, Roosevelt urged Americans to rededicate themselves so as to "defend and perpetuate those inalienable rights which found true expression" in the Declaration of Independence.[24]

The internationalist reading of the Declaration of Independence resembled President Wilson's understanding of international cooperation. This perspective regarded the Declaration's statements about human rights to apply beyond the boundaries of the United States to the country's war allies. The Lend-Lease Act of 1941 was designed to meet the emergency subsistence and munitions needs of such countries as England, France, China, and the Soviet Union in exchange for lower trade tariffs. The program was not conceived solely in economic terms. Lending support to allies was also a means of keeping alive the promises of the Declaration of Independence throughout the world. One of the greatest journalists of his generation, Walter Lippmann, regarded the pursuit of happiness to be about more than self-fulfillment or property ownership. He thought it also required sacrifice for the sake of communities, and in the case of the war the community of nations. Louisiana Congressman F. Edward Herbert put this aspiration into words: "The lease-lend bill is an Insurance policy on the right to the pursuit of happiness which is guaranteed every American citizen by the terms of the Constitution." Shortly after the attack on Pearl Harbor, British Prime Minister Winston Churchill expressed his countrymen's gratitude by reflecting on how the mutual effort against the Axis powers brought the two countries closer than they had been before the signing of the Declaration of Independence. The humanistic opinion about the necessity of Allied victory coupled defense of American democracy with the need to safeguard human rights overseas; but it ignored that the lend-lease program supported democracies and one of the worst human rights abusers in the world, the Stalinist Soviet Union.[25]

Americans primarily regarded the war as one for national survival, thus ensuring the existence of a "haven of democracy, where every man, rich or poor, has the right to life, liberty and the pursuit of happiness." Preservation of these interests, as a lieutenant commander said at a 1943 Fourth of July celebration, required sacrifice for the flag. Besides the United States' interest in self-preservation, the nation's international image was at stake.[26]

Racism was irreconcilable with the principal ideals justifying U.S. participation in World War II. A black author warned that "fascist gangs in our own country," which were "spawned in the South," were stirring race hatred. Various federal bureaus signed off on a plan for the Mobile, Alabama, shipyards that allowed black laborers to work at some jobs, although on a segregated basis, but denied them the opportunity to occupy the best-paid positions. The *Pittsburgh Courier* commented, "The much-lauded compromise in which Government officials took such a prominent part is actually a surrender to the Nazi racial theory and another defeat for the principles embodied in the Declaration of Independence." Southern behavior was most egregious, but racism knew no boundaries. On August 1, 1944, in Philadelphia, the place where the Declaration was penned, ten thousand public transportation workers went out on strike when eight blacks were promoted to motormen. Rev. J. C. Wright wrote that Hitler must have laughed to see such raw prejudice at the "cradle of American liberty," where the framers set about guarding the "right of every man not only to life and liberty, but to the unimpeded 'pursuit of happiness.'" An American Seaman, Donald D. Giesy, observed that the Declaration of Independence was the "bone and sinew of America." He asserted that the nation's explicit commitment to universal, inalienable rights separated Americans from

FIGURE 15.2 *Pittsburgh Courier*, July 4, 1942, p. 6. "A New Independence Day." (Image Courtesy of the Library of Congress.)

fascists, whose core ideology was predicated on racial superiority. Despite this assurance there was a large segment of the population for whom racism was "as American as Apple pie." Just before the war, in 1939, Hollywood's big hit was *Gone with the Wind*, which, as a contemporary author put it, "repeats Ku Klux Klan slanders against Negroes."[27]

As often occurs during a period of national conflict, the war brought an opportunity to reflect on the country's achievements and shortcomings. James T. Taylor, the dean of men at the North Carolina College for Negroes in Durham, spoke of blacks and whites being dedicated "to the proposition that all men are created equal and are endowed by their Creator with certain unalienable rights." At the same time, Taylor drew attention to the sacrifices of black soldiers who did not enjoy the "full measure of the rights, opportunities and obligations which the Declaration of Independence and the Constitution guarantee to all Americans." At a 1943 founder's day address, William L. Imes, president of Knoxville College, sharply criticized Alabama Gov. Chauncey Sparks's advocacy for "keeping the black man in his place." In response, Imes invoked the Declaration, which he called "a sort of political and social Bible to guide us in these perilous times of world war" when blacks and whites were fighting "in the deserts of North Africa and the jungles of Guadalcanal." Imes was disheartened that even at a time of such patriotic unity, segregation continued to "strike a moral blow" against the Declaration's "great principles."[28]

In a very different camp was a small militant group. A minister from the Mount Zion Baptist Church in Altoona, Pennsylvania, called on blacks to refuse conscription into the military until "liberty, freedom and pursuit of happiness" become more than empty words in the United States. Racism continued to be palpable even for blacks in uniform. Despite making sacrifices for the country, a disproportionate number of them were assigned to the most tedious and servile of menial work. Until shortly before the end of the War, their mess, eating, and recreational facilities were usually segregated from those of white soldiers. In response to that brazen system of racial subordination, a few ordinary black Americans, such as Ernest Calloway, registered with the selective service board as "conscientious objectors against Jim Crow."[29]

On the whole, the effort to defeat Germany and Japan began as a struggle for national defense. However, war against the Axis Powers also evoked a moral framework for condemning the color line, racial domination, and employment discrimination in the United States. Moral explanations for American involvement in the war could be turned inward to condemn supremacists for eroding fundamental, democratic commitments to the Declaration of Independence. An editorial picked up on this theme, criticizing Americans for fighting oppression abroad while failing to live up to the promises of the Declaration to provide the "same education, the same housing, the same jobs, [and] the same opportunities." Joint white, Jewish, and black involvement in organizations such as the NAACP, Fellowship of Reconciliation, Congress of Racial Equality, American Council on Race Relations, and the American Jewish Congress emboldened interracial cooperation acting in "the best spirit of the Declaration of Independence" to bring about an end to racial inequality. Some members of these civil rights organizations went further, to also protest Japanese internment on the West Coast. The Declaration, for its simplicity, imparted a message of human entitlements. In 1943, a "young southern white girl" defied segregated seating arrangements on the Washington to New Orleans train. After being forcibly removed from the train in Attalla, Alabama, she justified her conduct by stating "The Declaration of Independence says 'all men are created equal.'" The following year, Irene Morgan, traveling to

Baltimore, refused to yield her seat to a white passenger in Virginia. Her willingness to challenge southern racial standards led to victory in *Morgan v. Virginia*, which held that states could not enforce their segregation laws against interstate travelers.[30]

Contrary to expectation, however, the Declaration was not commonly invoked in arguably the most race-based U.S. policy during the war, the internment of Japanese on the West Coast. Opposition to presumptions of Japanese disloyalty relied on the Fifth Amendment, with its incorporation of the Equal Protection Clause, even though resort to either the tyrannical or the human rights clauses of the Declaration of Independence would have also been pertinent. Indiscriminate use of executive power against a whole ethnic group might have led as well to comparison of the British monarchy's conduct toward colonists with the Roosevelt administration's policies toward the Japanese.

After having fought a war clearly targeting international tyranny, the unfortunate reality remained that racism was still the norm in many American communities. A 1945 *Negro Digest* poll found that 76 percent of respondents, of all races, "believe in the doctrine of the Declaration of Independence that 'all men are created equal.'" The same poll discovered that 73 percent of respondents thought "whites were superior to Negroes." Focusing only on southern responses, 92 percent regarded blacks to be inferior to whites.[31]

Roosevelt's policies through works programs and creation of the Fair Employment Practices Committee, which investigated and redressed employment discrimination, were significant social and economic achievements. Although unable to end the depression before the commencement of war, Roosevelt's administration initiated relief programs for the unemployed and public insurance coverage for the elderly and debilitated. In later years, the widowed Eleanor Roosevelt explained her late husband's motives: "While my husband was in Albany [as governor of New York], and for some years after coming to Washington, his chief interest was in seeing that the average human being was given a fairer chance for 'life, liberty and the pursuit of happiness.'" But local control of programs such as the AAA or the Tennessee Valley Authority made success woefully incomplete because it permitted regional and even municipal prejudices to influence administration of federal programs.[32]

World War II pushed the Declaration of Independence even further onto the world stage. Establishment of the United Nations, it was hoped, would prevent another worldwide conflagration. The UN's Universal Declaration of Human Rights drew heavily from the Declaration of Independence; the preamble began with "Whereas recognition of the inherent dignity and of the equal and inalienable rights of all members of the human family is the foundation of freedom, justice and peace in the world," echoing the universal human rights of the American document. There was also a clear resemblance in other clauses, such as Article 1: "All human beings are born free and equal in dignity and rights." The UN document's mention of dignity, and other specifics such as gender and marital consent, went much further than the Declaration of Independence. The Declaration of Human Rights embraced women's rights, children's rights, the right to work, the right to travel freely, and other essential human interests. Enumerating these human entitlements dated the more general statements of the Declaration of Independence as well as the French Declaration on the Rights of Man. Despite the grand design of the United Nations, countries could join without showing any compliance with the equal human rights so eloquently pledged by its charter. What's more, the persistence of racially motivated violence, employment discrimination, and gender inequality in the United States left the country open to criticism for failing in its core commitments.

16

INDEPENDENCE PRINCIPLES
IN THE CIVIL RIGHTS ERA

REVOLUTIONARY NOTIONS OF UNIVERSAL RIGHTS INFORMED AND inspired social activism after World War II. During the Civil Rights Era, as never before, all three branches of government advanced the principle of universal equality embedded in the Declaration of Independence: Congress passed a variety of laws, such as the Civil Rights Act of 1964, providing federal recourse against discriminatory practices; the Executive Branch desegregated the military and interstate transportation; and the Supreme Court asserted its role in protecting individuals against prejudice born of stigma and stereotype.

The 1960s were a period of the greatest advances in civil rights since the Reconstruction Era. The patriotic furor against communism led to widespread evaluation of whether the United States was true to the anti-authoritarian and human rights legacy of the Declaration of Independence.

Long after natural rights philosophy had gone out of vogue in the United States, the statement of national purpose in the Declaration of Independence remained the benchmark for representative governance. The failure to address injustices, such as lynching, employment discrimination, and immigration quotas favoring Europeans, exposed the United States to foreign criticism. In 1946 the London *Sunday Pictorial* quoted from the Declaration and the Constitution, observing that "America has nerve" to criticize British colonialism in Africa while failing to prosecute a recent lynching in Monroe, Georgia. Likewise, Elmer A. Carter of the National Urban League marveled that the United States would try to teach democracy to the defeated Germans and Japanese. He posited that school children studying the Declaration of Independence in those two countries would likely ask teachers how a nation purporting to believe Jefferson's maxim that "all men are created equal" could be home to people who claim that members of the "white race are superior to the Negro." Writing of Independence Day in 1949, a journalist pointed out some remaining vestiges of inequality:

> Floggings in Alabama and violence in Georgia; injustice in prison camps and police brutality in our cities; Klan infiltration into our police departments and government, the duplicity of law enforcement officers with floggers…are only a few of the ominous signs of an America far short of the ideals, aims and aspirations set forth in our Declaration of Independence.

Justice begins at home, the article went on to say, and preaching abroad on the morality of the Declaration of Independence while maintaining inequality in the United States was unacceptable. Before "world brotherhood" could be achieved, said T. C. Johnson of the Lumberton, North Carolina, Rotary Club, there needed to be "community brotherhood," where "men can work to guarantee to each person the right to life, liberty and the pursuit of happiness." But speaking in the South, Johnson dared not directly challenge segregation. That part of the country had continuously interpreted the phrase of the Declaration of Independence to refer only to whites, a legacy that appeared prominently, a century before, in the Supreme Court decision of *Dred Scott*.[1]

There was reason to hope that better days lay ahead. In 1948, President Harry S. Truman issued an executive order requiring the armed services to provide "equality of treatment and opportunity to persons in the armed services without regard to race, color, religion, or national origin." At the Howard University commencement in 1952, Truman described the need to integrate the army and to advance additional civil rights initiatives, such as desegregation of the federal civil service, as part of the government's obligation to "live up to the ideals professed in the Declaration of Independence and the duties imposed upon it by the Constitution." In a 1951 Independence Day speech, Truman explained the root of national obligation and its link to humanity's destiny: "Anyone who undertakes to abridge the rights of any American to life, liberty, or the pursuit of happiness commits three great wrongs. He wrongs the individual first, but in addition, he wrongs his country and he betrays the hopes of mankind." In this formulation, the Declaration was conceived as a national baseline for the respect of human rights.[2]

Such broad understandings of the Declaration of Independence were rare in the 1940s and 1950s. For the most part, during those years politicians and ordinary citizens who mentioned the document used it as a rhetorical device for attacking communism. Political statements that made mention of it were often short on content and filled with breast-beating patriotism. A Christian minister in Peoria, Illinois, tried to gain traction for his views by calling the Truman administration socialist. Rather than tackling specifics of Truman's Fair Deal—which included welfare proposals such as national health insurance, additional civil rights legislation, and educational aid—the minister criticized the administration for trying to guarantee individual "happiness" rather than simply allowing people to pursue it on their own terms.[3] This antiregulatory interpretation of the Declaration opposed the growth of government programs and resembled a similar line of thought that had been popular with conservatives during the New Deal.

Those engaged in Cold War polemics represented the Declaration as a model of popular governance that was antithetical to totalitarianism. Indictments made in the Declaration of Independence against King George III—such as the accusation that he "destroyed the lives of our people...He has excited domestic insurrections amongst us"—were leveled against "the kind of tyranny now prevalent in the world, communism." This model not only trumpeted Americanism and internationalized the Declaration but also served as the ultimate political counterargument. Anticommunist rhetoric, however, was often visceral and short on substance. The 1946 commencement speaker at the Arkansas Medical School told graduates that enactment of Truman's proposed national health insurance would be a first step to "socialization of the county," amounting to having "our life, liberty and pursuit of happiness taken away from us." Rather than providing a thoughtful contrast between the precepts of government outlined in the Declaration and those of the "communist doctrine," it was easier to resort to clichés characterizing Marxism as "phony as a patent medicine man's patter at a county fair." The axiom of the United States that "all men are created equal" was contrasted with the ideologies of communist countries, where "distinctions are drawn between...the party members and the non-Communists." A slew of speeches distinguished between the safeguards for individual rights in the Declaration of Independence and communism's promotion of class struggle. Writing in a conservative Texas daily, the *Pamapa News*, a columnist asserted that communism denies human freedom and independence, as it is run by "those with the greatest force [to] enslave others and take from others part of the fruits of their labor." On the other hand, the "Declaration of Independence was the embodiment of the American way," the columnist continued, for obtaining "just powers from the consent of the governed" while "there are no principles whatsoever in communism."[4]

There were diplomatic costs for virulent anticommunism. The Soviet Union and China could not but understand the subversive message contained in statements supporting popular uprisings. President Dwight D. Eisenhower urged Americans to put tears into the Iron Curtain by staying true to the Declaration's revolutionary purposes. To make his meaning clear, during an informal speech on the subject Eisenhower quoted: "Whenever any form of government becomes destructive...it is the right of the people to alter and abolish it, and to institute new government, laying its foundations on such principles and organizing its powers in such form as to them shall seem most likely to effect their safety and happiness." Just as advocates of worldwide proletarian revolution invoked the Communist Manifesto, proponents of worldwide democracy drew on the inflammatory and subversive statements of the Declaration of Independence. In this sense, the Declaration was both a source of pride and a wedge between peoples.[5]

The House Committee on Un-American Activities, in contrast to most news items of the day, did offer one of the clearest distinctions between the two political systems. It stated that the Declaration of Independence established the principle that everyone is entitled to inalienable rights, which include "freedom of worship; freedom of speech; freedom of the press; freedom of assemblage; freedom to work in such an occupation as the experience, training and qualifications of a man enabled him to secure and hold." This was a very broad understanding of the terms of the Declaration of Independence, grounded on the progress of American history rather than solely the revolutionary period. The committee contrasted this social ethos with communism's rejection of religious freedoms, private property, political diversity, and representative governance.[6]

The same committee blacklisted Americans who were purportedly linked to communists, raising serious doubt about its own commitment to representative democracy, speech, and assembly. Anyone branded a communist by this or another congressional investigatory entity found opportunities to pursue the happiness of choosing an occupation, speaking openly about politics, and holding elective office severely reduced. Even some of the people who opposed communism considered the "political paranoia" of communist hunters such as Sen. Joseph McCarthy to consist of a "long train of abuses and usurpations" that were as harmful to the American public as the British monarchy had been to the colonists.[7]

In one of the most sensational stories of the day, the Illinois Bar Association denied George Anastaplo bar membership because he refused to respond to questions about his political leaning. In later years, he would become a professor at the Loyola University School of Law in Chicago. But for eleven years he was unable to practice law because the bar inquiry board became suspicious when Anastaplo (who was actually politically conservative) defended the statement on revolution in the Declaration of Independence. Anastaplo explained that if a tyranny like Nazism came to power in the United States and encroached on inalienable rights, "it would be the patriotic right of Americans to revolt." The committee then demanded that Anastaplo reveal if he was a communist, to determine whether he was a member of a subversive organization. Though he had no communist ties, Anastaplo refused to answer and was disqualified from the bar in Illinois. The Supreme Court of the United States upheld the right of state bar associations to set their own criteria for admission. In dissent, Justice Hugo Black wrote that the anticommunist campaign had led "the Government ... [to] being permitted to strike out at those who are fearless enough to think as they please and say what they think."[8]

Civil rights leaders working during the Red Scare persistently invoked the Declaration of Independence in their calls for fundamental reforms. In 1953 Frederick D. Patterson, the president of the Tuskegee Institute in Alabama, cautioned students about the intemperate political climate. He believed that indifference to the ideals of the Declaration of Independence made civil rights progress more difficult; even someone complaining about housing and employment discrimination might be labeled a communist. The Central Conference of American Rabbis condemned Jim Crowism, expressing a "sense of brotherhood with the colored races." Participating rabbis defended the birthright of the people to enjoy "the equality of all men before God and in the principles of the Declaration of Independence and of the Constitution of the United States." At another event, Robert W. Searle, of the Greater New York Federation of Churches, explained the importance of antidiscrimination employment policy, noting that without equal economic opportunities blacks could not hope to enjoy the promises of life, liberty, and the pursuit of happiness. Similarly, the 1952 Democratic Party Platform asserted that national governance was predicated on "the ideals of the Declaration of Independence and must exercise the powers vested in it by the Constitution." More specifically, it noted that "our country is founded on the proposition that all men are created equal. This means that all citizens are equal before the law and should enjoy equal political rights."[9]

The decision of the two most popular political parties to connect the Declaration to political rights mirrored others' increasingly comprehensive understanding of the document. At the 175th anniversary of the Declaration of Independence, one author went so far as to tie "the pursuit of happiness" to matters that would have been inconceivable to the framers, including Securities and Exchange Commission protections of bank deposits, social security, unemployment payments, minimum wage laws, and farm subsidies.[10] That interpretational breadth was linked to reformulation of the Declaration of Independence during Roosevelt's New Deal. This broad-ranging perspective reinvigorated the founding document to meet the needs of a more industrial age. It recognized that federal policies on such matters as communication, transportation, and media had a greater impact on individual rights than anyone might have imagined in 1776.

To be true to the principles in the Declaration of Independence, national policy was also necessary on matters of civil rights. By 1952 both of the main political parties in this country supported a variety of civil rights advancements. But there was great divergence between principles and practices. A 1956 survey by the *Catholic Digest* found that even though eight of every ten white Americans agreed with the Declaration's statement that "all men are created equal," only four of ten would entertain the idea of living next door to black neighbors, and only five in ten would live in an integrated neighborhood. In order to push the envelope, the NAACP set an aspirational deadline for ending segregation; the date coincided with the centennial of the Emancipation Proclamation. The "Free by '63" movement, as a reporter from the African American–owned newspaper *L. A. Sentinel* saw it, was "just like the Declaration of Independence, . . . a rallying force to inspire the best of our efforts—to unite us in a common cause."[11]

During the Cold War, the trend toward pluralism was not confined to the Democratic Party. The 1948 Republican Party Platform similarly asserted: "One of the basic principles of this Republic is the equality of all individuals in their right to life, liberty, and the pursuit of happiness. This principle is enunciated in the Declaration of Independence and embodied in the Constitution of the United States." Yet the platform listed only a couple instances of the applicability of the principle to political policy making, which included the party's commitment to desegregating the military and ending poll taxes. On numerous occasions, Gov. Earl Warren of California, who in 1948 was a Republican candidate for the vice presidency, endorsed the party platform and quoted the portion of it that cited the Declaration. And later, when he was confirmed to be the Chief Justice of the U.S. Supreme Court, Warren's ideological commitment translated into his decision making. After a decade on the High Court, Warren told an audience at a Georgetown University honorary degree ceremony, "We must discover the way to make meaningful in every respect the great principles that are symbolized in the words 'All men are created equal' and in the words 'equal protection of the laws.'" Fittingly, he guided the Court through a series of desegregation cases.[12]

What he meant by that vision came through in his written opinion in the seminal case on elementary school desegregation, *Brown v. Board of Education* (*Brown I*). Although his majority opinion did not mention the Declaration of Independence, the chief justice made clear through speeches that the document influenced his thinking. Nevertheless, judicial neglect of the document limited its precedential value. In a rare exception, an Arizona trial court in 1953 invalidated the state's local segregation statute, explaining that "democracy rejects any theory of second-class citizenship. There are no second-class citizens in Arizona. And the trend from the time of the enunciation in the Declaration of Independence of the principle 'That all men are created equal' has been to constantly reconsider the status of minority groups and their problems." Although mentioned rarely in reported cases, in public pronouncements judges made clear that the Declaration had an impact on their thinking. Retired Judge J. Waties Waring gave voice to his sense of ideological purpose while presiding over a district court in South Carolina. He advocated use of judicial force, especially through Supreme Court decision making, "to make the South observe the simple tenets of human decency." At an event convoked at Chicago's Sherman Hotel in his honor, Waring said that segregation and prejudice violated the "Declaration of Independence and the Constitution of the United States and especially those amendments [that] guarantee to all persons the equal protection of the laws." Beyond additional judicial clarity, Waring believed statutory reform was needed to guarantee equal suffrage, employment parity, and property rights. At another award ceremony, Justice William J. Brennan, one of the most influential jurists of the Supreme Court, admitted that "law had for a time isolated itself from the currents of life," but he said "it was now responding to human needs." Brennan chose wording reminiscent of the Declaration of Independence to call on "religion, education, and law" to "make yet more fruitful their pursuit of the age-old dream for recognition of the inherent dignity and of the equal and inalienable rights of all members of the human family."[13]

The NAACP Defense Fund's first legal breakthrough against segregation came in 1938, when the Supreme Court found Missouri in violation of black litigants' Equal Protection rights by failing to provide them with an in-state legal education. Other victories followed. In 1954 seventeen states still mandated racial segregation in public schools. All that changed when the Supreme Court held in *Brown I* that primary school segregation violates the Equal Protection Clause. In a letter to the editor of the *New York Times,*

James A. Farrell hailed the unanimous court decision for "finally giv[ing] the force of law to the holding of the Declaration of Independence that it is a self-evident truth that all men are created equal." Rather than abiding by the literal meaning of the Equal Protection Clause, which earlier higher education cases had found separate but equal education to satisfy, *Brown I* reconciled the Equal Protection Clause's neutral-sounding text with the universal principles of human equality and dignity in the Declaration of Independence.[14]

Another article published in the *New York Times* proclaimed *Brown I* to be predicated on the second paragraph of the Declaration, which it believed had foreshadowed "a system of human rights." The Court's historic accord with the American credo stepped away from its earlier narrow interpretation of racially separate equality. It challenged the nation to put its founding commitment to equality into practice. In the wake of the Court's decision, a student from West End High School (in Birmingham, Alabama), the site of later white supremacist protest, asserted in a public letter that "segregation deprives a citizen of equal rights and privileges" and is against the cherished "ideal that is stated in our Declaration of Independence that all men are created equal, and that color is no criterion of assets and liabilities." A letter to the editor of the *Chicago Defender* hailed black students in the south for "trying to remind America of her creed of equality and essential dignity of man" that "echoed" the "'humanitarian idealism of the Declaration of Independence.'" In light of the decision, the U.S. ambassador to the United Nations, James J. Wadsworth, issued an official communiqué proclaiming that educational integration would demonstrate to the world that America had "been moving steadily forward toward the translation into reality of the proposition that 'all men are created equal.'" Wadsworth's language showed how much the Declaration informed understanding of *Brown I* even though the decision never explicitly quoted from the document. The NAACP regarded the victory in *Brown I* to be as great in magnitude for the country "as the Declaration of Independence and Lincoln's Emancipation Proclamation" had been.[15]

Yet the Declaration of Independence was ambiguous enough for opponents of desegregation to also make reference to it. The contrarian interpretation resembled the states' rights version of the document that had informed Confederate leaders such as Jefferson Davis. A Virginian argued that "consent of the governed" referred to the consent of a state's citizens, not to a national consensus. The notion that southern state residents would desegregate on their own was far-fetched. Writing several months after the Court published its constitutional decision, Betty Walter, a resident of Salisbury, Maryland, who proudly proclaimed she cherished her black friends, conjectured that if the framers of the Declaration could have anticipated that their words would be so misunderstood, they would have muffled the equality portion of the manifesto. As Imogene McMurtry of Marysville, California, saw it, segregationists had an inalienable right not to associate with blacks. Hers was an exclusionary vision of individual liberty. Prejudice also showed itself in statements that warned of how racially mixed education would lead to more intimate relations between races. A two-time Pulitzer Prize winner, historian Allan Nevins, welcomed the idea that abiding by "the precepts of the declaration of independence" would likely lead to more pluralism and a higher rate of intermarriage. Such talk struck at the heart of taboos that had existed socially and legally for more than a hundred years before independence.[16]

In 1955, the Supreme Court issued the remedy portion of its decision, commonly known as *Brown II*. It ordered school boards to integrate with "all deliberate speed" rather than mandating them to do so immediately. The Court's use of this ambiguous term created administrative uncertainty among federal courts. Some southern schools deployed a variety of devices—school choice, transfer, pupil assignments—not to comply with desegregation. A group of southern congressmen issued a Declaration of Constitutional Principles vowing to impede compliance. Only in 1968 did the Court, in *Green v. County School Board*, demand that every school board develop a plan that "promises realistically to work, and promises realistically to work now."[17]

Benjamin E. Mays, who was the president of Morehouse College and a mentor of Martin Luther King, Jr., declared in 1955 that if governments failed to police schools refusing to comply with the tenets of student dignity in *Brown I*, the country might as well "tell the world honestly that we do not believe that part of the Declaration of Independence which says in essence that all men are created equal." An author of a historically black newspaper opined on the outlook of Thurgood Marshall, the lead counsel for the NAACP team who argued the *Brown* cases in court, at the prospect of gradual desegregation. It noted that he might have been just as impatient to cancel the long shadow of segregation as the framers of the Declaration had been to end British tyranny. But Marshall said that even though it might take a while to end separation in schools, "the period of time will be a much shorter time than it would have been without these Supreme Court decisions." Judge Waring expressed hope that "the true voice of America" would come "through to implement the teachings of our Declaration of Independence that all men are created equal" by complying with the Supreme Court's attack against racial bias.[18]

Even a one-day delay was regrettable, given the daily stigma black students experienced as a result of educational segregation. As an editorial in the *Pittsburgh Courier* put it, "Over 180 years after the Declaration of Independence, we find mobs of grown people preventing groups of two, six or a dozen Negro youngsters from entering public schools supported by the taxes of black and white alike, and regardless of the supreme law of the land."[19] Supreme Court leadership and social activism was needed to convince legislators to incorporate the longstanding statements of the Declaration of Independence into law.

Unable to win in the courts, extremists turned to violence. In November 1958, a dynamite blast tore through a high school in Clinton, Tennessee. Fortunately no one was hurt, with the blast leaving only structural damage. A journalist who visited the scene noticed that amid the destruction there still hung a picture of Abraham Lincoln, "who once proclaimed a nation 'dedicated to the proposition that all men are created equal.' Hanging from on high, his image looked down on the broken plaster, the twisted cinderblock, the glass and dust of a school where children had been studying together as equals." Hate crimes posed a danger at home and harmed the U.S. image abroad. Overt discrimination in schools, jobs, and businesses was even more endemic than violence.[20]

President Eisenhower sought to avoid direct confrontation with states that had not complied with *Brown*. But southern school districts' intransigence and outright violations placed his administration in the uncomfortable position of resorting to military power to enforce the decision. At the NAACP's 1954 Freedom Fulfillment Conference, the president pledged $1 million a year to abolish discrimination and live up to Lincoln's assertion that the nation was dedicated to achieving the equality promised by the Declaration of Independence. At first Eisenhower tried personal suasion of southern officials such as South Carolina Gov. James F. Byrnes, but that achieved little. Alabama was one of the most troubled spots. Editors of the *New York Amsterdam News* urged Eisenhower to act; "The Negro" could not enjoy "his God given freedom to life, liberty and the pursuit of happiness" with the looming threat of violence. Shortly after the beginning of the Montgomery bus boycott of 1955, a city bus was hit with gunfire; the house of a supporter of Reverend King was bombed; between December 26, 1956, and January 9, 1957, shooters hit four buses with gunfire, with one of the shots piercing both legs of a pregnant Rosa Jordan; on January 19, 1957, bombs were set off in four black churches and two homes; and on January 27, 1957, a black home and gas station were hit by gunfire. The *Amsterdam News* called the violence "a national disgrace." The president admonished the nation to keep in mind that "the Negro people of the South are American citizens. And as American citizens they are fully entitled to the life, liberty and pursuit of happiness guaranteed them." The outcry and southern brazenness pushed Eisenhower to act.[21]

Now in his second term of office, Eisenhower decided to demonstrate presidential resolve. Conflict began shortly after the Little Rock School Board agreed to desegregate its public school system. Arkansas Gov. Orval E. Faubus called out the state National Guard to prevent implementation of the plan, which was to begin with integration of Little Rock Central High School. In response to the governor's clear attempt to impede execution of *Brown II*'s remedy, the president federalized the Arkansas Guard and sent the 101st Airborne Division to secure admission for nine blacks to Central in September 1957. At the height of these events, Ike expressed the belief that the political phrase "all men are equal," which the framers had enshrined in the Declaration of Independence, was part of America's social religion. In the midst of a tense standoff, the president wrote the Episcopal bishop of Arkansas, asking that he continue to support the U.S. government's decision to stay "strong and vital" in its devotion to "the concepts that inspired the signers of our Declaration of Independence." Going a step further that year, Eisenhower spoke at the Augusta National Golf Club, an area that was once at the heart of the Confederacy. He reminded the Deep South of "the ringing pronouncements of our American Declaration" about human equality. Putting an end to segregation would not only help those Americans who were disadvantaged by systematic discrimination but also increase the talent pool essential for regional and national economic development.[22]

The Supreme Court's statement in *Cooper v. Aaron* (1957) that its interpretation of the Constitution was binding on state governments was a defense of federal power. On a popular front, the Constitution did not specify any particular sphere of authority to the people comparable to the judicial or executive branches. But the Declaration of Independence was interpreted in popular media as a source of national morality that superseded state prejudices. Finding relevance for the document in a context that the framers had never fathomed demonstrated the extent to which the meaning of inalienable rights, equality, consent of the governed, and the pursuit of happiness had both molded and been molded by U.S. culture.

The Declaration was a source of national pride as well as self-criticism. Pulitzer Prize winning journalist Edgar Ansel Mowrer questioned how the United States expected to convince mankind to shun communism. According to him, Governor Faubus's actions had become a source of shame for the country in the international arena; the pages of foreign newspapers were filled with coverage of the surrounding events. Overseas, America's claims about the gravitas of the Declaration's statements on freedom and equality could appear to be hollow rhetoric so long as segregation went unabated. The violence accompanying the Little Rock nine would be followed in the early sixties by violence directed at pacifist protestors seeking to desegregate restaurants and the means of interstate travel. The backlash, as another popular journalist pointed out, gave some credence to Soviet propaganda to the effect that the United States paid lip service to the Declaration in order to obfuscate its racial "mess."[23]

Ultimately, the tragic confrontation in Little Rock did lead to integration of the public schools there, and the blanket news coverage of the events reminded many Americans of their own communities' shortcomings. What could surely be said of the United States, as noted by a black Milwaukee attorney who won an interfaith human rights award from B'Nai Brith in 1957, was that black Americans' knowledge "that there was a Declaration of Independence which pronounced the equality of man has done much to encourage them to the truism that they, too, are included in the immortal document." Words were, of course, not enough to halt traditional forms of discrimination; but the document's language of universal equality set the baseline for national hope, aspiration, and reassessment. Passage of the Civil Rights Act of 1957, with Eisenhower's strong backing, also showed American resolve. Political syndicated columnist Holmes Alexander pointed out that the Declaration of Independence allowed government to reflect on "the decent opinion of mankind." Demonstrating resolve against segregation along with enactment of the first civil rights law since Reconstruction helped polish America's tarnished image.[24]

On May 17, 1957, about thirty thousand people assembled at the Lincoln Memorial in Washington, D.C., to celebrate the third anniversary of *Brown I*. Martin Luther King, Jr., who was one of the speakers, told those in attendance that recent achievements in the South, notably the desegregation of public transportation in Montgomery, were occasions ranking "in American history with the Declaration of Independence." The Supreme Court's holding in favor of equality sent an unmistakable message about the nation's core commitments that inspired others to work on behalf of justice. The National Conference of Christians and Jews issued a statement saying that "while the dictum of the Declaration of Independence that 'all men are created equal' and 'are endowed by their Creator with certain unalienable rights' does not yet command universal acceptance throughout the United States, very great progress has been made in recent years": lynching had almost disappeared, employment discrimination had diminished, and trade unions had admitted blacks in increasing numbers. These were accomplishments indeed; but the victories were still incomplete.[25]

After serving two terms as president, Eisenhower was constitutionally ineligible to run again in 1960. As at no period since Reconstruction, the nation seemed on the verge of a breakthrough. Both the Republican and Democratic platforms quoted from the Declaration of Independence to emphasize their commitment to civil rights. The Democratic Party tied domestic progress to foreign policy. It contrasted the nation's founding "proposition...that all men are created equal," which it took to refer to American respect for "human dignity," with "the closed totalitarian society of the Communists." Its Republican counterpart agreed that racial discrimination had no place in "a nation dedicated to the proposition that all men are created equal." Real differences existed, however, with liberals calling for government to support social and economic initiatives necessary for all individuals to have the wherewithal to pursue happiness.

Conservatives, on the other hand, believed government efforts to equalize conditions were outside the scope of congressional power and infringed on the liberties of the well-off.[26]

Democrats chose the Senate majority leader from Texas, Lyndon Johnson, to be John F. Kennedy's running mate. The choice was a logical one because Johnson's presence on the ticket increased Democratic chances of winning southern electoral votes, a region where the candidate from Massachusetts could otherwise hope to receive but little support. In his early political career, as the Texas director of the New Deal National Youth Administration, Johnson showed determined commitment to equality in education, albeit within the confines of the segregated system in that state. But his record was mixed; in the 1940s Johnson voted against antilynching and anti-poll-tax bills, but he voted for the Civil Rights Acts of 1957 and 1960. His sincerity in achieving political equality was tempered by political opportunism. Commenting on the Arkansas governor's standoff with Eisenhower, Johnson toed the line between constituents. He chided the South for being "a little late in...recognizing that all men are created equal" but disapproved of Eisenhower sending paratroopers to end the Little Rock standoff. To the happy surprise of black leaders, as the NAACP's executive secretary Roy Wilkins put it, once he was the vice president Johnson "began to emerge [on civil rights] during the Kennedy Administration...and to the delight of the civil rights forces" became deeply involved in the issues.[27]

A few months before the presidential election, Democratic Platform Committee Chairman Chester Bowles promised that if elected the new administration would "create a sense of national purpose." Better standards for public behavior would include "an affirmative new atmosphere in which to deal with racial division and inequalities" that would put an end to abuses undermining the human dignity guaranteed by the Declaration's proposition that all men are created equal. Bowles also recognized that to distinguish itself from communist regimes, the United States would need to unequivocally protect the people's inalienable rights.[28]

After Kennedy's victory, ordinary citizens propelled change at a quicker rate than politicians would have chosen to proceed on their own. In the South, segregation had set blacks and whites apart, forcing them to live in parallel countries, unable to share drinking fountains, bibles in courthouses, phone booths, bathrooms, medical facilities, benches, tables at restaurants, hotel rooms, and many other forms of public accommodation. In a letter to the editor of an Ohio newspaper, the owner of an engineering company reflected on how "the Negro has been stripped of his inalienable rights, deprived of various opportunities for advancement and then shoved into the background of American society," being segregated "in schools, buses, [and] public places." Speaking before the Sheboygan Evening Optimist Club in Wisconsin, social worker Theodore Mack indicted discrimination in employment, education, and housing because it "effectively denied Negroes their rights to 'life, liberty and the pursuit of happiness.'"[29]

The 1960s were a monumental time, when discontent with discrimination was at the breaking point, the tension having been brought on by the activism of such leaders as W.E.B. Du Bois and Martin Luther King, Jr., and the Supreme Court's ethical clarity in the *Brown v. Board of Education* decision. Four black college freshmen, students at North Carolina Agricultural and Technical College, sped up the impending change when they boycotted the Greensboro Woolworth's Five and Dime lunch counter for refusing to serve them on racial grounds. The protest spread rapidly, with professional civil rights organizations such as the NAACP, Student Nonviolent Coordinating Committee (SNCC), Congress of Racial Equality (CORE), and Southern Christian Leadership Conference providing logistical support. In Rock Hill, South Carolina, where eleven demonstrators had been imprisoned for conducting a sit in, protestors came to prison demanding a visit with them. Afterward, a mass meeting voted to send a letter to U.S. Attorney General Robert Kennedy requesting that he tour Rock Hill "to witness trials and obstacles to life, liberty and the pursuit of happiness of a vast section of the South Carolina population." A group of Columbia University students from New York wrote a letter to the mayors of Rock Hill and Denmark, South Carolina, adjuring them to defend "the right of all citizens to life, liberty and the pursuit of happiness" by prohibiting segregation. Protest spread north as well, where students from the University of Wisconsin picketed the W. T. Grant and F. W. Woolworth stores to protest the companies' lunch counter segregation in the South. The picketers distributed handbills encouraging pedestrians to practice the principles of the Declaration and the Constitution by not patronizing the stores and thereby giving tacit approval to enforced segregation.[30]

Antisegregation protests of public transportation and lunch counters quickly spread to other areas of public life. The Declaration's statement that all the people have a right to freely pursue happiness provided an easily recognizable statement of national purpose, ideologically knitting together opponents of public housing and park segregation. Rather than relying solely on the Equal Protection Clause, as the Court did in *Brown v. Board of Education* to strike at segregation of schools, ordinary people understood that the Declaration's second paragraph was also relevant to their cause. In a speech before a clothing workers union, Alexander J. Allen, associate director of the National Urban League, asserted that, "Today we are all being challenged to achieve in actual practice the principles which have been on paper since the Founding Fathers signed the Declaration of Independence." He commended college students who were conducting sit-ins for trying to live up to those standards and helping destroy racist stereotypes. Civil rights activists, among them the Freedom Riders, were no longer willing to wait patiently. Freedom Riders of 1961 rejected Attorney General Robert Kennedy's call for a cooling-off period. Like the framers of the Declaration of Independence, they were unwilling to suffer "a long train of abuses." Arthur M. Schlesinger, Jr., a historian and special assistant to John Kennedy, thanked the Freedom Riders for reminding the nation of its commitment to the Declaration of Independence.[31]

The people could press for change, but undoing cultural prejudice was inconceivable without efforts at the highest echelons of government. A year and a half into John Kennedy's presidency, Robert Kennedy commented as attorney general on the administration's civil rights record. He boasted about the number of voter fraud cases the Justice Department had brought under the Civil Rights Act of 1957 and about the Interstate Commerce Commission's order to desegregate interstate carriers and accommodations, which led relatively quickly to hundreds of "for whites only" signs coming down at bus depots and airline terminals as well as bus, train, and railway stations. Like so many other members of the cabinet, Bobby Kennedy spoke of how important civil rights progress was for strengthening the influence of the United States around the globe: "We are not going to be able to convince people in other lands that we mean what we say in the Declaration of Independence and in our Constitution if a large number of our citizens are denied their full rights." At a Colorado Young Democrats banquet, Schlesinger praised black citizens for compelling the government to begin fulfilling the Declaration's promise of equality. He spoke of the "blood and agony" that had gone into the long struggle and of how much remained undone. Bobby Kennedy also understood that other groups were the object of racism as well; at a Slovak Catholic Convention, Bobby decried anti-Semitic barriers Jews encountered in their pursuit of happiness.[32]

By the summer of 1963, President Kennedy was becoming more decisive on the issues. Despite the potential for a negative backlash from southern Democrats, he began planning a new statute. He spoke forcefully about every American's obligation to "examine his conscience" and determine whether he was hindering the nation's "worldwide struggle" to protect the "principle that all men are created equal." For his part, Kennedy promised to send Congress a bill to prohibit segregation in public places such as stores, hotels, and restaurants; to ask for more federal power to desegregate schools; and to bring added muscle to securing blacks' right to vote. At the same time, Kennedy federalized Alabama national guardsmen to enforce a federal district court order enjoining the University of Alabama at Tuscaloosa from barring enrollment of black students.[33]

Efforts to advance equal treatment and opportunity heightened public awareness of the need to move ahead rapidly to implement democratic principles. After dealing with violent attacks on Freedom Riders in Birmingham and Montgomery, and on students at the University of Mississippi, Kennedy was convinced that only federal legislation could secure the enjoyment of equal human dignity. An editorial published in a southern Illinois newspaper decried the "persecution of the Negro because of his skin color." The author thought it shameful that "we whites call ourselves Americans" while excluding blacks from enjoying the privileges the framers carved into the Declaration of Independence. Newspaper coverage of various protests made ordinary Americans increasingly aware that local school boards and thugs were challenging integration of black students into schools, where the most meaningful unification might have occurred in conformity with the proposition that "all men are created equal." President Kennedy challenged the nation to change the stark reality: "No American who believes in the basic truth that 'all men are created equal, that they are endowed by their Creator with certain inalienable rights,' can fully excuse, explain or defend the picture these statistics portray." Younger black mortality and dropout rates, lower earnings, and higher unemployment belied the notion that America had done enough to live up to its egalitarian ideals. As a major step toward closing existing gaps between America's aspirations and its practices, Kennedy's proposed bill was meant to streamline relief against disfranchisement, provide technical and financial assistance for education desegregation, expand federal oversight of employment discrimination, support community desegregation, and use government funds for a variety of other incentives.[34]

At a Fourth of July celebration held at Independence Hall, Vice President Johnson called on "today's generation" to "implement the Declaration of Independence...for all Americans!" He deplored the indignity people suffered at being forced to sit at the back of a bus or being relegated to substandard facilities. Johnson asserted that enough time had been spent parsing the words of the Declaration; time had come "to honor and fulfill their meaning." Johnson and Kennedy were able to muster sufficient support to bring about significant changes. Although Kennedy would not live to see enactment of the law, he jump-started the process.[35]

Progress hinged on whether the long-deferred equality of the Declaration of Independence (which many thought had been incorporated into the foundation of the Constitution) would or could become an immediate reality after centuries of hesitation and outright infringement. Reverend King, for one, believed that the Declaration, the Constitution, and ordinary law could be effectively conjoined to combat discrimination. His speech during the 1963 March on Washington, with its quotes of and references to the Declaration, elevated the nation's conscience and made it easier for Johnson to pass the Civil Rights Act of 1964. The time for "all deliberate speed" had ended, as the Court put it; indeed, there had never been any justification for delay. Speaking against the closing of Prince Edward County schools in Virginia, which refused to abide by a court order to integrate, King told the animated audience, "all men are created equal—the universalism at the center of the American dream—has been scarred and bruised and never achieved. America proudly professed the principles of democracy but sadly practiced the antithesis of those principles."[36] There was too much at stake for the individuals suffering from economic, housing, and school segregation to continue waiting for the states to come into line with national and international goals.

Not everyone around the country saw it that way. Many in the South still believed that unequal education was racially justifiable. "Only the ignorant would attempt to argue that all men are created equal, intellectually," retorted a Texas newspaper. This statement brings to mind John

C. Calhoun's proslavery attack of the nineteenth century against the idea that "all men are born free and equal" as "the most false and dangerous of all political error." Although a century earlier the final nail had been hammered into the coffin of the institution of slavery, racism and segregation did not die by moral suasion alone. When Jefferson was drafting the Declaration of Independence, prejudiced whites refused to free slaves, although as we saw at the beginning of the book many contemporaries realized that it would be the inevitable consequence of the document's principles. In 1963, those who still denied that the Declaration's statement applied to blacks sought to perpetuate prejudice by ignoring or outright defying the Court's order in *Brown*.[37]

Overt racism was sometimes couched in democratic, but antipluralistic, terms. Opponents of housing desegregation argued that whites were in the majority and allowed to pursue their happiness in neighborhoods free of blacks. According to this perspective, the federal government was not allowed to encroach on the Declaration's guarantee of the freedom of an owner to enjoy real property.[38]

Alongside the libertarian argument, there were those who believed the federal government's power simply did not extend to protection of inalienable rights. This minimalist school of thought believed only state governments could pass legislation inspired by the life, liberty, and pursuit of happiness clause of the Declaration of Independence. To its adherents, sit-down strikes, bus boycotts, and lunch counter demonstrations seemed like bullying tactics, not efforts to expand rights. Even worse, several newspaper authors claimed, forcing employers to treat people as if they were all created equal by paying them the same salary for the same work bore a resemblance to the standardization of communism.[39]

The 1963 report of the U.S. Commission on Civil Rights noted that the "nation was founded on the ringing affirmation that all men are created equal" and "has traditionally served as a haven of freedom in a world plagued by oppression." The United States could not "continue to deny equality to Negro and other minority groups" without "eroding the moral foundation" that had made it a leader in the free world. Countries throughout the world, filled as they were with multiplicities of races, were scrutinizing whether America would be true to its "moral foundation" or merely preach to countries around the world. Just the year before, black army veteran James Meredith's success at breaking the color barrier by enrolling at the University of Mississippi was met by violence that left two dead.[40]

Ordinary Americans, such as Carol J. A. Axtman of Billerica, Massachusetts, were "rapidly losing faith in humanity, and in democracy" for saying "all men are created equal" while "doing the opposite." Bayard Rustin, who had been a prominent member of the civil rights movement since his participation in the Journey of Reconciliation in 1947 and had served as co-director for the March on Washington in 1963, expressed similar sentiments. The Declaration of Independence would not be a noble instrument until it was used to promote an economic system committed to justice rather than to property rights.[41]

After John Kennedy was shot to death, Lyndon Johnson vigorously took up lobbying efforts to pass the civil rights bill. The new president assumed that the American Revolution had been fought in vindication of a Declaration of Independence that promised equality to mankind. "Those are not just clever words or empty theories," Johnson told a Joint House and Senate Session on Civil Rights. Rather, they "are a promise to every citizen that he shall share in the dignity of man.... To apply any other test—to deny a man his hopes because of his color or race, his religion or the place of his birth—is not only to do injustice, it is to deny America and to dishonor the dead who gave their lives for freedom."[42]

The most prominent opponent of the bill was the Republican Party candidate for president in 1964, Barry Goldwater. Even though he enthusiastically agreed that the wording of the Declaration meant that "citizens have rights common to all mankind," Goldwater rejected federal civil rights legislation. Unlike Johnson's vision, Goldwater's perspective was libertarian and oriented to states' rights. For those who supported him, the notion of equality at birth (meaning the federal government had the right to end public discrimination) was tantamount to communism because it threatened to infringe upon business owners' right to reject unwanted customers. Extending federal power to traditionally local matters, said Rep. August E. Johansen of Michigan, would encroach on the "live-and-let-live tolerance" that "is necessary if there is to be either domestic tranquility or any meaningful pursuit of happiness." To others of this individualistic ilk, among them Sen. James O. Eastland of Mississippi, even the existence of the Civil Rights Commission was troubling because it contained "the seeds of federal bureaucracy" that would impose on private citizens its interpretation of appropriate pursuits of happiness.[43]

The *Aiken Standard and Review,* a newspaper serving a small community in South Carolina, expressed the sentiments of many southerners. Rather than viewing the desegregation portion of the civil rights bill as a leveler, the *Review* claimed blacks wanted to exact special privileges from whites and receive extra safeguards for their rights to life, liberty, and the pursuit of happiness. It mocked the idea that the abstract proclamations of the Declaration of Independence granted the federal government any enforcement authority.[44]

Articles and speeches that relied on the Declaration to express opposition to increased federal administration were reminiscent of conservative statements against New Deal legislation. The issues were different but the rhetoric was similar. In 1964, the Mississippi senate judiciary committee complained that civil rights law threatened to impose "federal control over affairs specifically reserved to the States by the Constitution." The bill was also "iniquitous," the committee went on to say, because it "proposed to thwart the right and choice of the individual, or the majority, to the pursuit of happiness without Federal control." Sen. A. Willis Robertson had a similar view, telling the Senate Committee on Banking that the bill's attempt to bring about actual equality did a grave injustice to Jefferson's equality formulation in the Declaration and could lead to "ultimate dictatorship." Alabama Gov. George C. Wallace said the bill threatened to sanction all "21 charges of tyranny listed in the Declaration of Independence." Sen. Russell B. Long of Louisiana, the son of Sen. Huey P. Long, also rejected the idea that "equality" in the Declaration was ever meant to be "equality of the leveler." The statements of that document, Long said, in words clouded by unmistakable prejudice, could never change natural human inequalities. Coming from members of a privileged race and a culture that justified racial inequality by declaring it to be an objective fact rather than an imposed norm, these sentiments might have been expected. The *North Adams Transcript,* published in a Massachusetts city that in the early nineteenth century was a hotbed of radical abolitionism, mocked the younger Long for holding a view tantamount to diminishing the Declaration's statement of equality to only white American and British gentlemen rather than humanity as a whole.[45]

A southerner with a very different perspective, former Florida Gov. Leroy Collins, who was then president of the National Association of

Broadcasters, urged southerners to become supportive players in the nation's efforts to end racial injustices. He regarded civil rights legislation as an important means of treating the phrase "all men are created equal" as an influential principle rather than an empty cliché. After passage of the Civil Rights Act of 1964, President Johnson appointed Collins to direct the federal Community Relations Service in troubleshooting local racial tensions. The mighty idea of the Declaration, as Collins saw it, supported efforts to protect national standards of human dignity against localized prejudices, racist customs, hatreds, violence, and outrages. This was a major step forward for Collins, who, a decade earlier, after the *Brown* decision was issued, had openly tried to retain segregation in Florida. Provisions in the proposed civil rights law went much further in undermining school discrimination than the Court had been able to reach in *Brown*. The bill prohibited invidious discrimination in public places such as bathrooms, lunch counters, restaurants, movie theaters, hospitals, clothing stores, ice cream parlors, drug stores, schools that received federal funding, and places of employment engaged in interstate commerce.[46]

Just as the Declaration played a prominent role in debate on passage of the Reconstruction Amendments, so too congressmen repeatedly claimed that the Civil Rights Act of 1964 was important for fulfilling the nation's founding pledge "that all men are created equal; that they are endowed equally with unalienable rights; that they are entitled to equal opportunity in the pursuit of their daily lives." After the Civil War, congressmen used the lens of the Declaration of Independence to better understand how to amend the Constitution and thereby more closely align it with the nation's enduring purpose. With the work of Reconstruction left undone, congressional debate in 1964 returned to the Declaration. Supporters of the civil rights bill refocused the debate away from private interests and property rights to the "immortal ideals...put forth with simple eloquence in the second paragraph of the Declaration of Independence"[47]

States' rights arguments, thought Senator Edward V. Long of Missouri, were off target. Attention should instead be drawn to answering how the nation could adopt into law its "devotion to the concept of the dignity of the individual and to the principles of human rights and equal justice" as they were expressed by "our Declaration of Independence." This perspective regarded the second paragraph of the document as more than merely aspirational. Its statement of universal human rights was thought to be a skeleton of just governance that future generations needed to flesh out. Members of Congress such as Sen. Hubert Humphrey, who would become vice president after Lyndon Johnson won the election of 1964, believed the statute was needed to guarantee the civil liberties, civil rights, and human rights secured by adoption of the Declaration of Independence and the Constitution.[48]

Strong support for the bill in Congress reflected the attitude of ordinary people. Religious leaders of various faiths lobbied congressmen to honor the Declaration's recognition that "all men … are endowed by their creator with certain inalienable rights." Almost two centuries after the Declaration had given homage to universal equality, most of the country (except portions of the lower South) was anxious to approve a new law built on the nation's cornerstone rather than on persisting biases among the states. The nation had kept its freedom intact from external aggression, but only in 1964 did it reach the point in history of fighting for full equality at home. There was also the revolutionary aspect of the Declaration, which gave reason for concern. After all, the document had been written to assert the people's right to rise up and throw off an existing government in order to establish a new order to protect their inalienable rights.[49]

Lyndon Johnson signed the Civil Rights Act of 1964 into law on July 2, on the date when the Continental Congress had declared independence. That declaration had forever been coupled, of course, with July 4, when the colonists explained their decision to establish a nation beholden to the consent of the governed and the principle of universal rights. The colonists refused to remain second-class British citizens. After gaining independence, states passed and enforced oppressive laws that contravened the Declaration's fundamental statement of governance. Now President Johnson addressed the nation, surrounded by the leaders from both political parties: "One hundred and eighty-eight years ago," he said, with the declaration of independence,

> a small band of valiant men began a long struggle for freedom. They pledged their lives, their fortunes, and their sacred honor not only to found a nation, but to forge an ideal of freedom—not only for political independence, but for personal liberty—not only to eliminate foreign rule, but to establish the rule of justice in the affairs of men.… We believe that all men are created equal. Yet many are denied equal treatment. We believe that all men have certain unalienable rights.

Yet many Americans do not enjoy those rights. We believe that all men are entitled to the blessings of liberty. Yet millions are being deprived of those blessings—not because of their own failures, but because of the color of their skin.

The law, he said, would "promote a more abiding commitment to freedom, a more constant pursuit of justice, and a deeper respect for human dignity." Members of the black community expressed contrasting views. James L. Farmer, Jr., who had been the national director of CORE and later served in President Richard Nixon's administration, hailed the Act because it gave "hope to Negroes that the American people and Government mean to redeem the promise of the Declaration of Independence and the Emancipation Proclamation." But Malcolm X, a nationalist and racialist leader, predicted that it "will do nothing but build up the Negro for a big letdown." The continued effectiveness of the Act would prove Farmer correct.[50]

Other challenges loomed. In 1968 Congress would pass the Fair Housing Act, to prohibit racial impediments to real estate sales, rentals, and financing. Passage of this law demonstrated willingness to reconsider the inalienability of property as a right to enter into ownership rather than exclude groups from ownership. Its enforcement would continue to test whether a country "conceived in liberty and dedicated to the proposition that all men are born equal" would live up to its ideals.[51]

Debate on the Voting Rights Act of 1965 was couched in the ideology of government by consent of the people and their intrinsic equality. Congressmen who spoke of the inalienability of voting rights did not encounter the antagonism that met Thaddeus Stevens when he made the same claim during debate on the Fifteenth Amendment. In the words of one congressman, the right to vote was as imbedded in the pledges of the Declaration of Independence, "that all men are created equal... [and] endowed equally with unalienable rights," as were the rights to enjoy public accommodations and integrated schools. The Civil Rights Act of 1964 was the most sweeping civil rights statute since the Civil Rights Act of 1875, but some states continued to treat blacks as second-class citizens by imposing literacy tests, poll taxes, and fraudulent voter registration. Enforcement of the Voting Rights Act was critical to increasing registration of black voters because it suspended literacy test requirements, empowered federal examiners to register voters, created preclearance standards for states with a history of franchise discrimination, allowed federal officials to observe elections, and authorized the Justice Department to file federal lawsuits challenging poll tax provisions. These legislative advances brought hope for a future that would be truer to the Declaration's stated source of government, the consent of the people. Martin Luther King, Jr., expressed the hope that the same nation that "electrified a world with the words of the Declaration of Independence" would make a brighter future not only in "the Negro family but in the family of man."[52]

The evolving black power movement did not share King's optimistic enthusiasm. Malcolm X's speeches fueled a growing sense of despondent anger in black communities. An aggressive cadre—led by Stokely Carmichael, who popularized the term "black power," and later the even more divisive H. Rap Brown—disavowed King, Johnson, and their praises of the Declaration of Independence. The black power movement refused to wait for America to renounce racism. The movement demanded its birthright immediately.

Even members of organizations such as CORE and SNCC, both of which had been committed to nonviolence as late as 1965, were turning to violent protests. A field worker at CORE's Midwest Task Force paraphrased the Declaration: "When an oppressed people have tried every peaceful means of redress to grievances, they have no choice but to pick up arms in defense of freedom." H. Rap Brown, who decades later was convicted of murdering a black police officer, advised black youths to keep a copy of the Declaration in their pocket while they fought street battles, in order to give their destructive efforts a sense of purpose. Some pronouncements took on a decidedly secessionist tone, with groups such as the Nation of Islam and the National Committee of Black Churchmen calling for a black declaration of independence from "white racism and repression and genocide." An outpouring of lawlessness followed two centuries in which blacks were systematically denied the opportunity to participate in governance, despite the Declaration's proclamations about governance by consent.[53]

Violent street riots came at an inopportune time, however. They alienated white support for civil rights reform, ground down the pace of civil rights legislation, gutted black neighborhoods by arson, and led to the flight of businesses from at-risk areas. The black power movement was

too ideologically diffuse to have any sustaining effect, with views ranging from communism to authoritarianism, nationalism, pan-Africanism,
separatism, paternalism, and community self-defense. Some in the black
power movement, most prominently Malcolm X, also had a decidedly racist and anti-Semitic bent that was as offensive to the Declaration's ideal of
universal rights as white racism was. Bayard Rustin bemoaned that out of
frustration with continued obstruction of the achievement of black equality "there have been some who in their despair have attacked those very
people who have been the closest allies of the Negro struggle—namely, the
Jews," contrary to the "moral authority" of "the great American documents
such as the Declaration of Independence and the Constitution." Malcolm
X's slow evolution to a more tolerant form of protest was eventually cut
short by assassins' bullets.[54]

Violent riots and peaceful demonstrations for civil rights raised concerns
at the highest echelons of the U.S. government. America's criticism of the
human rights records of other nations and its self-image as the beacon
of democracy exposed the country to outside scrutiny. The liberation of
African nations (such as Rhodesia in 1965) from colonial rule and international acquiescence to the UN Charter set off a slew of articles bemoan-
ing how tyrannies prevented whole populations from pursuing happiness.
What's more, these journalistic writings pointed the accusing finger back
at the United States to show how it did not live up to the Declaration's philosophy of equal opportunity.[55]

   There were stark differences between mass labor camps and murders
(in such countries as the Soviet Union, Cuba, and mainland China) and
continued discrimination in the states, yet the image of equality that the
Declaration of Independence painted for the United States was never a
reality and it exposed the country to world criticism. Chinese oppression
of Tibetans, Soviet control of Eastern Europeans, Belgian plunder of the
Congo, and British brutality in Kenya were substantially different from the
racial divide in the United States. Nevertheless, the spotlight on human
rights, made brighter by the growing role of the United Nations, exposed the
United States to sustained criticism for claiming its declaration of independence provided fundamental principles while countenancing voting, educational, economic, and judicial discrimination. Under the circumstances,
civil rights legislation was both a domestic and a diplomatic necessity.[56]

By differentiating itself from the Communist Bloc of countries, the United States inadvertently exposed its own shortcomings. A former Columbia University professor, George S. Counts, sardonically quipped that rather than preaching anticolonialism to Far East Asians and Africans, "Maybe we ought to revoke the Declaration of Independence. Then we wouldn't have so much trouble living up to it." Robert Kennedy told those in attendance at an Associated Press conference that throughout the world he had been "asked about the question of civil rights." For instance, Carlos P. Romulo, soon to be Philippine secretary of foreign affairs, told the attorney general that unless the United States could move ahead with civil rights at home, it "cannot possibly win in the struggle with communism throughout the world, because people are just not going to accept or believe the fact that we believe in the Constitution of the United States or the Declaration of Independence if we treat part of our population as inferior human beings." Kennedy agreed with this assessment at the acceptance ceremony for an award from the American Jewish Congress: "We will not win the struggle just by confronting the enemy, but what we do at home, in the final analysis, is just as important....We must accelerate our efforts to banish religious prejudice, racial discrimination and any intolerance which denies to any Americans the right guaranteed them by the Declaration of Independence and the Constitution." Secretary of State Dean Rusk similarly told the Senate Commerce Committee that the "our failure to live up to the pledges of our Declaration of Independence and our Constitution 'embarrasses our friends and heartens our enemies.'"[57]

Curiously, prominent members of the judiciary, who had always been reluctant to rely on the Declaration of Independence in their written decisions, invoked it in public speeches. At the University of Judaism, which later became the American Jewish University, Justice William O. Douglas asked rhetorically, "Will a people who practice discrimination at home be eager evangelists of racial equality abroad?" He believed that enjoyment of individualism at home with an eye to how it influenced relations abroad could help resolve foreign policy dilemmas in the Congo, East Berlin, Cuba, and Laos. "If the mood of this day reflected the spirit of the Declaration of Independence," as he put it, "the renaissance would have arrived." Chief Justice Earl Warren revealed how the document affected his understanding of constitutionalism. A statement he made in 1969 clearly identified the role the Declaration played in American cultural and constitutional life:

> What is the American ideal? It is simply and precisely stated thusly in the Declaration of Independence—"We hold these truths to be self-evident, that all men are created equal, that they are endowed by their Creator with certain inalienable rights, that among these are life, liberty and the pursuit of happiness!" This noble language, fortified by the implementing language of the 14th Amendment, makes the picture complete.... Isn't it about time that it be made a reality?

Warren's comments are telling because they are a window onto his thinking as a judge and they demonstrate how a document that was initially drafted to explain American independence had become intrinsic to post-Civil War Reconstruction, and later to the civil rights movement.[58]

17

EPILOGUE

THE DECLARATION OF INDEPENDENCE LOOMS LARGE IN AMERICAN history. Although it lacks any explicit enforcement clause, the manifesto's statement of national purpose has inspired generations of Americans. Social movements have incorporated the Declaration's second paragraph and consent clauses into their demands for recognition of inalienable rights. The takeaway point from this book is not meant to be nostalgic but to provide clearer understanding of how the manifesto's core values have informed the U.S. public, its leaders, and even foreign nations as to the nature of justice, civility, and governance.

The signers of the Declaration of Independence contributed a lasting vision of liberty and equality that transcended their own practices and times. Paradoxically, the same men who excluded blacks, Native Americans, propertyless white laborers, indentured servants, and women from the seats of governance created the document that gave these and other disadvantaged groups hope of securing equality.

The country's past has always informed contemporary customs, institutions, politics, morals, regulations, and norms. The Declaration of Independence has made its way into the social conscience both as an heirloom of a bygone era and a treasure trove of wisdom with cultural salience. The natural rights theory of the framers is no longer popular, but the human rights aspects of the document have never become obsolete. Its core ideas about the structure of political justice have informed and shaped American perspectives, prudential considerations, and self-assessments. This analytical description lends insight into how the United States has dealt with tensions between its image and reality. The significance of the Declaration of Independence to national identity also helps in understanding how the country has evolved, moderated extremists, renounced past practices, and resolved internal divisions.

According to the founding document, the legitimacy of governance derives from the will of the people. The Declaration makes clear that a representative government must act in accordance with the consent of the real source of power: ordinary people, whose lives are profoundly affected by statutes, regulations, and judicial opinions. Arbitrary state actions committed against racial or nationality groups, women, religious minorities, propertyless persons, and other politically disempowered individuals undermines the purpose for which the government was formed: protection of human equality. The very act of constitution making, which resulted in a document with several clauses sheltering the institution of slavery, violated the Declaration's universal rights principles.

The second paragraph—which unlike most foreign declarations of independence includes a statement of inalienable human interests, the pursuit of happiness, and natural equality—has profoundly influenced progressive movements throughout the world. Other authors, most prominently David Armitage and Pauline Maier, have downplayed the extent to which the Declaration's statement about human dignity influenced the founding generation. In their view, its main function was to criticize King George III and proclaim sovereignty. They place less emphasis on the significance of clauses about individual rights.[1] My research raises doubts about their description.

The Continental Congress voted for independence on July 2, 1776. Two days later, Congress passed the Declaration of Independence to explain its decision and serve as the statement of national purpose. The core meaning of the Declaration of Independence resides in its explanation of which rights are inalienable, how Britain infringed them, and why a popular government is needed to prevent tyranny and autocracy. Armitage and Maier would agree with me that later generations interpreted the Declaration to be a statement of rights. Unlike them, however, I believe that from the very beginning Americans understood and intended it to carry that message.

Although the Declaration of Independence asserted that the United States broke from the monarchy to protect inalienable human rights, only a decade later the Constitutional Convention capitulated to southern demands for the preservation of slavery. By countenancing inequalities, state and federal governments undermined central aspects of the Declaration. So too, enforcing property voting requirements breached the Declaration's principle of political consent. The national statement of purpose inspired groups working to achieve a more egalitarian and pluralistic future. Contrary to the views of thinkers such as Rogers Smith, who in his book *Civic Ideals* argued that inegalitarian values are just as much a part of American ideology as egalitarian ones,[2] abolitionists and civil rights activists believed the Declaration of Independence to be the sole statement of national ideals. Deviations from them, on the part of the founding generation and contemporary society, do not taint the premise of human equality on which the nation is established. For every John Calhoun, who argued that the Declaration of Independence applied only to whites, there was Quaker David Cooper, revolutionary Samuel Adams, President Abraham Lincoln, Sen. Charles Sumner, suffragette Elizabeth Cady Stanton, or the Rev. Martin Luther King, Jr., who proclaimed that the document applied universally to all people, without regard to race, nationality, or gender.

Disputes about the meaning of federalism persistently raised questions regarding the interaction between national and state governments. Expansion of U.S. borders to the west in the early and middle nineteenth century placed strains on the county's unity. The Civil War was in large part an ideological battle about the moral characteristics of the American union. President Lincoln echoed this sentiment in his great speech in Gettysburg: "Fourscore and seven years ago," he said referring to 1776, "our fathers brought forth on this continent a new nation, conceived in liberty and dedicated to the proposition that all men are created equal. Now we are engaged in a great civil war, testing whether that nation or any nation so conceived and so dedicated can long endure." Victory, following bloodshed and devastation, enabled leaders in Congress to shepherd three constitutional amendments into ratification. They provided legislators with authority to implement laws for promoting values of the Declaration. But the Reconstruction Amendments—with their promises of equal protection, due process, liberty, citizenship, and suffrage—did not end debate about how best to protect fundamental interests. In fact, every generation advances this ever-evolving debate.

Social activists turned foremost to provisions of the Declaration of Independence to justify progressive, philanthropic, and humanitarian causes. The document was crucial to abolitionists, suffragists, and labor activists. So too, congressmen who fought for additional constitutional amendments and legislative reforms invoked paragraphs of the American manifesto. Even inclusion of the Equal Protection Clause in one of the Reconstruction Amendments proved to be insufficient for overturning systematic class, racial, and gender privileges such as segregated public transportation and employment discrimination. Besides being an instrument for identifying fundamental rights, the Declaration has helped reformers bring about structural changes that expanded voting rights and thereby augmented ordinary people's participation in governance by consent.

To those who believed in the Declaration's relevance to the evolution of American law and culture, the document offered a higher order of norms than the Constitution, ordinary laws, or agency regulations. At various times, it inspired objectors to the slave trade, the Fugitive Slave Act, school segregation, racial immigration classifications, and gendered family laws. The Declaration of Independence became a national statement of purpose that placed limitations on the exercise of federal and state prerogatives. For instance, the Declaration has appeared often in polemics about voting, first with white manhood suffrage, then black suffrage and women's suffrage. The people, through their elected representatives, were the final arbiters of the Declaration's meaning. The manifesto of equal liberty is not static; rather, later generations animated its meaning by enacting such statutes as the Civil Rights Acts of 1866, 1871, 1875, 1957, 1964, and 1965. In this way, the Declaration has both informed and been informed by challenges undreamed of by its signers.

The Declaration can also help to illuminate today's great political debates, ranging from homosexual discrimination, felon disfranchisement, freedom of conscience, disability rights, antipoverty programs, and gerrymandering to humanitarian laws and customs. Today's activists and politicians rarely invoke the Declaration of Independence in the context of these contemporary issues. This is a significant shift from the focus of previous generations. Of course, references to the values held in the Declaration periodically appear, as in 1990, when President George H. W. Bush and

Rep. Steny H. Hoyer discussed it when the Americans with Disabilities Act became law. But such elaborations of the foundational law are the exception rather than the rule. Loyalists involved in today's most popular social movements, the Tea Party and Occupy Wall Street, tend to mention the Declaration for patriotic effect rather than for its substantive relevance to their causes. The document's statements about inalienable rights, voting privileges, and equality rarely inform modern political debate.

The trend of merely praising the Declaration of Independence but not parsing it within the context of recent events can be traced to the end of the 1960s, where the narrative of this book ends. By that point the Supreme Court had established a cohesive body of civil rights jurisprudence that was well grounded in constitutional provisions, such as the Equal Protection and Due Process Clauses of the Fourteenth Amendment. For instance, the Court used the judicially created doctrine of substantive due process rather than the inalienable rights clause of the Declaration of Independence to protect interests in marriage, birth control, travel, association, child rearing, and religious practice. Organizations then relied on this body of substantive due process jurisprudence—with its various levels of judicial scrutiny that are meant to test the justice of governmental regulation—to develop their own lobbying and litigation strategies. With the Court functioning as a countermajoritarian institution, it seemed only logical to follow its rulings. But allowing the justices to be the only branch of government that can define rights loses track of the Declaration's maxim that rights derive from the people and not from common or statutory law.

In the two centuries since the Declaration's adoption, it has stood for the principle that the people are sovereign. Legislators are to function as their representatives to safeguard rights that are essential to every person. At the core of the Fourteenth Amendment's grant of congressional power is the older foundation of the Declaration of Independence that life, liberty, and the pursuit of happiness are innate human rights. Protection of those rights is the essential purpose of government.

The Declaration of Independence is no mere ornament of the past, as it has mostly been treated since the early 1970s. I believe that constitutional theory should be understood through the lens of the Declaration of Independence. For example, the Due Process Clause is a neutral provision unless it is understood to integrate the Declaration's humanistic values. The doctrine of substantive due process combines the principle that justice must be administered fairly with one that requires government to protect people's inalienable rights. This integration of constitutional and independence doctrines yields a national ethos against discrimination and inequality. Such a perspective helps explain why the Supreme Court, in cases such as *Griswold v. Connecticut*, has recognized privacy to be constitutionally protected under the Due Process Clause. The process is not the end but the means to safeguarding the rights that the Declaration of Independence recognizes to be the purpose of nationhood.

The Declaration's guarantee of liberty is coupled with its recognition of human equality. This combination gainsays the Supreme Court holding, in *Dred Scott v. Sandford*, which found that the Declaration of Independence recognized a liberty interest in slaves. That racialized interpretation of the document entirely overlooked its statement that people are created equal. Individual liberty, therefore, is no excuse for discriminatory inequality.

The Equal Protection Clause also gains clarity through the prism of the Declaration of Independence. For instance, the Court's opinion in *Brown v. Board of Education*, which found that segregated public education violates equal protection, has been criticized by scholars such as Herbert Wechsler for not following simple neutral principles to decide the case.[3] The Equal Protection Clause is indeed a neutral provision, which the Court used in *Plessy v. Ferguson* to defend separate but equal facilities in public places.[4] However, the Declaration's statement about a government obligation to safeguard people's equal rights is clearly connected to the substantive values of life, liberty, and the pursuit of happiness. The Court's unfortunate failure to rely on the Declaration to parse cases like *Brown* is reflected in contemporary culture, where the document remains a symbol of a bygone era but is now rarely regarded as an interpretive tool.

This neglect of the founding document is unfortunate. The Declaration's guarantee of representative self-governance, for instance, appears to run counter to the Supreme Court's recent holding in *Citizens United v. Federal Election Commission*. In that case, the majority held that corporations have the same rights to election-related free speech as natural people. The Court's characterization is questionable because it elevated the rights of corporations, which are artificial persons, with natural persons' inalienable right of political expression. During oral arguments, Justice Ruth Bader Ginsburg warned that the Court not treat corporations as if they were endowed with inalienable rights like ordinary people, but the Declaration of Independence did not figure in the final opinion or dissent.[5]

Debates on a variety of other contemporary issues could likewise gain clarity from a renaissance of Declaration of Independence populism. Some of the most hot-button topics—like welfare reform, affordable education and health care, and voting rights—easily lend themselves to the Declaration's substantive framework of governance by the people. Long ago the framers of that document laid the foundations for pluralistic safety and happiness. The Declaration of Independence left it to every succeeding generation to seek legal and cultural changes to end oppressions that undermine liberal equality.

The Declaration of Independence now stands at the National Archives in Washington, D.C. It has come a long way from being rolled up and kept in storage with ordinary government documents to being singled out, along with the Constitution and Bill of Rights, for public display behind bulletproof glass under the protective eyes of armed guards. What matters, though, is not the physical document but the significance of its enduring text to the American people.

ACKNOWLEDGMENTS

I am deeply indebted to the many scholars, librarians, and students who have helped to guide my steps through the process of research and writing. The Declaration of Independence is a subject of such broad interest that my universe of intellectual confidants extended from the classroom to faculty lounges, coffee shops, restaurants, and mountain trails.

Each conversation enriched me and helped me think through primary and secondary resources. Luminaries have taught me much not only about how to improve the manuscript but also about how to provide generous assistance. At the nascent stage of the project, Marcia McCormick, Brett M. Frischmann, Michael S. Pardo, and Spencer Waller carefully proofed the basic outline of the work. David Brion Davis, with his profound erudition, helped me set the introduction for the entire work. Susan Ferber, of Oxford University Press, made invaluable comments on my book proposal. As research began, the initial outline was revised numerous times to accurately reflect the gems I discovered through library and electronic researching, but I never lost track of their initial counsel. Throughout the whole process of development, friends kept me imbibed with ideas. Whether on a tour bus with Jack Balkin; at a conference with Shannon Gilreath; or by phone with Gordon Hylton, Heather Cox Richardson, and Michael Kent Curtis, the wealth of ideas I received kept me plied with insights about inalienable rights and equality.

Gathering research materials is always enjoyable, but it is made doubly so in the company of acquaintances. Librarians helped by directing me whenever I hit a dead end in the stacks or on the Internet. At the Loyola University-Chicago, C. Frederick LaBaron, Jr., and Jeannette Pierce always seemed ready to help fill a variety of requests and resource inquiries. I also received valuable assistance from Sarah Haight of Southern Methodist

University, Mike Millner at the University of North Carolina Library, Trevor Hughes of the Wake Forest University School of Law, Maria Bonn from the University of Michigan Library, Vincent L. Golden of the American Antiquarian Society, and the Special Collections staff at the Northwestern University Library. I would be remiss not to mention the student research assistants—Andrew Epstein, Jeremy Moorehouse, Charmaine Stanislaw, Christin Lanham, Nathan Sellers, Jean Godfrey, Patrick Chinnery, Amber Battin, Joshua Rubin, Joseph Schaedler, Elizabeth A. Coyne, and Courtney Lane–who over the years double-checked primary sources.

I owe the greatest debt to those friends who read chapters or the entire manuscript of the book. They all generously took time out of their own busy writing and teaching schedules to offer me sage advice. I cannot adequately stress just how tremendously George Rutherglen, Mark Tushnet, Neil S. Siegel, Eric Foner, James McPherson, and Andrew Taslitz helped me with their enriching comments on multiple chapters. They provided me with the guidance necessary to rewrite parts of the book. Each of them gently guided me to improve the analysis and discard extraneous materials. Michael Vorenberg sent me pages of comments on the entire manuscript, helping to identify places in need of reorganization and refocus. My editor at Oxford University Press, David McBride, has been phenomenally encouraging and insightful, from the time I first pitched the book to him to the point at which he sent me his deeply thought-out comments on the entire manuscript. From Oxford University Press, I also received helpful anonymous reviews, which furnished thoughtful guidance. Tom Finnegan carefully line edited the final draft. What mistakes remain are entirely my own fault.

The administration at the Loyola University, School of Law-Chicago has been generous in supporting this project. I am grateful to Dean David Yellen for ever being willing to supply me with the resources necessary to conduct my research. Associate Dean Michael Kaufman has demonstrated a remarkable knack for helping me design a teaching schedule that enriches my scholarly agenda.

My wife, Alexandra Roginsky Tsesis, is a wellspring of ideas. I am blessed to be married to so deep an intellectual. She is a constant source of inspiration and vitality. Time spent with her and our children, Ariel and Ruth, enlivened me with the mental and physical strength that kept my tank full of energy throughout this project.

APPENDIX

THE DECLARATION OF INDEPENDENCE

IN CONGRESS, July 4, 1776.

The unanimous Declaration of the thirteen united States of America,

When in the Course of human events, it becomes necessary for one people to dissolve the political bands which have connected them with another, and to assume among the powers of the earth, the separate and equal station to which the Laws of Nature and of Nature's God entitle them, a decent respect to the opinions of mankind requires that they should declare the causes which impel them to the separation.

We hold these truths to be self-evident, that all men are created equal, that they are endowed by their Creator with certain unalienable Rights, that among these are Life, Liberty and the pursuit of Happiness.—That to secure these rights, Governments are instituted among Men, deriving their just powers from the consent of the governed,—That whenever any Form of Government becomes destructive of these ends, it is the Right of the People to alter or to abolish it, and to institute new Government, laying its foundation on such principles and organizing its powers in such form, as to them shall seem most likely to effect their Safety and Happiness. Prudence, indeed, will dictate that Governments long established should not be changed for light and transient causes; and accordingly all experience hath shewn, that mankind are more disposed to suffer, while evils are sufferable, than to right themselves by abolishing the forms to which they are accustomed. But when a long train of abuses and usurpations, pursuing invariably the same Object evinces a design to reduce them under absolute Despotism, it is their right, it is their duty, to throw off such Government, and to provide new Guards for their future security.—Such has been the patient sufferance of these Colonies; and such is now the necessity which constrains them to alter their former Systems of Government. The history of the present King of Great Britain is a history of repeated injuries and usurpations, all having in direct object the establishment of an absolute Tyranny over these States. To prove this, let Facts be submitted to a candid world.

He has refused his Assent to Laws, the most wholesome and necessary for the public good.

He has forbidden his Governors to pass Laws of immediate and pressing importance, unless suspended in their operation till his Assent should be obtained; and when so suspended, he has utterly neglected to attend to them.

He has refused to pass other Laws for the accommodation of large districts of people, unless those people would relinquish the right of Representation in the Legislature, a right inestimable to them and formidable to tyrants only.

He has called together legislative bodies at places unusual, uncomfortable, and distant from the depository of their public Records, for the sole purpose of fatiguing them into compliance with his measures.

He has dissolved Representative Houses repeatedly, for opposing with manly firmness his invasions on the rights of the people.

He has refused for a long time, after such dissolutions, to cause others to be elected; whereby the Legislative powers, incapable of Annihilation, have returned to the People at large for their exercise; the State remaining in the mean time exposed to all the dangers of invasion from without, and convulsions within.

He has endeavoured to prevent the population of these States; for that purpose obstructing the Laws for Naturalization of Foreigners; refusing to pass others to encourage their migrations hither, and raising the conditions of new Appropriations of Lands.

He has obstructed the Administration of Justice, by refusing his Assent to Laws for establishing Judiciary powers.

He has made Judges dependent on his Will alone, for the tenure of their offices, and the amount and payment of their salaries.

He has erected a multitude of New Offices, and sent hither swarms of Officers to harrass our people, and eat out their substance.

He has kept among us, in times of peace, Standing Armies without the Consent of our legislatures.

He has affected to render the Military independent of and superior to the Civil power.

He has combined with others to subject us to a jurisdiction foreign to our constitution, and unacknowledged by our laws; giving his Assent to their Acts of pretended Legislation:

For Quartering large bodies of armed troops among us:

For protecting them, by a mock Trial, from punishment for any Murders which they should commit on the Inhabitants of these States:

For cutting off our Trade with all parts of the world:

For imposing Taxes on us without our Consent:

For depriving us in many cases, of the benefits of Trial by Jury:

For transporting us beyond Seas to be tried for pretended offences

For abolishing the free System of English Laws in a neighbouring Province, establishing therein an Arbitrary government, and enlarging its Boundaries so as to render it at once an example and fit instrument for introducing the same absolute rule into these Colonies:

For taking away our Charters, abolishing our most valuable Laws, and altering fundamentally the Forms of our Governments:

For suspending our own Legislatures, and declaring themselves invested with power to legislate for us in all cases whatsoever.

He has abdicated Government here, by declaring us out of his Protection and waging War against us.

He has plundered our seas, ravaged our Coasts, burnt our towns, and destroyed the lives of our people.

He is at this time transporting large Armies of foreign Mercenaries to compleat the works of death, desolation and tyranny, already begun with circumstances of Cruelty & perfidy scarcely paralleled in the most barbarous ages, and totally unworthy the Head of a civilized nation.

He has constrained our fellow Citizens taken Captive on the high Seas to bear Arms against their Country, to become the executioners of their friends and Brethren, or to fall themselves by their Hands.

He has excited domestic insurrections amongst us, and has endeavoured to bring on the inhabitants of our frontiers, the merciless Indian Savages, whose known rule of warfare, is an undistinguished destruction of all ages, sexes and conditions.

In every stage of these Oppressions We have Petitioned for Redress in the most humble terms: Our repeated Petitions have been answered only by repeated injury. A Prince whose character is thus marked by every act which may define a Tyrant, is unfit to be the ruler of a free people.

Nor have We been wanting in attentions to our Brittish brethren. We have warned them from time to time of attempts by their legislature to extend an unwarrantable jurisdiction over us. We have reminded them of the circumstances of our emigration and settlement here. We have appealed to their native justice and magnanimity, and we have conjured them by the ties of our common kindred to disavow these usurpations, which, would inevitably interrupt our connections and correspondence. They too have been deaf to the voice of justice and of consanguinity. We must, therefore, acquiesce in the necessity, which denounces our Separation, and hold them, as we hold the rest of mankind, Enemies in War, in Peace Friends.

We, therefore, the Representatives of the united States of America, in General Congress, Assembled, appealing to the Supreme Judge of the world for the rectitude of our intentions, do, in the Name, and by Authority of the good People of these Colonies, solemnly publish and declare, That these United Colonies are, and of Right ought to be Free and Independent States; that they are Absolved from all Allegiance to the British Crown, and that all political connection between them and the State of Great Britain, is and ought to be totally dissolved; and that as Free and Independent States, they have full Power to levy War, conclude Peace, contract Alliances, establish Commerce, and to do all other Acts and Things which Independent States may of right do. And for the support of this Declaration, with a firm reliance on the protection of divine Providence, we mutually pledge to each other our Lives, our Fortunes and our sacred Honor.

NOTES

CHAPTER 1

1. See, e.g., John Hart Ely, *Democracy and Distrust: A Theory of Judicial Review* 49 (1980).
2. Morton White, *The Philosophy of the American Revolution* (1978); Michael Zuckert, *Natural Rights and the New Republicanism* (1994).
3. Alexander Tsesis, "Self-Government and the Declaration of Independence," 97 *Cornell Law Review* 693 (2012).

CHAPTER 2

1. "From the Pennsylvania Packet, Political Observations," *Essex Gazette* (Salem, MA), Dec. 20, 1774, at 2; Letter from Samuel Adams to Arthur Lee, Apr. 4, 1774, reprinted in Richard Henry Lee, *Life of Arthur Lee, LL.D.* 218, 219 (1829).
2. *Journal of the Continental Congress* 26 (1904); Henry's remarks of Sept. 5, 1774, and Duane's of Sept 8, 1774, in *Debates*, 2 *The Works of John Adams*, 357–58, 366–67, 371 (1865); Samuel Ward, diary, Sept. 9, 1774, in 1 *Letters of Members of the Continental Congress* 27 (Edmund C. Burnett ed., 1921); *Declaration and Resolves of the First Continental Congress* (Oct. 1774; http://www.let.rug.nl/usa/D/1751–1775/independence/decres.htm).
3. Harry M. Tinkcom, "The Revolutionary City, 1765–1783," in Russel F. Weigley, *Philadelphia: A 300 Year History* 120 (1982); Edwin Wolf, 2d, "Introduction" to *Journal of the Proceedings of Congress, 1774*, at 2 (1974); 1 *Letters of Members of the Continental Congress*, 1, 7 (Edmund C. Burnett ed., 1921); Joyce Appleby, *Thomas Jefferson* 13 (2003); Norman K. Risjord, *Thomas Jefferson: American Profiles* 27 (1994); 2 *Journals of the Continental Congress, 1774–1789*, at 101 (1905); *Alexander H. Everett, An Oration Delivered at ... Boston, on the 5th of July, 1830*, at 7 19 (1830, quoting Adams).
4. James Parton, *Life of Thomas Jefferson* 163–64 (7th ed. 1883); 1 Benson J. Lossing, *Harpers's Popular Cyclopædia of United States History* 318 (revised & enlarged ed., 1892); John Ferling, *A Leap in the Dark* 135 (2003); Colin Bonwick, *The American Revolution* 87 (1991).
5. John Adams, *Autobiography, in* 2 *The Works of John Adams* 503 (Charles F. Adams ed., 1850); Robert A. McGuire, "The Founding Era, 1774–1791," in *Government*

  and the American Economy: A New History 61–62 (2007); *Declaration of the Causes and Necessity of taking up Arms,* July 6, 1775 <http://www.let.rug.nl/usa/D/1751–1775/war/causes.htm>.

 6. *The Annual Register or a View of the History of Politics and Literature* 186 (December 1775) (2nd ed. 1778); letter from Benjamin Franklin to Joseph Priestley, May 16, 1775, in 1 *The Private Correspondence of Benjamin Franklin* 403, 403 (William T. Franklin ed., 3rd ed. 1818); letter from General Greene to Governor Samuel Ward, Oct. 23, 1775, in *Sketches of the Life and Correspondence of Nathanael Greene* 42 (William Johnson ed., 1822), see also letter from Nathanael Greene to Jacob Greene, Dec. 20, 1775, in id. 49, 50; letter from Benjamin Franklin to Charles W. F. Dumas, Dec. 9, 1775, in 1 *The Private Correspondence of Benjamin Franklin,* supra, at 425, 426.

 7. Carl F. Kaestle, "The History of Literacy and the History of Readers," in *Perspectives on Literacy* 109 (Eugene R. Kintgen et al. eds., 1988); Andrew R. Heinze, *Jews and the American Soul: Human Nature of the 20th Century* 88 (2004); Richard Middleton, *Colonial America: A History, 1565–1776,* at 269 (3rd ed. 2002); Ross W. Beales and E. Jennifer Monaghan, "Literacy and Schoolbooks," in 1 *The Colonial Book in the Atlantic World* 380–81 (Hugh Amory and David D. Hall eds., 2000); Butler, supra, at 111.

 8. Letter from Samuel Adams to Thomas Paine, Nov. 30, 1802, in 3 *The Life and Public Services of Samuel Adams* 372 (1865); Samuel Bryan, "Introduction" to Thomas Paine, *Common Sense* 3 (1844); Joseph Lewis, *Thomas Paine: Author of the Declaration of Independence* (1947); Albert W. Bergen, "Thomas Paine–The Declaration of Independence," May 11, 1881, *Boston Investigator,* at 5; "Liberal Principles," *Boston Investigator,* Apr. 12, 1876, at 3.

 9. Richard Price, *Observations on the Nature of Civil Liberty, the Principles of Government, and the Justice and Policy of the War with America* 3, 4, 6, 30–31 (1776); Jerome R. Reich, *British Friends of the American Revolution* 93 (1997).

 10. "Letter from a Member of the Virginia Convention," in 1 *Diary of the American Revolution* 204 (Frank Moore ed., 1860); 2 David K. Watson, *The Constitution of the United States* 1039–43 (1910); Gerard J. Mangone, *United States Admiralty Law* 29 (1997); 1 George Tucker, *The History of the United States, From Their Colonization to the End of the Twenty-sixth Congress, in 1841,* at 163 (1856).

 11. Hugh F. Rankin, *The North Carolina Continentals* 54 (2005).

 12. 1 William P. Hazard, *Annals of Philadelphia* 335 (duel) (1881); David L. Swain, "British Invasion in 1776," in *Revolutionary History of North Carolina in Three Lectures* 125–26 (William D. Cooke ed., 1853); Alan D. Watson, *Wilmington North Carolina, to 1861,* at 34–35 (2003); see also Iredell's June 1776 "Essay" in 1 *Life and Correspondence of James Iredell* 283 (Griffith J. McRee ed., 1857); Sally E. Hadden, *Slave Patrols: Law and Violence in Virginia and the Carolinas* 155 (2001).

 13. John Ferling, *Almost a Miracle: The American Victory in the War of Independence* 126 (2007); Drayton quoted in "The Charge to the Grand Jury," in 1 *American Eloquence: A Collection of Speeches and Addresses by the Most Eminent Orators of America* 50, 54, 56 (Frank Moore ed., 1859); Francis Jennings, *The Creation of America* 167 (2000).

14. Moderator, "Mr. Humphreys, Please Give the Following a Place in Your Next Paper," *Pennsylvania Ledger* (Philadelphia), Apr. 27, 1776, at 2, 3; Curtis P. Nettels, *The Emergence of a National Economy, 1775–1815*, at 13 (1962); Evarts B. Greene, *The Foundations of American Nationality* 451 (1922); "Cassandra to Cato. Number III," *Pennsylvania Ledger*, Apr. 27, 1776, at 2; "To the Honorable the Representatives of the Freemen of the Province of Pnnnsylvania [sic]," *Pennsylvania Evening Post*, May 23, 1776, at 260; A Watchman, "To the Common People of Pennsylvania," *Dunlap's Pennsylvania Packet* (Philadelphia), June 10, 1776, at 1.

15. 4 *Journals of the Continental Congress* 342, 358 (Worthington C. Ford ed., 1906); Gordon S. Wood, *The Creation of the American Republic* 132 (1969); "Laying the Corner Stone," May, 23, 1825, *Boston Commercial Gazette* 2, quoting 6 *Boston Records* 49 (May 23, 1776); National Archives Administration, found at *Declaration of Independence: A History* <http://www.archives.gov/exhibits/charters/declaration_history.html>.

16. *A Source Book in American History to 1787*, at 443, 444 (Willis M. West ed., 2007) (1913); "Resolution of the Convention of Virginia, Instructing Their Representatives in Congress To Propose a Declaration of Independence," in 1 *Statutes at Large Being a Collection of All the Laws of Virginia* 7–8 (William W. Hening ed., 1823); letter from Lee to Landon Carter, May 19, 1776, in *Lee of Virginia, 1642–1892*, at 225 (Edmund Jennings Lee ed., 1895); *Scots Magazine* 370 (July 1776).

17. 5 *Journals of the Continental Congress* 425 (1906) (June 7, 1776); letter XXIX, May 20, 1776, in William Eddis, *Letters from America* 275–76 (1792); J. H. Elliot, *Empires of the Atlantic World* 347 (2007); Michael A. McDonnell, *The Politics of War: Race, Class, and Conflict in Revolutionary Virginia* 215 (2007); Charles Campbell, *History of the Colony and Ancient Dominion of Virginia* 661–62 (1860); Paul C. Nagel, *The Lees of Virginia: Seven Generations of American Family* 4–5 (1992).

18. 1 Tucker, supra, at 167–71 (1856); John Dickinson, "To My OPPONENTS in the Late Elections of Councillor for the County of Philadelphia," *Philadelphia Packet*, Dec. 31, 1782, at 1 (Dickinson's explanation that he supported independence but disagreed with the timing of the motion).

19. James W. Fraser, *A History of Hope: When Americans Have Dared to Dream of a Better Future* 11 (2002); Charles J. Stillé, *The Life and Times of John Dickinson* 14–31 (1891); Jack P. Greene, "Law and the Origins of the American Revolution," in *The Cambridge History of Law in America* 464 (M. Grossberg & C. Tomlins eds., 2008); Ida M. Tarbell, "The Story of the Declaration of Independence," 17 *McClure's Magazine* 223, 225 (1901); Jedidiah Morse, *Annals of the American Revolution* 247 (1824); Merrill Jensen, *The Articles of Confederation* 249 (1970); 1 David Ramsay, *The History of the American Revolution* 431–32 (1811); Esmond Wright, *Franklin of Philadelphia* 245 (1988); Merrill D. Peterson, *Thomas Jefferson and the New Nation* 86–87 (1970).

20. 5 *Journals of the Continental Congress* 428–29, 431 (Worthington C. Ford ed., 1906); C. Edward Quinn, *Roots of the Republic: Signers of the Declaration of Independence* 123 (1996); Charles Campbell, *History of the Colony and Ancient Dominion of Virginia* 661–62 (1860).

21. *Virginia Declaration of Rights*, <http://avalon.law.yale.edu/18th_century/virginia.asp>; Eric Slauter, *The State as a Work of Art* 215–16 (2009).

22. Darrin M. McMahon, *Happiness: A History* 318 (2006); Joseph Ragland Long, *Government and the People* 96 (1922).

23. Alexander Tsesis, *We Shall Overcome: A History of Civil Rights and the Law* 33–34 (2008); Jeff Broadwater, *George Mason: Forgotten Founder* 235 (2006); 2 Stephen F. Miller, *The Bench and Bar of Georgia* 399 (1858); Douglas R. Egerton, *Death or Liberty: African Americans and Revolutionary America* 129 (2009); Richard R. Beeman, *The Varieties of Political Experience in Eighteenth-Century America* 63 (2006); *An Act for Regulating the Election of Burgesses …* (1769), in 8 *The Statutes at Large being a Collection of All Laws of Virginia* 307 (William W. Henning ed., 1821); Michael Kent Curtis, "St. George Tucker and the Legacy of Slavery," 47 *Wm. & Mary L. Rev.* 1157, 1181 (2006); 2 *Encyclopedia of Homelessness* 583 (David Levinson ed., 2004); letter from Jefferson to [probably Edmund Pendleton], Aug. 13, 1776, in 2 *The Writings of Thomas Jefferson* 78, 83 (Paul L. Ford ed., 1893).

24. *The Public Record of the Colony of Connecticut: From May, 1775 to June, 1776*, at 415 (Charles J. Hoadly ed., 1890).

25. Joel Parker, *The Domestic and Foreign Relations of the United States* 17 (1862); *Report of the Trial and Acquittal of Edward Shippen … on an Impeachment* 79 (William Hamilton ed., 1805); letter from Adams to William Plumer, Mar. 28, 1813, in 1 *Letters of Members of the Continental Congress* 537 (Edmund C. Burnett ed., 1921).

26. "Declaration of Independence," *Sandusky Clarion* (Sandusky, OH), Aug. 1, 1829, at 1; letter from Adams to Timothy Pickering, Aug. 6, 1822, in 2 *The Works of John Adams* 512, 514 (1865); John Adams, *Autobiography*, in id. at 513–15; letter from Jefferson to James Madison, Aug. 30, 1823, in 3 *Memoir, Correspondence, and Miscellanies from the Papers of Thomas Jefferson* 376 (1829).

27. *St. Louis Globe-Democrat*, Mar. 12, 1883, at 4 col. A; 5 *Journals of the Continental Congress*, supra at 491.

28. Tarbell, supra, at 30 (quoting Jefferson); "Declaration of Independence," *Sandusky Clarion* (Sandusky, OH), Aug. 1, 1829, at 1; 5 *Journals of the Continental Congress*, supra at 504–5.

29. David McCullough, *John Adams* 129 (2001) (about Rodney); "Declaration of Independence," *The Torch Light and Public Advertiser* (Hagers-town, MD), Aug. 3, 1826, at 1; diary, Sept. 3, 1774, 2 *The Works of John Adams* 364 (Charles Francis Adams ed., 1865); E. Digby Baltzell, *Puritan Boston & Quaker Philadelphia* 180–81 (1996); Thomas W. Balch, "Thomas Willing of Philadelphia," 46 *Pa. Mag. of Hist. and Biography* 1, 7–8 (1922); "The Declaration of Independence–Statements of Thomas McKean and Thomas Jefferson Compared," 5 *Potter's American Monthly* 650, 651 (1875); F. Burdge, "New York in the Continental Congress," 6 *Mag. Am. Hist.* 459, 459 (1881); John A. Doyle, *History of the United States* 252 (1876); John Ferling, *Setting the World Ablaze* 134 (2000); 5 *Journals of the Continental Congress*, supra at 507.

30. Ferling, supra, 175; letter to John Adams to Abigail Adams, July 3, 1776, in Philadelphia, July 3, 1776, *Norwich Courier* (Norwich, CT), Aug. 2, 1826, at 2.

31. "Mr. Jefferson Used to Relate," *Daily Evening Bulletin* (San Francisco), June 3, 1872, col. E; "Signing the Declaration," *Yenowine's Illustrated News* (Milwaukee, WI), Sept. 15, 1894, at 6.

32. "Declaration Of Independence," *Independent Chronicle & Boston Patriot*, Aug. 31, 1822, at 4. For a more thorough treatment of the subject see Carl Becker, *The Declaration of Independence: A Study in the History of Political Ideas* 135–93 (2nd ed. 1942) and Pauline Maier, *American Scripture: Making the Declaration of Independence* 97–153 (1997).

33. Thomas Jefferson, *Autobiography, in* 1 The Writings of Thomas Jefferson 28 (Albert E. Bergh ed., 1907) (1821); Act of Mar. 2, 1807, ch. 22, 2 Stat. 426 (forbidding slave importation into the United States as of Jan. 1, 1808); David H. Fischer, *Liberty and Freedom* 125–26 (2004).

34. "Anecdote of Dr. Franklin, Related by Mr. Jefferson in a Letter of the 4th of December, 1818," *Portsmouth Oracle* (Portsmouth, NH), Apr. 29, 1820, at 1.

35. Abraham Lincoln, "Speech in Springfield, Illinois, June 26, 1857," in 2 *Complete Words of Abraham Lincoln* 331 (John G. Nicolay and John Hay eds., 1894).

36. "Sang Froid," *New London Gazette* (New London, CT), Aug. 12, 1835, at 2. For a Connecticut delegate's similar understanding that his many connections to the rebel cause might lead to his hanging see "Annecdote [sic] of the Revolution," *Lowell Daily Citizen and News* (Lowell, MA), Feb. 14, 1859, at col F.

37. *New Hampshire Patriot & State Gazette* (Concord, NH), Nov. 18, 1847, at 4 col. A.

38. "Not on the Fourth," *Bismarck Daily Trib.*, Mar. 13, 1885, col D; 1 *Journals of the American Congress from 1774–1788*, at 410 (1823); <http://www.loc.gov/exhibits/declara/images/dunlap.jpg> (Dunlap Broadside of the original Declaration); John H. Hazelton, *The Declaration of Independence: Its History* 193–219 (1906); Charles Thornton Adams, *Matthew Thornton of New Hampshire* 45 (1903); Roberdeau Buchanan, *Genealogy of the McKean Family of Pennsylvania* 46–48 (1890); Garry Wills, *Inventing America* 326–27 (1978); *Public Ledger Almanac* 9 (1876); "Declaration of Independence," *Torch Light and Public Advertiser* (Hagers-Town, MD), Aug. 3, 1826, at 1.

CHAPTER 3

1. Daniel T. Rodgers, *Contested Truths: Keywords in American Politics Since Independence* 66–67 (1987); 5 *Journal of the Continental Congress* 516 (Worthington C. Ford ed., 1906); National Archives Administration, *Declaration of Independence: A History*, http://www.archives.gov/exhibits/charters/declaration_history.html.

2. Charles D. Deshler, "How the Declaration Was Received in the Old Thirteen," 84 *Harper's New Monthly Magazine* 179, 168 (June 1892).

3. "Biography, Cæsar Rodney," in *Delaware Register and Farmers Magazine* 19, 25 (Feb. to July 1838); 1 John T. Scharf, *History of Delaware: 1609–1888*, at 236 (1888); *Sanderson's Biography of the Signers of the Declaration of Independence* 448–49 (revised by Robert T. Conrad, 1846); Thomas F. Bayard, *Proceedings on Unveiling the Monument to Cæsar Rodney* 51 (1889).

4. *New Jersey in the American Revolution, 1763–1783: A Documentary History* 219–20 (Larry R. Gerlach ed., 1975); Letter, Major F. Barber to Rev. James Caldwell, July 17, 1776, in 5 *Proceedings of the New Jersey Historical Society: 1850–1851*, at 168 (1851); Frank Moore, *Diary of the American Revolution* 279–81 (1860) (quoting speech by the physician, Dr. Elmer).

5. 2 Martha J. Lamb et al., *History of the City of New York* 90–93 (1896); 2 Benson J. Lossing, *The Pictorial Field-Book of the Revolution* 801 n. 2, 802 (1852); 2 Gideon H. Hollister, *The History of Connecticut* 263–66, quote on 266 (2nd ed., 1857); "Extract of a Letter from a Young Man in the Army at New-York, to His Father In Town," *American Gazette, or, The Constitutional Journal* (Salem, MA), July 23, 1776, at 24, col. 2.

6. *Royal Gazette* (New York), Sept. 22, 1779, at 2, col. c (Loyalist account of the New York events).

7. *The New-York Journal* (New York), Aug. 8, 1776, at 1, 4.

8. "How the Declaration Was Received at Portsmouth, N.H.," *New York Times*, July 4, 1871, at 2; John A. Brown & Charles H. Bell, *A Hand-Book of Exeter, New Hampshire* 6 (1888); *A Historical Collection of the Part … Sustained by Connecticut During the War of the Revolution* 95 n. (Royal R. Hinman ed., 1842).

9. "The Proclamation of Independence," *Boston Daily Advertiser*, July 15, 1876, at 2 (Worcester); *American Gazette, or, The Constitutional Journal* (Salem, MA), July 23, 1776, at 24, col. 1; Susan Wilson, *An Essential Guide to Historic Landmarks In and Around Boston* 5 (revised. and updated 2004); *Proceedings of the American Antiquarian Society* 246 (1926); George F. Scheer and Hugh F. Rankin, *Rebels and Redcoats* 153 (1957).

10. George W. Howard, *The Monumental City, Its Past History and Present Resources* 20 (1873).

11. Henry Howe, *Historical Collections of Virginia* 114 (1852); *Virginia Gazette*, Aug. 10, 1776, in *Historical Collections of Virginia* 313 (Henry Howe ed., 1845).

12. R. D. W. Connor, "Cornelius Harnett: The Pride of Cape Fear," 5 *The North Carolina Booklet* 171, 195–96 (July 1905); Jo. Seawell Jones, *A Defence of the Revolutionary History of the State of North Carolina* 268–69 (1834).

13. Deshler, supra, at 181; 7 *Rhode Island Historical Magazine* 77–78 (July 1886).

14. Lossing, supra, at 757 n. 4; Joseph Johnson, *Traditions and Reminiscences: Chiefly of the American Revolution in the South* 188–190 (1851).

15. F. D. Lee and J. L. Agnew, *Historical Record of the City of Savannah* 43 (1869); William Bacon Stevens, *A History of Georgia from its First Discovery by Europeans to the Adoption of the Present Constitution* 151–52 (1859); 2 Stephen F. Miller, *The Bench and Bar of Georgia* 399 (1858); Betty Wood, *Slavery In Colonial America, 1619–1776*, at 73 (2005); Donald L. Grant, *The Way It Was In the South: The Black Experience in Georgia* 13 (Jonathan Grant ed., 2001).

16. Letter from S. Adams to John Pitts, July 1776, in James K. Hosmer, *Samuel Adams* 350 (6th ed., 1887); 2 *The Life of Paul Revere* 621 (1891); 3 *The Writings of Samuel Adams (1773–1777)*, at 221, 222 (Harry A. Cushing ed., 1904) ("Declaration of Independency … " and "declaration of Independence").

17. Letter from Joseph Barton to Henry Wisner, July 9, 1776, in http://slic.njstatelib.org/slic_files/imported/NJ_Information/Digital_Collections/

NJInTheAmericanRevolution1763–1783/7.9.pdf; letter from Tristram Dalton to Gerry, July 19, 1776, in *The Life of Elbridge Gerry: With Contemporary Letters* 209 (James T. Austin ed., 1828); letter from an Old Friend [Benjamin Rush] to Charles Lee, July 23, 1776, in *Memoirs of the Life of the Late Charles Lee* 267–68 (1792).

18. 2 Egerton Ryerson, *The Loyalists of America and their Times* 125–26 (2nd ed. 1880).

19. "House of Commons," Oct. 31, 1776, 38 *Scots Magazine* 574 (Nov. 1776); A. J. Langguth, *Patriots: The Men Who Started the American Revolution* 364 (1989) (*Public Advertiser*).

20. Samuel Johnson, "Taxation No Tyranny, An Answer to the Resolutions and Address of the American Congress, 1775," in 14 *The Works of Samuel Johnson* 144 (1903); Stanley Weintraub, *Iron Tears: America's Battle for Freedom, Britain's Quagmire: 1775–1783*, at 71 (2005) (quoting *Gentleman's Mag.*); Christopher Hibbert, *Redcoats and Rebels* 117 (2002); Vigilans, "A Dialogue between a Modern Patriot and a Friend to His Country," *Morning Chronicle and London Advertiser*, Dec. 6, 1776, at 1.

21. Despite the Declaration's frequent appearance in newspapers, pamphlets, and speeches beginning in 1776, Philip F. Detweiler's seminal article claimed that the Declaration played little role in early American politics. He linked the Declaration's popularity to the improved relations with Britain after the War of 1812. Philip F. Detweiler, "The Changing Reputation of the Declaration of Independence: The First Fifty Years," 19 *William and Mary Q.* 557, 571 (1962). Prominent scholars, including David Armitage, Pauline Maier, and Garry Wills, interpolated Detweiler's influential argument into their books. In his work on the Declaration's international influences, Armitage dated the document's iconic status "only after the War of 1812. ... The first engravings and reprintings of the document were produced for display in homes and official buildings in 1817." David Armitage, *The Declaration of Independence* 25, 92 (2007). Pauline Maier likewise writes, "What began as a Republican property became a national icon after the War of 1812." Maier, *American Scripture: Making the Declaration of Independence* 154, 168–69 (1997); Maier, "Introduction," to *The Declaration of Independence and the Constitution of the United States* (reissue 2008). Wills also relies on Detweiler's theory in his *Inventing America: Jefferson's Declaration of Independence* 324 (2002, 1978).

22. For published versions of the Declaration during the time period in question, see *Connecticut Journal* (New Haven), July 17, 1776, at 2; *New England Chronicle* (Boston), July 18, 1776, at 1; *Pennsylvania Mercury and Universal Advertiser* (Philadelphia), Oct. 22, 1784, at 1; *Pennsylvania Packet, and Daily Advertiser* (Philadelphia), July 4, 1787, at 2; *Dunlap's American Daily Advertiser* (Philadelphia), July 4, 1791, at 2; *General Advertiser* (Philadelphia), July 23, 1794, at 2; *Philadelphia Gazette & Universal Daily Advertiser*, July 3, 1797, at 2; *Times and District of Columbia Daily Advertiser* (Alexandria, VA), July 2, 1802, at 2; *Eastern Argus* (Portland, ME), June 28, 1805, at 4; *National Intelligencer and Washington Advertiser* (Washington, DC), July 3, 1805, at 2; and *Kline's Carlisle Weekly Gazette* (Carlisle, PA), June 30, 1809, at 3.

23. "Philadelphia, March 18," *Independent Chronicle and the Universal Advertiser* (Boston), Apr. 3, 1777, at 3; "In General Assembly of Pennsylvania, May 25, 1778," *Pennsylvania Packet or the General Advertiser* (Philadelphia), May 27, 1778, at 2; "London: House of Commons, Nov. 7," *New-London Gazette* (New London, CT), Apr. 18, 1777, at 1; "Considerations upon Granting Independence in America," *Edinburgh Advertiser* (Edinburgh, Midlothian), Sept. 3, 1779, at 1.

24. Henry Steward, *Equality, the First Principle of Government in the United States* 7 (1804); *Chisholm v. Georgia*, 2 Dallas 419, 470 (1793); Friends to the Liberties of America, "From the New-York Journal," *Independent Gazetteer* (Philadelphia), July 2, 1791, at 2; "New-York, July 2. Celebration of the Fourth of July," *New-York Daily Gazette*, July 2, 1791, at 2; "The Laws of the United States of America," *General Advertiser* (Philadelphia), Oct. 18, 1791, at 4; letter from Thomas Mifflin to the State Societies of the Cincinnati, *Federal Gazette* (Philadelphia), June 7, 1790, at 2, 3; "Philadelphia, July 5," *Mail* (Philadelphia), July 5, 1792, at 2–3; *Greenleaf's New York Journal*, July 9, 1794, at 3.

25. See, e.g., Martin Post, *An Oration Delivered At Jerico, On the Anniversary of American Independence, July Fourth, Eighteen Hundred and Four* 7 (1804).

26. Letter from Thomas Jefferson to Henry Lee (May 8, 1825), in 10 *The Writings of Thomas Jefferson* 342, 343 (Paul Leicester Ford ed., 1899); letter from Thomas Jefferson to James Madison (Aug. 30, 1823), in id. at 266, 267–68; John Locke, "An Essay Concerning the True Original Extent and End of Civil Government," in *Two Treatises of Government* 193, 279 (6th ed. 1764); letter from John Adams to Timothy Pickering (Aug. 6, 1822), in 2 *The Works of John Adams* 512, 514 (Charles Francis Adams ed., 1850).

27. Anonymous [Moses Mather], *America's Appeal to the Impartial World* 7–9 (1775); John Dickinson, *An Essay on the Constitutional Power of Great-Britain over the colonies in America; with the Resolves of the Committee for the Province of Pennsylvania* 68–72 (1774); David Griffith, *Passive Obedience Considered* 18 (1776); Enoch Huntington, *The Happy Effects of Union* 17, 20, 26 (1776).

28. Columbian Patriot [Mercy Otis Warren], *Observations on the New Constitution*, 4 (1788); "Observations on the Federal Procession on the Fourth of July, 1788, in the City of Philadelphia," *Am. Museum*, July 1788, at 75; Christopher Manwaring, "Republicanism & Aristocracy Contrasted ... Delivered At New London," (CT) July 4th, 1804, at 6 (1804); "Salem, July 6," *Federal Gazette* (Philadelphia), July 14, 1790, at 3; A Friend of the People, "Miscellany, From the *Baltimore Evening Post*," *Oracle of the Day* (Portsmouth, NH), Nov. 9, 1793, at 1.

29. Samuel Stillman, "A Sermon Preached Before the Honorable Council" 8–9 (1779); Richard Price, "Additional Observations on the Nature and Value of Civil Liberty, and the War with America" 11–12 (1778) ("the natural equality of mankind"); "Result of the Convention of Delegates Holden at Ipswich in the County of Essex 1778," in Theophilus Parsons, *Memoir of Theophilus Parsons* at 11–12 (Boston, 1861, 1778) ("classes of men"); "History of the American Revolution," *Universal Asylum & Columbian Mag.*, Mar. 1791, at 169.

30. See an example of this type of thinking in "Result of the Convention of Delegates," supra, 359, 362, 365–66.

CHAPTER 4

1. Quoted in Winthrop D. Jordon, *The White Man's Burden: Historical Origins of Racism in the United States* 118 (1974).
2. "Constitution of Georgia; February 5, 1777," in *The Constitutions of the Several Independent States of America* 344 (2nd ed. 1783); "Constitution of South Carolina—March 19, 1778," in id. at 314; also available at http://avalon.law.yale. edu/subject_menus/statech.asp.
3. "Memorial of a Convention Held at Lebanon, N.H., July 27, 1779," in 2 *Records of the Governor and Council of the State of Vermont* 171–73 (E. P. Walton ed., 1874); Zadock Thompson, *History of Vermont, Natural, Civil, and Statistical Part II*, at 50 (1842); Henry W. De Puy, *Ethan Allen and the Green-Mountain Heroes '76*, at 378–81 (1861); "Vermont's Declaration of Independence," in *The Geography, History, Constitution and Civil Government of Vermont* 192 (6th ed. 1915); Constitution of Vermont—July 8, 1777, http://avalon.law.yale.edu/subject_menus/statech.asp.
4. New Hampshire Bill of Rights, June 2, 1784, http://www.nh.gov/constitution/billofrights.html.
5. Constitution of New York 1777, http://avalon.law.yale.edu/subject_menus/statech.asp.
6. *Thomas Paine to the Citizens of Pennsylvania on the Proposal for Calling a Convention* (1805); Constitution of Pennsylvania—September 28, 1776, at § 6, http://avalon.law.yale.edu/18th_century/pa08.asp; John G. McCurdy, "The Origins of Universal Suffrage: The Pennsylvania Constitution of 1776," 8 *Historical Society of Pennsylvania Legacies* 6 (2008); The Constitution of the Commonwealth of Pennsylvania (1790) art IX § 1, http://www.duq.edu/law/pa-constitution/constitutions/1790.cfm.
7. Constitution of the Commonwealth of Massachusetts 1780, http://www.mass.gov/legis/const.htm#cart106.htm; John Quincy Adams, "Letter from J. Q. Adams," *Liberator*, Aug. 20, 1841, at 134; *Commonwealth v. Jennison* (1783), quoted in Philip S. Foner, 1 *History of Black Americans* 353 (1975).
8. See, e.g., North Carolina Ratifying Convention, Declaration of Rights and Other Amendments, Aug. 1, 1788, http://press-pubs.uchicago.edu/founders/documents/bill_of_rightss10.html; Ratification of the Constitution by the State of Virginia; June 26, 1788, http://avalon.law.yale.edu/18th_century/ratva.asp.
9. A Jerseyman, "Address to the Citizens of New Jersey on the New Constitution," *Am. Museum*, Nov. 1787, at 436; Stanley Griswold, *Overcoming Evil with Good* 30 (1801); John Leland, *An Elective Judiciary* (1805); Dan Himmelfarb, "The Constitutional Relevance of the Second Sentence of the Declaration of Independence," 100 *Yale L.J.* 169, 174–75 (1990).
10. 4 *The Debates in the Several State Conventions on the Adoption of the Federal Constitution* 202 (Jonathan Elliot ed., 1836) (Lenoir); 2 id. at 311 (Melancton Smith); John Smilie, Speech in the Pennsylvania Ratification Convention, Nov. 28, 1787, in *Pennsylvania and the Federal Constitution, 1787–1788*, at 250–51 (John B. McMaster and Frederick D. Stone eds., 1888); 4 Debates in the Several State ..., supra, at 136 (Spencer); Cato, No. IV, "Mr. Humphreys," *Pennsylvania*

Mercury (Philadelphia), Apr. 12, 1788, at 3; see also An American Citizen, "On the Federal Government," *Salem Mercury* (Salem, MA), Oct. 16, 1787, at 1; Philadelphiensis, No. 8, "For the Freeman's Journal," *Freeman's Journal* (Philadelphia), Jan. 23, 1788, at 2, 3.

11. 2 Debates in the Several State . . . , supra, at 457 (Wilson); 1 id. at 66; "Extract from an Address of 'A Citizen of Pennsylvania' to the People of America," *Maryland Journal*, Oct. 19, 1787, at 2.

12. New York Weekly Museum (New York), June 13, 1789, at 2 (Madison's proposal).

13. See Charles L. Black, *A New Birth of Freedom: Human Rights, Names & Unnamed* 34–35 (1997) (discussing Declaration in context of Ninth Amendment).

14. John Hart Ely, *Democracy and Distrust: A Theory of Judicial Review* 49 (1980); letter from James Madison to Thomas Jefferson, Feb. 8, 1825, in 9 *The Writings of James Madison* 218, 221 (Gaillard Hunt ed., 1910); "Speech of Samuel Adams, in Domestic Occurrences," *Mass. Mag.*, Jan. 1794, at 59, 62–64.

15. James Madison, *Manifestations of the Beneficence of Divine Providence towards America* 8 (1795); William L. Brown, "An Essay on the Natural Equality of Men" iv, 46–47, 50 (1793).

16. Richard Price, *Additional Observations on the Nature and Value of Civil Liberty, and the War with America* 11–12 (1778).

17. William Hunter, *An oration, delivered in Trinity Church, in Newport on the Fourth of July, 1801*, at 9–10 (1801).

18. Letter from Abigail Adams to John Adams, Mar. 31, 1776, http://www.thelizlibrary.org/suffrage/abigail.htm; Mary Wollstonecraft, *A Vindication of the Rights of Women* 247 (1792).

19. [Written by a Lady], An Oration Delivered on the Fourth Day of July 1800 4, 5, 11 (Springfield: Henry Brewer 1808).

20. *Pennsylvania Packet*, May 16, 1780, at 3. For examples of offers for runaway apprentices, see id., Aug. 4, 1781, at 3.

21. Gordon S. Wood, *The Radicalism of the American Revolution* 186–87 (1991); David B. Davis, "American Slavery and the American Revolution," in *Slavery and Freedom in the Age of the American Revolution* 262, 275–77 (Ira Berlin and Ronald Hoffman eds., 1983); Benjamin Quarles, "The Revolutionary War as a Black Declaration of Independence," id. at 283, 290. For an example of a black petition relying on the Declaration's natural rights principles, see James Foster, *Letters from a Man of Color* (1813). The author provides multiple arguments to show a proposed Pennsylvania law "to prevent the immigration of people of color into this state."

22. "American Intelligence," 58 *Universal Magazine* 159, 161 (Sept. 1776); *Gentleman's Magazine* 434 (Sept. 1776); 57 *Monthly Review* 252 (Sept. 1777); "In General Assembly of Pennsylvania, May 25, 1778," *Pennsylvania Packet* (Philadelphia), May 27, 1778, at 2; Crito, "Letter to the Editor of the *Providence Gazette*," *Providence Gazette*, Oct. 6, 1787, at 1; "To the Printer," *Freeman's Journal*, June 29, 1785, at 2.

23. *The American in Algiers, or The Patriot of Seventy-six in Captivity* 23–25 (1797).

24. [David Cooper], *A Serious Address to the Rulers of America on the Inconsistency of Their Conduct Respecting Slavery* 6–13 (1783).

25. George Buchanan, *An Oration upon the Moral and Political Evil of Slavery* 13–14 (July 4, 1791); The Constitution of the New-Jersey Society, for Promoting the Abolition of Slavery … passed the 2d of March, 1786, and supplement … the 26th of November, 1788, at title page and 3 (1793); Joseph Bloomfield et seq., "Notice," *General Advertiser* (Philadelphia), Feb. 2, 1793, at 1.

26. "For the Connecticut Journal," *Connecticut Journal* (New Haven, CT), June 12, 1793, at 2; Constitution and Act of Incorporation of the Pennsylvania Society, for Promoting the Abolition of Slavery and the Relief of Free Negroes, Unlawfully Held in Bondage. and for Improving the Condition of the African Race 34 (1800); Alexander Tsesis, *We Shall Overcome: A History of Civil Rights and the Law* 28, 32 (2008); "For the Argus," *Argus* (New York), Feb. 3, 1796, at 2.

27. Robert J. Branham and Stephen J. Hartnett, *Sweet Freedom's Song: "My Country 'Tis of Thee" and Democracy in America* 108 (2002); A Republican, "For the North-Carolina Journal," *North Carolina Journal* (Halifax), July 4, 1796, at 4; Crito, "On the African Slave Trade," *Pennsylvania Mercury* (Philadelphia), Nov. 23, 1787, at 1; "The Pedlar, No. VI," *Evening Fire-Side*, Aug. 30, 1806, at 274.

28. Warner Mifflin, "Serious Expostulation with the Members of the House of Representatives of the United States," *Dunlap's American Daily Advertiser* (Philadelphia), Feb. 19, 1793, at 2; Alexander McLeod, *Negro Slavery Unjustifiable* 18–19 (1802); Henry Steward, *Equality, the First Principle of Government in the United States* 8–9, 20–25 (1804).

29. Thomas Branagan, *The Penitential Tyrant: Or Slave Trader Reformed* x, 147–48 (1807); John Parrish, *Remarks on the Slavery of the Black People* 3, 45–46, 49–51 (1806).

30. Id.; letter from James Forten to Congressman George Thatcher, in John Parrish, *Remarks on the Slavery of the Black People* 51–52 (1806).

31. 2 Stat. 426, ch. 22 (Importation of Slaves Prohibited After January 1, 1808); "Support of Government," *Raleigh Register and North-Carolina State Gazette*, Jan. 28, 1808, at 1 (Jefferson's letter); Humanitas, *Reflections on Slavery with Recent Evidence of Its Inhumanity* (1803); *Annals of Cong.*, 9th Cong., 2nd Sess. 225–27 (Dec. 29, 1806); "The Petition of the Inhabitants of the Town of New Haven to James Madison," *National Intelligencer* (Washington, DC), June 20, 1811 ("important grievance … ").

CHAPTER 5

1. James Cheetham, *Life of Thomas Paine* 53 n. (g) (1809); letter from John Adams to Timothy Pickering (Aug. 6, 1822), in 2 *The Works of John Adams* 512, 514 (Charles Francis Adams ed., 1850); letter from Thomas Jefferson to James Madison (Aug. 30, 1823), in 10 *The Writings of Thomas Jefferson* 266, 267–68; letter from Thomas Jefferson to Henry Lee (May 8, 1825), in 10 *The Writings of Thomas Jefferson* 342, 343 (Paul Leicester Ford ed., 1899); "Col. Pickering's Remarks," *Middlesex Gazette* (Middletown, CT), July 31, 1823, at 2.

2. Letter from Thomas Jefferson to Roger C. Weightman, June 24, 1826, http://www.loc.gov/exhibits/declara/rcwltr.html; Daniel Walker Howe, *What Hath*

God Wrought: The Transformation of America, 1815–1848, at 243 (2007); *The Torch Light and Public Advertiser*, July 13, 1826, at 2; "A Great Man Has Fallen in Israel," *Edwardsville Spectator* (IL), Aug. 4, 1826, at 4.

3. Eugene M. Waite, *America and the War of 1812*, at 155 (1999); Donald R. Hickey, *The War in 1812: A Forgotten Conflict* 256 (1989); Ferdinand Ellis, "A Discourse, Adapted to the Present Situation" 11–12 (1812); John G. Jackson, "An Oration Pronounced in Clarksburg, On the Fourth of July 1812" (1812); Virginia Resolution, http://avalon.law.yale.edu/18th_century/virres.asp; Kentucky Resolution, http://avalon.law.yale.edu/18th_century/kenres.asp.

4. Rossiter Johnson, *A History of the War of 1812–1815*, at 346 (1882); Kendric C. Babcock, *The Rise of American Nationality* 185, 202 (1906); David H. Fischer, *Liberty and Freedom* 207–8 (2005); praise for painting, "The Splendid … ," *Ohio Repository* (Canton), Mar. 12, 1819, at 3 col. c; "Trumbull's Painting," *Mercantile Advertiser* (New York), Sept. 28, 1818, at 2; and criticism, "Col. Trumbull's Painting," *American Beacon* (VA) Feb. 27, 1819, at 2 col. c.

5. Letter from Joseph M. Sanderson to Thomas Jefferson, Dec. 9, 1818, in 1 *Collections of the Massachusetts Historical Society* 273–74 (7th Ser. 1900); "Proposal," *Republican Compiler* (Gettysburg, PA), Mar. 10, 1819, at 1.

6. "Declaration of Independence," *Sioux County Herald* (Orange City, IA), Mar. 27, 1884, at 3.

7. *Franklin Monitor* (Charlestown [Boston], MA), July 10, 1819, at 3 (about Springfield and New London); "Celebration: Baltimore Independent Volunteers," *Baltimore Patriot*, July 9, 1819, at 2 col. c; "Independence," *Adams Centinel* (Gettysburg, PA), July 12, 1820 (quoting Adams); "American Independence," *Northern Sentinel* (Burlington, VT), July 9, 1819, at 1 col a.

8. "The Traveller [sic]," *Village Record* (West Chester, PA), June 24, 1818, at 2; "Letter from Louisiana," *National Advocate* (New York), July 24 1819, at 2.

9. Minutes of the Sixteenth American Convention for Promoting the Abolition of Slavery and Improving the Condition of the African Race 7–9, 19 (1819).

10. American Colonization Society, "A View of Exertions Lately Made For the People of Colonizing the Free People of Colour" 6–7 (1817).

11. "Columbia Land of Library," *Providence Gazette*, Feb. 14, 1821, at 2–3 (slave trade).

12. William J. Cooper, Jr., *Liberty and Slavery: Southern Politics to 1860*, at 134–35 (2000); Asa E. Martin, *Anti-Slavery Movement In Kentucky, Prior to 1850*, at 18 et seq. (1918) (concerning Kentucky anti-Slavery movement 1792–1800); 2 Alexander Johnston, *American Political History, 1763–1876*, at 36–37 (1905); Duncan J. MacLeod, *Slavery, Race and the American Revolution* 56 (1974); Lacy Ford, "Reconsidering the Internal Slave Trade," in *The Chattel Principle: Internal Slave Trades in Americas* 143, 157 (Walter Johnson ed., 2004). Alabama's 1819 Constitution provided, in part, "The general assembly shall have no power to pass laws for the emancipation of slaves, without the consent of their owner, or without paying their owners, previous to such emancipation, a full equivalent in money for slaves so emancipated." Constitution of the State of Alabama–1819, in 2 *Code of Alabama* 63, 80, *Slaves* § 1 (1907).

13. *Annals of Cong.*, 15th Cong., 2nd Sess. 1211 (Feb. 16, 1819).

14. *Annals of Cong.*, 15th Cong., 2nd Sess. 1166, 1170 (Feb. 15, 1819); see Don E. Fehrenbacher, *The South and Three Sectional Crises* 15 (1980) (characterizing the Tallmadge Amendment).

15. *Annals of Cong.*, 15th Cong., 2nd Sess. 1180–81 (Feb. 15, 1819).

16. Id. at 1203, 1208, 1211. Thomas Jefferson's draft of the Declaration accused King George III of acting "against human nature itself" by keeping open an international slave trade that violated the "rights of life and liberty in the persons of a distant people." Quoted in Tania Tetlow, "The Founders and Slavery: A Crisis of Conscience," 3 *Loyola J. Pub. Int. L.* 1, 11 (2001).

17. *Annals of Cong.*, 15th Cong., 2nd Sess. 1214 (Feb. 17, 1819) (House); id. at 273 (Feb. 27, 1819) (Senate); id. at 279–80 (Mar. 2, 1819) (Senate).

18. Letter from Jefferson to John Holmes (Apr. 22, 1820), in 10 *The Writings of Thomas Jefferson* 157 (Paul L. Ford ed., 1899); "Dissolution of the Union," *Middlesex Gazette* (CT), Aug. 12, 1819, at 3 col. b; "Missouri Territory," *Commercial Advertiser* (New York), May 24, 1819, at 2 (St. Louis grand jury).

19. Letter of John Jay to the New-Jersey Committee, on the subject of the Restriction of Slavery in the State of Missouri, reprinted in *New-York Daily Advertiser*, Dec. 15, 1819, at 2; "The Missouri Question," *Repertory* (Boston, MA), Nov. 27, 1819, at 4, col. b.

20. *St. Louis Enquirer*, Aug. 16, 1820, at 3, col. c.

21. "Philadelphia, Jan. 4," *Boston Daily Advertiser*, Jan. 8, 1820, at 2, col. a (reporting on the content of a letter about Cincinnati); "From the Connecticut Mirror," *Commercial Advertiser* (New York), Dec. 7, 1819, at 2, col. b, and *Annals of Cong.*, Appendix, 16th Cong., 1st Sess. 2457–58 (Jan. 18, 1820); "Further extract of a Letter from a Gentlemen in this City," *Connecticut Journal* (New Haven), Dec. 12, 1820, at 3.

22. "Legislature of New York," *Times* (Hartford, CT), Jan. 25, 1820, at 2, col. b; David B. Davis, *Inhuman Bondage: The Rise and Fall of Slavery in the New World* 176–77 (2006).

23. *Vermont Intelligencer* (Bellows Falls), Mar. 13, 1820, at 3 ("every new state"); "A Citizen of Illinois, Mr. Spooner," *New York Columbian*, Feb. 11, 1820, at 2; "The Substance of Two Speeches on the Missouri Bill Delivered by Mr. King in the Senate of the United States," in 6 *The Life and Correspondence of Rufus King* 690, 699 (1900 [Feb. 11, 1820]).

24. *Annals of Cong.*, 16th Cong., 1st Sess. 119, 128 (Jan. 17, 1820) (Roberts); "Missouri Question," *Providence Gazette*, Feb. 14, 1820, at 2 (Raymond).

25. *Albany Gazette* (NY), Jan. 20, 1820, at 2, col. a ("the rights … "); *Annals of Cong.*, 16th Cong., 1st Sess. 1195–96 (Feb. 9, 1820) (Rep. John Sergeant of PA).

26. Liam Riordan, *Many Identities, One Nation: The Revolution and Its Legacy in the Mid-Atlantic* 227 (2007); *Annals of Cong.*, 16 Cong. 1st Sess. 301–2 (Jan. 28, 1820) (Van Dyke); id. at 1025 (Reid); *Commercial Adviser* (New York), Jan. 19, 1820, at 2, col. e ("the preamble … ").

27. *Annals of Cong.*, 16th Cong., 1st Sess. 405 (Feb. 15, 1820) (Pinkney); id. at 1025 (Feb. 1, 1820) (Rep. Reid, GA).

28. Id. at 225, 227 (Jan. 20, 1820) (Macon); *Annals of Cong.*, 16th Cong., 2nd Sess. 57–59 (Dec. 8, 1820) (Smith).

29. *Annals of Cong.*, 16 Cong., 1st Sess. 201 (Jan. 20, 1820) (Lowrie); Lemuel Shaw, "Slavery and the Missouri Question," 10 *N. Am. Rev.* 137, 142–43 (1820); Robert Ernst, *Rufus King: American Federalist* 372 (1968) (quoting King).
30. 3 Stat. 544 (Mar. 3, 1820) (Maine admission); 3 Stat. 545 esp. § 8 (Mar. 6, 1820) (Missouri admission).

CHAPTER 6

1. "Extract of a Letter from Washington to the Editor of the American Republican," *Cherry-Valley Gazette* (NY), Feb. 29, 1820, at 1.
2. David Ress, *Governor Edward Coles and the Vote to Forbid Slavery in Illinois, 1823–1824* (2006); "For the Spectator," *Edwardsville Spectator* (IL) July 19, 1823, at 2; letter from Thomas Jefferson to Edward Coles, Aug. 25, 1814, in 11 *The Works of Thomas Jefferson* 416–19 (Paul L. Ford, ed., 1905); S. P. Wheeler, "Edward Coles Second Governor of Illinois," in *Transactions of the Illinois State Historical Society for the Year 1903*, at 104 (1904).
3. "We Are All Born Equal," *Edwardsville Spectator* (IL), May 29, 1821, at 1.
4. "For the Sun," *Pittsfield Sun* (MA), Dec. 10, 1835, at 3; "Legislature of Tennessee: Report of the Committee on Slavery," *Pittsfield Sun* (MA), Nov. 28, 1821, at 1; Oliver Perry Temple, *East Tennessee and the Civil War* 110 (1899); Asa Earl Martin, "The Anti-Slavery Societies of Tennessee," 1 *Tenn. Hist. Mag.* 261, 269 (1915); Isaac Candler, *A Summary View of America* 259 (1824).
5. "Celebration in Poland," *Eastern Argus* (Portland, ME), July 19, 1831, at 2 (the title of the article seems to be a misprint for Portland).
6. "From the Baltimore Morning Chronicle: Right to Office," *Connecticut Courant* (Hartford), Nov. 20, 1821, at 3 (e.g., lauding Sherman); "Mr. Lefever," *Republican Compiler* (Gettysburg, PA), Sept. 17, 1823, at 2; James Cheetham, *A Dissertation Concerning Political Equality* vi, 25 (1800); "Speech," *Pittsfield Sun* (MA), Sept. 22, 1831, at 1; "Town of Enfield," *Republican Chronicle* (Ithaca, NY), Apr. 18, 1821, at 3.
7. Franklin [pseudonym], "For the Colombian," *New York Colombian*, Sept. 14, 1820, at 2, col. B; Alexander Keyssar, *The Right To Vote: The Contested History of Democracy in the United States* 24 (2000).
8. Charles L. Zelden, *Voting Rights on Trial* 46 (2002); David M. Ricci, *Good Citizenship in America* 89 n.41 (2004); "Letter III: From a Republican in the Country to a Federalist in Baltimore," *Baltimore Patriot*, Aug. 3, 1820, col. a. ("in the year 1801 ... "); "Constitution of the State of Massachusetts art. ix," in *Official Papers, Printed for the Common Council of the City of Boston* 23, 28 (1822); *Journal of Debates and Proceedings in the Convention of Delegates, Chosen to Revise the Constitution of Massachusetts, Begun and Holden at Boston, November 15, 1820, and Continued by Adjournment to January 9, 1821*, at 172, 483 (revised and corrected 1853) (some of the references to Declaration); "Town of Enfield," *Republican Chronicle* (Ithaca, NY), Apr. 18, 1821, at 3; "N.Y. State Constitution of 1821 art. II," in *The Constitution of the State of New York* 59, 60–61 (Robert C. Cumming et al. eds., 1894); Reports of the Proceedings and Debates of the Convention of 1821, Assembled for the Purpose of Amending the Constitution

of the State of New York 178, 235 (Nathaniel H. Carter and William L. Stone. eds., 1821).

9. Dixon R. Fox, *The Decline of Aristocracy in Politics in New York* 353 (1919); "From the Philadelphia Gazette," *Daily National intelligencer* (Washington, DC), Mar. 8, 1820, at 2; "A Citizen, Letter to the Editor," *Providence Gazette*, May 1, 1820, at 1–2; *Annals of Cong.*, 17th Cong., 2nd Sess. (1823) (Johnson).

10. Alexander Tsesis, *We Shall Overcome: A History of Civil Rights and the Law* 39–40 (2008).

11. "Ladies Celebration," *Essex Register* (Salem, MA), Aug. 18, 1825, at 2.

12. Richard H. Chused, "Married Women's Property Law: 1800–1850," 71 *Georgetown L.J.* 1359 (1983); Linda K. Kerber, "From the Declaration of Independence to the Declaration of Sentiments," 6 *Human Rts.* 115 (1976); The Public Statute Laws of the State of Connecticut 1, 351 (1835); Laws of the State of Delaware 1, 556 (1829); Public Laws of the State of Rhode-Island 10, 231–32, 260 (1844).

13. Edward D. Mansfield, *The Legal Rights, Liabilities and Duties of Women* 124–25 (1845); "The People," 9 *Yale Literary Mag.* 275, 276–77 (April 1844); "Rights of Woman," *Ohio Repository*, (Canton, OH), Feb. 9, 1843, at 1.

14. First Annual Report of the Board of Managers of the New-England Anti-Slavery Society 49, 52–53 (1833) (comments of Prof. Charles Follen); 1 *Society in America* 148–49 (1837); *Literary Gazette, and Journal of the Belles Lettres*, May 13, 1837, at 297, 298 (book review).

15. Harriot K. Hunt, *Glances and Glimpses* 295–96, 318–19 (1856).

16. Daniel W. Howe, *What Hath God Wrought: The Transformation of America, 1815–1848*, at 562 (2007); "The Rail Road & the Canal," *Torch Light and Public Advertiser* (Hagers-Town, MD), July 17, 1828, at 1.

17. "First American Railroad and Car," *Atchison Daily Globe*, May 31, 1895, at 7; "Charles Carroll or Carrollton," *Huron Reflector* (Norwalk, OH), Sept. 19, 1831, at 4; "Charles Carroll," *Torch Light and Public Advertiser*, May 27, 1830, at 1; "Charles Carroll of Carrollton. August 2nd, 1826," reprinted in George W. Howard, *The Monumental City, Its Past History and Present Resources* 385 (1873) ("to the present ... "); "Transatlantic Sketches," in *The West of Scotland Magazine and Review* 464, 469 (April 1858).

18. "Transatlantic Sketches," supra, at 469; *County Court v. Baltimore & Ohio R. Co.*, 35 F. 161, 164 (1888) (source of charter); Dionysius Lardner, *Railway Economy: A Treatise on the New Art of Transport* 366 (1850); Jack Gieck, *A Photo Album of Ohio's Canal Era, 1825–1913*, at 4 (1992); *Middlesex Gazette* (Middletown, CT), Aug. 17, 1825, at 1 (Ohio and Erie Canal); *Life and Public Services of John Quincy Adams, Sixth President of the United States* 219, 222–23 (1849) (Adams's speech).

19. "Life and Character of Andrew Jackson," in Levy Woodbury, *Writings of Levi Woodbury* 372 (1852) (reprinted eulogy of July 2, 1845).

20. Thomas Jefferson, "First Inaugural Address," in 33 *The Papers of Thomas Jefferson* 148–52 (Barbara B. Oberg and J. Jefferson Looney eds. in chief 2006); "The Course of Civilization," 6 *United States Democratic Rev.* 208, 212–13 (1839); "Great Democratic Congressional Celebration of the Fourth of July," *Ohio*

Statesman (Columbus), July 17, 1838, at 2 ("apostle … "); "Mr. Bancroft's Oration: Delivered Before the Democracy of Springfield, and the neighboring Towns, on the 4th of July," 1836, *Pittsfield Sun* (MA), Sept. 22, 1836, at 1, 2.

21. [Fisher Ames], *The Influence of Democracy on Liberty, Property, and the Happiness of Society, Considered* 57 (1835); Francis J. Grund, *The Americans in Their Moral, Social, and Political Relations* 404 (1837); Patrick Shirreff, *A Tour Through North America* 296 (1835).

22. *The Life of Major-General William Henry Harrison* 21 (1840); Sean Wilentz, *Andrew Jackson* 107 (2006); Jon Meacham, *American Lion: Andrew Jackson in the White House* 267 (2008); Robert V. Remini, *Andrew Jackson* 183–84 (1969); Letter from F. H. Elmore to Planning Committee to Volunteer and States Rights Barbacue, Jan. 15, 1834, in *Columbia Telescope* (SC), Mar. 8, 1834, at 1 (e.g., of remark on Jackson's "tyrannical" style); "Public Meeting Of Authors, Editors, Booksellers, Publisher, Printers, Bookbinders, &c," *United States' Telegraph* (Washington, DC), Mar. 14, 1834, at 1 ("the usurpation … "); letter from a gentleman in Albany to his friend in New York, Mar. 23, 1834, in "Interesting Correspondence," *New-York Spectator* April 3, 1834, at 3 ("My worst fears, with respect to Gen. Jackson, are realized; and he stands confessed to all eyes … a Usurper and a Tyrant."); "Extract of a Letter from South Carolina," *United States' Telegraph* (Washington DC), May. 16, 1834, at 1; "General Jackson," *United States' Telegraph* (Washington, DC), June 17, 1834, at 1.

23. "From the Sentinel-Extra. National Republican Meeting," *Republican Compiler* (Gettysburg, PA), Nov. 13, 1832, at 2.

24. The Society of Friends of the People, which formed in Philadelphia in 1805 to protect the working poor against exploitations endemic to preindustrialization, was an early labor organization that unified around the principles of the Declaration of Independence. Its constitution embraced the public good for all people, irrespective of their religions and nationalities. After quoting the preamble's statement on human equality and unalienable rights, the Society's constitution required new members to pledge their commitment to the "wholesome and essential principles contained in the Declaration of Independence." Constitution of the Democratic Society of Friends of the People, Established At Philadelphia 13th April, 1805 (1805).

25. John B. McMaster, *The Acquisition of Political Social and Industrial Rights of Man in America* 56–60 (1903); *Maryland: A Guide to the Old Line State* 78 (1940); *Trenton Federalist* (NJ), July 13, 1818, at 2.

26. *We, the Other People: Alternative Declarations of Independence by Labor Groups, Farmers, Woman's Rights Advocates, Socialists, and Blacks, 1829–1975*, at 47–49 (Philip S. Foner ed., 1976); Edward Pessen, *Most Uncommon Jacksonians: The Radical Leaders of the Early Labor Movement* 26–33 (1967).

27. Thomas Skidmore, *The Rights of Man to Property! Being a Proposition to Make it Equal among the Adults* 242 (1829); "Returning the Bank Bill to the Senate with His Objections," in *Annual Messages, Veto Messages, Protests, & c. of Andrew Jackson* 244 (2nd ed. 1835); "The Working Men of the City of New York … ," *Illinois Gazette* (Shawnee-town), Aug. 7, 1830, at 4, col. b ("The political text … "); Theodore Sedgwick, *Public and Private Economy* 85 (1838) (part second); Seth Luther,

"An Address to the Working Men of New England on the State of Education and the Condition of the Producing Classes in Europe and America" 27 (2nd ed. 1833).

28. "To the People of South Carolina, by Their Delegates in Convention," in *Journal of the Convention of the People of South Carolina* 57 (1833); "Address to the People of South Carolina by Their Delegates," reprinted in *Register of Debates, Appendix*, 22d Cong., 2nd Sess. 164 (1833); "Messages of the Governor of Virginia, Dec. 3, 1833," in *Journal of the Senate, of the Commonwealth of Virginia* 7, 24 (1833).

29. "The Virginia and Kentucky Resolutions of 1798 and '99 ... also Madison's Report, Calhoun's Address Resolutions of the Several States in Relation to State Rights" (1833); Register of Debates, 22d Cong., 2nd Sess. 1624 (Feb. 5, 1833) (Patton); "Debates in the Senate," *Niles Weekly Register*: Supplementary to Volume XLIII 66 (1833) (Bibb).

30. Register of Debates, 22d Congress, 2nd sess. 1612–13 (Feb. 4, 1833) (Adams on compact theory and privilege); "Great Meeting of the Friends of the Protective System," *Connecticut Courant* (Hartford), June 5, 1832, at 2; *Salem Gazette* (MA), Dec. 21, 1832, at 2 (" ... philosophical dream ... "); "Proclamation of Andrew Jackson, President of the United States," *Adams Sentinel* (Gettysburg, PA), Dec. 18, 1832, at 6.

31. "Legislature of North Carolina," *Richmond Enquirer*, Jan. 1, 1833, at 4; "Harrison County Clarksburg (VA) Dec. 29," *Richmond Enquirer*, Jan. 10, 1833, at 1–2.

32. David Brion Davis, *The Problem of Slavery in the Age of Revolution, 1770–1823*, at 60 (1999); "Slavery Laws of Mexico," in N. Doran Maillard, *The History of the Republic of Texas* 508 (1842); Richard Bruce Winders, *Crisis in the Southwest: The United States, Mexico, and the Struggle over Texas* 80 (2002) (quoting 1827 laws); "Legislature of Ohio," *Emancipator* (New York), Feb. 1, 1839, at 154; Will Fowler, *Santa Anna of Mexico* 174 (2007); David Lee Child, "Texas," 1 *Quarterly Anti-Slavery Magazine* 202 (Elizur Wright ed., Jan. 1836); *Mobile Mercantile Advertiser*, "'Liberty': The Image and Superscription on Every Coin Issued by the United States of America" 73 (1837).

33. "Texas," *Floridian and Journal* (Tallahassee), Apr. 2, 1836, at 2; "Constitution of Texas—1845," in 6 *Federal and State Constitutions* 3563 (Francis N. Thorpe ed., 1909).

34. "John Quincy Adams," *Daily Atlas*, Oct. 17, 1842, at 1; "The Texas Question–Extracts from J. Q. Adams' Speech," *Liberator*, July 20, 1838, at 1; [Benjamin Lundy], *The War in Texas* 14 (2d ed. 1837).

35. "Slavery–New Hampshire Resolution," in 8 *Latter-Day Saints' Millennial Star* 118 (1846).

36. Resolutions and Private Acts: Passed by the General Assembly of the State of Connecticut, May Session, 1845, at 21 (1845); Laws of the State of Delaware, Passed at Session of the General Assembly ... On Tuesday the Seventh Day of January ... One Thousand Eight Hundred and Forty-five 90–91 (1845).

37. *Register of Debates*, 24th Cong., 1st Sess. at 4277 (June 9, 1836).

38. "National Anniversary," *City of Washington Gazette*, July 5, 1820, at 2; "General La Fayette," *Richmond Enquirer*, July 31, 1821, at 4; [No title], *New London Gazette* (CT), Jan. 5, 1831, at 3, col. A.

39. *Cong. Globe*, 28th Cong., 2nd Sess. 169 (Jan. 21, 1845); John Quincy Adams, "Speech of John Quincy Adams of Massachusetts upon the Right of the People,

Men and Women, to Petition" 83 (1838); Horace Mann, *Slavery: Letters and Speeches* 3–4 (1851); "Mr. Stanton's Speech At the N.E.A.'s Convention," *Liberator,* June 11, 1836, at 94.

CHAPTER 7

1. See, e.g., "General Sentiments," *Ohio Repository* (Canton), July 12, 1848, at 3.
2. *Biography of an American Bondman, by His Daughter* (1856) (about William W. Brown); Richard Hildreth, *Despotism in America* 15 (1840) ("Who could ... "); Joseph E. Sprague, "An Oration, Delivered At Salem, On the Fourth of July, 1810," at 4 (1810); William Craft, *Running a Thousand Miles for Freedom* iii (1860).
3. Alice D. Adams, *The Neglected Period of Anti-Slavery in America (1808–1831),* at 116–39, 154–94, 250 (1908); Lacy Ford, *Deliver Us from Evil: The Slavery Question in the Old South* (2009).
4. William Lloyd Garrison, "Incendiary Doctrines," *Liberator,* Mar. 18, 1837, at 1.
5. "To the Editor of the Traveller," *Vermont Gazette* (Bennington), July 21, 1829, at 3.
6. J. D., "The Ever-glorious Fourth," *North Star* (Rochester, NY), July 13, 1849.
7. Alexander Tsesis, *The Thirteenth Amendment and American Freedom* (2004); *The Promises of Liberty: A History and Contemporary Relevance of the Thirteenth Amendment* (Alexander Tsesis ed., 2010).
8. "American Ingratitude and Inconsistency," *Emancipator* (Boston), Feb. 21, 1839, at 174.
9. "Anti-Slavery Windowblinds," *Colored American* (New York), June 29, 1839; "Declaration of Sentiments of the American Anti-Slavery Society," in *The Platform of the American Anti-Slavery Society and Its Auxiliaries* 7 (1855); William E. Channing, *Slavery* 21, 27, 32, 46 (1835); see generally on self-cultivation "Self-Culture: An Address ... Boston, Sept. 1838," in *The Works of William E. Channing* 14–15 (American Unitarian Association ed., 1891); "Three Abstract Principles," *Liberator,* Apr. 5, 1834, at 1 ("meanest individual ... "); "Principles of the Anti-Slavery Society," in *The American Anti Slavery Almanac* 30–31 (1837 ed.); Euthymus, "Letter to the Editor: Thoughts on Color," *Liberator,* Aug. 27, 1831, at 138.
10. William Lloyd Garrison, "The Cause of Emancipation," in *The Liberty Bell* 98–99 (American Anti-Slavery Society, 1839); "Address of the Executive Committee of the American Anti-Slavery Society to the Friends of Freedom and Emancipation in the United States," in 3 *William Lloyd Garrison, 1805–1879: The Story of His Life Told by His Children* 129–32 (1889); 2 Charles Elliot, *Sinfulness of American Slavery* 129–30, 253–55 (1850).
11. Baptist, "View of Slavery," *Liberator,* Mar. 1, 1834, at 1 (e.g., antislavery thought).
12. "Letters on Slavery From John Rankin to Thomas Rankin," *Liberator,* Oct. 20, 1832, at 1; Robert B. Hall, "Slavery and the Means of Its Removal," *Liberator,* Apr. 14, 1832, at 1.
13. "Address of the National Convention of Abolitionists Held in Albany, July 31, 1839," *Liberator,* Aug. 23, 1839, at 1; Archibald H. Grimke, *William Lloyd Garrison: The Abolitionist* 354 (1891).

14. "Constitution of the Cambridgeport Anti-Slavery Society," *Liberator*, Aug. 29, 1835, at 138 ("the principles … "); "A Noble Document," *Emancipator* (New York), June 21, 1838, at 32 (Annual Convention …); "Address of the Rochester Anti-Slavery Society," *Liberator*, Jan. 11, 1834, at 1, with this address concluded in id., Jan. 18, 1834, at 1; "The Dangers from Slavery," *Emancipator* (Boston), June 14, 1848, at 1; William E. Channing, *Slavery* 34, 46 (1835) ("his own and other's … " and "spoke in the name … ").

15. "New England Anti-Slavery Convention," *Liberator*, Aug. 30, 1834, at 138; Proceedings of the Anti-Slavery Convention, Assembled at Philadelphia, Dec. 4, 5, and 6, 1833, at 5–6, 13–14 (1833); "Declaration of Sentiments on Behalf of the Illinois State Anti-Slavery Society, Formed Oct. 28, 1937, At Alton" *Emancipator*, Mar. 8, 1838, at 176; "Anniversary of the Rhode-Island Anti-Slavery Society," *Liberator*, Nov. 19, 1836, at 1, 2 (Tappan); "Speech of Professor Follen," *Liberator*, Apr. 5, 1834, at 54; Robert Alexander Young, *The Ethiopian Manifesto* 5 (New York, 1829).

16. "Address of the New York State Convention of Colored Citizens to the People of the State," *Colored American*, Dec. 19, 1840; see also "Should Colored Men Vote," *Colored American*, Dec. 5, 1840; "Right of Suffrage," *North Star* (Rochester, NY), Feb. 8, 1850, at 1; "From the Mobile Register & Journal," *Georgia Telegraph* (Macon), Oct. 13, 1846, at 1.

17. Letters from John Rankin to Thomas Rankin, supra; Alexander Tsesis, *We Shall Overcome: A History of Civil Rights and the Law* 46 (2008); Daniel J. Flanigan, "Criminal Procedure in Slave Trials in the Antebellum South," 40 *J. South. Hist.* 537, 540, 543–44 (1974); Peter W. Bardaglio, "Rape and the Law in the Old South: 'Calculated to Excite Indignation in Every Heart,'" 60 *J. South. Hist.* 749, 761–62 (1994) (see accompanying notes); George M. Stroud, *A Sketch of the Laws Relating to Slavery in the Several States of the United States of America* 90 (1856); "The Liberator and Slavery," *Liberator*, Jan. 7, 1832, at 1 ("For thirty-two … "); "Letter from the Editor of the *Dublin Freeman*, James Haughton," *Liberator*, Nov. 14, 1845, at 1.

18. 11 *Register of Debates*, 23rd Cong., 2nd Sess. 1131–35 (Feb. 2, 1835) (eight-hundred-person petition); 12 *Register of Debates*, 24th Cong., 1st Sess. 500–03 (Feb. 15, 1836) (Quaker petitions); "Petition to Congress," *Liberator*, Feb. 11, 1832, at 23; "District Of Columbia," *Liberator*, Jan 1, 1831, at 1; William Jay, "A View of the Action of the Federal Government in Behalf of Slavery (2d ed.)," in *Miscellaneous Writings on Slavery* 216 (1853) (Sept. 1839); "The Anti-Slavery Meeting," *Daily National Intelligencer* (Washington, DC), Oct. 7, 1833 (detailing formation of the New York City Anti-Slavery Society).

19. William Lloyd Garrison, "To the Public," *Liberator*, Jan. 1, 1831, at 1 ("full of … "); William L. Garrison, "An Address Delivered before the Old Colony Anti-Slavery Society, at South Scituate, Mass., July 4, 1839," at 17 (1839).

20. 2 *The Letters of William Lloyd Garrison: A House Dividing against Itself* 566 (1971) (quoting Jay).

21. "Whittier's Reply," *Liberator*, Aug. 17, 1833, at 1; "The Synod of Kentucky," *Sun* (Pittsfield, PA), Dec. 10, 1835, at 3 (disavowing immediatism and embracing gradualism).

22. A. B., "Selected," *Philadelphia Nat'l Enq.*, July 11, 1839, at 2; "Liberty Platform of 1844," in *National Party Platforms, 1840–1960*, at 4–8 (Donald B. Johnson ed., 1978); Letter from Alvan Stewart to Dr. Bailey [editor of *The Philanthropist*], Apr. 1842, in *Writings and Speeches of Alvan Stewart, on Slavery* (Luther Rawson Marsh ed., 1860); David E. Swift, *Black Prophets of Justice: Activist Clergy Before the Civil War* 140 (1989); Letter of Alvan Stewart to the Liberty Party, 1846, in *Writings and Speeches of Alvan Stewart, on Slavery* 44, 266–67 (Luther Rawson Marsh ed., 1860).

23. "Whigery and Abolitionism," *Greenville Mountaineer* (SC), Nov. 6, 1846, at 1; Allen O. Myers, *Bosses and Boodle in Ohio Politics* 81 (1895); Frederic M. Holland, *Frederick Douglass: The Colored Orator* 210–11 (rev. ed. 1895).

24. Henry Clay, speech of Jan. 18, 1848, in *Thirty-First Annual Report of the American Colonization Society* 25 (1848); Robert V. Remini, *Henry Clay, Statesman for the Union* 696 (1991); "Henry Clay and African Colonization," *Liberator*, Jan. 28, 1848, at 14; "Resolutions," *Liberator*, Apr. 5, 1839, at 54.

25. "The American Colonization Society—No. 1," *Independent Inquirer* (Brattleboro, VT), Jan. 4, 1834, at 1.

26. "An Address to the Citizens of New-York," *Liberator*, Feb. 12, 1831, at 1; "Address of the Free People of Color of the Borough of Wilmington, Delaware," *Liberator*, Sept. 24, 1831, at 1; "Address," *Liberator*, Sept. 10, 1831, at 146; "The Anti-Colonization Meeting in Exeter Hall, London," *Liberator*, Nov. 16, 1833, at 1 (Rev. Paul).

27. Tsesis, supra, at 61–63 (2008); William Wiecek, *The Sources of Antislavery Constitutionalism in America, 1760–1848*, at 249–75 (1977).

28. James Williams, *Letters on Slavery from the Old World: Written During the Canvass for Presidency of the United States in 1860*, at 78–80 (1861); William A. Smith, *Lectures on the Philosophy and Practice of Slavery: As Exhibited in the Institution of Domestic Slavery in the United States* 69 (1856); William Harper, "On Slavery", in *The Pro-Slavery Argument; As Maintained by the Most Distinguished Writers of the Southern States*, (1852); John H. Hopkins, *Scriptural, Ecclesiastical, and Historical View of Slavery* 17–21, 90 (1864).

29. "All Men Are by Nature Free," *Daily Picayune* (New Orleans, LA), July 31, 1845, at 2; Hopkins, supra, at 26 (1864).

30. Letter from Calhoun to Ellwood Fisher, July 21, 1848, *The Papers of John C. Calhoun, 1847–1848*, at 608, 638 (1999); "Speech of John C. Calhoun," *North Star* (Rochester, NY), July 7, 1848, at 1; John C. Calhoun, "A Disquisition on Government (1851)," in 1 *The Works of John C. Calhoun* (Richard K. Cralle ed., 1883); John L. Carey, *Some Thoughts Concerning Domestic Slavery* 34, 44 (1838).

31. Thornton Stringfellow, *Scriptural and Statistical Views in Favor of Slavery* 144 (1856).

32. Letters from Rev. Frederick A. Ross to Rev. A. Barnes, [not dated], in *Frederick A. Ross, Slavery Ordained of God* 103–104, 122–26, 139, 174 (1857).

33. J. K. Paulding, *Slavery in the United States* 37, 40, 42–43, 46, 95, 125, 130–31, 184–85 (Harper & Brothers, 1836); W. B. Hartgrove, "The Negro Soldier in the American Revolution," 1 *J. Negro Hist.* 110 (1916).

34. Samuel Seabury, *American Slavery Distinguished from the Slavery of English Theorists and Justified by the Law of Nature* 34, 39–40, 128–29 (1861); 7 Thomas

Smyth, *The War of the South Vindicated and the War Against of South Condemned*, in *Complete Works of Rev. Thomas Smyth, D.D.* 563, 590 (J. Wm. Flinn ed., 1910); B. M. Palmer, *The Life and Letters of James H. Thornwell* 473 (1875).

35. *Cong. Globe*, 24th Cong., 1st Sess. app. 9 (Dec. 1, 1835) (Kendall's report to Congress); Defensor, *The Dispersion of the State Anti-Slavery Convention* 11–13 (1835) (President Jackson backed Kendall); Andrew Jackson, "Seventh Annual Message to Congress," in 3 *A Compilation of the Messages and Papers of the Presidents 1789–1897*, at 176 (James Richardson ed., 1896); "To the Public," *New Hampshire Sentinel*, Aug. 27, 1835, at 2 (May's Speech); "Calhoun's Gag Law," *Liberator*, Apr. 2, 1836, at 1 (paraphrasing *Boston Daily Advocate*); "Auburn Free Press" *Liberator*, Nov. 26, 1831, at 3.

36. "Calhoun's Gag Law," *Liberator*, Apr. 2, 1836, at 1; David Christian, *Imperial and Soviet Russia: Power, Privilege, and the Challenge of Modernity* 66 (1961) (regarding censorship under Nicholas I); Jane Clapp, "Art Censorship under French King Louis Philippe," in *Art Censorship: A Chronology of Proscribed and Prescribed Art* 120–24 (1972).

37. "The Freeman," *Philadelphia National Enquirer*, Dec. 27, 1838, at 1.

38. "Letter of John Quincy Adams on Slavery," *Berkshire County Whig* (Pittsfield, MA), Aug. 31, 1843, at 1; *Letters of Theodore Dwight Weld, Angelina Grimké Weld, and Sarah Grimké* 899 (1965).

39. "Mr. Adams' Second Letter," *Emancipator* (Boston), June 13, 1839, at 25.

40. John Quincy Adams, "Miscellaneous," *Liberator*, Feb. 25, 1837, at 36; "Rescinding and Expunging," *Philadelphia National Enquirer*, Mar. 15, 1838, at 3.

41. "Mr. Adams' Letter of the Right of Petition," *Emancipator* (New York), May 16, 1839, at 1; "Proceedings in Congress," *Daily National Intelligencer*, Dec. 24, 1838, at 1, Jan. 11, 1839, at 1, Jan. 23, 1839, at 2, Mar. 14, 1839, at 2, Apr. 23, 1839, at 2; "Right to Petition," *Liberator*, Mar. 11, 1837, at 44.

42. *Cong. Globe*, 26th Cong., 1st Sess. 102 (1840) (Cooper); *Cong. Globe Appendix*, 27th Cong., 1st Sess. 72 (June 1841) (Rep. Charles J. Ingersoll of PA); *Cong. Globe Appendix*, 27th Cong., 2nd Sess. 337–38 (Campbell) (Apr. 15, 1842).

43. George Wingate Chase, *The History of Haverhill, Massachusetts* 516 (1861) (quoting petition read by Adams); *Cong. Globe*, 27th Cong. 2nd Sess. 168 (Jan. 27, 1842); "Tom Marshall of Kentucky," 35 *Harper's Magazine* 354, 355 (1867) (about Henry Clay); "Abolition Dissolution," *Ohio Statesman* (Columbus), Feb. 4, 1842, at 3.

44. *Cong. Globe*, 27th Cong., 2nd Sess. 170 (Jan. 25, 1842); "Washington, Tuesday, Jan. 25th, 1842," *Daily Atlas* (Boston), Jan. 29, 1842, at 2; "Debate on the Motion to Censure Mr. Adams," *Daily Atlas*, Jan. 31, 1842, at 1.

45. Casey Olson, "John Quincy Adams's Congressional Career," U.S. Capitol Historical Society, http://uschscapitolhistory.uschs.org/articles/uschs_articles-01.htm (Wise statement); *Cong. Globe*, 27th Cong., 2nd Sess. 214–15 (Feb. 7, 1842).

46. 3 *History of the United States: From the Earliest Discovery of America to the End of 1902*, at 239 (1903).

47. "Ladies Petition," *Emancipator and Republican* (Boston, MA), Feb. 24, 1835, at 3–4 (e.g., of women's petition); "Meeting of the Colored People in New-Bedford," *Liberator*, June 5, 1840, at 2.

48. Declaration of Sentiments, http://www.library.csi.cuny.edu/dept/history/lavender/2decs.html (Declaration of Independence and Declaration of Sentiments side by side); "Woman Suffrage Jubilee," *Sunday Inter Ocean*, Apr. 1, 1888, at 2; 1 *A History of Woman Suffrage, 1848–1861*, at 70–71 (Elizabeth Cady Stanton ed., 1881); Benjamin Quarles, "Frederick Douglass and the Woman's Rights Movement," 25 *J. Negro Hist.* 35 (1940); *Proceedings of the Woman's Rights Conventions Held at Seneca Falls and Rochester N.Y., July and August, 1848* (1848); Gerda Lerner, "The Meaning of Seneca Falls, 1848–1998," in *Women's America: Refocusing the Past* (5th ed., Linda K. Kerber and Jane Sherron DeHart, 2000); "Breaking the Trail for Woman Suffrage," *Kansas City Star* (MO), Aug. 20, 1920, at 26.

49. "Meeting of the Colored People in New-Bedford," *Liberator*, June 5, 1840.

50. "Ladies Department," *Liberator*, Apr. 19, 1834, at 1; 3 *William Lloyd Garrison, 1805–1879: The Story of His Life Told by His Children* 310 (1889) (reprinting a Garrison article from an 1850 *Liberator*); "Woman's Rights," in Wendell Phillips, *Speeches, Lectures, and Letters* 11–13 (1863); "Natural Equality: The Abolitionists Hold with the Declaration," *Colored American*, Mar. 3, 1838.

51. Ernestine L. Rose, *A Lecture on Woman's Rights* (Oct. 19, 1851).

52. "Women's Rights Tracts, ... Number 4, Oct. 29th, 1850," reprinted in *Woman's Rights Commensurate with Her Capacities and Obligations* 1–3 (1853); *Proceedings of the Woman's Rights Convention, Held At Worcester, October 15th and 16th, 1851*, at 11 (1852).

53. *Proceedings of the Ohio Women's Convention Held at Salem, April 19th, and 20th, 1850*, at 6–8 (1850).

CHAPTER 8

1. "Speech for Union Among Men of All Parties Against the Slave Power ... at Worcester, June 28, 1848," in 2 *Orations and Speeches by Charles Sumner* 253 (1850); *Cong. Globe Appendix*, 29th Cong. 2nd Sess. 171 (Feb. 4, 1847) (Tilden); Thomas G. Cary, "An Oration Delivered before the Authorities of the City of Boston at the Celebration of the Declaration of Independence, July 5, 1847," at 6–7 (1847); "Anti-Slavery Gathering Fourth of July at Norton," *Emancipator*, July 7, 1847; "Fourth of July—Celebration at Monticello," *Floridian* (Tallahassee), July 10, 1847, at 2; "4th of July Celebration," *Raleigh Register* (NC), July 21, 1847.

2. Letter from Ahmed, No. 48, in *Liberty Chimes* 124–25 (1845); "Connecticut on Annexation," *Sun* (Baltimore, MD), July 11, 1845, at 1; *Emancipator* (Boston), Nov. 19, 1845, at 119 (Roxbury); "The Hon. Alexander H. Stephens' Opinion on Slavery," *Georgia Telegraph* (Macon), Feb. 25, 1845, at 3; "Commend the Poisoned Chalice to Their Own Lips!" *Daily Madisonian* (Washington, DC), Mar. 7, 1845, at 2.

3. "Free Soil State Convention—Resolution," *New York Daily Tribune*, Sept. 18, 1848, at 1.

4. "Speech of Mr. Horace Mann, of Mass" 8 (1848); "Speeches in Congress: Speech of Mr. Corwin of Ohio," 74 *Niles' National Register* 282, 282 (1848); *Cong. Globe Appendix*, 30th Cong., 2nd Sess. 179–80 (Feb. 26, 1849) (Rep C. E. Stuart);

"The Three Million Bill: A Speech ... delivered on the 1st March, 1847," in *John A. Dix, Speeches and Occasional Addresses* 188 (1864); *Cong. Globe Appendix,* 30th Cong., 2nd Sess. 168–69 (Feb. 24, 1849) (Murphy).

5. "Magnificent Illumination in Honor of the Day!" *North Am. & United States Gazette* (Philadelphia), July 5, 1847; J. D., "The Ever-glorious Fourth," *North Star* (Rochester, NY), July 13, 1849, at 2.

6. Henry Montgomery, *The Life of Major General Zachary Taylor* 422 (1850).

7. "Higher Law," *Janesville Gazette* (WI), Dec. 11, 1851, at 4; Samuel T. Spear, *The Law Abiding Conscience and the Higher Law Conscience* 16 (1850); Charles Durkee, "Correspondence," *Wisconsin Free Democrat* (Milwaukee), Feb. 20, 1850, at 2.

8. Robert R. Russel, "What Was the Compromise of 1850?," 22 *J. Southern Hist.* 292 (1956); F. H. Hodder, "The Authorship of the Compromise of 1850," 22 *Miss. Valley Hist. Rev.* 525 (1936); "Speech of Theodore Parker to the New England Anti-Slavery Convention, May 29, 1850," *Liberator,* July 5, 1850, at 1.

9. Alexander Tsesis, *The Thirteenth Amendment and American Freedom* 26–29 (2004); Marion G. McDougall, *Fugitive Slaves* 112–15 (1967) (text of law); *Cong. Globe,* 31st Cong., 1st Sess. 525 (Mar. 15, 1850) (Sen. John P. Hale); "Jefferson Revised," *State Gazette* (Trenton, NJ), June 19, 1854, at 2.

10. "Speech at the New England Anti-Slavery Convention in Boston, May 29, 1850," in 3 *Speeches, Addresses, and Occasional Sermons, by Theodore Parker* 55 (1861).

11. "For the Farmers' Cabinet," *Farmers' Cabinet* (Amherst, NH), Nov. 14, 1850, at 3; "Baptists on the Slave Bill," *Pittsfield Sun* (MA), Oct. 17, 1850, at 3.

12. "From L. A. Hine," *Liberator,* Oct. 22, 1852, at 171 ("fathers appealed ..."); "Letter From John G. Whittier to Wm. Lloyd Garrison, May 13, 1850," *Liberator,* May 17, 1850, at 79 ("practical believers ... "); "A British Nobleman in America," *Sun,* Jan. 6, 1851, at 1.

13. William Wells Brown, *Three Years in Europe: or, Places I Have Seen and People I Have Met* 247–48 (1852); Samuel Ringgold Ward, *Autobiography of a Fugitive Negro: His Anti-slavery Labours in the United States, Canada, and England* 118–22 (1855); Frederick Douglass, "What to the Slave is the Fourth of July?: Extract from an Oration, at Rochester, July 5, 1852," in *Frederick Douglass, My Bondage and My Freedom* 441–42 (1857).

14. "Anti-Fugitive Slave Law Meeting," *North Star,* Jan. 23, 1851, at 1.

15. "Freedom National, Slavery Sectional: Speech in the Senate, on a Motion to Repeal the Fugitive Slave Act, Aug. 26, 1852," in 3 *The Works of Charles Sumner* 95, 111 (1875).

16. "Woman's Right Convention," *Liberator,* June 16, 1854, at 96.

17. Abraham Lincoln, "Speech at Peoria, Illinois, in Reply to Senator Douglas, Oct. 16, 1854," in 2 *The Writings of Abraham Lincoln* 190, 234–35 (Arthur B. Lapsley ed., 1905); *Cong. Globe,* 33rd Cong., 1st Sess., Appendix 268 (Feb. 24, 1854).

18. "A Contest of Principle," *Free Press,* Feb. 10, 1854; *Cong. Globe,* 34th Cong., 1st Sess. 1407 (June 16, 1856) (Clayton); "Kansas Legislature," *Liberty Weekly Tribune* (Liberty, MO), Aug. 3, 1855, at 2.

19. "Benjamin Franklin String Fellow," in *Two Tracts for the Times* 29 (1855); Albert T. Bledsoe, "An Essay on Liberty and Slavery" 102, 104 (1856); *Cong. Globe,* 33rd Cong., 1st sess. 214 (Feb. 20, 1854) (Pettit); *Speeches, Messages, and Other*

Writings of the Hon. Albert G. Brown 614 (M. W. Cluskey ed., 2nd ed. 1859) ("the helpless ... ").

20. "Self-Government," *New York Tribune*, Feb. 4, 1854; *Proceedings of a Public Meeting of the Citizens of Providence, Held in the Beneficent Congregational Church, March 7, 1854*, at 4, 13 (1854); *Cong. Globe*, 33rd Cong., 1st Sess. 199 (Feb. 13, 1854) (Weller).

21. Message of President Franklin Pierce, in *Cong. Globe Appendix* 4 (Dec. 31, 1855).

22. Letter from Rufus Choate to E. W. Farley, Aug. 9, 1856, in 1 *Samuel Gilman Brown, The Works of Rufus Choate with a Memoir of His Life* (1862).

23. Horace Greeley, *A History of the Struggle for Slavery Extension or Restriction in the United States* 132–33, 138 (1856); William Goodell, *The Kansas Struggle, of 1856, in Congress and in the Presidential Campaign* 34, 74 (1857).

24. *Report of the Board of Commissioners for the Investigation of Election Frauds* 21 (1858).

25. "The Minority Report of the Select Committee of Fifteen," in 1 *Reports of Committees of the House of Representatives Made During the First Session of the Thirty-fifth Congress* 104, 106–7 (1858).

26. *Cong. Globe*, 35th Cong., 1st Sess., at 778–79 (Feb. 18, 1858) (Rep. Sherrard Clemens, Democrat, VA).

27. Henry M. Flint, *Life of Stephen A. Douglas* 123 (1860) (quoting Douglas); *Cong. Globe*, 35th Cong., 1st Sess. 1014 (Mar. 9, 1858) (Keitt); id. at 897–98 (Feb. 26, 1858) (Giddings).

28. *Ableman v. Booth*, 62 U.S. (21 How.) 506, 515–17 (1859); *Prigg v. Pennsylvania*, 41 U.S. (16 Pet.) 539, 625–26 (1842); David Martin, *Trial of the Rev. Jacob Gruber* 43 (1819) (quoting "and hard ... "); Carl B. Swisher, *Roger B. Taney* 93–95, 154 (1935).

29. "The Dred Scott Case, J. COM." (Mar. 12, 1857), reprinted in *Dred Scott v. Sandford, A Brief History with Documents* 140–41 (Paul Finkelman ed., 1998); "Senator Douglas' Speech in Illinois," *New York Herald*, June 22, 1857, at 2; Stephen A. Douglas, Senator, speech at Springfield (July 17, 1858), reprinted in *Political Debates between Hon. Abraham Lincoln and Hon. Stephen A. Douglas* 52 (1860).

30. "From His Speech on the *Dred Scott* Decision. Springfield, Illinois. June 26, 1857," in *Speeches and Letters of Abraham Lincoln* (Merwin Roe ed., 1894).

31. "Selections: The Supreme Court of the United States," *Liberator*, Mar. 20, 1857; "Chief Justice Taney's Opinion," *Boston Daily Advertiser*, May 26, 1857, at 2; "Dred Scott," *Boston Daily Atlas*, Mar. 9, 1857, at 2; "Wickedness of the Decision in the Supreme Court against the African Race," *Independent* (New York), Mar. 19, 1857 reprinted in *Dred Scott v. Sandford, A Brief History with Documents* 151 (Paul Finkelman ed., 1998) (defending framers' character); "The Supreme Court Decision," *Milwaukee Daily Sentinel*, Mar. 19, 1857.

32. "State of New York Report of the Joint Legislative Committee on the Dred Scott Decision," *Boston Daily Advertiser*, Apr. 13, 1857; "The Dred Scott Resolution as They Pass," *Ripley Bee* (OH), May 2, 1857, at 1; Appendix to the *Journal of the Senate of the State of Ohio* 571 (1857); Appendix to the *Minutes of the House of Assembly of the State of New Jersey* 348–49 (1858); *Journal of the House of Representative*

[sic] of the State of Delaware 29, 30 (1859) (reprinting New Hampshire legislature pronouncement of Sept. 1, 1858).

CHAPTER 9

1. Speech at Peoria, Illinois, in 2 *The Collected Works of Abraham Lincoln* 276 (1953).
2. *Cong. Globe*, 34th Cong., 1st Sess. Appendix 400 (Apr. 9, 1856) (Seward); *Cong. Globe*, 33rd Cong., 1st Sess. Appendix 262 (Feb. 24, 1854) (Sumner); Joshua R. Giddings, *History of the Rebellion* 410 (1864) (Giddings); *Cong. Globe*, 33rd Cong., 1st Sess. Appendix 137 (Feb. 4, 1854) (Chase).
3. "Platform of the Fremont and Dayton Convention, Held In Philadelphia, June 16, 1856," in *An Address to the Voters of Burlington County, Upon the Importance of the Approaching Presidential Election, and the True Issue in the Contest* 13 (1856); "Platform of the Republican Party," in *Our Nation's Archives: The History of the United States in Documents* (Eric Braun and Jay Crosby eds., 1999).
4. *Cong. Globe*, 36th Cong., 1st Sess. 56 (Dec. 8, 1859) (Clay and Trumbull); *Cong. Globe*, 36th Cong., 1st Sess. 100–101 (Dec. 12, 1859) (Johnson).
5. Delegates to John Brown's Constitutional Convention of May 8, 1858, http://www.alliesforfreedom.org/Convention.pdf.
6. "Fraternity Lectures," *New York Herald*, Nov. 5, 1859, at 2; "Speech of Wm. Lloyd Garrison, At the Meeting of Tremont Temple, Dec. 2d ... ," *Liberator*, Dec. 16, 1859, at 198; "Legally Wrong, but Morally Right," *Newark Advocate* (OH), Dec. 16, 1859, at 1 (quoting the *State Journal*).
7. "John Brown and the American Slavery Question," *Reynold's Newspaper* (London), Jan. 8, 1860, at 16; "Leeds young Men's Anti-Slavery Society," *Leeds Mercury* (England), Dec. 24, 1859, at 7; "The London Times on the Harper's Ferry Affair," *Ripely Bee* (OH), Dec. 3, 1859, at 1.
8. *Cong. Globe*, 36th Cong., 1st Sess. 142 (Dec. 14, 1859).
9. Merrill D. Peterson, *John Brown: The Legend Revisited* 31 (2002) (quoting Lincoln and Seward in 1860); Redpath, *The Public Life of Capt. John Brown* 104–5 (1860).
10. Lincoln, letter to James N. Brown, Oct. 18, 1858, in 3 *The Collected Works of Abraham Lincoln* 327 (Roy P. Basler et al. eds., 1953); id. at 16 ("there is no reason ... "); Lincoln, "Speech at Peoria, Illinois, in Reply to Senator Douglas, Oct. 16, 1854," in 2 *The Works of Abraham Lincoln* 217 (Arthur B. Lapsley ed., 1905) (on the injustice of slavery); Lincoln, speech at New Haven, CT, in 4 *The Collected Works of Abraham Lincoln* 16–17 (Mar. 6, 1860).
11. *The Lincoln-Douglas Debates: The First Complete, Unexpurgated Text* 55 (Harold Holzer ed., 1993) (Aug. 21, 1858).
12. "Republic Meeting in Brooklyn: Speech of Hon. James Humphrey," *New York Times*, Aug. 24, 1860, at 5.
13. *Cong. Globe*, 36th Cong., 1st Sess., at 2513–15 (May 31, 1860) (Adams).
14. *Cong. Globe*, 36th Cong., 1st Sess., at 1166 (Mar. 15, 1860) (Leach).
15. Id. at 1679–80 (Apr. 12, 1860) (Clark); id. at 1685 (Apr. 13, 1860) (Wilson).
16. *Cong. Globe*, 36th Cong., 1st Sess. 1617 (Apr. 11, 1860) (Chesnut); *Cong. Globe* 36th Cong., 1st Sess. 1005 (Mar. 7, 1860) (Gallatin).

17. "The Status of the Negro at the Revolution," *Semi-Weekly Mississippian* (Jackson), June 26, 1860, at 1.

18. Eugene H. Berwanger, *The Frontier against Slavery* 136 (2002) (quoting Giddings); "The Republicans and the Doctrine of Negro Equality," *New York Times*, Aug. 28, 1860, at 4 (quoting *Guardian*); *Cong. Globe*, 35th Cong., 2nd Sess. 346 (Jan. 12, 1859) ("the devotion of the American ... ").

19. David Christy, *Pulpit Politics* 438 (1862); "The Republicans and the Doctrine of Negro Equality," *Daily Ohio Statesman* (Columbus), Sept. 2, 1860, at 2; "City Politics: Republican Mass Meeting," *New York Times*, Sept. 28, 1860, at 1.

20. "A Great Speech ... Speech of S. A. Douglass, at Springfield, Illinois, June 12, 1857," *Coshocton County Democrat* (OH), June 6, 1860, at 1; "Speech of Hon. Stephen A. Douglass, Delivered in Raleigh, Aug. 30, 1860," *North Carolina Standard* (Raleigh), Sept. 5, 1860, at 2.

21. "He says the Declaration of Independence Was Not Intended To Include 'All Men,'" *Chicago Press and Tribune*, Oct. 5, 1860, at 2; "Speech of the Hon. Stephen A. Douglas at Chicago, Oct. 5th," *Wisconsin Daily Patriot* (Madison), Oct. 10, 1860, at 1.

22. *Political Debates between Hon. Abraham Lincoln and Hon. Stephen A. Douglas* 37 (1860); D. W. Bartlett, *The Life and Public Services of Hon. Abraham Lincoln* 177 (1860); "The Address of the Hon. Abraham Lincoln: in Vindication of the Policy of the Framers of the Constitution" 29 (1860); *The Life, speeches, and public services of Abram [sic] Lincoln* 62 (1860); M'Kean Miner (PA), Oct. 6, 1860, at 1; "The Lincoln's Apostrophe on the Declaration of Independence," *Chicago Press and Tribune*, May 15, 1860, at 2.

23. "More Discussion Nonsense," *New York Times*, Aug. 11, 1860, at 4; "Southern Sentiment on Lincoln's Election: Letter from Mr. Keitt, of South Carolina," *New York Herald*, Oct. 3, 1860, at 2.

24. "Disunion In Georgia," *New York Times*, Nov. 27, 1860, at 1 (Hill); http:// freepages.genealogy.rootsweb.ancestry.com/~ajac/gatroup.htm (Hill's slave ownership).

25. "Proposed Declaration of Independence of South Carolina," *New York Times*, Nov. 14, 1860, at 1; *Declaration of the Immediate Causes Which Induce and Justify the Secession of South Carolina from the Federal Union*, http://avalon.law.yale. edu/19th_century/csa_scarsec.asp.

26. *Banner of Liberty* (Middletown, NY), Jan. 9, 1861, at 10–11, col. c ("never compromise"); *Cong. Globe*, 36th Cong., 2nd Sess. 1373 (Mar. 4, 1861) (Wigfall); id. at 666 (Jan. 30, 1861) (Wigfall).

27. 3 *Meliora* 194 (1861); letter from Governor R. K. Tall, of Florida to John S. Littell, Feb. 12, 1861, at 27 (1861); "The Chicago Platform," *New York Herald*, Jan. 21, 1861, at 4; Joel Parker, *The Right to Secession: A Review* 12–14 (1861); James D. B. DeBow, *The Interest in Slavery of the Southern Non-Slaveholder* 8–9 (1860).

28. *Cong. Globe*, 36th Cong., 2nd Sess. 406 (Jan. 16, 1861) (Simmons); *Burlington Hawk-Eye* (IA) Apr. 17, 1863, at 1 (Everett).

29. "One Day Later: From Europe," *Boston Daily Advertiser*, July 12, 1862, at 1; "From Europe," *Semi-Weekly Raleigh Register* (NC), Nov. 8, 1862; "Letter From George Thompson, Esq. to William Lloyd Garrison," *Liberator*, Feb. 21, 1862, at

30 ("any attempt ... "); "The Two Declarations," *Burlington Hawk-Eye* (IA), Oct. 21, 1863, at 2.

30. Declaration of Causes of Seceding States, http://sunsite.utk.edu/civil-war/reasons.html.

31. "Mr. Lincoln's Movement," *Lowell Daily Citizen and News* (MA), Feb. 23, 1861, at 2; Abraham Lincoln, "Message to Congress in Special Session," in 4 *The Collected Works of Abraham Lincoln* 438 (Roy P. Basler ed., 1953) (July 4, 1861).

32. "Governor Ellis's Message to the Honorable General Assembly of N. Carolina," *Fayetteville Observer* (NC), May. 6, 1861, at 2; "The Tories of 1776 and the Abolitionists of 1863," *Mountain Democrat* (Placerville, CA), Apr. 18, 1863, at 4; "Interview with Jeff. Davis," *Daily Evening Bulletin* (San Francisco), Sept. 12, 1873, at 4; 1 *Rebellion Record* 384 (Frank Moore ed., 1861) (quoting Stephens).

33. *Cong. Globe*, 36th Cong., 2nd Sess. 1285 (House vote) (Feb. 28, 1861), 1364 (text of proposed amendment) (Mar. 2, 1861), 1402–3 (Senate vote) (Mar. 2, 1861); R. Alton Lee, "The Corwin Amendment in the Secession Crisis," 70 *Ohio Hist. Q.* 1 (1961); 1 John W. Forney, *Anecdotes of Public Men* 152–53 (1873) (quoting Slidell).

34. Alexander H. Stephens, *The Reviewers Reviewed* 141–42 (1872); "Southern Views ... Speech of Jefferson Davis ... Delivered in the Senate of the United States, May 7th, 1860," *Coshocton Democrat* (OH), Dec. 23, 1863, at 1; Albert T. Bledsoe, *Is Davis a Traitor: or, Was Secession a Constitutional Right Previous to the War of 1861?* at 143–44 (1866).

35. *Milwaukee Daily Sentinel*, July 18, 1864, at 1, col. c (quoting *Richmond Dispatch*); "Men Are not Born to Equal Rights," *Liberator*, Oct. 7, 1864, at 163 (quoting *Richmond Enquirer*); letter from Hon. John Bell, of Tennessee, Dec. 30, 1865, *Macon Daily Telegraph* (GA), Jan 17, 1866, at 1.

36. 1 Alexander H. Stephens, *A Constitutional View of the Late War Between the States* 62 (1868).

37. Wesson G. Miller, *Thirty years in the Itinerancy* 238 (1875); A Clergyman of the North-West, *The Foundation of Civil Government Self-Evident, And Men Should Not Kill Each Other About It* (1865) ("fundamental political ... ").

38. "The War: Lecture by Wendell Phillips, Esq., at the Cooper Institute, New York," *Liberator*, Dec. 27, 1861, at 206, 207.

39. "The Patriot," *Wisconsin State Journal* (Madison), June 26, 1863, at 1; "Abolitionism Becoming Respectable," *Liberator*, Dec. 19, 1862, at 7; Eric Foner, *Free Soil, Free Labor, Free Men* 119 (1995); *Cong. Globe*, 37th Cong., 2nd Sess. 329 (Jan. 16, 1862) (Julian).

40. "Who are the Traitors," *Wisconsin Daily Patriot* (Madison), Feb. 25, 1863, at 2.

41. "The Speech of Vice-President Stephens," *New York Times*, Dec. 8, 1862, at 4; *Cong. Globe*, 37th Cong., 2nd Sess., at 3356 (July 15, 1862) (Sumner).

42. 12 Stat. 319 (1861) (First Confiscation Act); 3 *Official Records of the Union and Confederate Armies* 466–67 (Robert N. Scott ed., Ser. 1, 1882); Paul Finkelman, "Lincoln and the Preconditions of Emancipation," in *Lincoln's Proclamation* 13, 25 (Willam A. Blair and Karen Fisher Younger eds., 2009).

43. 12 Stat. 589, 591 (Second Confiscation Act) (July 17, 1862); "The Confiscation Bill Passed," *Chicago Tribune*, July 15, 1862, at 2; *Brown v. United States* 12

U.S. 110 (1814); "Thirty-Seventh Congress," *North American and United States Gazette* (Philadelphia), Apr. 19, 1862, at 2, col. c; *Cong. Globe Appendix*, 37th Cong., 2nd Sess. 117–18 (Apr. 23, 1862).

44. "By Telegraph," *Boston Daily Advertiser*, July 12, 1862, at 1.

45. 12 Stat. 597, 599 (July 17, 1862).

46. *Cong. Globe Appendix* 37th Cong., 2nd Sess., at 322 (July 11, 1862) (Harlan).

47. "Reply to the President by the Colored People of Newtown, L.I.," *Liberator*, Sept. 12, 1862, at 148.

48. "What Can and Ought To Be Done," *Liberator*, Aug. 2, 1861, at 122.

49. "The Year of Jubilee," *Daily Evening Bulletin*, Jan. 3, 1863, at 2; "The Following Resolutions...," *Vermont Watchman and State Journal* (Montpelier), July 3, 1863, at 1; "The Proclamation—A Comparison," *Richland County Observer* (WI), Feb. 6, 1863, at 3; "The Declaration of Independence," *Burlington Weekly Hawk Eye* (IA), Jan. 17, 1863, at 2; Letter from Colonel Robert G. Shaw, in *Soldiers' Letters, from Camps, Battle-field and Prison* 255 (Lydia Minturn Post ed., 1865).

50. "By Whom Promulgated," *Mountain Democrat* (Placerville, CA), Feb. 7, 1863, at 6; Observer [pseudonym], Editorial, "Will the Abolition of Slavery Restore Peace to the Country?," *Compiler* (Gettysburg, PA), Jan. 19, 1863, at 1.

51. Hondon B. Hargrove, *Black Union Soldiers in the Civil War* 116–19 (1988); John D. Smith, "Let Us All Be Grateful That We Have Colored Troops That Will Fight," in *Black Soldiers in Blue: African American Troops in the Civil War Era* 51 (John D. Smith ed., 2002); Carleton, "A Step in the Right Direction," *Liberator*, May 13, 1864, at 1.

52. Henry T. Johns, *Life with the Forty-Ninth Massachusetts Volunteers* 329 (1864); "Independence Day," *Boston Daily Advertiser*, July 4, 1864, at 2; "Letter From R. D. Mussey to W. S. Cheatham, July 3, 1864," *Liberator*, July 29, 1864, at 124.

53. "Great speech of Gen. Carl Schurz," *Janesville Weekly Gazette* (WI), Oct. 21, 1864, at 7.

54. Michael Foley, *American Credo: The Place of Ideas in U.S. Politics* 366–67 (2007); Gettysburg Address, http://avalon.law.yale.edu/19th_century/gettyb.asp.

CHAPTER 10

1. "The Great Victory," *Boston Daily Advertiser*, Apr. 11, 1865, at 1, 4; Charles Sumner, "The Promises of the Declaration of Independence," *Eulogy on Abraham Lincoln* 7, 57–58 (1865).

2. "The President's Remains in Philadelphia," *Daily Cleveland Herald*, Apr. 24, 1865, at 1; John G. Shea, *The Lincoln Memorial...* 174–75 (1865); "Mr. Sumner's Resolution," *Daily Citizen and News* (Lowell, MA), Dec. 8, 1866, at 2; "Anti-Slavery Gathering in Framingham," *Boston Daily Advertiser*, July 6, 1866, at 1 (Phillips); "Death of the Oldest Pioneer In the West," *Daily Evening Bulletin* (San Francisco), Mar. 30, 1864, at 2; National Archives Administration, Declaration of Independence: A History, http://www.archives.gov/exhibits/charters/declaration_history.html.

3. William Henry Singleton, *Recollections of My Slavery Days* 1–2 (1922, 2000), http://docsouth.unc.edu/neh/singleton/singleton.html; "A Ramble through

Petersburg," *Boston Daily Advertiser*, Apr. 8, 1865, at 1; "The Negro Canaan," *Macon Daily Telegraph* (GA), July 31, 1866, at 4.

4. 2 *Committees in the U.S. Congress, 1789–1946*, at passim (David T. Canon et al., eds., 2002); *Cong. Globe*, 42nd Cong., 2d Sess., at 728 (Jan. 31, 1872) (Sumner).

5. "The German Radical Convention," *Daily Cleveland Herald*, Oct. 24, 1863, at 3.

6. Alexander Tsesis, *The Thirteenth Amendment and American Freedom: A Legal History* (2004); "What for?," *Weekly Patriot and Union* (Harrisburg, PA), Oct. 26, 1865, at 4 (quoting *Tribune*); *Cong. Globe*, 38th Cong., 1st Sess. 1443 (1864) (Hale); id. at 1461 (Henderson).

7. See id. at 1424; *Cong. Globe*, 38th Cong., 2nd Sess. 260 (1865) (Rollins); *Cong. Globe*, 38th Cong., 1st Sess. 1420, 1422 (1864) (Johnson).

8. Id. at 1319 (Wilson); id. at 2989; see, e.g., *Cong. Globe*, 39th Cong., 1st Sess. 476 (1866).

9. *Cong. Globe*, 38th Cong., 1st Sess. 521 (1864); id. at 1483. (Sumner); id. at 1457 (Hendricks).

10. *Cong. Globe*, 38th Cong., 1st Sess. 2989 (1864); *Cong. Globe*, 39th Cong., 1st Sess. 570 (1866).

11. "The Constitutional Amendment Abolishing Slavery," *Waukesha Freeman* (WI), Feb. 14, 1865, at 2; 4 *William Lloyd Garrison, 1805–1879: The Story of His Life Told by His Children* 129–30 (1889); Samuel May, Jr., "The Amendment Adopted," *Liberator*, Dec. 22, 1865, at 202.

12. "The Social Problem," *Georgia Weekly Telegraph* (Macon), Aug. 6, 1866, at 8; Henry C. Carey, "The Iron Question: Letters to the Hon. Schuyler Colfax, Jan. 16, 1865," in *Miscellaneous Works by Henry C. Carey* (1865).

13. "Republican Governments for the South," *Daily Miners' Register* (Central City, CO), Jan. 29. 1867, at 1; Address by Daniel Ullman, L.L.D., ... Delivered at Albany, February 5, 1868, at 13 (1868); "The National Security and the National Faith ... Speech of Hon. Charles Sumner" 13–14 (1865).

14. "Message of His Excellency Joseph E. Brown," *Macon Daily Telegraph* (GA), Mar. 12, 1864, at 1–2; "The Abolitionists are much devoted ... ," *Liberty Tribune* (Liberty, MO), May 4, 1866, at 2; "Senator Ashley's Reconstruction Bill," *Philadelphia Inquirer*, Dec. 20, 1865, at 4; "Mr. Sumner's Rules of Clemency," *Philadelphia Inquirer*, Nov. 28, 1865, at 8.

15. "John Stuart Mill," *Boston Daily Advertiser*, June 8, 1865, at 2; "A [Illegible] Republic," *Dawson's Fort Wayne Weekly Times* (IN), May 1, 1864, at 1.

16. Alexander Tsesis, *Promises of Liberty: The History and Contemporary Relevance of the Thirteenth Amendment* (Alexander Tsesis ed., 2009); *Cong. Globe*, 39th Cong., 1st Sess. 129 (1866); Civil Rights Act, ch. 31, 14 Stat. 27 (1866); Second Freedmen's Bureau Act, ch. 200 § 14, 14 Stat. 173, 176–77 (1866).

17. *Cong. Globe*, 39th Cong., 1st Sess. 1159 (1866); id. at 474 (Trumbull).

18. Id. at 1159.

19. "Negroes Not Included in the Declaration of Independence," *Portsmouth Times* (OH). May 27, 1865, at 1 (quoting Johnson in 1859).

20. *Cong. Globe*, 39th Cong., 1st Sess. 1262 (Rep. Broomall).

21. *Cong. Globe*, 39th Cong., 1st Sess. 599–600 (1866).

22. "The Declaration of Independence and the Radicals," *Charleston Courier* (SC), Dec. 7, 1867, at 2.

23. Civil Rights Act, ch. 31, 14 Stat. 27 (1866); "Interview with Jeff. Davis," *Daily Evening Bulletin* (San Francisco), Sept. 12, 1873, at 4; "President Johnson, His Proclamation of Amnesty ... ," *Charleston Courier* (SC), Dec. 29, 1868, at 2; *Cong. Globe Appendix*, 42nd Cong., 2nd Sess. at 30 (Feb. 9, 1872) (Senator Allen Granberry Thurman).

24. "Do the Radicals Never Read the Declaration of Independence," *Constitution* (Atlanta, GA), June 23, 1868, at 3; "The Formation of Our Government," *New-Orleans Times*, July 26, 1866, at 8; *Cong. Globe*, 40th Cong., 2nd Sess., at 1067 (Feb. 8, 1868).

25. "*Democratic National Convention,*" *St. Joseph Herald* (MI), July 18, 1868; *Cong. Globe*, 40th Cong., 2nd Sess., at 1438 (Feb. 26, 1868) (Saulsbury).

26. "Civil Rights of Freedmen," *Philadelphia North American and United States Gazette,* Jan. 9, 1866, at 2.

27. Alexander Tsesis, "Principled Governance: The American Creed and Congressional Authority," 41 *Conn. L. Rev.* 679, 715–20 (2009); *Cong. Globe*, 39th Cong., 1st Sess. 2462 (May 8, 1866) (Rep. James Garfield counseling adoption of a constitutional amendment).

28. *Cong. Globe*, 39th Cong., 1st Sess. 2896 (1866); Civil Rights Cases, 109 U.S. 3 (1883); *United States v. Morrison*, 529 U.S. 598 (2000).

29. *Cong. Globe*, 39th Cong., 1st Sess. 2539 (1866).

30. *Cong. Globe*, 39th Cong., 1st Sess. 2961 (1866) (Sen. Poland); id. at 2539.

31. *Cong. Globe Appendix*, 34th Cong., 3rd Sess. 140 (1857); *Cong. Globe*, 39th Cong., 1st Sess. 2459 (May 8, 1866) (Stevens); id. at 2510 (May 9, 1866) (Miller).

32. Jeffrey W. Miller, "Redemption through Violence," 35 *Southern Literary Journal* 14, 20 (2002); Eric Foner, *Reconstruction: America's Unfinished Revolution* 267 (1988).

33. "An Act to Regulate the Elective Franchise in the District of Columbia," in *Compilation of the Laws in Force in the District of Columbia* 466–67 (1868); *A Hand Book of Politics for 1868*, at 154 (Edward McPherson, 1868); "The Suffrage Question in Connecticut," *Daily Palladium* (New Haven, CT), Aug. 23, 1865, at 1; History of African Americans in the Civil War, http://www.itd.nps.gov/cwss/history/aa_history.htm; "The Two Systems of Government Proposed for the Rebel States: Speech of Edward L. Pierce, at the Town House Milton, October 31, 1868," at 25–27 (1868); "The Constitutional Amendment," *Vermont Watchmen and State Journal* (Montpelier), Feb. 10, 1869, at 2.

34. *Cong. Globe*, 40th Cong., 3rd Sess., at 150 (Dec. 18, 1868) (Sumner's speech in memory of Stevens); *Cong. Globe*, 40th Cong., 2nd Sess., at 2053 (March 21, 1868) (Rep. Woodward); "Before the War ... ," *Daily Memphis Avalanche* (TN), Sept. 12, 1866, at 2; George P. Fisher, "Of the Distinction Between Natural and Political Rights," 23 *New Englander and Yale L. Rev.* 25–26 (1864); *Cong. Globe*, 39th Cong., 2nd Sess., at 478 (Jan. 15, 1867) (Stevens); Letter from Sumner to John Bright, May 27, 1867, in 4 *Memoir and Letters of Charles Sumner* 319, 319 (Edward L. Pierce, ed. 1893).

35. "Our Washington Correspondence," *Charleston Courier* (SC), Mar. 24, 1868, at 3; *Cong. Globe*, 39th Cong., 2nd Sess., at 339 (Jan. 8, 1867) (Howard); Leo Alilunas, "A Review of Negro Suffrage Policies Prior to 1915," 25 *J. Negro Hist.*

153–55 (1940); "The Campaign In Ohio," *New Hampshire Statesman*, Sept. 6,1867, at 1; *Cong. Globe*, 40th Cong., 3rd Sess., at 95 (Jan. 29, 1869) (Bowen).

36. Gillette, *Retreat From Reconstruction, 1869–1879*, at 18–19 (1979); LaWanda and John H. Cox, "Negro Suffrage and Republican Politics," 33 *J. South. Hist.* 303, 318–20, 327–30 (1967); Alexander Keyssar, *The Right to Vote* 89 (2000).

37. *Cong. Globe*, 40th Cong., 3rd Sess., at 980 (Feb. 8, 1869) (Abbott); id. at 903 (Sumner); *Cong. Globe Appendix*, 40th Cong., 3rd Sess. at 200 (Loughridge); id. at 100 (Jan. 29, 1869) (Hamilton); id. at 117 (Feb. 5, 1868) (Senator Morrill).

38. *Cong. Globe Appendix*, 40th Cong., 3rd Sess. at 294 (Mar. 3, 1869) (Higby); *Cong. Globe*, 40th Cong., 2nd Sess. at 302–3 (March 21, 1868) (Newcomb); Caspar T. Hopkins, *A Manual of American Ideas* 40 (1872).

39. Ulysses S. Grant, "Message Mar. 30, 1870," in 7 *A Compilation of the Messages and Papers of the Presidents, 1789–1897*, at 55–56 (1898); *Boston Daily Advertiser*, Apr. 2, 1870, at 1; *Boston Daily Advertiser*, Apr. 11, 1870.

40. "One Hundred and Ten," *St. Louis Globe Democrat*, Dec. 26, 1876, at 6.

41. *Cong. Globe*, 40th Cong., 3rd Sess. at 861–62 (Feb. 4, 1869) (Warner); id. at 863 (Morton); id. at 1626–27 (Feb. 26, 1869) (Wilson).

42. James McPherson, *The Abolitionist Legacy* 16–21 (1976).

43. "Letter of Charles Sumner to Professor John M. Langston," *Dubuque Herald* (IA), Apr. 24, 1872, at 1.

44. *Cong. Globe*, 42nd Cong., 2nd Sess. at 728 (Jan. 31, 1872); id. at 825 (Feb. 5, 1872).

45. Id. at 730; id. at 761, 827 (Feb. 1, 1872) (Sen. Matthew H. Carpenter).

46. "Sumner's Death," *Evening Bulletin* (San Francisco), Mar. 12, 1874, at 1.

47. William Gillette, *Retreat from Reconstruction, 1869–1879*, at 18–19 (1979).

48. "Civil Rights in Trenton," *New York Times*, Mar. 26, 1875, at 12; Civil Rights Cases, 109 U.S. 3 (1883); "Civil Rights No Go," *Evening Gazette* (Cedar Rapids, IA), Oct. 17, 1883, at 6.

CHAPTER 11

1. National Archives Administration, *Declaration of Independence: A History*, , http://www.archives.gov/exhibits/charters/declaration_history.html.

2. *Milwaukee Sentinel*, Apr. 5, 1877, at 3; "The Autograph Sale," *Boston Daily Advertiser*, Nov. 13, 1879, at 1; *Titusville Herald* (PA), Oct. 8, 1886, at 3; "The Trade in Autographs," *Denver Evening Post*, Feb. 12, 1896, at 6.

3. "Presentation of a Valuable Historical Relic," *Boston Daily Advertiser*, Apr. 16, 1880, at 1; "An Interesting Ceremony," *Boston Daily Advertiser*, Apr. 26, 1880, at 2.

4. Xi Wang, *The Trial of Democracy: Black Suffrage and Northern Republicans, 1860–1910*, at 161 (1997); "The President and the Party," *Independent Statesman* (Concord, NH), Dec. 13, 1877, at 84; "Looking Facts in the Face," *Bangor Daily Whig and Courier*, July 14, 1877, at 2; "The Africo-American Convention," *Sunday Inter Ocean* (Chicago), Dec. 15, 1889, at 28.

5. "Mr. Donnelly's Address," *Emmett County Herald* (Estherville, IA), June 6, 1884, at 8.

6. "The Real Objection," *Logansport Journal* (IN), Jan. 7, 1880, at 4; "The Following From the San Jose," *Fort Wayne Daily Gazette* (IN), June 29, 1881, at 8; School

L. of California art. X §1669, at 20 (1878); Lisa M. Schenck, "Assault at West Point," 148 *Military L. Rev.* 274, 275 (1995); "West Point Outrage," *Independent Statesman* (Concord, NH), Apr. 29, 1880, at 244; "Our Heroic Dead," *New York Globe,* June 9, 1883, at 1.

7. J. S. A. Murphy, "A Solemn Protest," *New York Globe,* Oct. 18, 1884, at 2; "Twenty-Five Years of Freedom," *Daily Inter Ocean* (Chicago), Jan. 3, 1889, at 1.

8. Quoted in Vincent P. De Santis, *Republicans Face the Southern Question: The New Departure Years, 1877–1897,* at 100–101 (1959).

9. "Indianapolis Journal," *Independent Statesman* (Concord, NH), Oct. 16, 1879, at 20; *United States v. Cruikshank,* 92 U.S. 542, 553 (1876); *United States v. Reese,* 92 U.S. 214, 217 (1875).

10. "Opposing Civilizations," *Inter Ocean* (Chicago), Oct. 27, 1879, at 7; "The Cry for Change," *Courier* (Waterloo, IA), Aug. 13, 1884, at 7; "Mr. Downing's Advice to Colored Voters," *Boston Daily Advertiser,* July 22, 1880, at 1; "Reasons Why," *Bucks County Gazette* (Bristol, PA), Sept. 23, 1880; "Nobody can read . . . ," *Daily News* (Denver, CO), June 28, 1882, at 4.

11. "Drifting Toward Nullification," *Inter Ocean* (Chicago), Sept. 10, 1889, at 4.

12. "Mississippi's Constitution," *New Mississippian* (Jackson), Oct. 30, 1889, at 2; Stephen Cresswell, *Multiparty Politics in Mississippi, 1877–1902,* at 220–21 (1955); Earl M. Lewis, "The Negro Voter in Mississippi," 26 *J. Negro Ed.* 329, 336–38 (1957).

13. *Williams v. Mississippi* 170 U.S. 213 (1898); "Farmer Tillman," *Daily Picayune* (New Orleans). Dec. 5, 1890, at 2; 56 *Cong. Record,* 56th Cong., 1st Sess. 3223–24 (Mar. 23, 1900) (Tillman); John A. Roebling, "The Views of a Northern Man," *News and Observer* (Raleigh, NC), Aug. 24, 1899, at 192; "Congressman Underwood on the Suffrage Question," *Age Herald* (Birmingham, AL), Feb. 25, 1900, at 9.

14. "Hon. William H. Fleming Discusses Negro Question in Statesman like Manner Before University Alumni," *Macon Daily Telegraph* (GA), June 20, 1905, at 8.

15. "A Quietus to Railroad Discrimination," *New York Age,* May 25, 1889, at 2; "Alexandria as a Pest Hole," *Indiana Weekly Messenger* (PA), July 28, 1890, at 1.

16. "We Must Co-Operate," *Leavenworth Herald* (Kansas), Aug. 18, 1894, at 2; "Plea for the Negro's Rights," *Morning Oregonian,* Oct. 11, 1899, at 6.

17. Ray Stannard Baker, "An Ostracized Race in Ferment," 65 *American Magazine* 66 (May 1908).

18. "Two Tendencies Among Negroes," *Kansas City Star* (MO), Aug. 20, 1903, at 6; "Negro Problem's Peril," *New York Times,* Feb. 23, 1903, at 7.

19. Miller, *History of the World War for Human Rights* 550 (1919); "The Negroes' Great Day," *Evening News* (San Jose, CA), Jan. 3, 1918, at 4.

20. "For Needed Reforms in South Carolina," *State* (Columbia, SC), Feb. 9, 1914, at 13; "A Sermon for Memorial Day," *Charlotte Daily Observer* (NC), May 10, 1903.

21. Steven Hahn, *A Nation Under Our Feet* 445 (2003); George L. Sioussat, "Teaching the History of the New South," 7 *History Teacher's Magazine,* Oct. 1916, at 270, 274; Gilbert T. Stephenson, *Race Distinctions in American Law* 320 (1910).

22. Charles V. Roman, *American Civilization and the Negro,* at xii, 210 (1916).

23. Bloomfield Bergen, "South To Save the Union," *Chicago Defender*, May 8, 1915, at 8; Z. Withers, "Democracy on Trial," *Chicago Defender*, May 2, 1914, at 7; "Letter to the Editor by M. Marion Davis," *Chicago Defender*, June 7, 1913, at 4.

CHAPTER 12

1. Harriot K. Hunt, "Taxation Without Representation," *Liberator*, Jan. 3, 1862, at 3; Hunt, "Taxation Without Representation," *Liberator*, Dec. 23, 1864, at 208.
2. Lucinda B. Chandler, "Woman and Politics," *Daily Inter Ocean* (Chicago), Jan. 22, 1881, at 9; letter from Stanton to Smith (Jan. 1, 1866), in Ellen Dubois, *Feminism and Suffrage: The Emergence of an Independent Women's Movement in America, 1848–1869*, at 61 (1978); Carrie Chapman Catt and Nettie Rogers Shuler, *Woman Suffrage and Politics: The Inner Story of the Suffrage Movement* 37–41 (1923); William L. O'Neill, *Everyone Was Brave: A History of Feminism in America* 17 (1971) (Anthony).
3. "Lucy Stone's Speech," *Ohio Convention Reporter*, vol. 1, no. 2 (Feb. 1870); [Pillsbury], *Revolution*, Mar. 11, 1869; T.W.H., "The Use of the Declaration of Independence," *Woman's J.*, May 14, 1870, at 148.
4. Goodrich Willard, "The Situation," *Revolution*, Nov. 3, 1870, at 1; William West, "The New Democracy, or Political Commonwealth," *Revolution*, Sept. 30, 1869, at 3; George P. Fisher, "Of the Distinction Between Natural and Political Rights," 23 *New Englander and Yale L. Rev.* 1, 22 (1864).
5. "American Anti-Slavery Society," *National Anti-Slavery Standard*, May 13, 1865, at 2 (Phillips quote); Barbara Allen Babcock, "A Place in the Palladium: Women's Rights & Jury Service," 61 *U. Cincinnati L. Rev.* 1139, 1164–65 (1993) (Stanton); Letter from Stanton to Phillips, May 25, 1865, in 2 *Elizabeth Cady Stanton as Revealed in Her Letters, Diary and Reminiscences* 104–105 (Theodore Stanton and Harriot Stanton Blatch eds., 1922); [Susan B. Anthony], *Revolution*, July 2, 1868.
6. "Woman Suffrage," *Boston Investigator*, Oct. 16, 1867, at 190; "Extract From a Speech of William I. Bowditch at Brookline, Mass., July 4, 1876," *Daily Rocky Mountain News* (Denver, CO), Aug. 27, 1876, at 1; William I. Bowditch, *Taxation of Women in Massachusetts* 11, 18 (1875); "The Protection of the Ballot," *Daily Rocky Mountain News* (Denver, CO), Aug. 27, 1876, at 1.
7. *Cong. Globe*, 42nd Cong., 2nd Sess., at 973 (Feb. 12, 1872); "George Francis Train on Slavery and Universal Emancipation," in *George F. Train, Train's Union Speeches*, "Second series" 66, 69 (1862).
8. *Revolution*, Jan. 22, 1869; Edward R. Turner, "Women's Suffrage in New Jersey, 1790–1807," 1 *Smith College Studies* 165 (1916); William I. Bowditch, *Taxation of Women In Massachusetts* 11–13 (revised ed. 1875); Mary Philbrook, "Woman's Suffrage in New Jersey Prior to 1807," 57 *Proc. N. J. Hist. Soc'y* 87, 95–96 (1939); *Woman Suffrage In New Jersey: An Address Delivered by Lucy Stone, At a Hearing Before the New Jersey Legislature*, Mar. 6, 1867, at 23 (Boston: C. H. Simonds, 1867) (Stone); "Woman Suffrage at the State House," *Boston Daily Advertiser*, Feb. 18, 1870, at 4; "Report of the Special Committee on Woman Suffrage," *Vermont Chronicle* (Bellows Falls), Aug. 21, 1869, at 2.

9. "The Women Convention in Dayton," *Cleveland Daily Herald*, Apr. 30, 1870, at 2; 1 *Ohio Convention Reporter* 123 (1870).

10. "The Right of Suffrage: A Speech Made...July 19, 1867," in 1 *Orations and Addresses of George William Curtis* (Charles E. Norton ed., 1894); "Woman Suffrage—Again," *Vermont Watchman and State Journal* (Montpelier) Feb. 9, 1870, at 1; "Report on Woman Suffrage," *Vermont Watchman and State Journal*, Aug. 4, 1869.

11. "Susan B. Anthony," *Milwaukee Sentinel*, July 4, 1874, at 2; "She Wanted to Vote," *Morning Republican* (Little Rock, AR), June 2, 1870, at 3.

12. B. A. U., "The Second Declaration of Independence," *Daily Inter Ocean* (Chicago), Aug. 30, 1876, at 3; Catt, "Only Yesterday," in *Our Common Cause, Civilization...July 16–22, 1933*, at 235, 236–38 (1933); Excelsior, "Equality of Rights," *Jackson Sentinel* (Maquoketa, IA), July 27, 1876, 3; "Declaration of the Rights of Women," in 3 *The Selected Papers of Elizabeth Cady Stanton and Susan B. Anthony* 235 (Ann D. Gordon ed., 2003).

13. "Women about to Capture the Fourth of July, the Birthday of the Republic," *Woman's Exponent* (Salt Lake City, UT), Jan. 1, 1881, at 119; Stacy A. Cordery, "Women in Industrializing America," in *The Gilded Age: Essays on the Origins of Modern America* 111 (Charles W. Calhoun ed., 1996); "Suffrage," 6 *Flaming Sword* 337, 349 (1893).

14. The Declaration of Independence, para. 19; "Judge Wm. B. Mills at Breckenridge—His Speech on Woman Suffrage," *Rocky Mountain News* (Denver, CO), Sept. 14, 1877, at 4; "Woman Suffrage," *Boston Daily Advertiser*, Jan. 31, 1877, at 4; Lucinda B. Chandler, "The Declaration of Independence and the Fourteenth Amendment," *Woman's Tribune*, June 1886, at 1; "Proper Demand," *North American* (Philadelphia), Feb. 4, 1897, at 4; Victoria Claflin Woodhull and Tennessee C. Claflin, *The Human Body the Temple of God* 130–31 (1890).

15. "Citizenship Declaration of Principles Adopted By the Margaret Fuller Society," *Daily Inter Ocean* (Chicago), Oct. 30, 1880, at 12.

16. "Non-Combatants, Not Voters," *Morning Oregonian* (Portland), June 21, 1888, at 4; J. M. Buckley, "The Wrongs and Perils of Woman Suffrage," 48 *The Century; A Popular Q.* 613 (1894); "Difficulties in the Way of the Female Suffragists," *Boston Daily Advertiser*, Oct. 23, 1879, at 2.

17. "Report of Corresponding Secretary [Kate M. Gordon]," in *Proceedings of the Twenty-fifth Annual Convention of the American Woman Suffrage Association* 14 (Harriet Taylor Upton ed., 1893); "A Four Star Flag," *Milwaukee Journal*, Jan. 29, 1897, at 7; House of Representatives, Washington, D.C., January 28, 1896, Statement of Frances A. Williamson, of Nevada (Washington, GPO, 1896); "Woman Suffrage," *Morning Oregonian* (Portland), Aug. 13, 1889, at 2.

18. "Work and Women," *Daily Evening Bulletin* (San Francisco) Nov. 26, 1886, at 2 ("there never ... ").

19. Gail Laughlin, *Women Suffrage: Hearing Before the Select Committee on Woman Suffrage ... [February 18, 1902]* (Washington, GPO 1902); M.G.W., "Woman's Rights," *Woman's Tribune*, Feb. 7, 1891, at 47; Emily R. Meredith, "Equal Suffrage," *Daily News* (Denver, CO), Nov. 1, 1893, at 5 (Stephens); "I would say...," *Revolution*, Dec. 12, 1871; "Women's World in Paragraph," *Atchison Daily Globe* (KS), Sept. 1, 1891, at 2 ("obey"); "Unique Divorce Petition," *Galveston News* (Houston, TX), June 6, 1894, at 4.

20. "Woman Suffrage," *Bucks County Gazette* (Bristol, PA), Feb. 27, 1902, at 2; "Political Equality Club," *Dunkirk Evening Observer* (NY), Nov. 24, 1890, at 2.

21. Report: First International Woman Suffrage Conference 4 (1902); *The Woman Suffrage Year Book* 79 (Martha G. Stapler ed., 1917).

22. "An Open Letter to the Voters of Ohio," *Sandusky Daily Register* (OH), Aug. 1, 1890, at 1; "Can a Woman Rob Her Husband," *Philadelphia Inquirer*, July 26, 1901, at 8.

23. "Woman's Right To Vote," *Republican Herald* (Phoenix, AZ), Feb. 14, 1901, at 7; "A Declaration by Women," *Columbus Enquirer-Sun* (GA), May 6, 1914, at 2; "Letter from Annie I. Larkin of the Atlanta Equal Suffrage Assoc. to the Editor," *Atlanta Constitution*, Aug. 2, 1914, at 5.

24. "Suffs Will Win Ballot Asserts Kahn," *Fort Worth Star-Telegraph* (TX), Sept. 15, 1915, at 5; "Long Fight For the Ballot," *Kansas City Star* (MO), Oct. 19, 1915, at 12; "Miss Allen Speaks," *Elyria Democrat* (OH), Oct. 15, 1914, at 8.

25. Eugene V. Debs, "Social Democratic Party," *Independent*, Aug. 23, 1900, at 2019; Republican Party Platform of 1896, http://www.presidency.ucsb.edu/ws/index.php?pid=29629; Vance Thompson, "Woman," *Association Monthly*, Oct. 1918, at 395; "Why I Believe in Woman Suffrage," *Wilkes-Barre Times Leader* (PA), July 19, 1915, at 8; Oliver T. Beaumont, "Economic Freedom," 15 *American Federationist* 520 (1908).

CHAPTER 13

1. "The Sixteenth Amendment," *Revolution*, Apr. 29, 1869, at 266.

2. "The Coming Chinaman; and What Shall We Do With Him," 10 *Hours At Home* 276, 277, 283 (Jan. 1870).

3. David Heer, *Immigration in America's Future* 37 (1996); Matthew Josephson, *The Robber Barons* 86 (1934); *Cong. Globe*, 41st Cong., 2nd Sess. 5172–73 (July 4, 1870), see also id. at 5155–56.

4. *Cong. Globe*, 40th Cong., 2nd Sess. at 386 (Jan. 8, 1868) (Orth); id. at 42nd Cong., 2nd Sess., at 385 (Jan. 15, 1872) (Sumner).

5. Eric Foner, *Reconstruction* 313–14 ("the Republican ... "); Irish Citizen, "The Chinese Question," *Georgia Weekly Telegraph and Georgia Journal and Messenger* (Macon), July 26, 1870, at 1; *Cong. Globe*, 41st Cong., 2nd Sess. at 5156; "The Evening's Dispatches," *Daily Evening Bulletin* (San Francisco), July 5, 1870, at 2; *Cong. Globe*, 40th Cong., 2nd Sess. at 2055 (March 21, 1868); *Cong. Globe*, 41st Cong., 2nd Sess. at 5175 (July 4, 1870) (Sen. Oliver Morton of IN).

6. "San Francisco in Trouble," *Milwaukee Daily Sentinel*, Jan. 18, 1877, at 4; *Cong. Record* 45th Cong., 3rd Sess. at 1312 (Feb. 14, 1879); *Cong. Record*, 46th Cong., 2nd Sess. at 2858 (April 29, 1880) (Senator Hoar); *Cong. Record*, 47th Cong., 1st Sess. at 1705 (March 8, 1882) (Senator Platt).

7. "America for Americans," *Nevada State Journal* (Reno), Aug. 23, 1887, at 2.

8. "A Languid Canvass," *Galveston Daily News* (Houston, TX), Aug. 1, 1880, at 2; "Protest against the Bill," *Salt Lake Daily Tribune*, Feb. 23, 1879, at 1; "Very Select," in id., Feb. 23, 1879, at 1; "Thurlow Weed on the Chinese," *Titusville Morning Herald* (PA), Mar. 4, 1879, at 1; "Those Anti-Chinese Planks," *Galveston Daily News*, Aug. 7, 1880, at 2 (Beecher).

9. "The Meek Mongol," *Hutchinson News* (KS), Mar. 23, 1882, at 3; "Views Expressed Elsewhere," *Evening Bulletin* (San Francisco), Feb. 9, 1886, at 2.

10. "Halls of Congress," *Morning Oregonian* (Portland), Sept. 14, 1888, at 1; "When the declaration … ," *Eau Claire News* (WI), Feb. 27, 1886, at 1; "Repressive Legislation and American Liberty," *Galveston Daily News* (Houston, TX), Sept. 11, 1888, at 4; *Chae Chan Ping v. United States*, 130 U.S. 581 (1889); "Labor Speaks," *Milwaukee Journal*, Dec. 1, 1897, at 7; "Chinese Civil Rights League," *Daily Picayune* (New Orleans), Sept. 23, 1892, at 2.

11. "The People's Party," *Olean Weekly Democrat* (NY) Aug. 20, 1891, at 6; "The New York Truth," *Daily Globe* (Atchison, KS), Apr. 15, 1882, at 2; Henry George, "Problem of the Time," *Frank Leslie's Illustrated Newspaper*, June 23, 1883, at 279, 282; *see* Quentin R. Skrabec, Jr., *William McKinley: Apostle of Protectionism* 227–28 (2008) (discussing wealth and expenditures in the 1880s).

12. A Woman, "Too Long Hours," *Cedar Rapids Evening Gazette* (IA), Mar. 15, 1897, at 4; James W. Ely, Jr., *The Fuller Court* 4–5 (2003).

13. "Oracularity," *Mountain Democrat* (Placerville, CA), Apr. 10, 1886, at 2; "Right to Work," *Duluth News Tribune* (MN), Aug. 2, 1901, at 4; "Stanford on Strikes," *Daily Nevada State Journal* (Reno), Apr. 8, 1886, at 2; "Workingmen Should Stand Together Against Government by Injunction," *Newark Daily Advocate* (OH), Oct. 7, 1897, at 2.

14. "The Labor Question," *Decatur Daily Republican* (IL), Nov. 20, 1886, at 4; William H. Sylvis, Speech Delivered at Birmingham, PA., September, 1868, in *The Life, Speeches, Labors and Essays of William H. Sylvis, Late President of the Iron-Moulders' International Union; and also of the National Labor Union* 233 (James C. Sylvis ed., 1872); "A Committee of Illinois Farmers … ," *Rocky Mountain News* (Denver, CO), June 10, 1873, at 2; Solon J. Buck, *The Granger Movement* 86 (1913); Buck, *The Agrarian Crusade: A Chronicle of the Farmer in Politics* 33–34 (1921) (Illinois declaration); "Labor's Complaint," *Daily Inter Ocean* (Chicago), Aug. 24, 1877, at 8; Edward W. Martin [James D. McCabe, Jr.], *History of the Grange Movement; or, The Farmer's War against Monopolies* 521–22 (1874); "Anti-Monopolist Convention," *Evening Bulletin* (San Francisco), July 5, 1883, at 1; "Chicago Unemployed," *Emporia Daily Gazette* (Emporia, KS), Mar. 15, 1897, at 1.

15. "People's Party Platform," *Milwaukee Sentinel*, Sept. 1, 1898, at 3; "Questions for Workingmen," *Milwaukee Sentinel*, Nov. 8, 1886, at 4; "The Labor Problem," *Daily Republican Sentinel* (Milwaukee), Nov. 13, 1882, at 1.

16. Tom Goyens, *Beer and Revolution: The German Anarchist Movement in New York City, 1880–1914*, at 211 (2007); "Reds Talk Loudly," *Inter Ocean* (Chicago), July 11, 1892, at 2; "Anarchy Defined," *Milwaukee Sentinel*, Nov. 2, 1893, at 1; Terence V. Powderly, "Speech Delivered at the Session of the General Assembly, Richmond, Virginia, 1886," in *First Annual Report of the Bureau of Labor Statistics of the State of North Carolina* 221 (1887).

17. "Forming a New Party," *Milwaukee Sentinel*, Dec. 3, 1886, at 5; "Call for State Convention of the Union Labor Party of Pennsylvania," *Decatur Daily Republican* (IL), July 15, 1887, at 2; "The Labor Party," *Boston Daily Advertiser*, Dec. 6, 1886, at 2; Henry George, *Social Problems* 268 (1884).

18. "For Eight Hours," *Milwaukee Sentinel*, July 5, 1889, at 5.

19. "John W. Hayes (General Secretary-Treasurer Knights of Labor) Letter to the Editor," *North American* (Philadelphia), Sept. 4, 1899, at 1.

20. Michael Foley, *American Credo: The Place of Ideas in U.S. Politics* 266–67 (2007); "Federation of Labor," *News* (Frederick, MD), Dec. 12, 1892, at 1; "The Laboring Man Wants No Master," *Galveston Daily News* (Houston, TX), Dec. 18, 1893, at 4 (Gompers).

21. Id.; "Freedom of Anarchy," *Daily Evening Bulletin* (San Francisco), Sept. 27, 1877, at 2; "Indianapolis Journal," *Decatur Daily Republican* (IL), Aug. 15, 1877, at 2; "Stanford's Steal," *Rocky Mountain News* (Denver, CO), Jan. 23, 1881, at 6; "Equality of Conditions," *Milwaukee Sentinel*, Jan. 28, 1894, at 12.

22. "All Men Are Not Equal," *Milwaukee Sentinel*, Jan. 22, 1894, at 1; "Created Free and Equal," *Inter Ocean* (Chicago), Jan. 23, 1894, at 6.

23. "Seeking Harmony: How Shall Labor and Capital Be Reconciled," *Labor Advocate* (Birmingham, AL), Sept. 28, 1901, at 8.

24. "Ringing Platform Adopted," *Morning World-Herald* (Omaha, NE), Feb. 14, 1900, at 5; Nick Salvatore, *Eugene V. Debs: Citizen and Socialist* 192 (1984); "Speech at Battery D, Chicago, on his release from Woodstock Jail, Nov. 22, 1895," in *Debs: His Life, Writings and Speeches* 327 (1908); *Socialism in America* 380 (Albert Fried ed., 1992).

25. "Printers Adopt Resolution," *Charlotte Daily Observer* (NC), May 22, 1905, at 6; "Headquarters Central Trades and Labor Council," in H. R. 15651, Eight Hours for Laborers on Government Work 706 (1908); Florence Kelley, *Some Ethical Gains through Legislation* 264, 267 (1910); Robert H. Craig, *Religion and Radical Politics* 72 (1992); *Autobiography of Mother Jones* 143 (1925).

26. *Holden v. Hardy* 169 U.S. 366 (1898); *Lochner v. New York* 198 U.S. 45 (1905); http://www.historyplace.com/unitedstates/childlabor/, http://www.archives.gov/education/lessons/hine-photos/#documents (photos of child miners).

27. D. Hiden Ramsay, "Address of Welcome," 5 *Child Labor Bulletin* 6 (1916); "Democracy's Defender," *Wisconsin State Journal* (Madison) July 9, 1914, at 10; *Report of the National Society of the Daughters of the American Revolution* 45–46 (1913); "Remarks of Hon. William H. De Lacy," in *Proceedings of the Conference on the Care of Dependent Children* 33, 74–75 (1909); *Brooklyn Medical Journal* 544 (1901); Abram I. Elkus, "Working Conditions in Factories," 74 *Independent* 740 (Apr. 3. 1913).

28. Benjamin P. De Witt, *The Progressive Movement* 233 (1915); Congressman Samuel W. McCall, "Representative as against Direct Government," *Atlantic Monthly*, Oct. 1911, at 454, 455 (1913); Harley W. Brundige, "Democracy or Autocracy—Which?" *California Outlook*, June 24, 1911, at 212; *By the People* 26, 71 (Eltweed Pomeroy ed., 1900).

CHATPER 14

1. "Appeal for the Cubans," *New York Times*, Oct. 1, 1895, at 3; "America Must Liberate Cuba," *Denver Evening Post*, Dec. 3, 1897, at 1; "A National Disgrace," *Weekly News* (Denver, CO), Feb. 18, 1897, at 4.

2. "Letter to the Editor from John B. Walker," *News and Observer* (Raleigh, NC), Aug. 7, 1898, at 1; Oscar W. Coursey, *The Philippines and Filipinos* 100–101 (1914).

3. George A. Billia, *American Constitutionalism Heard Round the World, 1776–1989*, at 230 (2009); "Condemns Expansions," *Milwaukee Journal*, Nov. 2, 1898, at 1.

4. *Cong. Record Appendix*, 55th Cong., 2nd Sess., at 234 (Jan. 20, 1898); id. at 288 (Apr. 15, 1898); *Cong. Record*, 55th Cong., 2nd Sess., at 4034 (Apr. 18, 1898); id. at 5934 (June 14, 1898); "Car Empire's Survey," *Atchison Daily Globe* (KS), Dec. 8, 1898, at 3; *Cong. Record Appendix*, 55th Cong., 2nd Sess., at 544 (June 11, 1898) (Hartman); "Not a Natural Right," *Morning Oregonian* (Portland), Dec. 1, 1898, at 4; U.S. Bureau of Insular Affairs, *A Pronouncing Gazetteer ... of the Philippine Islands* 69 (1902).

5. "Theories Divorced from Facts," *Morning Oregonian* (Portland), Feb. 3, 1899, at 4; "The Mistakes of Logic," *Morning Oregonian*, Dec. 18, 1898, at 6; "Mr. Beveridge's Address," *Weekly Indiana State Journal* (Indianapolis), Feb. 22, 1899, at 2; "Senator Lindsay of Kentucky Defends Course in Philippines," *Milwaukee Journal*, Aug. 29, 1899, at 1.

6. *Cong. Record*, 55th Cong., 3rd Sess., at 108 (Jan. 26, 1899); id. at 833 (Jan. 20, 1899).

7. *Cong. Record*, 55th Cong., 3rd Sess., at 1943 (Feb. 16, 1899) (Spight); id. at 499 (Jan. 9, 1899) (Hoar); id. at 1482, 1538 (Feb. 6 and 7, 1899) (Allen); id. at 1429 (Feb. 3, 1899) (Daniel).

8. "The Philippines," *Weekly News and Courier* (Charleston, SC), Feb. 25, 1899, at 8; Michael Davitt, "An Insolent Challenge," *Irish World and Industrial Liberator* (New York), Jan. 7, 1899, at 4.

9. "Fourth of July Celebration At Manila," *Milwaukee Sentinel*, Aug. 20, 1899, at 18; "The Philippine Disgrace," *Irish World and American Industrial Liberator*, June 3, 1899, at 4; "Impeachment of Mr. McKinley," id., Oct. 21, 1899, at 6; "See the Perils of Empire," *Morning World-Herald* (Omaha, NE), Feb. 24, 1900, at 1.

10. "Bryan Finished In Chicago," *Sun* (Baltimore, MD), Nov. 5, 1900, at 8; Bryan, "Jefferson Versus Imperialism," in *The Second Battle or the New Declaration of Independence* 119 (1900).

11. "Independence Declared," *Bismarck Daily Tribune* (ND), June 22, 1898, at 1. Efforts at continued use of the Declaration of Independence to argue for Filipino independence: "The Course of Our Predecessors," *Morning World-Herald* (Omaha, NE), Mar. 6, 1901, at 4; "The Filipino Fourth of July," *Sunday World-Herald* (Omaha, NE), July 7, 1901, at 4; "The Application of Declaration," *Duluth News Tribune* (MN), Nov. 5, 1901, at 4; "The American Doctrine," *Morning World-Herald* (Omaha, NE), June 14, 1902, at 4; "The Proclamation and Its Effect," *State* (Columbia, SC), July 7, 1902, at 4.

12. *Statement of a Proper Military Policy for the United States ... Sept. 1915*, at 7 (1916).

13. "Birth of a Nation" Run Out of Philadelphia, *Chicago Defender*, Sept. 25, 1915, at 1, 1, 11.

14. "President's Independence Day Speech," Salt Lake Tribune (UT), July 5, 1914, at 11; "Roosevelt Says Wilson Policies Are 'Cowardly,'" *Star and Sentinel*, Oct. 7, 1916, at 7.

15. "Glorious Achievement of America Is Theme," *San Jose Mercury Herald*, Feb. 22, 1915, at 7; "The Program of the Pacifist," 78 *Advocate of Peace* 96, 97 (Apr. 1916); "Declaration of the Rights and Duties of Nations," id., at 170 (June 1916).

16. "A Proclamation: By the Governor," *Evening News* (Sault Sainte Marie, MI), Nov. 23, 1916, at 4.

17. Ralph W. Tyler, "Why Fight for a Flag Whose Folds Do Not Protect," *Chicago Defender*, Mar. 14, 1914, at 1; Talcott Williams, "The Real Issue," *Independent* (July 24–31, 1920), at 109; P. P. Watson, "Negroes Should Buy Liberty Bonds Now," *State* (Columbia, SC), Oct. 19, 1918, at 8.

18. James Davenport Whelpley, "America at War," 70 *Overland Monthly* 198 (Aug. 1917); "Second Independence Day," *Miami Herald*, Mar. 28, 1918, at 10; Sean D. Cashman, *America in the Age of the Titans* 533 (1988); *Anarchism on Trial* 64 (1917); "Making America Safe for Democracy," 6 *Viereck's* (Aug. 1, 1917), at 435; *Cong. Record*, 65th Cong., 1st Sess., at 5234 (July 18, 1917).

19. "Patriotism—The Love of an Ideal," *Belleville News-Democrat* (IL), Sept. 21, 1917, at 4; "A United World," *Ukiah Republican Press* (CA), Jan 15, 1915, at 16; "The Last Fight for Liberty," *Puerto Chieftain* (CO), Apr. 29, 1918, at 4.

20. "The President Prophetic Vision," *Fort Worth Star-Telegram*, Oct. 5, 1917, at 8; "British Celebrate Independence Day," *Dallas Morning News*, July 5, 1918, at 3; "The Declaration of 1918," *Charlotte Observer* (NC), July 5, 1918, at 4. Objectors to the war argued that America's principal aim was not humanitarian but commercial. They believed that the United States wanted to buttress Allied countries, which had borrowed more than $2 billion from American banking firms such as J. P. Morgan. Bankers were unlikely to recoup the debts if Germany emerged victorious.

21. "The American Mission in Russia," in 12 *The European War* 57, 58 (New York Times Company, 1917); David Armitage, *The Declaration of Independence: A Global History* 151 (2007); "Koreans Will Fight to Last Drop of Blood," *Idaho Sunday Statesmen*, Mar. 14, 1919, at 1; "Self Rule Is Goal of Irish Republic," *Morning Oregonian* (Portland), May 3, 1918, at 1; "Czecho Slovaks in Declaration of Own Liberty," *Evening News* (San Jose, CA), Oct. 19, 1918, at 2; "Korean Freedom Declaration Read At Independence Hall," *Grand Forks Herald* (ND), Apr. 17, 1919, at 1; "Place Jewish Flag with Allied Colors," *Dallas Morning News*, Dec. 17, 1917, at 2.

22. "Military Autocracy Must Be Destroyed or Made Harmless, Says President at Mt. Vernon," *Dallas Morning News*, July 5, 1918, at 1–2 ("America's Declaration …"); *A World League of Nations and Religions: Ninth Congress…* 76 (1919); "Declaration of Rights of Nations Is Promulgated," *Lexington Herald* (KY), Jan. 30, 1916, at 2; Eugene C. Brooks, *Woodrow Wilson as President* 503–4 (1916).

23. The Covenant of the League of Nations Art. 22, 23(a), http://avalon.law.yale. edu/20th_century/leagcov.asp#art22; "Wilson Address at Berkeley, Calif., Sept 18, 1919," in *Addresses of President Wilson on His Western Tour, September 4 to September 25, 1919*, at 262 (1919).

24. "Mothers, Wives, Workers, and More," in *World War I: Personal Perspectives* 278 (Timothy C. Dowling ed., 2006).

25. "Declaration of Independence Is Strong Woman Suffrage Argument," *Trenton Evening Times* (NJ), Feb. 14, 1914, at 5; Alexander Tsesis, *We Shall Overcome*

156–57 (2008); "Miss Allen Speaks," *Elyria Democrat* (OH), Oct. 15, 1914, at 8; "Votes for Women," *Racine Journal-News* (WI), Oct. 8, 1914, at 4; "Mrs. Squire Must Settle or Stand for a Lawsuit," *Anaconda Standard* (MT), Jan. 22, 1914, at 11; "Nevada Equal Franchise Society," *Nevada State Journal* (Reno), July 6, 1914, at 4.

26. Audrey Oldfield, *Woman Suffrage in Australia* 242 (1992); Michael Linfield, *Freedom under Fire* 41 (1990); "Raps Putting Own Country Ahead of Sex," *Idaho Daily Statesman* (Boise), Nov. 5, 1917, at 3.

27. *Cong. Record*, 64th Cong., 1st Sess., at 6776–77 (Apr. 25, 1916) (Shafroth); *Cong. Record*, 65th Cong., 2nd Sess., at 8345 (Apr. 12, 1918) (Shafroth); *Cong. Record*, 65th Cong., 2nd Sess., at 5001 (June 27, 1918) (Thomas); Letter from Irene M. Flint (WV), Jan. 7, 1918, in *Extending the Right of Suffrage to Women: Hearings before the Committee on Woman Suffrage* 317 (Washington, GPO 1918).

28. "The Original Declaration … ," *Milwaukee Journal*, Feb. 16, 1894, at 4.

29. National Archives Administration, *Declaration of Independence: A History*, http://www.archives.gov/exhibits/charters/declaration_history.html.

30. "July 4th, 1776–1926," *New York Amsterdam News*, July, 7, 1926, at 20; "Protest Plans for Independence Week," *Chicago Defender*, June 12, 1926, at A1.

31. *Houston Informer*, Oct. 11, 1919, and *Atlanta Independent*, Oct. 18, 1919, in *The Voice of the Negro* 34–35 (Robert T. Kerlin ed., 1920); Benjamin Brawley, *Your Negro Neighbor* 74–75 (1918).

32. "Dyer Anti-Lynching Bill," *Crisis*, Nov. 1922, at 23–24; Maxwell Bloomfield, *Peaceful Revolution: Constitutional Change and American Culture from Progressivism to the New Deal*, 94, 96 (2000) (quoting *City Times*).

33. "Negro Honor Student Reads Declaration," *New York Amsterdam News*, July 11, 1923, at 3; "In Rage at Raising of Race Issue," id., July 4, 1923, at 3.

34. Arthur E. Barbeau and Florette Henri, *The Unknown Soldiers: African-American Troops in World War I* 175 (Da Capo Press 1996, Temple U. Press 1974); *African American Lives* 212 (Henry L. Gates, Jr., and Evelyn Brooks Higginbotham eds., 2004); "The Klan Defies a State," 77 *Literary Digest* 12 (June 9, 1923).

35. "Slump in Nightgown Market Forecasted," *Woodland Daily* (CA), May 14, 1923, at 2; "Answer To Question Of What Is Americanism?," *Brookshire Times* (Brookshire, NY), Aug. 10, 1923, at 3; "Doing Away with Ku Klux Klan," *Ogden Standard-Examiner* (Ogden, UT), Nov. 12, 1923, at 4; "From A. Lincoln," *Capital Times* (Madison, WI), Oct. 29, 1923, at 24; "Current Comment," *Daily News Standard* (Uniontown, PA), Apr. 23, 1923, at 4.

36. "Ku Klux Defended by Pastor as 100 Percent American," *Janesville Daily Gazette* (WI), June 4, 1923, at 1; "Klan Claims It's 100 percent Pure," *Emporia Gazette* (KS), Feb. 9, 1923, at 1; "Malliett Discusses Prejudice," *Pittsburgh Courier*, (PA) July 12, 1930, at A1; "Make Replies To Klan Program," *Hamilton Daily News* (OH), Oct. 27, 1923, at 7; "Knights of the Ku Klux Klan And Their Ideals," *Freeport Journal Standard* (IL), May 18, 1923, at 17.

37. "Equal Rights League Meets In Baltimore," *Chicago Defender*, Oct. 17, 1925, at 3; "New Independence Declared July 4th," id., July 6, 1929, at 1; "The Suppression

of Lynching," *Columbus Enquirer-Sun* (OH), Sept. 19, 1919, at 4; "More Florida Justice," *Chicago Defender*, July 10, 1926, at 4.

38. Carl Abbott, *Political Terrain: Washington, D.C.* 88 (1999); "Ask Coolidge To Blot Out Segregation," *Chicago Defender*, July 10, 1926, at 4; "Ask Hoover to Abolish Federal Segregation," *Pittsburgh Courier*, July 6, 1929, at 2.

39. Paul D. Moreno, *Black Americans and Organized Labor* 152–56 (2006); Philip S. Foner, 9 *History of the Labor Movement in the United States*, 228 (1991).

40. Samuel Gompers, "Editorial," 28 *American Federationist* 568, 570 (July 1921); "Harding and the Constitution," 23 *International Horseshoers' Monthly Magazine*, Sept. 1922, at 5; "Anti-Unionists Quack Patriots," *Railway Brotherhood of Maintenance of Way Employes* [sic] *Journal*, Dec. 1920, at 25; "Strict Neutrality Observed by Troops In W. Va. Mine Area," *Columbus Ledger* (GA), Sept. 8, 1920, at 3; Frank J. Weber, "Voice of the People: A Prediction," *Capital Times* (Madison, WI), Sept. 20, 1929, at 16; "Manufacturers Adopt Platform," *Wisconsin State Journal* (Madison), May 21, 1920, at 9; "A Neglected 'Inalienable Right,'" *Wall Street Journal*, Aug. 17, 1920, at 1.

41. *Children's Hospital of District of Columbia v. Adkins* 284 F. 613, 615 (Court of Appeals D.C. 1922); affirmed by *Adkins v. Children's Hospital* 261 U.S. 525 (1923). In one case an appellate court reversed a judgment in favor of an injured minor employee, finding that the employer's right to jury, which was based on the same common law right invoked in the Declaration of Independence, had been violated. *McKeon v. Central Stamping Co.* 264 F. 385 (Ct. App. 3d Dist. 1920). The following is the list of the cases invoking the Declaration during this period: *Pierce v. Society of Sisters* 268 U.S. 510 (1925); *McCarthy v. Arndstein* 266 U.S. 34 (1924); *Heald v. District of Columbia* 259 U.S. 114 (1922); *Marcus Brown Holding Co. v. Feldman* 256 U.S. 170 (1921); *Schencks v. United States* 2 F. 2d 185 (Court of Appeals D. C. 1924); *Fulsom v. Quaker Oil & Gas Co.* 28 F.2d 398 (N.D. Ok. 1928); *United States ex rel. Valotta v. Ashe* 2 F.2d 735 (W.D. Pa. 1924); *The Mercedes De Larrinaga*, 293 F. 251 (D. Mass. 1923); In re Goldberg, 269 F. 392 (E.D. Mo. 1920); Ex parte Jackson, 263 F. 110 (D. Mt. 1920); *United States v. Steene* 263 F. 130 (N.D. N.Y. 1920). For a fuller discussion of Supreme Court references to the Declaration of Independence, see Alexander Tsesis, "Self-Government and the Declaration of Independence," 97 *Cornell L. R.* (forthcoming May 2012).

42. Robert S. McElvaine, *The Great Depression: America, 1929–1941*, at 21–22 (2d ed., 1993); Alan Dawley, *Struggles for Justice: Social Responsibility and the Liberal State* 338 (1991).

43. "Export Surplus Is Farmer Problem, Says [sic] Grain Men," *Hutchinson News* (KS), May 13, 1930, at 14.

44. Lewis F. Carr, "Middle West Is Middle West," 118 *Century Magazine* 41, 46 (May 1929) ("disease ..."); Robert W. Kelso, *Poverty* 7–8 (1929); G. Arthur Sabine, *Balance in Government* 66 (1930); S. Howard Patterson, *Social Aspects of Industry* 31–32 (1929).

45. "America's New Problem of Liberty," *Coshocton Tribune* (OH), Feb. 5, 1932, at 8; "On With Farm Strike," *Iola Daily Register* (KS), Sept. 26, 1932, at 1; F. J. Keilholz, "Farmers Call Him Best Booster," 9 *Banker-Farmer* 14, Oct. 1922, at 14.

CHAPTER 15

1. National Archives Administration, *Declaration of Independence: A History*, http://www.archives.gov/exhibits/charters/declaration_history.html.
2. "M'Adoo Voices Party Warning," *Billings Gazette* (MT), Jan. 5, 1933, at 3.
3. "Ickes Hits Public on Slum Neglect," *New York Times*, Sept. 30, 1934, at 33; "Farley Defends Air Mail Action," *Miami News Record*, Feb. 23, 1934, at 13 (Durham); "Farley Attacks New Deal Critics," *New York Times*, Sept. 29, 1934, at 8 (Chicago); "We Do Not Know," *Daily Capital News* (Jefferson City, MO), Aug. 30, 1934, at 4 (Roosevelt).
4. "Continue the Probe," *Daily Democrat* (Fayetteville, AR), Apr. 17, 1933, at 2; "Asserts New Deal Is Middle Course," *New York Times*, Feb. 28, 1935, at 2; Herbert J. Tily, "Business Under the NRA," in *America's Recovery Program* 201–2 (1934); Elmus Wicker, *The Banking Panics of the Great Depression* (1996).
5. National Industrial Recovery Act (NIRA) of 1933, ch. 90, 48 Stat. 195 (1933); Harry B. McMeal, 105 *Telephony* 18 (1933); 1 *Proceedings of the Thirty-Third Constitutional Convention of the United Mine Workers of America* 215 (1934); John L. Lewis, "Significance of American Membership in the I. L. O. to Labor," in *What the International Labor Organization Means to America* 68–69 (Spencer Miller, Jr. ed., 1936); "New Deal, New Code, New Era," 69 *International Molders' Journal* 530 (1933).
6. M. Bauer, "Letter to the Editor," *Chronicle-Telegram* (Elyria, OH), Mar. 24, 1933, at 16; *Cong. Record*, 73rd Cong., 1st Sess., at 2727 (May 2, 1933) (Keller); "Judge Gives Address as City Joins in Tribute," *Woodland Democrat* (CA), May 30, 1933, at 1; "Many Important Problems Yet To Be Solved," *Emmetsburg Democrat* (IA), Apr. 6, 1933, at 2; *A. L. A. Schechter Poultry Corp. v. United States* 295 U.S. 495 (1935).
7. Ward H. Rogers, "Sharecroppers Drop Color Line," 42 *Crisis* 168, 178 (June 1935); Mark Fannin, *Labor's Promised Land* 128 (2003).
8. Agricultural Adjustment Act (AAA), ch. 25, 48 Stat. 31 (1933); "FD Hits Back at Foes," *Brainerd Daily Dispatch* (MN), Sept. 28, 1935, at 1; Raymond Clapper, "Lasting AAA Pledged Farmers," *Washington Post*, Sept. 29, 1935, at 1.
9. *United States v. Butler* 297 U.S. 1 (1936); "Should the Constitution and United States Supreme Court Be Abolished?" 53 *Railroad Trainman* 89 (Feb. 1936).
10. "Congress Adjourns," *Chicago Defender*, June 23, 1934, at 14; Frank R. Crosswaith, "The Negro and Unemployment," *Chicago Defender*, Feb. 22, 1930, at A2; Sean J. Savage, *Roosevelt: The Party Leader, 1932–1945*, at 41 (1991); 2 Mary B. Norton et al., *A People & Nation* 682 (9th ed. 2012); "So This Is Independence Day," *Atlanta Daily World*, July 4, 1932, at 6.
11. Harold L. Ickes, "The Negro as a Citizen," 43 *Crisis* 230, 242 (1936); R. Q. Venson, "Letter to the Editor," *Pittsburgh Courier* (PA), July 9, 1932, at A2; John Wesley Neely, "Editorial," *Pittsburgh Courier*, May 12, 1934, at A2.
12. Abbott, "Disregard for Rights of Others an Old American Custom," *Chicago Defender*, Oct. 20, 1934, at 10; "Letter to the Editor," 43 *Crisis* 243 (1936).
13. "American Philosophy," *La Crosse Tribune* (WI), Sept. 10, 1934, at 3; George F. Oxley, "Introduction," *Earnest Greenwood, The Great Delusion* ix–x (1933); "Raskob to Expand Liberty League," *New York Times*, Feb. 1, 1936, at 1.

14. "A New Declaration," *Los Angeles Times*, July 4, 1936, at A4; "New Deal Goal Likened to that of King George," *Chicago Tribune*, Nov. 12, 1935, at 7; Doctor-Solon Uses Scalpel Upon New Deal," *Chicago Tribune*, Oct. 7, 1934, at 1; "Judge De Young Warns Against U.S. Despotism," *Chicago Tribune*, Sept. 21, 1934, at 7.

15. "Editorial of the Day," *Olean Times-Herald* (NY), Sept. 14, 1934, at 20; "Human Misery and Human Rights," *Morning Herald* (Uniontown, PA), Oct. 21, 1935, at 6; Robert Margo, "Interwar Unemployment in the United States," in *Interwar Unemployment in International Perspective* 326 (Barry Eichengreen and T. J. Hatton eds., 1988); Samuel Laufbaun, "Letter to the Editor," *New York Times*, Sept. 3, 1934, at 12.

16. "New Deal Is Made Campaign Target," *New York Times*, July 3, 1934, at 8; "Time for Public to Wake Up," *Wellsboro Agitator* (PA), Oct. 3, 1934, at 3; Raoul E. Desvernine, *Democratic Despotism* 16–17, 216–17 (1936); "Liberty and/or Civilization," 33 *Electrical Workers and Operators* 415(1934).

17. *Cong. Record*, 73rd Cong., 2nd Sess., at 3693 (Mar. 5, 1934) (Long); *Cong Record*, 73rd Cong., 1st Sess., at 5602 (June 10, 1933) (Sen. Josiah William Bailey, NC, supporting Long).

18. "Low Wages Makes Pension System For Aged a Necessity," *Cedar Rapids Tribune* (IA), Apr. 17, 1931, at 1 (Green); Abraham Epstein, *Social Security* 5 (1937); Old-Age Pension: Hearings, The Committee on Labor, House of Representatives 246 (1930); U.S. Dept. of Labor, *Handbook of Labor Statistics* 1936 Ed. (Bulletin No. 616), at 607 (1936).

19. *Helvering v. Davis* 301 U.S. 619 (1937); *Steward Machine Co. v. Davis* 301 U.S. 548 (1937).

20. "Kelly Miller Says," *Atlanta Daily World*, May 1, 1938, at 4; Selig Perlman, *A History of Trade Unionism in the United States* 279–81 (1937); "From L. U. No. 5991, Glen White, W. Va.," in 4 *Proceedings of the Unite Mine Workers of America* 200–201 (1936); Marion Catherwood, "Letter to the Editor," *New York Amsterdam News*, Mar. 21, 1936, at 12; "Labor and Wages," 54 *Conductor and Brakeman* 107 (Mar. 1937).

21. "Text of Ickes Broadcast Urging United Front Against Communism, Fascism," *Washington Post*, Feb. 23, 1938, at 4.

22. "Court Reform Proposal 'Evil,' Lowell Asserts," *Washington Post*, Feb. 11, 1937, at 3; "Senate Is Urged To Condemn Nazis," *New York Times*, June 16, 1933, at 4; James W. Wise, *Swastika: The Nazi Terror* 81–82, 84 (1933); "Justice Murphy on Intolerance," *Ironwood Daily Globe* (MI), June 20, 1944, at 4.

23. "'Calling America': A Special Number of *Survey Graphic* on the Challenge to Democracy" 100 (1939); "What It Means Today," *Charleston Gazette* (WV), July 4, 1942, at 6; Clapper, "American Was Born … ," *Panama City News-Herald* (FL), July 5, 1942, at 6.

24. John F. Hoyt, "Editorial: Democracy," *Portsmouth Herald* (NH), Mar. 1, 1939, at 4; "Check Hitlerism Now or Risk Peril Later, FDR Warns," *Charleston Gazette* (WV), May 28, 1941, at 8; "President Urges Rededication to Freedom on Fourth of July," *Titusville Herald* (PA), June 26, 1941, at 1.

25. Lippmann, "Editorial," Oakland Tribune (CA), June 8, 1941, at 2; 87 Cong. Record A839 (Feb. 25, 1941); "Britons Cheered by Churchill Talk," New York Times, Dec. 27, 1941, at 3.

26. "Everyone of us ... ," Lake Park News (IA), Mar. 5, 1942, at 7, col. a; "Thousands Throng...," Muscatine Journal and News-Tribune (IA), July 6, 1943, at 2; S. Burton Heath, "Letter to the Editor," Clearfield Progress (PA), June 30, 1943, at 4.

27. "Surrender in Mobile," Pittsburgh Courier, June 19, 1943, at 6; Rev. J. C. Wright, "From My Study Window," Atlanta Daily World (GA), Aug. 6, 1944, at 4; Harold Preece, "The Living South," Chicago Defender, Nov. 11, 1944, at 11; "Hollywood Goes Hitler One Better," Los Angeles Sentinel, Feb. 9, 1939, at 1; "A Resolution," Chicago Defender, Nov. 7, 1942, at 14.

28. James T. Taylor, "Letter to the Editor," New York Times, Apr. 19, 1942, at E9; "College Head Replies to Gov. Sparks," Chicago Defender, Apr. 17, 1943, at 22.

29. "Pastor Terry Resents Discrimination against Negro," Altoona Mirror (PA), July 10, 1942, at 4; "Won't Serve In U.S. Army; Cites Bias," Chicago Defender, Jan. 11, 1941, at 8; "Army, Navy Scored by Race Physicians," Atlanta Daily World (GA), Feb. 20, 1942, at 1.

30. "A New Independence Day," Pittsburgh Courier, July 4, 1942, at 6; "Breaking Down the Constitution From Two Angels," Indiana Evening Gazette (Indiana, PA), Apr. 24, 1944, at 3; J. A. Rogers, "Propaganda Breeds Hate Among Races," Pittsburgh Courier, May 9, 1942, at 7; "Jim Crow Rail Seating Defied By White Girl," Atlanta Daily World, Nov. 1, 1943, at 1; Morgan v. Virginia, 328 U.S. 373 (1946).

31. "Poll Finds Most Whites Believe in Superiority," Chicago Defender, Jan. 6, 1945, at 9.

32. "Forgotten Men Do Not Forget Man Who Remembered Them," Waukesha Daily Freeman (WI), Apr. 12, 1946, at 2.

CHAPTER 16

1. "Lynch Violence in America Hit in England," Chicago Defender, Aug. 31, 1946, at 20 (quoting Pictorial); Elmer A. Carter, "Plain Talk, Education After the War," New York Amsterdam News, May 15, 1943, at 10; "Independence Day," Atlanta Daily World (GA), July 3, 1949, at 4; "Declares Brotherhood Starts in Community," Robesonian (Lumberton, NC), Mar. 6, 1951, at 7.

2. Executive Order 9981, http://www.trumanlibrary.org/9981.htm; Harry S. Truman, "Commencement Address at Howard University: June 13, 1952," http://www.presidency.ucsb.edu/ws/index.php?pid=14160; "Address at the Ceremonies Commemorating the 175th Anniversary of the Declaration of Independence, July 4, 1951," http://www.trumanlibrary.org/publicpapers/index.php?pid=358&st=&st1=; George E. Sokolsky, "These Days," Altoona Mirror (PA), Feb. 22, 1960, at 8.

3. "Pursuit of Happiness," Newport Mercury and Weekly News (RI), Apr. 6, 1951, at 4.

4. "July Fourth's Glorious History Conveys Hope to All Oppressed," Long Beach Press-Telegram (CA), July 4, 1952, at 8; "Young Doctors Warned Against Socialization," Blytheville Courier (AK), June 25, 1946, at 3 (Arkansas speech);

Drew Pearson, "Editorial: Declaration of Independence Stresses the Dignity of Man," *Brownsville Herald* (TX), July 5, 1951, at 4; R. C. Homes, "Editorial: Better Jobs," *Pampa News* (TX), Mar. 11, 1951, at 18; Stefan Gusky, "Iron Curtain a World Tragedy," *Portsmouth Herald* (NH), Sept. 7, 1951, at 4; "More of the Declaration," *Pampa News* (TX), Feb. 11, 1945, at 4.

5. "On Preaching the Declaration of Independence," *Newport Daily News* (RI), Sept. 12, 1956, at 8; "Declaration of Independence Still is Grandiose Document," *Albuquerque Tribune* (NM), July 3, 1956, at 6.

6. "Two Definitions," *Anderson Herald* (IN), Dec. 2, 1961, at 4.

7. "'Irrational Attitude ... ,' Letter to the Editor," *New York Times*, May 29, 1954, at 14.

8. 366 U.S. 82 (1961).

9. "Dr. Patterson Urges 'New Global Concept,'" *Atlanta Daily World* (GA), June 4, 1953, at 3; "'Jim Crow Must be Abolished'—Rabbis," *Pittsburgh Courier* (PA), Feb. 3, 1945, at 4; "News in the World of Religion," *Daily Times-News* (Burlington, NC), Sept. 6, 1945, at 3.

10. Walter Shead, "The Declaration," *West Bend Journal* (IN), July 26, 1951, at 3.

11. "Democratic Party Platform of 1952," http://www.presidency.ucsb.edu/ws/index.php?pid=29600; "'They're Different' Key Chant of Survey," *Atlanta Daily World* (GA), July 31, 1956, at 1; "Freedom Is the Thing," *Los Angeles Sentinel*, July 1, 1954, at A9.

12. "Republican Party Platform of 1948," http://www.presidency.ucsb.edu/ws/index.php?pid=25836; "Warren Says FEPC Found in 1948 GOP Platform," *Atlanta Daily World* (GA), May 8, 1952, at 2; "Warren Cites Racial Views," *Pitt. Courier*, Oct. 10, 1953, at 1, 5; "Crisis on Rights Seen by Warren," *New York Times*, Oct. 29, 1963, at 19.

13. "Arizona Wipes Out School Segregation," *Atlanta Daily World* (GA), Feb. 17, 1953, at 1, 2–3; "Waring Challenges Politicians on Civil Rights," *Chicago Defender*, May 17, 1952, at 1; Arnold H. Lubasch, "Shift in the Law Seen by Brennan," *N. Y. Times*, Nov. 16, 1964, at 23.

14. *Missouri ex rel. Gaines v. Canada* 305 U.S. 337, 352 (1938); *Sipuel v. Bd. of Regents of the Univ. of Okla.* 332 U.S. 631, 633 (1948); *McLaurin v. Okla. State Regents of Higher Educ.* 339 U.S. 637, 641–42 (1950); *Sweatt v. Painter* 339 U.S. 629, 635–36 (1950); Thomas R. Dye and Harmon Zeigler, *The Irony of Democracy* 354 (2008); "Letter from James A. Farrell, May 18, 1954," *New York Times*, May 21, 1954, at 26.

15. "Comments of U.S. Press on Segregation Ruling," *Los Angeles Times*, May 19, 1954, at 8 ("a system ... "); "Letter to the Editor from Creola Armstead, Student of West End," *Pittsburgh Courier* (PA), Feb. 6, 1954, at 29; J. J. Peters, "Letter to the Editor," *Chicago Defender*, Apr. 9, 1960, at 10 ("trying to ... "); James J. Wadsworth, "The Problem of Apartheid in South Africa," 32 *Dep't. of State Bulletin* 1, 34 (1955); "Negroes to Mark Integration Day," *Washington Post*, May 13, 1955, at 10.

16. Homer Alexander, "Virginia Fights Supreme Court," *San Antonio Express* (TX), Jan. 23, 1956, at 4; "Letter from Betty Walter," *Salisbury Times*, Oct. 11, 1954, at 6; Imogene McMurtry, "Letter to the Editor," *Appeal Democrat* (Marysville, CA), Jan 29, 1959, at 15; David Lawrence, "Voting Demonstration," *Ironwood*

Globe (MI), Nov. 12, 1958, at 4 (Nevins); Peggy Pascoe, *What Comes Naturally: Miscegenation Law and the Making of Race in America* 19–20 (2009).

17. *Brown v. Board of Ed.* 349 U.S. 294, 300–301 (1955); "Southern Manifesto Will Impede Progress, Speaker Says," *Atlanta Daily World* (GA), Mar. 15, 1956, at 3; *Green v. County School Board* 391 U.S. 430, 439.

18. Benjamin E. Mays, "My View," *Pittsburgh Courier* (PA), Dec. 10, 1955, at A10; "Thurgood Says Court Did All It Could on Schools," *Pittsburgh Courier* (PA), July 2, 1955, at 6; J. Waties Waring, "Letter to the Editor," *New York Times*, May 22, 1955, at 225 (Magazine SM6).

19. "Editorial," *Pittsburgh Courier* (PA), Oct. 6, 1956, at A5.

20. "Dynamited Osage School Lost Only One Day Of Study," *Beckley Post Herald* (WV), Nov. 20, 1958, at 4; Joseph H. Nelson, "Letter to the Editor," *Atlanta Daily World* (GA), Mar. 4, 1956, at 4.

21. "Race Equality Aid Promised by Eisenhower," *Los Angeles Times*, Mar. 11, 1954, at 7; "Helpful and Appropriate," *New York Amsterdam News*, Feb. 9, 1957, at 14; "A National Disgrace," *New York Amsterdam News*, Jan. 19, 1957, at 1.

22. "Pessimistic Ike Decries School Ban," *Beckley Post-Herald* (WV), Sept. 26, 1958, at 1; "Letter from President Dwight D. Eisenhower to Bishop Robert R. Brown," *Syracuse Herald Journal* (NY), Oct. 6, 1957, at B6; "President Urges End of Job Bias," *New York Times*, Nov. 19, 1957, at 1.

23. *Cooper v. Aaron* 358 U.S. 1 (1958); Edgar Ansel Mowrer, "Editorial," *Daily Herald* (Albuquerque, NM), Sept. 18, 1957, at 14; Robert C. Ruark, "Not a Nice Feeling," *Newport Daily News* (RI), Oct 1, 1957, at 8 ("mess").

24. "Ultimate Solution Of The Integration Problem Seen By Lions Club Speaker," *Sheboygan Press*, (WI), Feb. 18, 1959, at 14; Holmes Alexander, "On the National Front," *Reno Evening Gazette* (NV), Sept. 6, 1957, at 5.

25. "Anti-Segregation Move On Capital," *Laurel Leader-Call* (MS) May 17, 1957, at 19; Merrill D. Peterson, *Lincoln in American Memory* 353 (1994); "Brotherhood Week," *Rocky Mount Evening Telegraph* (NC), Feb. 15, 1957, at 4A.

26. Democratic Party Platform of 1960, http://www.presidency.ucsb.edu/ws/index.php?pid=29602; Republican Party Platform of 1960, http://www.presidency.ucsb.edu/ws/index.php?pid=25839; Mortimer J. Adler, "Inequalities Do Not Alter Men Being Equal 'As Men,'" *Charleston Gazette* (WV), Oct. 8, 1960, at 5.

27. "Sen. Johnson Raps Forced Integration," *Newport Daily News* (RI), Dec. 13, 1958, at 1; Lyle C. Wilson, "Convention Window," *Daily News* (Huntington, PA), July 26, 1960, at 12; Monroe Billington, "Lyndon B. Johnson and Blacks: The Early Years," 62 *J. Negro Hist.* 26, 29–30, 33 (1977); Garth Pauley, "The Genesis of a Rhetorical Commitment: Lyndon B. Johnson, Civil Rights, and the Vice Presidency," in *Civil Rights Rhetoric and the American Presidency* 157, 160 (James A. Aune and Enrique D. Rigsby eds., 2005) (quoting Wilkins).

28. "Sweeping Provisions Included In Disputed Civil Rights Proposal," *Avalanche-Journal* (Lubbock, TX), July 13, 1960, at 15.

29. Edwin V. Anderson, "Letter to the Editor," *Chronicle Telegram* (Elyria, OH), Oct. 2, 1963, at 2; "Social Worker Hits Discrimination Against 'The Unwanted America,'" *Sheboygan Press* (WI), Oct. 11, 1963, at 4.

30. Alexander Tsesis, *We Shall Overcome: A History of Civil Rights and the Law* 261–63 (2008); "Police Block Negro Visit," *Arizona Republican* (Phoenix), Feb. 13, 1961, at 40; "Columbia Group Sends Telegrams to S.C. Mayors," *Florence Morning News* (SC), Mar. 5, 1960, at 3; "Students Here Picket Stores, Cite South," *Wisconsin State Journal*, Feb. 28, 1960, at 1–2; "Wisdom of Reno Picketing Incident, Is Questionable," *Nevada State Journal* (Reno), June 14, 1960, at 6.

31. Lillian E. Herz, "Plea Referred to Attorney for Opinion," *Galveston Daily News* (TX), July 15, 1960, at 1, 5; "A Great Anniversary," *Record-Eagle* (Traverse City, MI), June 23, 1962, at 4; "Cites New Urge in Race Relations," *Chicago Defender*, June 25, 1960, at 9; Robert C. Power, research director, Elephant Club, "Letter to the Editor," *Chicago Defender*, June 28, 1961, at 10; "Kennedy Aids [sic] Praises NAACP Freedom Riders," *Pittsburgh Courier* (PA), Oct. 28, 1961, at 9; David Niven, *The Politics of Injustice* 125 (2003).

32. Robert F. Kennedy, "Kennedy Sums Up His Civil Rights Record," *Chicago Defender*, Aug. 11, 1962, at 8; "Robert Kennedy Deplores Prejudice Against Jews," *New York Times*, July 15, 1963, at 30.

33. "Transcript of President [Kennedy]," *New York Times*, June 12, 1963, at 20.

34. "Column of Comment," *Ada Evening News* (OK), Mar. 28, 1961, at 3; James C. Young (Elkville)," Letter to the Editor," *Southern Illinoisan* (Carbondale, IL), Nov. 13, 1963, at 4; "Texts of the President's Statements on Rights and on Labor Day," *New York Times*, Aug. 29, 1963, at 16; John F. Kennedy, Special Message to the Congress on Civil Rights (Feb. 28, 1963), http://photo.pds.org:5005/advanced/document?id=dc310101&st=%22daniel+boone%22+or+%22emancipation+proclamation%22+or+%22davy+crockett%22%20uses%20term%94all%20men%20are%20created%20equal

35. "'Implement The Declaration of Independence,' Johnson Urges," *Chicago Defender*, July 6, 1963, at 2; "Live Up to Meaning of Holiday, Says Johnson," *Los Angeles Times*, July 5, 1963, at 2; "LBJ Urges More Action on Rights," *Big Spring Daily Herald* (TX), July 5, 1963, at 8.

36. "Negroes Demonstrate, Ask Virginia To Open Schools," *Corpus Christi Times* (TX), Jan. 2, 1960, at 8.

37. "Intellectual Inequality," *Corpus Christi Caller-Times* (TX), Aug. 6, 1961, at 2b; *The Papers of John C. Calhoun, 1847–1848*, at 534 (1999, 1848); Reinder Van Til, "Letter to the Editor," *Hammond Times* (IN), Aug 9, 1963, at B2.

38. William L. Ingersoll, "Sacred Right," *Indiana Evening Gazette* (PA), July 27, 1963, at 6.

39. Irving B. Edelstein, "Letter to the Editor," *Chicago Tribune*, June 3, 1963, at 20; Alta Lee Pilon, "Letter to the Editor," *Montana Standard Post* (Butte), Mar. 3, 1963, at 4; "Letter to the Editor from Paul Hortzman," *Capital Times* (Madison, WI), July 8, 1963, at 32; David Lawrence, "Treatment Of Negroes In The South," *Big Spring Daily Herald* (TX), Mar. 10, 1963, at 26; Lawrence, "Law On Public Accommodations Could Wreck Retail Businesses," *Panama City Herald* (FL), July 10, 1963, at 6.

40. "Text of Preface to Civil Rights Commission's Report," *New York Times*, Oct. 1, 1963, at 20.

41. Axtman, "Letter to the Editor," *Lowell Sun* (MA), Mar. 5, 1964, at 6; "Rustin Calls for Rights Fight to Turn to Broader Movement," *New York Amsterdam News*, July 18, 1964, at 13.

42. "LBJ Calls On Youth To Enrich Mankind," *Newport Daily News* (RI), Feb. 22, 1965, at 1–2; "Text of President Johnson's Rights Talk," *Arizona Republican* (Phoenix), Mar. 16, 1965, at 32.

43. "The Heart of a Man Looks Across This Land," *Fairbanks Daily News* (AK), Oct. 21, 1964, at 10; David Lawrence; "Confusion For Retailers," *Kingsport News* (TN), July 10, 1963, at 4; 109 *Cong. Record* 18469 (Oct.1, 1963) (Eastland).

44. "The Fog Lift," *Aiken Standard and Review* (SC), May 29, 1964, at 4; "The Shattering Policy," *Aiken Standard and Review* (SC), June 1, 1966, at 4.

45. 110 *Cong. Record* 2400 (Feb. 7, 1964); letter from Robertson to U.S. Senate Committee on Banking, reprinted in *Laurel Leader* (MS), Mar. 11, 1964, at 4; "Civil Rights Bill Is Tyranny: Wallace," *Sandusky Register* (OH), June 12, 1964, at 3; 112 *Cong. Record* 22311 (1966) (Long); James Marlow, "The Struggle Grows," *High Point Enterprise* (NC), May 11, 1964, at 4; "Rewriting the Declaration," *North Adams Transcript* (MA), Mar. 16, 1964, at 6.

46. "Collins Demands End of Bigotry," *New York Times*, Dec. 4, 1963, at 19; 110 *Cong. Record* 1538–39 (Jan. 31, 1964) (Rep. Peter W. Rodino, Jr., of NJ).

47. 110 *Cong. Record* 1593 (Feb. 1, 1964) (Rep. Jeffrey Cohelan: "that all men are ... "); 110 *Cong. Record* 1627 (Feb. 1, 1964) (Rep. Seymour Halpern of NY); 110 *Cong. Record* 23438 (Oct. 7, 1964) (Rep. James C. Corman of CA); 110 *Cong. Record* 3190–91 (Feb. 19, 1964) (Rep. Ronald B. Cameron of CA).

48. 110 *Cong. Record* 7001 (Apr. 6, 1964) (Long); 110 *Cong. Record* 89–90 (Jan. 8, 1964).

49. "Our Nation's Birthday," *Chronicle Telegram* (Elyria, OH), July 3, 1964, at 40; Edward L. Caum, "Independence and Freedom?" *Fairbanks Daily News-Miner* (AK), July 3, 1964, at 4; "Church Leaders Urge Support of Idahoans for Rights Bill," *Idaho State Journal* (Pocatello), Mar. 20, 1964, at 11; "The Civil Right Bills, Editorial," *El Paso Herald-Post* (TX), Feb. 11, 1964, at B2; Arthur N. Perkins, "Letter to the Editor," *Independent* (Long Beach, CA), Nov. 19, 1964, at B2; "Council on Human Relations of the Cedar Rapids-Marion Area," *Cedar Rapids Gazette* (IA), May 19, 1964, at 9; "Negroes Gain Allies in Long Struggle," *Daily Review* (Hayward, CA), May 11, 1964, at 4.

50. *President Lyndon B. Johnson's Radio and Television Remarks Upon Signing the Civil Rights Bill July 2, 1964*, Lyndon Baines Johnson Library and Museum (National Archives and Records Administration), http://www.lbjlib.utexas.edu/johnson/archives.hom/speeches.hom/640702.asp; Martin Arnold, "CORE Plans Tests," *New York Times*, June 20, 1964, at 1, 10.

51. Fair Housing Act of 1968, 42 U.S.C. §§ 3601–3631; Stanley Robertson, "Another 'Trick' of the Race Haters," *Los Angeles Sentinel*, Apr. 14, 1960, at A6; "NAREB Urging Defeat of Rights Bill," *Lake Charles American Press* (LA), May 26, 1964, at 16; Robert A. Bell, 112 *Cong. Record* 18124 (Aug. 3, 1966) (Rep. William A. Barrett of PA); 112 *Cong. Record* 17554 (July 28, 1966) reprinting press release of the Detroit Real Estate Brokers Association; "Oak Park Citizen Fights For Open Occupancy," *Chicago Defender*, June 25, 1966, at, 10; "Double-Barrelled Holiday," *Appleton Post* (WI), July 10, 1964, at 31.

52. 110 *Cong. Record* 1538–39 (Rep. Peter W. Rodino of NJ); 110 *Cong. Record* 1593 (Feb. 1, 1964) (Rep. Jeffery Cohelan of CA); 111 *Cong. Record* 5351 (Mar. 18, 1965) (Rep. Sidney Yates of IL); "Enforcing Rights," *Raleigh Register* (Beckley, WV), Dec. 15, 1965, at 4; 111 *Cong. Record* 16270 (July 9, 1965) (Rep. Samuel S. Stratton of NY); *Lassiter v. Northampton County Bd. of Elections* 360 U.S. 45, 53–54 (1959) (literacy tests). Cf. *Breedlove v. Suttles* 302 U.S. 277 (1937) (upholding poll tax) and *Harper v. Virginia State Bd. of Elections* 383 U.S. 663 (1966) (find that a poll tax violated the Equal Protection Clause of the Fourteenth Amendment); *State of S.C. v. Katzenbach* 383 U.S. 301, 314 (1966); "County Is Ready For Race Bias Atonement," *Chicago Defender*, Nov. 27, 1965, at 35 (King).

53. 114 *Cong. Record* 916–17 (Jan. 24, 1968); James Kilpatrick, "How Things Change," *Athens Messenger* (OH), Aug. 26, 1966, at 4; "Natl. CORE Backs up St. Louis," *New York Amsterdam News*, Oct. 7, 1967, at 42; "Issue Declaration," *New York Amsterdam News*, July 4, 1970, at 18; "Hot Summer Begins In Spring—Gregory," *New York Amsterdam News*, Feb. 24, 1968, at 30; "Black Nationalists Form Own Government," *Chicago Defender*, Apr. 2, 1968, at 8; Floyd McKissick, "Respect and Fear of the Law," *New York Amsterdam News*, Nov. 29, 1969, at 13.

54. Bayard Rustin, "On Blacks and Jews," *New York Amsterdam News*, Feb. 8, 1969, at 14; "Reduce the Fever but Treat Riot Cause Too," *Salina Journal* (KS), July 26, 1967, at 4; 112 Cong. Rec. 17752 (Aug. 1, 1966) (Rep. Lucius M. Rivers of SC).

55. "Half the Race To Go," *Record-Eagle* (Traverse City, MI), July 3, 1958, at 4; "Says America's Racial Curtain Helps 'Iron Curtain,'" *Atlanta Daily World* (GA), July 6, 1956, at 4; "UN Human Rights Day," *Hutchinson News* (KS), Dec. 10, 1961, at 4.

56. N. Lloyd, "Letter to the Editor," *Port Angeles Evening News* (WA), Apr. 2, 1963, at 2; James Marlow, "'All men Created Equal'" Not Practiced By Many," *Baytown Sun* (TX), July 4, 1961, at 2.

57. "Expert on USSR Warns Racism Will Hurt U.S.," *Pittsburgh Courier* (PA), Aug. 12, 1961, at A7; "U.S. Must Lead in Civil Rights-Bob Kennedy," *Pittsburgh Courier*, Apr. 28, 1962, at 1; "Links Bias to Russian Tension," *New York Amsterdam News*, Nov. 3, 1962, at 32.

58. "The Possibilities of Freedom," *Chicago Defender*, Nov. 10, 1962, at 8; Frank L. Stanley, "People, Place, Problems," *Chicago Defender*, Feb. 21, 1970, at 10.

CHAPTER 17

1. David Armitage, *The Declaration of Independence: A Global History* 17–18, 92–93 (2007); Pauline Maier, *American Scripture: Making the Declaration of Independence* 160–64, 213–15 (1997).

2. Rogers M. Smith, *Civic Ideals* 9 (1997).

3. Herbert Wechsler, "Toward Neutral Principles of Constitutional Law," 73 *Harv. L. Rev.* 1 (1959).

4. *Plessy v. Ferguson* 163 U.S. 537 (1896).

5. *Citizens United v. Federal Election Commission* 130 S. Ct. 876 (2010); "Self-Government and the Declaration of Independence," 97 *Cornell Law Review* 693 (2012).

INDEX

The abbreviation "DOI" stands for "Declaration of Independence." Page numbers in italics denote illustrations.